BROOKLANDS BOOKS

LOTUS CORTINA
Gold Portfolio
1963~1970

Compiled by
R.M. Clarke

ISBN 1 85520 0457

Distributed by
Brooklands Book Distribution Ltd.
'Holmerise', Seven Hills Road,
Cobham, Surrey, England
Printed in Hong Kong

BROOKLANDS BOOKS

BROOKLANDS ROAD TEST SERIES

AC Ace & Aceca 1953-1983
Alfa Romeo Alfasud 1972-1984
Alfa Romeo Alfetta Coupes GT, GTV, GTV6 1974-1987
Alfa Romeo Giulia Berlinas 1962-1976
Alfa Romeo Giulia Coupes 1963-1976
Alfa Romeo Spider 1966-1987
Allard Gold Portfolio 1937-1958
Alvis Gold Portfolio 1919-1969
American Motors Muscle Cars 1966-1970
Aston Martin Gold Portfolio 1972-1985
Austin Seven 1922-1982
Austin A30 & A35 1951-1962
Austin Healey 100 & 100/6 Gold Portfolio 1952-1959
Austin Healey 3000 Gold Portfolio 1959-1967
Austin Healey 'Frogeye' Sprite Col No.1 1958-1961
Austin Healey Sprite 1958-1971
Avanti 1962-1983
BMW Six Cylinder Coupes 1969-1975
BMW 1600 Col. 1 1966-1981
BMW 2002 1968-1976
Bristol Cars Gold Portfolio 1946-1985
Buick Automobiles 1947-1960
Buick Muscle Cars 1965-1970
Buick Riviera 1963-1978
Cadillac Automobiles 1949-1959
Cadillac Automobiles 1960-1969
Cadillac Eldorado 1967-1978
High Performance Capris Gold Portfolio 1969-1987
Chevrolet Camaro SS & Z28 1966-1973
Chevrolet Camaro & Z-28 1973-1981
High Performance Camaros 1982-1988
Camaro Muscle Cars 1966-1972
Chevrolet 1955-1957
Chevrolet Impala & SS 1958-1971
Chevrolet Muscle Cars 1966-1971
Chevelle and SS 1964-1972
Chevy Blazer 1969-1981
Chevy EL Camino & SS 1959-1987
Chevy II Nova & SS 1962-1973
Chrysler 300 1955-1970
Citroen Traction Avant Gold Portfolio 1934-1957
Citroen DS & ID 1955-1975
Citroen 2CV 1949-1988
Shelby Cobra Gold Portfolio 1962-1969
Cobras & Replicas 1962-1983
Corvair 1959-1968
Chevrolet Corvette Gold Portfolio 1953 1962
Corvette Stingray Gold Portfolio 1963-1967
High Performance Corvettes 1983-1989
Datsun 240Z 1970-1973
Datsun 280Z & ZX 1975-1983
De Tomaso Collection No.1 1962-1981
Dodge Charger 1966-1974
Dodge Muscle Cars 1967-1970
Excalibur Collection No.1 1952-1981
Ferrari Cars 1946-1956
Ferrari Cars 1973-1977
Ferrari Dino 1965-1974
Ferrari Dino 308 1974-1979
Ferrari 308 & Mondial 1974-1984
Ferrair Collection No.1 1960-1970
Fiat-Bertone X1/9 1973-1988
Fiat Pininfarina 124 + 2000 Spider 1968-1985
Ford Automobiles 1949-1959
Ford Bronco 1966-1977
Ford Bronco 1978-1988
Ford Cortina 1600E & GT 1967-1970
Ford Fairlane 1955-1970
Ford Falcon 1960-1970
Ford GT40 Gold Portfolio 1964-1987
Ford RS Escorts 1968-1980
High Performance Escorts Mk1 1968-1974
High Performance Escorts Mk II 1975-1980
High Performance Mustangs 1982-1988
Honda CRX 1983-1987
Hudson & Railton 1936-1940
Jaguar Cars 1957-1961
Jaguar Cars 1961-1964
Jaguar Mk2 1959-1969
Jaguar E-Type Gold Portfolio 1961-1971
Jaguar E-Type 1966-1971
Jaguar E-Type V-12 1971-1975
Jaguar XKE Collection No.1 1961-1974
Jaguar XJ6 1968-1972
Jaguar XJ6 Series II 1973-1979
Jaguar XJ6 & XJ12 Series III 1979-1985
Jaguar XJ12 1972-1980
Jaguar XJS Gold Portfolio 1975-1988
Jaguar XK120.XK140.XK150 Gold Portfolio 1948-1960
Jeep CJ5 & CJ6 1960-1976
Jeep CJ5 & CJ7 1976-1986
Jensen Cars 1946-1967
Jensen Cars 1967-1979
Jensen Interceptor Gold Portfolio 1966-1986
Jensen Healey 1972-1976
Lamborghini Cars 1964-1970
Lamborghini Cars 1970-1975
Lamborghini Countach Col No.1 1971-1982
Lamborghini Countach & Urraco 1974-1980
Lamborghini Countach & Jalpa 1980-1985
Lancia Stratos 1972-1985
Land Rover 1948-1973 - A Collection
Land Rover Series II & IIa 1958-1971
Land Rover Series III 1971-1985
Land Rover 90 & 110 1983-1989
Lincoln Gold Portfolio 1949-1960
Lincoln Continental 1961-1969
Lotus and Caterham Seven Gold Portfolio 1957-1989
Lotus Cortina Gold Portfolio 1963-1970
Lotus Elan Gold Portfolio 1962-1974
Lotus Elan Collection No.2 1963-1972
Lotus Elite 1957-1964
Lotus Elite & Eclat 1974-1982
Lotus Turbo Esprit 1980-1986
Lotus Europa 1966-1975
Lotus Europa Collection No.1 1966-1974
Lotus Seven Collection No.1 1957-1982
Marcos Cars 1960-1988
Maserati 1965-1970
Maserati 1970-1975

Mazda RX-7 Collection No.1 1978-1981
Mercedes 190 & 300SL 1954-1963
Mercedes 230/250/280SL 1963-1971
Mercedes Benz SLs & SLCs Gold Portfolio 1971-1989
Mercedes Benz Cars 1949-1954
Mercedes Benz Cars 1954-1957
Mercedes Benz Cars 1957-1961
Mercedes Benz Compention Cars 1950-1957
Mercury Muscle Cars 1966-1971
Metropolitan 1954-1962
MG TC 1945-1949
MG TD 1949-1953
MG TF 1953-1955
MG Cars 1959-1962
MGA Roadsters 1955-1962
MGA Collection No.1 1955-1982
MGB Roadsters 1962-1980
MGB GT 1965-1980
MG Midget 1961-1980
Mini Moke 1964-1989
Mini Muscle Cars 1961-1979
Mopar Muscle Cars 1964-1967
Mopar Muscle Cars 1968-1971
Morgan Three-Wheeler Gold Portfolio 1910-1952
Morgan Cars 1960-1970
Morgan Cars Gold Portfolio 1968-1989
Morris Minor Collection No.1
Mustang Muscle Cars 1967-1971
Oldsmobile Automobiles 1955-1963
Old's Cutlass & 4-4-2 1964-1972
Oldsmobile Muscle Cars 1964-1972
Oldsmobile Toronado 1966-1978
Opel GT 1968-1973
Packard Gold Portfolio 1946-1958
Pantera Gold Portfolio 1970-1989
Plymouth Barracuda 1964-1974
Plymouth Muscle Cars 1966-1971
Pontiac Tempest & GTO 1961-1965
Pontiac GTO 1964-1970
Pontiac Firebird 1967-1973
Pontiac Firebird and Trans-Am 1973-1981
High Performance Firebirds 1982-1988
Pontiac Fiero 1984-1988
Pontiac Muscle Cars 1966-1972
Porsche 356 1952-1965
Porsche Cars in the 60's
Porsche Cars 1960-1964
Porsche Cars 1964-1968
Porsche Cars 1968-1972
Porsche Cars 1972-1975
Porsche Turbo Collection No.1 1975-1980
Porsche 911 1965-1969
Porsche 911 1970-1972
Porsche 911 1973-1977
Porsche 911 Carrera 1973-1977
Porsche 911 Turbo 1975-1984
Porsche 911 SC 1978-1983
Porsche 914 Gold Portfolio 1969-1976
Porsche 914 Collection No.1 1969-1983
Porsche 924 Gold Portfolio 1975-1988
Porsche 928 1977-1989
Porsche 944 1981-1985
Range Rover Gold Portfolio 1970-1988
Reliant Scimitar 1964-1986
Riley 11/2 & 21/2 Litre Gold Portfolio 1945-1955
Rolls Royce Silver Cloud 1955-1965
Rolls Royce Silver Shadow 1965-1981
Rover P4 1949-1959
Rover P4 1955-1964
Rover 3 & 3.5 Litre 1958-1973
Rover 2000 + 2200 1963-1977
Rover 3500 1968-1977
Rover 3500 & Vitesse 1976-1986
Saab Sonett Collection No.1 1966-1974
Saab Turbo 1976-1983
Shelby Mustang Muscle Cars 1965-1970
Stubebaker Gold Portfolio 1947-1966
Stubebaker Hawks & Larks 1956-1963
Sunbeam Tiger & Alpine Gold Portfolio 1959-1967
Thunderbird 1955-1957
Thunderbird 1958-1963
Thunderbird 1964-1976
Toyota MR2 1984-1988
Triumph 2000. 2.5. 2500 1963-1977
Triumph GT6 1966-1974
Triumph Spitfire 1962-1980
Triumph Spitfire Col No.1 1962-1982
Triumph Stag 1970-1980
Triumph Stag Collection No.1 1970-1984
Triumph TR2 & TR3 1952-60
Triumph TR4-TR5-TR250 1961-1968
Triumph TR6 1969-1976
Triumph TR6 Collection No.1 1969-1983
Triumph TR7 & TR8 1975-1982
Triumph Vitesse & Herald 1959-1971
TVR Gold Portfolio 1959-1988
Volkswagen Cars 1936-1956
VW Beetle Collection No.1 1970-1982
VW Golf GTi 1976-1986
VW Karmann Ghia 1955-1982
VW Kubelwagen 1940-1975
VW Scirocco 1974-1981
VW Bus. Camper. Van 1954-1967
VW Bus. Camper. Van 1968-1979
VW Bus. Camper. Van 1979-1989
Volvo 120 1956-1970
Volvo 1800 1960-1973

BROOKLANDS ROAD & TRACK SERIES

Road & Track on Alfa Romeo 1949-1963
Road & Track on Alfa Romeo 1964-1970
Road & Track on Alfa Romeo 1971-1976
Road & Track on Alfa Romeo 1977-1989
Road & Track on Aston Martin 1962-1984
Road & Track on Auburn Cord and Duesenburg 1952-1984
Road & Track on Audi & Auto Union 1952-1980
Road & Track on Audi 1980-1986
Road & Track on Austin Healey 1953-1970
Road & Track on BMW Cars 1966-1974
Road & Track on BMW Cars 1975-1978
Road & Track on BMW Cars 1979-1983

Road & Track on Cobra, Shelby & GT40 1962-1983
Road & Track on Corvette 1953-1967
Road & Track on Corvette 1968-1982
Road & Track on Corvette 1982-1986
Road & Track on Datsun Z 1970-1983
Road & Track on Ferrari 1950-1968
Road & Track on Ferrari 1968-1974
Road & Track on Ferrari 1975-1981
Road & Track on Ferrari 1981-1984
Road & Track on Fiat Sports Cars 1968-1987
Road & Track on Jaguar 1950-1960
Road & Track on Jaguar 1961-1968
Road & Track on Jaguar 1968-1974
Road & Track on Jaguar 1974-1982
Road & Track on Jaguar 1983-1989
Road & Track on Lamborghini 1964-1985
Road & Track on Lotus 1972-1981
Road & Track on Maserati 1952-1974
Road & Track on Maserati 1975-1983
Road & Track on Mazda RX7 1978-1986
Road & Track on Mercedes 1952-1962
Road & Track on Mercedes 1963-1970
Road & Track on Mercedes 1971-1979
Road & Track on Mercedes 1980-1987
Road & Track on MG Sports Cars 1949-1961
Road & Track on MG Sprots Cars 1962-1980
Road & Track on Mustang 1964-1977
Road & Track on Peugeot 1955-1986
Road & Track on Pontiac 1960-1983
Road & Track on Porsche 1961-1967
Road & Track on Porsche 1968-1971
Road & Track on Porsche 1972-1975
Road & Track on Porsche 1975-1978
Road & Track on Porsche 1979-1982
Road & Track on Porsche 1982-1985
Road & Track on Porsche 1985-1988
Road & Track on Rolls Royce & B'ley 1950-1965
Road & Track on Rolls Royce & B'ley 1966-1984
Road & Track on Saab 1955-1985
Road & Track on Toyota Sports & GT Cars 1966-1984
Road & Track on Triumph Sports Cars 1953-1967
Road & Track on Triumph Sports Cars 1967-1974
Road & Track on Triumph Sports Cars 1974-1982
Road & Track on Volkswagen 1951-1968
Road & Track on Volkswagen 1968-1978
Road & Track on Volkswagen 1978-1985
Road & Track on Volvo 1957-1974
Road & Track on Volvo 1975-1985
Road & Track - Henry Manney at Large and Abroad

BROOKLANDS CAR AND DRIVER SERIES

Car and Driver on BMW 1955-1977
Car and Driver on BMW 1977-1985
Car and Driver on Cobra, Shelby & Ford GT 40 1963-1984
Car and Driver on Corvette 1956-1967
Car and Driver on Corvette 1968-1977
Car and Driver on Corvette 1978-1982
Car and Driver on Corvette 1983-1988
Car and Driver on Datsun Z 1600 & 2000 1966-1984
Car and Driver on Ferrari 1955-1962
Car and Driver on Ferrari 1963-1975
Car and Driver on Ferrari 1976-1983
Car and Driver on Mopar 1956-1967
Car and Driver on Mopar 1968-1975
Car and Driver on Mustang 1964-1972
Car and Driver on Pontiac 1961-1975
Car and Driver on Porsche 1955-1962
Car and Driver on Porsche 1963-1970
Car and Driver on Porsche 1970-1976
Car and Driver on Porsche 1977-1981
Car and Driver on Porsche 1982-1986
Car and Driver on Saab 1956-1985
Car and Driver on Volvo 1955-1986

BROOKLANDS PRACTICAL CLASSICS SERIES

PC on Austin A40 Restoration
PC on Land Rover Restoration
PC on Metalworking in Restoration
PC on Midget/Sprite Restoration
PC on Mini Cooper Restoration
PC on MGB Restoration
PC on Morris Minor Restoration
PC on Sunbeam Rapier Restoration
PC on Triumph Herald/Vitesse
PC on Triumph Spitfire Restoration
PC on VW Beetle Restoration
PC on 1930s Car Restoration

BROOKLANDS MOTOR & THOROGHBRED & CLASSIC CAR SERIES

Motor & T & CC on Ferrari 1966-1976
Motor & T & CC on Ferrari 1976-1984
Motor & T & CC on Lotus 1979-1983

BROOKLANDS MILITARY VEHICLES SERIES

Allied Mil. Vehicles No.1 1942-1945
Allied Mil. Vehicles No.2 1941-1946
Dodge Mil. Vehicles Col. 1 1940-1945
Military Jeeps 1941-1945
Off Road Jeeps 1944-1971
Hail to the Jeep
US Military Vehicles 1941-1945
US Army Military Vehicles WW2-TM9-2800

BROOKLANDS HOT ROD RESTORATION SERIES

Auto Restoration Tips & Techniques
Basic Bodywork Tips & Techniques
Basic Painting Tips & Techniques
Camaro Restoration Tips & Techniques
Custom Painting Tips & Techniques
Engine Swapping Tips & Techniques
How to Build a Street Rod
Mustang Restoration Tips & Techniques
Performance Tuning - Chevrolets of the '60s
Performance Tuning - Ford of the '60s
Performance Tuning - Mopars of the '60s
Performance Tuning - Pontiacs of the '60s

BROOKLANDS BOOKS

Part 1

CONTENTS

Contents for Part Two will be found on Page 101

BROOKLANDS BOOKS

ACKNOWLEDGEMENTS

We produced our first book on the Lotus Cortina — Lotus Cortina 1963-1970 early in 1983. It went out of print last year and since that time we have received many requests to make it available once more. We decided to expand the Lotus Cortina story by adding a further 80 pages to the original book and issuing it as a Gold Portfolio.

The forward I wrote in 1983 is reprinted below for your interest:

> 'At the time the Lotus Cortina was at the height of its fame I was attending a well known business school. They taught me through an absorbing game how to recognise win-win, win-lose and lose-lose situations. It would seem that representatives from Dagenham and Cheshunt had been there before me as the emergence of the Lotus Type 28/Ford 125E (the 1963 Lotus Cortina) had all the characteristics of a classic win-win ploy.
>
> It established Ford of Britain on the track, and later the international rally circuits, and started a succession of winning competition models such as the twin-cam Escorts, the RS. 1600s, 1800s and 2000s, the sporting Capris and the GT40 which took top honours at Le Mans on four separate occasions.
>
> Colin Chapman during this period took Lotus from modest facilities at Cheshunt to a new factory near Norwich and entered the seventies with an enviable track record and two successful production models, the Elan and Europa.'

The Lotus Cortina Register encouraged us to publish the first book and have given us every assistance with this enlarged Portfolio. For further information see their notice on page 36.

Our books are printed in small numbers as works of reference for those that indulge in the hobby of automobile collecting and restoration. We exist firstly because there is a need by owners for this information and secondly because the publishers of the worlds leading automotive journals generously assist us by allowing us to include their copyright articles in these anthologies.

We are indebted in this instance to the management of Autocar, Australia Motor Sports, Autosport, Auto Topics, British Car, Car Life, Cars and Car Conversions, Cars Illustrated, Classic and Sportscar, Custom Car, Ford Times, Modern Motor, Motor, Motoring News, Motor Sport, Motor Trend, Performance Ford, Practical Classics, Road & Track, Small Car, Sports Car Graphic, Sports Car World, Thoroughbred & Classic Cars, Wheels and Worlds Fastest Sports Cars for their ongoing support.

R.M. Clarke

THE announcement of a new ultra-high performance saloon by Ford is exciting news indeed. The basis of the car is the 1,500 c.c. version of the Cortina, of which the engine, transmission, suspension, brakes and equipment have all been modified by Lotus and Cosworth for high speed road work and touring car racing.

The basic Ford 1,500 c.c. engine carries the Lotus twin-overhead-camshaft light alloy cylinder head that was designed by Harry Mundy and is manufactured by J.A.P. The camshafts are chain-driven and operate the valves through inverted pistons, the sparking plugs being vertical on the central axis but set back or forward over alternate bores to clear the inclined valves. The crankshaft is specially balanced for high revolutions and the pistons are designed by Cosworth.

Two Weber twin-choke carburetters supply the gas, and a built-in cold air supply carries an air filter. The exhaust system features four matched pipes which are first paired and then run in together under the car. The machine is properly silenced.

Special close ratios are fitted to the all-synchromesh gearbox. Alternative final drive ratios are available but with the standard 3.90 to 1 axle the overall ratios are 3.90, 4.797, 6.396 and 9.750 to 1. Speeds around 115, 92, 69 and 45 m.p.h. are obtained at 6,500 r.p.m. A short central remote control gear lever is mounted on a central console. Naturally, a special 8 ins. clutch is used with this transmission, and the propeller shaft has a 3 ins. diameter tube. The differential housing is in light alloy, and special light alloy parts are also used for the clutch housing, gearbox extension and remote gear change.

A considerable use of light alloys also occurs in the body construction, the outer panels of the body, doors and bonnet being in aluminium. The shape is identical to that of the standard Cortina but the body is white with green flashes and a green-on-

THE PERFORMANCE CORTINA MODIFIED BY LOTUS

BY
JOHN
BOLSTER

yellow Lotus crest. The interior trim is in black vyanide with racing-type heavily padded bucket seats and crash pads. Most important, the wood-rimmed steering wheel operates a special high-geared steering box.

The binnacle houses a speedometer, rev. counter, oil pressure, water temperature and fuel gauges.

The car is considerably lowered, the front suspension units being different and the front wheels without any camber. At the rear, the semi-elliptic springs have gone, making way for helical springs. The axle is located on trailing arms each side, and underneath the centre there is an A-shaped tubular member. Thus, the beam is located in both directions and the torque reaction is absorbed.

A vacuum servo is applied to the hydraulic operation of the brakes; 9½ ins. discs are fitted in front and 9 ins. × 1¾ ins. drums at the rear, the linings being to competition specification. A stiffer anti-roll bar is fitted and the special wheels, which carry 6.00 × 13 ins. tyres, have the very wide rim size of 5½ ins. for stability.

As supplied, the engine develops 105 b.h.p. (nett) at 5,500 r.p.m. on a compression ratio of 9.5 to 1. As much as 140 b.h.p. has already been obtained in tuned form. Obviously, the potentialities of this car are very great indeed, and it is understood that over 1,000 are already in course of assembly, so homologation is assured.

Team Lotus announce that "works" cars will be driven in touring car races by Jim Clark, Trevor Taylor and Peter Arundell. In addition, they will develop cars for the Competitions Department of the Ford Motor Company, which will be entered in rallies. It is certain that the demand for these cars from enthusiasts will be very heavy, and for really fast road work or competitions these machines are very desirable indeed. In spite of the very high performance available it is impressive that standard Ford parts figure largely in the specification, which is a great advantage from the point of view of service.

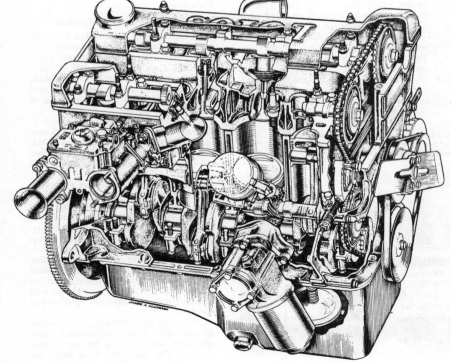

AND NOW...

FORD CORTINA LOTUS

IN Great Britain the success of improved performance cars has been phenomenal; it is seldom appreciated that the suspension, steering and brakes on the modern mass-produced cars have such a degree of inherent safety that considerable increases in performance can be made with relatively minor changes. Moreover, the higher engine powers obtained are not usually accompanied by any significant shortening of working life in most instances.

Several factors undoubtedly have contributed to the Ford decision to produce a high-performance sports saloon based on the recently announced Cortina, with the help of Colin Chapman and his young and virile Lotus organization. Unquestionably, the decision of the American parent company in Dearborn to pursue a policy of active competition with works-sponsored cars has filtered through to Dagenham. Also, the success of the small, over-square four-cylinder engines, developed to an outstanding degree by Keith Duckworth and Mike Costin, of Cosworth Engineer-ing, has been responsible for Ford taking advantage of the enormous publicity given to these achievements.

When these engines were first used for formula Junior racing, Ford did not actively oppose the projects, neither did they actively support them; in later days this attitude changed completely, and experimental cylinder blocks with five main bearings were made available to Lotus and Cosworth at a very early stage.

Finally, the Lotus twin-overhead camshaft conversion of the 1·5-litre 116E engine, which performed sensationally in the 1962 1,000 Kilometre Race at the Nürburgring when first fitted to the Lotus 23 sports car—and later used also for the new Lotus Elan—opened up immense possibilities. Early prototypes of this engine were fitted in standard production cars to speed the development period. This led Colin Chapman to appreciate the potentialities of the Cortina, with slight modifications, as a high-performance road car, with an eye on its future possibilities for production car racing and similar sporting events.

It is also not unreasonable to imagine that Sir Patrick Hennessy and his managerial colleagues at Dagenham became envious of the success of the Mini-Cooper in competition and mindful of the resulting publicity. A combination of the above factors has led to a working arrangement between Ford and Lotus to produce the Cortina-Lotus. It is powered by a 1,558 c.c. version of the twin-overhead camshaft engine. Considerable modifications have been made to the suspensions and brakes, and weight has been saved by the greater use of aluminium; along with other changes, this has contributed to a better weight distribution, to provide a car with a claimed top speed of nearly 115 m.p.h., the fastest British Ford ever marketed.

Lotus Works Extended

These cars will be modified from the basic production units in a newly completed extension to the Cheshunt works of Lotus Cars Ltd., and will be marketed through the normal Ford channels. Home price has not yet been announced but we expect it to be in the region of £1,100 including tax.

The twin overhead camshaft engine is basically similar to the original Lotus unit described in *Autocar* of 1 June 1962, but there are differences resulting from the closer co-operation now existing with the Ford Motor Company.

Briefly, that engine utilizes a production Ford cylinder block with crankshaft, connecting rods, pistons, camshafts and drives for the oil pump and distributor; the standard head assembly, push rods, front cover and water pump casing are discarded. The new components consist of an aluminium-alloy twin-overhead camshaft cylinder head with opposed valves separated at an included angle of 54 degrees and operated directly through inverted piston-type tappets.

The original camshaft and sprocket are retained. Two more standard chain sprockets are used for the new camshafts. The drive to them from the

A veritable wolf in sheep's clothing. Suspension changes made to the Cortina-Lotus are particularly apparent from the way the rear end has been lowered by approximately 3·5in. The standard colour is white with a green flash along each side

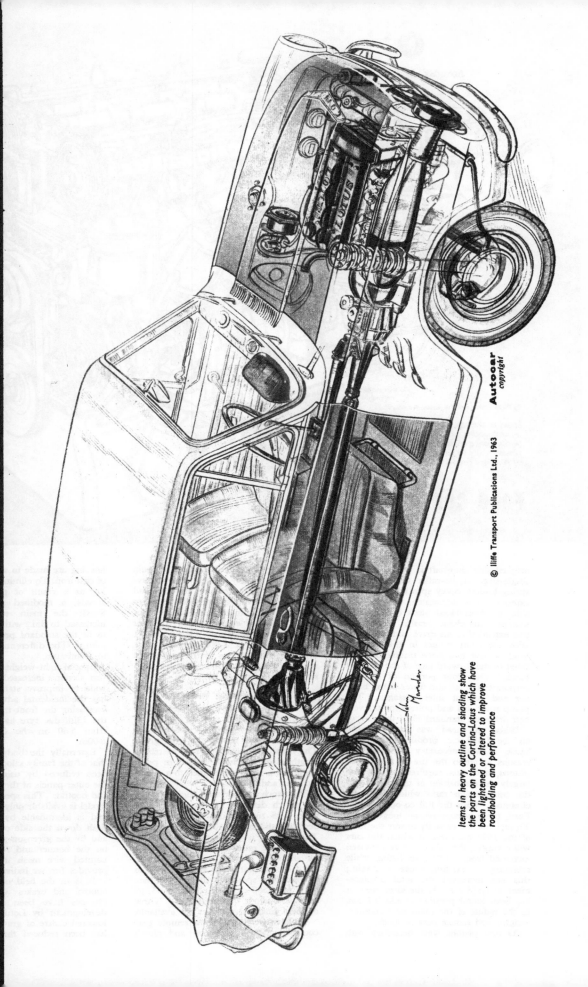

Items in heavy outline and shading show the parts on the Cortina-Lotus which have been lightened or altered to improve roadholding and performance

© Iliffe Transport Publications Ltd., 1963

Autocar
copyright

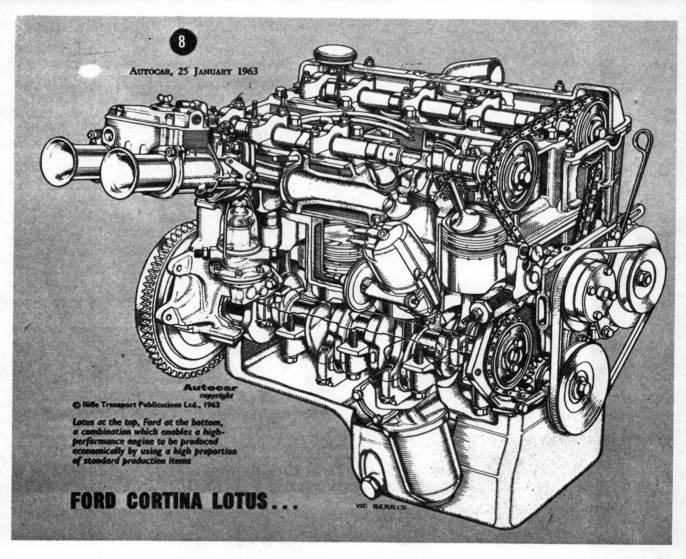

Lotus at the top, Ford at the bottom, a combination which enables a high-performance engine to be produced economically by using a high proportion of standard production items

FORD CORTINA LOTUS...

VIC BERRIS

original side camshaft is by means of a single-stage single-roller chain, with a spring-loaded jockey sprocket having an external screw adjustment on the slack side; a rubber-faced block on the tight side prevents chain thrash. To enclose this extended chain drive and match-up with the front tunnel in the cylinder head, a new two-piece timing cover is fitted to the forward face of the cylinder block. The front portion of this incorporates the fan and water pump bearing and coolant inlet passages. The pump rotor seal and pulleys for the vee-belt drive are standard Ford units.

When the head was first designed on the 1,499 c.c. production cylinder block, it was necessary for economic reasons to retain the use of flat-topped pistons, and this requirement dictated largely the disposition of the valves and the compression ratio which could be obtained. With the full co-operation of Ford, these parameters no longer exist. To increase the capacity nearer the limit of the 1600 c.c. class in which the cars will compete, the cylinder bore has been increased from 3·187in. to 3·25in. while retaining the existing stroke of 2·86in.; this has increased the total displacement to 1,558 c.c. At the same time, it has been found possible to add 0·375in. to the radius of the crankshaft counter-weights and reduce bearing loads.

As new pistons were necessary with this change, it has been possible to equip them with slightly domed crowns having shallow valve clearance cut-outs, and thus increase the compression ratio to 9·5 to 1. Maximum net power output of the standard engine is 105 b.h.p. at 5,500 r.p.m. with a peak b.m.e.p. of 171 p.s.i. recorded at 4,000 r.p.m. More highly tuned versions of the engine are under development and these are currently producing 140 b.h.p.

Twin-choke Webers

Two 40mm twin-choke Weber carburettors are fitted and air is fed to them through a large silencer box and a cleaner mounted behind the front grille. The exhaust system uses four matched-length pipes which are joined in pairs, ending in a single pipe taken to a resonator box and muffler.

To absorb the increased engine power, the clutch diameter has been increased from 7·25 to 8in. dia. and the latest design of diaphragm spring type is used. The gearbox is equipped with a set of special close ratios different from those for any other Cortina or Classic model. With the standard axle ratio of 3·90 to 1, maximum speeds in the intermediate gears (at 6,500 engine r.p.m.) are 45, 69 and 92 m.p.h. respectively. Three optional final drive ratios are available. To save weight, the new remote gear control, gearbox extension and clutch

housing are made in aluminium, instead of cast iron. To eliminate possible whirling as a result of the higher engine speeds, a modified propeller shaft is fitted; the main tube diameter is increased to 3in., with the ends swaged to fit the standard production universal joints. The differential housing is also of aluminium.

Special light-weight steel wheels have rim sections increased from 4 to 5·5in. wide to improve stability; this change has the incidental advantage of slightly increasing the front track. Sections for the 13in. dia. tyre have been increased from 5·60 on the Cortina Super to 6·00in.

Externally the body looks similar to that of the family saloon, but weight has been reduced by using aluminium for the outer panels of the doors, the bonnet and bootlid. This special Cortina-Lotus model is available only in two-door form and is identifiable by a striking green flash down the side of the white body, and by the green-on-yellow Lotus crest on the bonnet and rear flanks; black-painted wire mesh in the front grille provides further individuality.

It is in the field of suspension, ride control and brakes where considerable changes have been made during the development by Lotus. To provide a lowered centre of gravity, the ride level has been reduced throughout, in con-

junction with higher rate springs and stiffer dampers. At the front, the wheel camber has been reduced to zero by modifying the front suspension units and using lowered track control arms; these are now steel forgings in place of the back-to-back pressed steel channel sections used on the production cars. Roll has been reduced by using a stiffer 1⅝in. dia. anti-roll bar at the front, which also acts as a lower wishbone member. A new steering box assembly raises the overall gearing by approximately 12 per cent.

The normal half-elliptic leaf springs on the rear suspension have been discarded. The springing is by coils surrounding heavy duty telescopic dampers and the live axle is controlled by trailing radius arms at each side and a widely based "A" bracket for lateral location.

Because of the suspension changes it has been necessary to make detailed modifications to the body structure. As the car is now set lower, additional bump clearance above the axle has been provided and there are stiffening tubes extending from the wheel arches to the frame extensions at each side in the boot. This has necessitated removing the spare wheel from behind the left wheel arch to a horizontal position on the floor; also, the battery has been moved to a position behind the left rear wheel, to make way for the new carburettor air cleaners and improve weight distribution.

Servo Brakes

Girling vacuum-servo-assisted brakes are fitted, the equipment comprising 9·50in. dia. discs at the front and 9in. × 1·75in. wide drums and shoes at the rear, the same as those fitted to the heavier Classic. The parking brake is operated by a pistol grip lever mounted beneath the facia.

Internal trim is carried out entirely in black Vynide. The frames of the front bucket seats are standard Cortina components, but the backrests are provided with greater rake and the cushions more heavily padded for lateral support, to match the car's sporting character.

A trimmed cover encloses the central remote gear lever linkage and an exten-

sion of it forms a small compartment, the lid of which is padded to serve as a central arm rest. A new instrument binnacle is clamped on the existing facia in front of the steering wheel, and houses a speedometer, tachometer, oil pressure and water temperature gauges and fuel contents gauge. Arm reach has been improved by shortening the steering column and fitting a non-dished three-spoked aluminium wheel having a wooden rim 15in. in diameter.

To date, only a few prototype vehicles have been produced and no weights have been released, but Lotus estimate that the modifications made will effect a reduction of approximately 100lb.

This co-operation between a big manufacturer and a small company which has established itself in the forefront of competitive motoring has obvious benefits for both. It enables Ford to market a small series of high performance cars economically without disruption to normal production; for Lotus it means an almost undreamed of production stability.

Team Lotus, the company formed to undertake the racing activities of Lotus Cars, have announced the formation of a team to compete with these new cars in all suitable touring car competitions. Their drivers, Jim Clark, Trevor Taylor and Peter Arundell, are a formidable trio in other racing spheres. In addition to their circuit racing activities, Team

The Lotus badge on the bonnet adds to the confusion of names already adorning the car. Black-painted wire mesh replaces the bright metal grille seen on this early prototype

Lotus will also prepare rally cars for the use of the Ford Competition Department as works entries.

Specification

ENGINE
No. of cylinders	...	4 in line, water-cooled
Bore	...	3·25in. (82·6mm)
Stroke	...	2·86in. (72·75mm)
Displacement	...	1,558 c.c. (95·1 cu in.)
Valve gear	...	Twin o.h.c. chain driven
Compression ratio		9·5 to 1
Max. b.h.p. (net)	...	105 at 5,500 r.p.m.
Max. b.m.e.p. (net)		171 p.s.i. at 4,000 r.p.m.
Max. torque (net)		108 lb ft at 4,000 r.p.m.
Carburettors	...	Two twin-choke Weber, type 40 DCOE2
Fuel pump	...	AC mechanical
Tank capacity	...	8 Imp. gallons (36 litres)
Sump capacity	...	6·5 pints (3·7 litres)
Cooling system	...	Fan, pump and thermostat
Battery	...	12 volt, 38 amp hr.

TRANSMISSION
Clutch	...	Diaphragm type single plate 8·0in. dia
Gearbox	...	Four speeds, synchromesh on all forwards ratios, central floor change
Overall gear ratios (std)		Top, 3·90; 3rd, 4·80; 2nd, 6·40; 1st, 9·76
Final drive	...	Hypoid bevel; std. ratio 3·90 to 1. Optional ratios 3·77, 4·10, 4·43

CHASSIS
Brakes	...	Girling hydraulic with vacuum-servo assistance. Discs front, drums rear
Disc dia.	...	9·50in.
Drum dimensions		9·0in. dia. x 1·75in. wide shoes
Suspension	...	Front, independent MacPherson strut type, coil springs and anti-roll bar. Rear, live axle, located by radius arms and A-frame. Coil springs mounted co-axially with dampers
Dampers	...	Armstrong telescopic F and R
Wheels	...	Bolt-on steel discs; 4 studs 5·5in. rim width
Tyre size	...	6·00—13in. tubeless nylon speed
Steering	...	Ford-Burman recirculating ball
Steering wheel	...	Three-spoke, 15in. dia.
Turns lock to lock		3

DIMENSIONS (Manufacturer's figures)
Wheelbase	...	8ft 2·4in. (249·9cm)
Track	...	Front 4ft 3·6in. (131 cm) Rear, 4ft 1·5in. (125·5 cm)
Overall length	...	14ft 0·3in. (428 cm)
Overall width	...	5ft 2·5in. (159cm)
Overall height	...	4ft 5·4in. (136cm) unladen
Ground clearance		5in. (12·7cm)

PERFORMANCE DATA
Top gear m.p.h. per 1,000 r.p.m.	Std. ratio	17·9
	3·77 to 1 ratio,	18·5
	4·10 to 1 ratio,	17·0
	4·43 to 1 ratio,	15·8
Torque lb ft per cu in. engine capacity		1·14
Brake surface area swept by linings		282 sq in.

Main internal changes comprise a new instrument cluster, Lotus steering wheel, central padded tunnel and competition-type seats which, like the rest of the car, are trimmed in black plastic cloth

Top Speed: 115 mph! 0-100 mph in under 30 sec!

FORD BUILDS A FLIER - WITH

ON the eve of the fourth Annual Racing Car Show in London the Ford Motor Company announced its latest addition to the already large range — the Consul Cortina Sports Special, a 105 bhp and 115 mph version of the current medium-sized family hack. This is the fastest sedan produced by the Ford Company of England and brings together Ford's production capabilities and the high performance know-how of the Lotus firm.

Bodily, this sports model differs little from the standard Cortina. Identification is by the open front grille, the Lotus badge, and the color scheme. They are all finished in white with a brilliant green flash down each side. The body panels are mostly made from aluminium and offer a great saving in weight. All the outer panels of the doors, body, and bonnet lid are also aluminium.

Bucket seats are fitted to the front, shaped

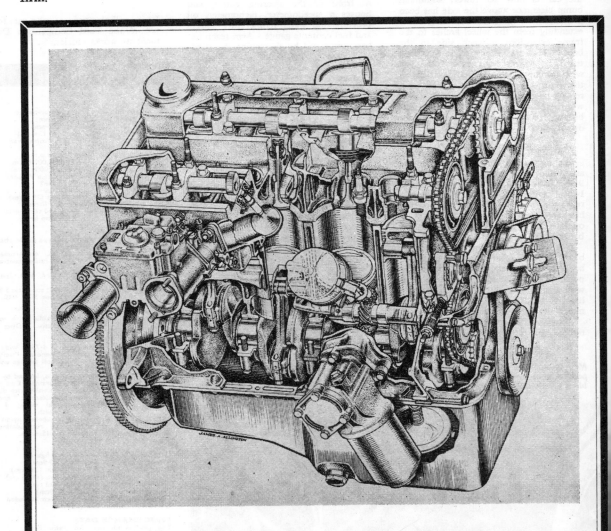

Sectional view of the Lotus/Ford twin-cam engine, which uses standard Ford components apart from cylinder head, pushrods, timing cover and water pump.

From DAVID M. PALMER

Lotus' Help

and well padded to offer the best crash padding, support. With the trim panels and crash padding, they are covered in black vynide. A non-dished small diameter wood-rimmed steering wheel and the neat instrument nacelle directly in front of the driver make the pilot's position very business-like. Instruments include speedometer, tachometer, oil pressure and water temperature gauges and fuel gauge. Warning lights are used to indicate the state of the charging circuit and show when the headlamps are on high beam. The battery is mounted in the luggage boot, presumably in an effort to have a little weight over the rear wheels, for the car appears to be nose-heavy. There is a centred console between the front seats which embodies a driver's armrest and provision for further instrumentation. The short remote-control gear lever protrudes from this console.

Driving force of this Cortina sports is the Classic 1½-litre engine, specially developed and bored out to 1558 cc and fitted with the Lotus twin-cam cylinder head and two twin-choke Weber carburettors. This is the engine from the recently announced Lotus Elan sports car. In standard form it develops 105 bhp at 5500 rpm and 108 lb/ft torque at 4000 rpm. As many enthusiasts will remember, this unit last year had a really startling debut in the Nurburgring 1000 Km Race, but then it was propelling a Lotus 23 sports racer.

Development work was carried out in great secrecy last year, one of the test drivers being none other than Jim Clark, seen here putting prototype through its paces at Silverstone.

For an engine conversion such as this to be successful, it has to retain as many of the original parts as possible to take care of the spares situation. This is what Lotus, in conjunction with the well known Ford engine tuners, Cosworth Engineering Ltd, have done. The engine uses all standard parts, except for the cylinder head, push rods, timing cover and water pump. The head has circular combustion chambers, large valves, and rather narrow valve angle of 54 degrees. Valve operation is by inverted bucket-type tappets operating directly in the alloy head, while each camshaft is through-drilled and pressure-fed from the main system to keep the four bearings adequately lubricated.

Two standard Ford sprockets drive the camshafts, a single roller chain with spring-loaded jockey sprocket connecting these, this having an

CONTINUED ON PAGE 25

Different grille, side paint flash, half-bumpers and lowered bodywork outwardly distinguish Cortina Special. Note Lotus badge under Consul emblem.

What might be described as everybody's cup of Coffey, the Lotus Cortina comes only in white with green flash.

A WOLF IN SHEEP'S CLOTHING

CORTINA IN LOTUS-LAND

By PAUL HIGGINS

The results of improving the breed are illuminated in this exclusive road test of the first Lotus-Cortina to reach Australia. Hereinafter the reaction will be: "That's a Lotus-Cortina — wasn't it?"

WHAT is the most exclusive high-performance road car in Australia today? Certainly not Aston Martin or Maserati. Or Jaguar E-types — they're 10 a penny. Or the highly-desirable Ferrari Berlinetta, a couple of which have been booming around for some time.

Corvette or Avanti? The answer again is no.

Top of the list is an almost insignificant-looking car that can be parked in a busy city street without tempting a second glance from the crowds that cluster around anything novel.

The car? A Lotus Cortina, the one and only in this country. Essentially, it is a Cortina body with the twin-cam Lotus-modified 1500 cc engine.

Owner is 28-year-old Melbourne businessman Peter Coffey, who brought the car to Australia in July after completing a 10-month working assignment with Ford at Dagenham. Although no stunner in looks — functional efficiency, not chromium-plated glamor has been the aim — the Lotus Cortina certainly leaves the traffic gasping.

Some time before its release in January of this year, Lotus head Colin Chapman played a trick on his No 1 works driver, Jim Clark, by dropping the twin-cam engine into the factory's hack Anglia without telling Clark. Clark couldn't believe what was happening when he put his foot down on the journey up the MI turnpike towards his home in Scotland. A quick look under the bonnet told the story. But his disbelief was nothing compared to that of the driver of a 3.8 Jaguar sitting smugly on 100 miles an hour, who found a seedy-looking Anglia in his slipstream and pulling out to pass. The poor man probably hasn't recovered yet.

I know how much of a kick Clark must have had out of it because I found my "Jaguar" while testing the Lotus. Only it wasn't a Jaguar, but an MG-A. The A-type ranged alongside at traffic lights heading out of the city limits. The driver could afford only one patronising glance before smoothing down his stringbacks and sprinting through the de-restriction signs on Victoria's M1, the Geelong Road.

A couple of miles further on and the Lotus burbled past him at an easy 90. The cat and mouse game was on. It lasted for more than 20 miles until 1 pulled off the road for petrol. Seconds later the MG, smelling pretty hot, drew up. Out got Stringbacks wearing the defensive "there-must-be-something-wrong-with-my-speedo" frown that seems standard behavior among sports car drivers.

A close look at the Coffey car and 10 minutes of

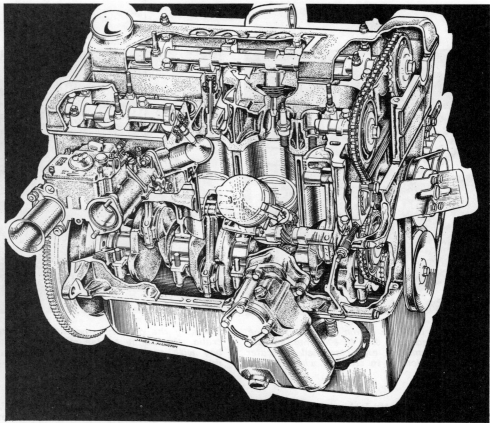

Schematic illustration of the twin-cam 1500 cc Ford engine; it uses standard Ford components, apart from cylinder head, pushrods, timing cover and water pump.

Invitation to exhilaration: The Lotus interior demonstrates competition breeding in wood-rimmed wheel, short gearlever, and beautiful bucket seats trimmed in black. Central console houses a lockable glovebox.

questions — then he left, a much humbler man. Who can blame him?

There is no doubt that the wedding of Ford's rather orthodox Cortina to Chapman's genius has produced a safe and spirited offspring. There's no doubt, too, that it has the balance, feel and manners of a track car. Below 3000 revs the 1.6-litre twin-cam motor is almost dead. When it comes on the cam, things really start to move. Taken up to the red-banded 6500 segment on the tachometer results in 45 mph in first gear, 68 in second, 92 in third and 107 in top. The standing quarter scurries under the wide-rim wheels in 18.2 seconds, and 0-80 takes only 20 seconds.

All of this seems pretty impressive. But the outstanding thing of all is that the car has received only routine servicing since becoming Peter Coffey's property, 7000 miles before. It was used as an everyday family car by Peter and his wife Jean during their stay in Britain, with a quick 4000-mile dash through Europe before it was loaded aboard ship for Australia. In a better state of tune the car should shave seconds off its acceleration times. Engine output is 105 brake horsepower. When raced by the factory, power goes up to 140 bhp.

Price of the milder version landed here is about £2000. That's pretty hefty, so a more than critical look was given to the Lotus Cortina.

Finish inside and out is good with the possible

In front of the driver are (from left) fuel gauge, tachometer segmented from 6500 to 8000 rpm, speedometer with trip odometer, and combined oil/water gauge. Lotus emblem is in steering wheel boss.

Probably the only twin-cam engine extant in Australia, the Coffey engine sits neatly in the Cortina bay with reasonable elbow room. Cam covers are finished in crackle-type blue and Webers can be seen.

exception of the rather tatty-looking facia padding. Paintwork is deep and smooth and there are no signs of blemishes or roughness in the bodywork. Ford Australia could pick up a few tips here.

Lowered almost two inches all round, the car looks purposeful, if not downright aggressive. Quarter bumpers guard the front fenders, tyres are fat 600 x 13 Dunlop C-41s on 5½ inch rims — tubeless tyres mark you, and that's what Chapman specifies — and an olive green sash sweeps along the waistline and on to the bottom panel of the boot. This breaks up the tendency towards slabbiness, the prime color of white can give to the body.

Yellow and green Lotus badges can be found on the radiator grille, back wheel panels, gear lever knob, and steering wheel boss. But there is not a mention of Ford anywhere on the car. The nearest it comes to acknowledging the relationship is the flat vee Consul legend on the bonnet.

Inside, the layout has obviously been planned to put all vital controls and instruments within easy look or reach of the driver. A 140 mph speedometer and 8000 rpm tachometer share pride of place in a hooded binnacle dead ahead of the driver. Flanking them on the left is the fuel gauge, while oil pressure and water temperature share a dial to the right. All markings are white on black for legibility.

In fact black is the predominant color inside the car . . . from the superbly comfortable bucket seats, over the dash, and onto the door trims. Even the between-the-buckets console, that starts off as a padded arm rest — hidden under the pop-up lid is a box for odds and ends — and becomes a tunnel for the remote control gearshift, is covered in good quality vinyl. Rubber mats, again black, are used on the floor.

The 15-inch wood-rimmed steering wheel feels good, acts quickly and lightly, and gives a fine alertly-relaxed driving position. Strangely, the foot brake and throttle pedals are too far apart for heeling and toeing.

Race-breeding is clearly shown in the design of the two front seats. The backs are curved and grip the shoulders firmly and softly. Raised folds on the cushions stop any sliding when travelling through fast corners. This means the driver can concentrate on controlling the car and not on trying to keep himself from vanishing through the window. Nearest approach to this set-up would be to use a tightly-

drawn lap belt in the family runabout. The back seat of the car is the same as the under-£1000 Cortina, apart from the trim.

A heater-demister and screenwashers are standard, and the windscreen is laminated glass. Wipers are single-speed electric, and seem too sluggish to cope with more than a sprinkling of rain at high speed.

The battery is in the boot — for two reasons: it stays cooler there and helps to improve weight distribution. But the luggage area is still big enough for a bundle of suitcases.

To get the car's weight down to 14¾ cwt, the boot lid, bonnet and doors are made of alloy. Door locks are the zero torque type that need just a gentle one-finger push to click home. Under-bonnet working room is good although at first sight there appears to be a bit of a crush with the brake servo unit, and the long silencer box that feeds air to the twin-choke 40 mm Weber carburettors, taking up a fair bit of space.

In full view is the alloy twin-cam head, with Lotus written boldly on the crackle-blue cam covers. The head was designed by Harry Mundy, famed for his brilliant work on competition Jaguars, and is built by J. A. Prestwich, better known as the J.A.P. engine makers.

Initial impressions behind the wheel of the Lotus Cortina are a little frustrating, even disappointing. The clutch return spring is strong enough to have a mind of its own, and calls for exact control. There's no messing about. The clutch is either in or out. The bite is immediate and it can't be slipped. Trying to take off from rest needs a bootful of revs — maximum torque doesn't show up until 4000 rpm are posted — or the engine will fade and the transmission buck and snatch.

Town driving confines itself mostly to first and second gears, with the occasional use of third. Top gear is definitely open road stuff. This is one of the prices that must be paid when tactability is sacrificed for performance. Yet it's not such a sacrifice at that for the all-synchromesh close-ratio gearbox is one of the great joys of the car.

The truly enthusiastic driver will revel in the rapid, silent changes. No matter how fast he is at stirring the six-inch high gear lever he won't catch out the synchromesh. However, there is a fair amount of travel across the gate.

Continued on page 36

wheels ROAD TEST

TECHNICAL DETAILS

OF THE

LOTUS-CORTINA

SPECIFICATIONS

Cylinders	Four, in-line
Bore and stroke	82.55 mm by 72.746 mm
Cubic capacity	1558 cc
Compression ratio	9.5 to 1
Valves	Overhead camshafts
Carburettor: Two twin-choke 40 DCOE2 Weber sidedraught	
Power at rpm	105 bhp at 5500
Maximum torque	108 lb/ft at 4000 rpm

TRANSMISSION:

Type	Manual, floor-mounted remote lever

RATIOS:

First	9.75
Second	6.369
Third	4.797
Top	3.9
Rear axle	3.9 to 1

SUSPENSION:

Front	Coils
Rear	Trailing arm A-frames, coils
Dampers	Telescopic

STEERING:

Type	Recirculating ball
Turns, 1 to 1	3.25 to 1
Circle	36 ft

BRAKES:

Type	Discs front, drums rear, servo assisted

DIMENSIONS:

Wheelbase	8 ft 2½ in
Track, front	4 ft 3½ in
Track, rear	4 ft 1½ in
Length	14 ft 0¼ in
Width	5 ft 2½ in
Height	4 ft 5½ in

TYRES:

Size	600 x 13 on 5½ in rims

WEIGHT:

Dry	14¾ cwt

PERFORMANCE

TOP SPEED:

Fastest run	108 mph
Average of all runs	107 mph

MAXIMUM SPEED IN GEARS:

First	45 mph
Second	68 mph
Third	92 mph
Top	107 mph

ACCELERATION:

Standing Quarter-mile:

Fastest run	18.2 secs
Average of all runs	18.3 secs
0 to 30 mph	3.9 secs
0 to 40 mph	5.3 secs
0 to 50 mph	8.2 secs
0 to 60 mph	11.1 secs
0 to 70 mph	15.1 secs
0 to 80 mph	20 secs
20 to 40 mph	4.9 (2nd) 6.9 (3rd) secs
30 to 50 mph	6.8 (3rd), 9.6 (top) secs
40 to 60 mph	7.4 (3rd), 10 (top) secs

GO-TO-WHOA:

0-60-0 mph	15.4 secs

SPEEDO ERROR:

Indicated	Actual
30 mph	31 mph
40 mph	40.5 mph
50 mph	50 mph
60 mph	60 mph
70 mph	69.7 mph
80 mph	79.1 mph
90 mph	88.9 mph

FUEL CONSUMPTION:

Cruising speeds	'26-28
Overall for test	22.5 over 153 miles driven hard

AUTOSPORT, JANUARY 3, 1964

JOHN BOLSTER

tests a

LOTUS

FORD

CORTINA

IN a journal of the calibre of AUTOSPORT, there is no need to write a lengthy introduction to the Lotus Cortina. After the Cortina G.T., with pushrod engine and semi-elliptic springs, had made a habit of victory for most of the 1963 season, the Lotus version was homologated. This model, with its twin-cam engine and helical rear springs, proved to be even faster, and it is now available on the open market in road-going tune.

The basis of the car is the standard pressed steel saloon body, which is stiffened at the rear and has aluminium for the unstressed panels, such as the doors, bonnet, and boot lid. (The latter tends to bend or dent if closed sharply.) The front suspension has a very thick anti-roll bar, but at the rear a complete re-design has taken place. The axle is now located on trailing arms, with an A-bracket for lateral positioning. At the apex of this member, the trunnion has a grease nipple to ensure that no friction here can cause roll resistance.

Wheels with extra wide rims are set out to increase the track. The Girling brakes, with discs in front, have vacuum servo assistance. The body is carried appreciably lower than that of the standard car, the battery being moved back into the boot where the spare wheel is now bolted flat on the floor.

The engine is the Ford five-bearing four-cylinder unit, enlarged to 1,558 c.c. It has a light-alloy, twin overhead camshaft head, with two inclined valves per cylinder, and the drive for the camshafts is by chains. Two double-choke Weber carburetters, type 40DCOE 18, make an impressive sight under the bonnet.

Exceptionally close ratios are employed in the gearbox, the excellent Ford synchromesh being retained on all gears. The bottom gear is quite remarkably high for a saloon, but the good torque of the engine in the middle revolution ranges ensures certain restarting on steep hills—the diaphragm spring clutch will stand plenty of slipping. The remainder of the car follows Ford practice, though some components are of aluminium to counteract the extra weight of the twin-cam power unit.

The interior of the body is upholstered in

black Vynide, the seats being much more comfortable than the standard ones and giving good lateral location. The seating position is fairly high, the driver taking up a commanding posture behind his wood-rimmed steering wheel. All the controls are well placed for fast, long-distance driving.

The engine is an instant starter, even after a frosty night in the open. After a few seconds, the choke may be released, no accidental stalling taking place. By no means as flexible as the G.T. unit, the twin-cam engine can nevertheless be relied upon not to foul its sparking plugs or overheat during extended traffic driving. It is perhaps a little "lumpy" when idling and objects to pulling at less than 2,000 r.p.m., but thereafter, gives a most satisfying "punch" up to its peak speed of 5,500

r.p.m. It will reach about 6,200 r.p.m. on top gear and can touch 6,500 r.p.m. on the indirects, at which velocity a red mark is found on the rev.-counter dial. Actually, the relatively large "four" is just about running out of breath at such a rate, possibly due to pre-ignition of the very versatile sparking plugs.

The clutch is fairly heavy to operate and grips very firmly, but it never judders when slipped deliberately on the high bottom gear. This ratio is equivalent to second speed on most saloons, so it must be employed a great deal during traffic driving, when one seldom goes higher than the 70 m.p.h. second gear of the Cortina Lotus. The gear change is superb, which removes any objection to the frequent use of first speed. The gearbox and rear axle are both audible, but the noise level is not unduly high.

Except on very bad roads, the car rides remarkably well. The steering has a "competition" feel about it, allowing the machine to be pulled back onto its line when one has inadvertently run wide on a corner. At Brands Hatch, on Clearways, it is possible to get back onto the chosen line after over-sliding and dropping down the outer camber. With most saloons, the corner is irreparably spoilt if this mistake is made. The handling characteristic is an under-steering one, but the tail may be "flicked out" with the steering, or power may be used to break the rear end loose.

On very sharp corners, particularly where there are bumps, some rear wheel bounce and a tendency for the inside tyre to lift emphasize the presence of a rigid axle. The brakes, with servo assistance and discs in front, are smooth, dependable, and very powerful. The parking brake is a somewhat utilitarian pull-out handle but it holds well on hills.

The acceleration is very good indeed, aided by the closeness of the gear ratios. The engine seems to prefer hard driving and on average British roads this Ford is a hard one to beat. The acceleration continues strongly right up to 100 m.p.h., and consequently this is a speed which is often seen. When driven with abandon, the Lotus Cortina may consume fuel at the rate of a gallon for less than 20 miles. This consumption is not outrageous, having regard to the outstanding performance, but the size of the fuel tank is rather inadequate.

The silencing of the engine is worthy of praise and the unit is not mechanically noisy. The whole character of the car encourages fast driving, the acceleration being more than a surprise to many other road users. The cream paint, with green flashes, gives the game away, but I would

URGE DEPARTMENT. The engine (right) is a five-bearing, four-cylinder, twin-cam unit of 1,558 c.c. Power output is 105 b.h.p. at 5,500 r.p.m., which is quite healthy for any sort of motor car.

CUTAWAY DRAWING of the Lotus Ford Cortina (below), a high performance car developed jointly by Lotus and Ford. The changes from the original Ford Cortina can be seen.

prefer to spray the body in one colour, when one would have a real wolf in sheep's clothing!

The Lotus Cortina is a roomy four-seater saloon, with a large boot and plenty of interior parcel space. It is practical rather than luxurious, but has quite adequate equipment and a very good heater. The man who drives mostly in towns or traffic would probably prefer the more flexible G.T. and would certainly use less petrol. For really going places on the open road, however, the Lotus model, with its fierce acceleration and its speed of well over 100 m.p.h., is incomparably the better car and is made to be exploited by the press-on driver.

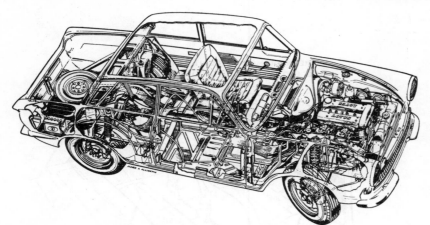

INSIDE of the car (below), showing the wood-rim steering wheel, the remote control gear-change and the instrument panel, which includes a speedometer, a rev.-counter and oil pressure, water temperature and fuel gauges.

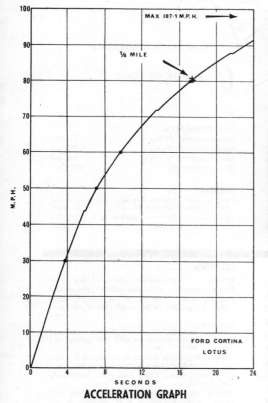

ACCELERATION GRAPH

SPECIFICATION AND PERFORMANCE DATA

Car Tested: Lotus Ford Cortina saloon, price £1,100 3s. 1d, including P.T.

Engine: Four-cylinders 82.55 mm. × 72.75 mm. (1,558 c.c.), twin overhead camshafts. Two double-choke side-draught Weber carburetters. Compression ratio 9.5 to 1. 105 b.h.p. (net) at 5,500 r.p.m. Lucas coil and distributor.

Transmission: Single dry plate diaphragm spring clutch. Four-speed all-synchromesh gearbox with short central lever, ratios 3.90, 4.79, 6.40, and 9.75 to 1. Open propeller shaft. Hypoid rear axle.

Chassis: Combined body and chassis. Independent front suspension with MacPherson struts, wishbones, and anti-roll torsion bar. Burman re-circulating ball steering gear. Rear axle on trailing arms and A-bracket. Helical springs and telescopic dampers all round. Girling hydraulic brakes, discs front, drums' rear. Bolt-on disc wheels, fitted 6.00—13 in. Dunlop tubeless tyres.

Equipment: 12-volt lighting and starting. Speedometer. Rev. counter. Oil pressure, water temperature, and fuel gauges. Heating and demisting. Windscreen wipers and washers. Flashing direction indicators.

Dimensions: Wheelbase 8 ft. 2½ ins. Track (front) 4 ft. 3½ ins., (rear) 4 ft. 2½ ins. Overall length 13 ft. 10 ins. Width 5 ft. 2½ ins. Weight 16 cwt. 1 qtr. Turning circle 38 ft.

Performance: Maximum speed 107.1 m.p.h. Speeds in gears, 3rd 88 m.p.h., 2nd 72 m.p.h., 1st 44 m.p.h. Standing quarter-mile 17.2 secs. Acceleration: 0-30 m.p.h. 3.8 secs.; 0-50 m.p.h. 7.1 secs., 0-60 m.p.h. 9.7 secs., 0-80 m.p.h. 17.2 secs.

Fuel Consumption: 19-23 m.p.g.

THE Motor

MAKE: Ford *TYPE: Lotus Cortina*

MAKERS: Ford Motor Co. Ltd. Dagenham, England

ROAD TEST ● No. 5/64

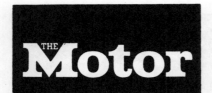

TEST DATA:

CONDITIONS: *Weather: Dry, cold, fresh wind 10-20 m.p.h. (Temperature 42°F., Barometer 29.5 in Hg.). Surface: Dry tarmacadam. Fuel: Super premium grade pump petrol (101 Octane by Research Method).*

MAXIMUM SPEEDS

Mean of six opposite runs	103·0 m.p.h.
Best one-way ¼-mile time equals	109·1 m.p.h.

"Maximile" speed: (Timed quarter mile after one mile accelerating from rest)

Mean of four opposite runs	105·1 m.p.h.
Best one-way time equals	107·2 m.p.h.

Speed in gears: (at approx. 6,500 r.p.m.)

Max. speed in 3rd gear	93 m.p.h.
Max speed in 2nd gear	70 m.p.h.
Max speed in 1st gear	46 m.p.h.

ACCELERATION TIMES
From standstill

0-30 m.p.h.	3.9 sec.
0-40 m.p.h.	5·8 sec.
0-50 m.p.h.	7·8 sec.
0-60 m.p.h.	10·1 sec.
0-70 m.p.h.	13·3 sec.
0-80 m.p.h.	18·1 sec.
0-90 m.p.h.	24·5 sec.
0-100 m.p.h.	33·5 sec.
Standing quarter mile	17·7 sec.

On upper ratios

	Top gear	3rd gear
10-30 m.p.h.	—	—
20-40 m.p.h.	—	5·9 sec.
30-50 m.p.h.	8·0 sec.	6·3 sec.
40-60 m.p.h.	8·5 sec.	6·3 sec.
50-70 m.p.h.	8·7 sec.	6·2 sec.
60-80 m.p.h.	9·7 sec.	7·2 sec.
70-90 m.p.h.	11·8 sec.	10·5 sec.
80-100 m.p.h.	15·3 sec.	—

HILL CLIMBING
Max. gradient climbable at steady speed

Top gear	1 in 9·7 (Tapley 230 lb./ton)
3rd gear	1 in 7·2 (Tapley 310 lb./ton)
2nd gear	1 in 4·7 (Tapley 460 lb./ton)

FUEL CONSUMPTION
Overall Fuel Consumption for 2,127 miles, 99·8 gallons, equals 21·3 m.p.g. (13·25 litres/100 km.)

Touring Fuel Consumption (m.p.g. at steady speed midway between 30 m.p.h. and maximum, less 5% allowance for acceleration) 21·15 m.p.g.
Fuel tank capacity (maker's figure) 8 gallons

Top Gear

48½ m.p.g.	at constant 30 m.p.h. on level
41½ m.p.g.	at constant 40 m.p.h. on level
32 m.p.g.	at constant 50 m.p.h. on level
23½ m.p.g.	at constant 60 m.p.h. on level
22 m.p.g.	at constant 70 m.p.h. on level
21 m.p.g.	at constant 80 m.p.h. on level
18½ m.p.g.	at constant 90 m.p.h. on level
16½ m.p.g.	at constant 100 m.p.h. on level

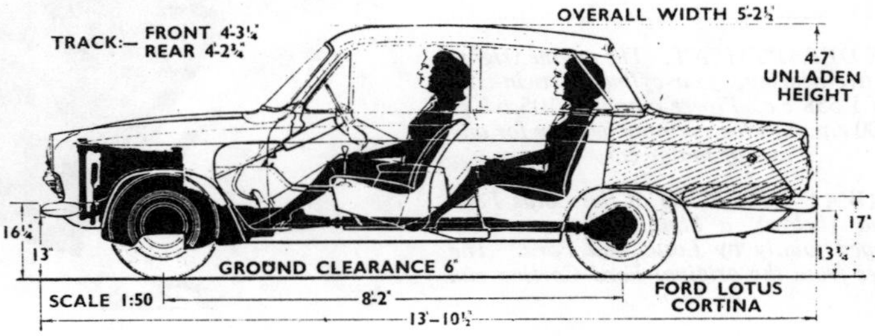

TRACK:— FRONT 4'-3¼" REAR 4'-2¾"
OVERALL WIDTH 5'-2½"
4'-7" UNLADEN HEIGHT
16¼"
13"
GROUND CLEARANCE 6"
17"
13¼"
SCALE 1:50
8'-2"
13'-10½"
FORD LOTUS CORTINA

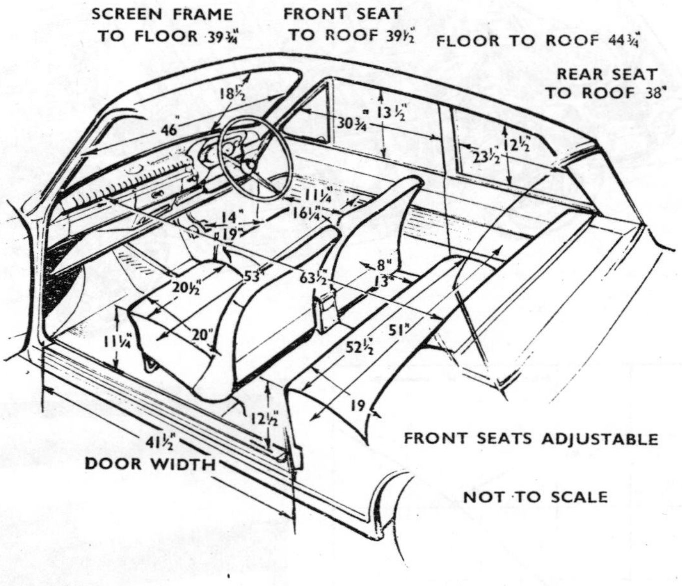

SCREEN FRAME TO FLOOR 39¾"
FRONT SEAT TO ROOF 39½"
FLOOR TO ROOF 44¾"
REAR SEAT TO ROOF 38"
18½
46"
30¾
13½"
12½
23½"
11¼
16¼"
14"
19"
8"
13"
53"
63½"
20½"
20"
11¼
51"
52½
19
12½"
41½"
DOOR WIDTH
FRONT SEATS ADJUSTABLE
NOT TO SCALE

BRAKES
Deceleration and equivalent stopping distance from 30 m.p.h.

0·31 g with 25 lb. pedal pressure	(97 ft.)
0·72 g with 50 lb. pedal pressure	(42 ft.)
0·90 g with 75 lb. pedal pressure	(33 ft.)
0·93 g with 90 lb. pedal pressure	(31 ft.)

STEERING
Turning circle between kerbs:

Left	34½ ft.
Right	34½ ft.
Turns of steering wheel from lock to lock	3

INSTRUMENTS

Speedometer at 30 m.p.h.	3% fast
Speedometer at 60 m.p.h.	2% fast
Speedometer at 90 m.p.h.	3% fast
Distance recorder	2% slow

WEIGHT

Kerb weight (unladen, but with oil, coolant and fuel for approximately 50 miles)	16½ cwt.
Front/rear distribution of kerb weight	54½/45½
Weight laden as tested	20¼ cwt.

Specification

ENGINE

Cylinders	4
Bore	82·55 mm.
Stroke	72·75 mm.
Cubic Capacity	1558 c.c.
Piston area	33·15 sq. in.
Valves	Inclined, operated by twin o.h.c.
Compression ratio	9·5/1
Carburetter	Two Weber 40 DCOE/18 twin choke compound side draught
Fuel pump	A.C. mechanical
Ignition timing control	Centrifugal and vacuum
Oil filter	Full flow — AC Tecalemit or Purolator
Maximum power (net)	105 b.h.p.
at	5,500 r.p.m.
Maximum torque (net)	108 lb. ft.
at	4,000 r.p.m.
Piston speed at maximum b.h.p.	2625 ft./min·

TRANSMISSION

Clutch	8 in. Ford/Borg and Beck s.d.p. diaphragm
Top gear (s/m)	3·90
3rd gear (s/m)	4·80
2nd gear (s/m)	6·40
1st gear (s/m)	9·75
Reverse	10·96
Propeller shaft	B.R.D. single piece open
Final drive	Hypoid bevel
Top gear m.p.h. at 1,000 r.p.m.	17·2
Top gear m.p.h. at 1,000 ft./min. piston speed	36·0

CHASSIS

Brakes .. Ford/Girling, disc front, drum rear

Brake dimensions 9½ in. discs and 9×1¾ in. drums

Friction areas .. 76 sq. in. of friction lining working on 282 sq. in. swept area of discs and drums

Suspension:
Front: Independent by Macpherson struts and lower wishbones with coil springs and anti-roll bar.
Rear: Rigid axle located by A bracket and two trailing radius arms with coil springs.

Shock absorbers: Front and rear, Armstrong telescopic.

Steering gear: Ford-Burman recirculating ball

Tyres: 6·00-13 Dunlop C.41 tubeless 4 ply

FORD LOTUS CORTINA

THE Lotus Cortina is a car of very strong personality—like most of its kind its good and bad points are prominent, not smoothed off to that level of consistent mediocrity which ordinary cars achieve. The right sort of buyer, the man who really wants a fast sports car but who is compelled to buy a saloon for family or business reasons, will be prepared for some sacrifices in flexibility, noise and refinement in return for the things which really matter to him.

We would certainly not advise anybody to buy one as a car for pottering around town. There is plenty of torque well down the speed range but below 2,000 r.p.m. roughness discourages its use. Some delicacy of clutch and throttle use is essential to avoid clonks from the rear axle locating members and prolonged running in city traffic brings symptoms of incipient plug fouling.

But when the towns are left behind the performance is found to be even more striking on the road than it is on paper and, with the aid of one of the best close ratio gearboxes we have met, the car seems to arrive at every destination well ahead of schedule. Excellent front seats and a good driving position make for the best possible use of steering, road holding and handling, which, although they fall short of the top class, are excellent for a saloon and good enough to make full use of the performance exhilarating rather than frightening. Firmer suspension, and tyres which improve cornering power at the expense of cushioning ability, bring a rather harsher but much more positive feeling of contact with the road for which one pays only a small penalty in riding comfort. Even the most blase motorist is likely to find himself seeking an excuse for a dice round the local roads but it remains a practical car for long distance travel.

We also had the opportunity of a short run in the Special Equipment conversion which Lotus offer at a slightly higher price and a few notes on this will be found on p. 67.

Performance and economy

LOTUS modifications for the Ford Cortina 1500 engine are extensive; a small increase in bore raises the capacity to 1,558 c.c. and a twin camshaft cylinder head with two double-choke Weber carburetters increases the power output by more than 75 per cent and the torque by 33 per cent in the middle speed range. It is this tremendous surge of mid-range acceleration which makes the performance so vivid—there is no need to use the extreme top end of the rev range to make the car go, but it revs so freely and smoothly that few drivers will be able to resist doing so. Although many people have commented that the power seems to fall right off at 6,500 r.p.m. it is not generally realized that there is a good reason for

this; to counter over-enthusiasm Lotus fit an ingenious rotor arm in the distributor with a spring-restrained centrifugal bob weight which cuts the ignition at this speed.

The performance figures show a mean maximum speed of 108 m.p.h. and an ability to reach 60 m.p.h. from rest in just over 10 seconds and 100 m.p.h. in 33.5 seconds. Very few four-seater saloons of any size or price can accelerate much faster than this and nearly all of them have engines of twice the capacity or more.

At the other end of the scale we found starting immediate, warm-up quick and idling fairly smooth although rather fast. Below 2,000 r.p.m. the engine vibrates harshly on its flexible mountings at large throttle openings. This corresponds to about 30-35 m.p.h. in top gear but there is little excuse for accelerating in top at this speed when it can be exceeded by a large margin in any of the other gears—even reverse.

Fuel consumption is very dependent on speed but we cannot imagine that anyone is going to buy a Lotus Cortina to drive it slowly. Driven really fast and using the whole rev range in the gears it returned only about 19 m.p.g. but on long main road runs at 80-90 m.p.h. cruising speeds some 23 m.p.g. was obtainable, our average for the whole 2,000 mile test falling slightly above the mean of these figures; with an 8-gallon tank it is necessary to refuel with irritating frequency on long journeys. We used Super Premium (101 Octane rating) fuel for most of our test because this is recommended by the manufacturers, but there was not much pinking on French petrol which is roughly equivalent to our ordinary Premium grade. Engine modifications have not appreciably affected the oil consumption (around 4,000 m.p.g.) and although at first we wondered whether the oil pressure was below normal, we found that 30-35 lb. (hot) is the standard figure for this unit.

Transmission

THIS very close ratio version of the standard Ford gearbox is for connoisseurs who will derive endless pleasure from its continual use—the temptation is to use it far more than necessary. A light

In Brief

Price (as tested) £910 plus purchase tax £190 2s. 11d. equals £1,100 2s. 11d.	
Capacity	1,558 c.c.
Unladen kerb weight	16½ cwt.
Acceleration:	
30-50 m.p.h. in top gear	8.0 sec.
0-50 m.p.h. through gears	7.8 sec.
Maximum top gear gradient	1 in 9.7
Maximum speed..	108 m.p.h.
Overall fuel consumption	21.3 m.p.g.
Touring fuel consumption	21.15 m.p.g.
Gearing: 17.2 m.p.h. in top gear at 1,000 r.p.m.	

FORD LOTUS CORTINA

(Above) **The colour treatment and reduction in overall height achieved by lowering the suspension makes the Lotus Cortina look longer and much more purposeful.** *(Right)* **Both the driving position and the front seats are just as comfortable as they look. With one seat tilted forward part of the useful storage box between them can be seen.**

flywheel, a clutch which is smooth but grips too firmly to encourage much slipping and a very high first gear all combine to make it a very easy car to stall when taking off from rest, but this difficulty is soon dispelled by practice. It is only just possible to re-start on a 1 in 4 gradient, but on level ground it rockets off the line without a trace of wheelspin and will run straight up to over 45 m.p.h. in bottom gear; in speed limits it is often convenient to change directly from first gear into top and conversely one soon gets used to changing down into the synchronized first gear in ordinary town driving.

The change is very light and very fast indeed; any lack of smoothness on the driver's part elicited a clonk from the rear end of our test car which suggested some looseness in the A bracket or radius arm bearings—the process of locating the back axle has made the drive line much more rigid and much less forgiving of slight clumsiness. It seems also to have increased the transmission of noise so that from 55 to 70 m.p.h. there is quite a loud low pitched whine from the rear axle.

Handling and braking

IN its general feel this saloon remains a Cortina rather than a Lotus although Lotus chassis modifications have converted it into a car which handles well enough to match its formidable performance. The steering has strong self-centring, but the initial impression of heaviness disappears as soon as it is properly on the move. Higher gearing and wide-rimmed wheels make the steering positive and accurate, but with the standard tyre pressures of 20 lb. sq. in. all round there is a very pronounced understeer which demands a sweeping and forceful approach to wheel movements when cornering hard. We preferred much higher pressures of 28 lb. all round and even then it was possible to break the front wheels away on fast corners—on slower ones enough power could be found in the lower gears to bring the tail round.

The pleasure of very hard driving is greatly enhanced by the absence of appreciable roll, lurch or tyre squeal, by the general stability and safety on wet roads or dry and by its ability to hold a straight course at high speeds on most roads. The fast bumpy roads of France, however, made it wander at speed but confirmed that the firm location and lower unsprung weight of the rigid rear axle had improved its roadholding to a very satisfactory level.

The brakes are entirely in keeping with the performance—the pedal has a short travel and a hard, solid feel and even brutal treatment on a closed circuit produced no perceptible fade. A vacuum servo keeps the pressure light but on our test car it produced a rather irritating clonk from under the bonnet every time it was energized. Although the pull and twist handbrake held the car on a 1 in 3 gradient, some drivers felt that it was not really in character.

Comfort and control

AT first the Lotus Cortina feels harder sprung than it really is; the rear suspension attachments transmit more road noise than a standard Cortina and the high tyre pressures we used for much of the time accentuated a few minor rattles on cats' eyes and small pot-

holes. But this slight harshness, mainly noticeable at low speeds, is rather misleading since the suspension, although firm, gives a comfortable ride with none of the excessive choppiness which accompanies abnormally hard damping.

It is, in fact, a car in which really long journeys can be made without fatigue even on Continental roads. The rear seats are quite standard, but the front ones, although based on standard frames,

The boot differs in three respects from that of an ordinary Cortina. Tubes run to the top of the wheel arches to stiffen the top mountings of the coil spring damper units; the nearside tube displaces the spare wheel from its vertical position behind the wheel and the battery has been transferred from under the bonnet to improve the weight distribution.

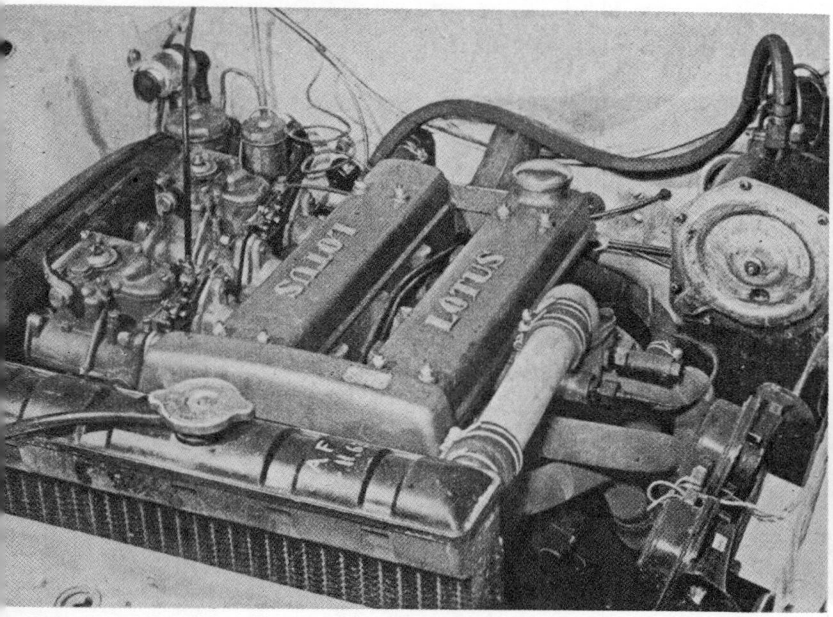

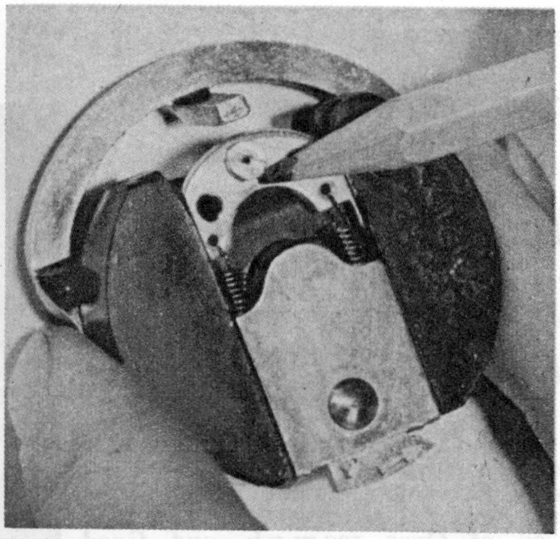

(*Left*) The twin o.h.c. head, two double-choke Webers, four branch exhaust system and vacuum servo brake unit completely obscure the Ford origin of the engine. (*Above*) You can't over-rev it—at 6,500 r.p.m. the spring-loaded bobweight in the special ignition rotor arm centrifuges out and cuts the ignition.

have been re-upholstered and re-shaped to combine luxuriously soft support with adequate side location. There is no rake adjustment for the backrests but the fore and aft movement tilts the whole seat further back as it moves forward—this makes it rather more comfortable for people of medium height and below than it is for the very tall. A small diameter wood-rimmed wheel in just the right position for a medium-stretch arm position, very good forward visibility and well-placed pedals add the finishing touches which make a driver feel at home and in command to an exceptional degree. The relationship of accelerator and brake pedals made heel and toe operation impracticable although in another example which we drove, with slightly different adjustments, it was possible. The only mechanical trouble which we suffered in well over 2,000 miles was the failure of a throttle return spring.

At idling speeds and above 5,500 r.p.m. the engine sounds clattery, but between these limits it is tolerably quiet and the exhaust is silent enough to make the full performance useable without attracting public attention.

For some unknown reason the Lucas sealed beam headlights seemed to be particularly effective on this car. The windscreen wipers also sweep a good arc, but at very high speeds they tend to lift off the glass.

Fittings and furniture

ONLY one colour scheme is available, white with a green flash which extends right round the tail of the car, and black vynide upholstery inside. Below the facia there is full-width parcel shelf, a large dashboard locker faces the front passenger and between the front seats there is a most useful box to absorb gloves, maps, sweets, cigarettes etc. The normal Cortina heating system is retained and is very effective.

Behind the small wood-rimmed steering wheel is a projecting instrument nacelle which contains a speedometer, rev. counter, fuel gauge and combined oil pressure gauge/water thermometer, all of which are clearly calibrated and easily read. Projecting from the right of the steering column is the usual Cortina stalk, carrying lamp and indicator controls, the former shortened to lessen risk of confusion between the two. There was no headlamp flasher on our test car but this has become a standard fitting on cars made within the past few weeks; it is operated by the present horn button on the side stalk, the horn control being transferred to the centre of the wheel.

The use of light alloys in various places helps to compensate for weight increases in others so that the Lotus Cortina weighs ¼ cwt. more than the standard 1500 Super and ¾ cwt. less than the Cortina GT. But the aluminium panels used for the bonnet, boot lid and doors are very easily damaged—in car parks the doors quickly get dented by careless opening of other heavier doors.

Coachwork and Equipment

Starting handle .. .. None
Battery mounting: Off side of luggage compartment
Jack .. .. Screw type
Jacking points — Two under each side of body
Standard tool kit: Jack, wheelbrace, hub cap remover
Exterior lights: Two head, two side, two tail/stop, number plate lamp.
Number of electrical fuses: One for flashers and one for radio (if fitted).
Direction indicators .. Self-cancelling flashers
Windscreen wipers — Twin self-parking electric
Windscreen washers .. Manual plunger type

Sun visors .. .. Two
Instruments: Speedometer (with total and decimal trip mileage recorders), rev. counter, fuel gauge, oil pressure gauge and thermometer.
Warning lights: Main beam, generator, oil pressure, flashers.
Locks: With ignition key — Driver's door and boot
With other keys .. .. None
Glove lockers: One in facia panel and one between front seats.
Map pockets .. .. None

Parcel shelves: One below facia and one behind rear seat.
Ashtrays .. One above facia, one on rear tunnel
Cigar lighters .. .. None
Interior lights .. .. One above mirror
Interior heater — Standard fitting—fresh air type
Car radio — Optional extra—push button or manual
Extras available .. Radio, safety belts
Upholstery material .. .. .. P.V.C.
Floor covering .. .. .. Moulded rubber
Exterior colours standardized .. .. One only
Alternative body styles .. .. .. None

Maintenance

Sump: 5¾ pints, S.A.E. 20W/30 (plus ¾ pint in filter)
Gearbox .. .. .. 1¾ pints, S.A.E. 80
Rear axle .. .. .. 2 pints, S.A.E. 90
Steering gear lubricant .. .. S.A.E. 90 EP
Cooling system capacity 10½ pints (2 drain taps) plus 2 pints in heater.
Chassis lubrication: By grease gun to 5 points after 500 miles and then every 2,500 miles.
Ignition timing .. .. .. 14° b.t.d.c.

Contact breaker gap .. 0.014 to 0.016 in.
Sparking plug type .. .. Lodge 2HLN
Sparking plug gap .. .. 0.023 to 0.028 in.
Valve timing: Inlet opens 22° b.t.d.c. and closes 62° a.b.d.c. Exhaust opens 62° b.b.d.c. and closes 22° a.t.d.c.
Tappet clearances (cold): Inlet 0.005-0.006 in.; exhaust 0.006-0.007 in.

Front wheel toe-in .. .. $\frac{1}{16}$ to $\frac{1}{8}$ in.
Camber angle .. .. .. 0° 40′
Castor angle .. .. 0° 36′ negative
Steering swivel pin inclination .. .. 5° 54′
Tyre pressures: Front .. .. .. 20 lb.
Rear .. .. .. 20 lb.
Brake fluid .. Castor oil/polyglycolether mixture
Battery type and capacity — 12-volt 38 amp-hour

ROAD TEST—

THE LONG-AWAITED TWIN-CAM FORD LOTUS-CORTINA

A £1,100 Competition Saloon Which is Also a Very Practical Road Car, Possessing Extremely Usable Acceleration, Very Powerful Girling Brakes, a Top Speed of Over 100 m.p.h. and Good Handling Qualities.

FAST FORD.—The twin-cam Lotus-Cortina is distinguished in side view by the colour-flash along the body.

SOON after that man Chapman had been signed on by British Ford, Dagenham announced the Lotus-Cortina, which was to have a 1½-litre twin-cam 105 b.h.p. engine in a Consul Cortina 2-door saloon body-shell using light-alloy doors, bonnet top and boot-lid, a close-ratio gearbox, modified suspension with a properly-located back axle with aluminium differential housing sprung on Chapman coil-spring struts, Corsair-size servo-assisted front disc brakes, larger tyres and other modifications to improve performance and handling. This Lotus-Cortina was announced enthusiastically in MOTOR SPORT last February, when I remarked that it sounded like the most exciting British car since the Jaguar E-type.

Team Lotus were to run a trio of these Fords in saloon-car races, but the project was a long time coming to fruition, probably because the twin-cam engines were needed for Lotus Elans before they found a place in Cortina body-shells. And competition work with these exciting new cars, for which a top speed of 115 m.p.h. and 0-100 m.p.h. in around 30 sec. is still hinted at in Ford publicity material, was not possible until they had been homologated, which meant that at least 1,000 had to be built. Ford Dealers, promised these fast Cortinas, grew restive, the Ford Board wrathful, but gradually these outwardly normal-looking Cortinas with the colour-flash along the bodyside began to appear on the roads and, occasionally, by the date of Oulton Park's Gold Cup meeting, on the circuits, while Henry Taylor drove one in the recent R.A.C. Rally.

At last, late in November, a test car was placed at our disposal for a brief period, and let me say right away that we were not disappointed! The Lotus-Cortina is a very commendable all-round car of truly excellent performance, the acceleration being an outstanding feature, very usable from the low speeds at which the average motorist drives, and going on and on most impressively as upward gear changes are made, so that overtaking is rendered not only safe but a positive pleasure!

This Ford is not a 100 m.p.h. car in the sense that the "ton" can be attained almost anywhere, but it achieves an easy 85-90 m.p.h. on give-and-take roads and certainly has a three-figure top speed. Such performance will leave behind, say, a Porsche 1600 Super or Mini-Cooper S or Alfa Romeo Giulia T1, and it is accomplished without sense of fuss or stress, merely that nice "hard" sound of busy but efficient machinery associated with a twin o.h.c. engine. However, although the r.p.m. limit is set between 6,500 and 8,000 r.p.m., the engine in the test car would not go beyond the first of these figures.

Road-holding is another strong feature of Colin Chapman's modified Cortina, the standard being extremely satisfactory, remembering that the basis of the exercise is a low-priced family saloon. The back suspension creaks a bit but the combination of coil springs, tying up the axle and reducing its weight has transformed the mediocre handling of the bread and margarine Cortina.

Cornering is mainly neutral, with a tendency to understeer, probably accentuated by the small-diameter wood-rimmed steering wheel, which makes the steering ratio seem rather low geared on acute corners; in fact, the wheel calls for 3½ turns, lock-to-lock,

including some sponge not noticeable when on the move. On normal bends the gearing feels just right and the steering very accurate and positive. Roll on fast corners is very moderate. The front-end feels softly sprung if sudden changes of direction or a heavy application of the brakes are made, when the weight of the twin-cam engine tends to be noticeable, but even over bad surfaces the front wheels retain firm adhesion with the road and the ride is comfortable. Even at 80 m.p.h. over a bad road the ride is very reasonable and the car in full control. At high speed there is a slight weaving action, accentuated by rough going, as if the back axle resents the restraint Colin Chapman has wisely put on it, but this does not develop into anything serious. Round fast, wide-radius bends the Lotus-Cortina holds the desired line most commendably, even with the inner wheels running along a rough verge, while the car goes exactly where it is directed when tucking in quickly after overtaking. There is some lost movement in the transmission, probably another product of restricting rear axle movement, just as the absence of a propeller shaft accentuates harshness of take-up in rear-engined cars. Had Chapman been

The impressive twin-cam 1,558-c.c. engine of the Ford Lotus-Cortina, which Harry Mundy so generously designed for the Lotus Elan sports car and which Colin Chapman was able to give to Ford of Dagenham for their fastest Cortina model. Note the dual Weber carburetters with cold-air box, which kept on coming adrift on the test car, and the brake-booster on the near-side.

Business-like interior of the Lotus-Cortina, with good, grouped instruments, " racing " wheel, and matt-black upholstery and trim. Note the improved driving-seat.

THE FORD LOTUS-CORTINA SALOON

Engine: 4 cylinders, 82.5 × 72.75 mm. (1,558 c.c.). Inclined overhead valves operated by twin overhead camshafts. 9.5 to 1 compression ratio. 105 (net) b.h.p. at 5,500 r.p.m.
Gear ratios: 1st, 9.75 to 1; 2nd, 6.40 to 1; 3rd, 4.79 to 1; top, 3.90 to 1.
Tyres: 6.00 × 13 Dunlop Gold Seal C41 tubeless, on bolt-on steel disc wheels.
Weight: 16¼ cwt. (kerb weight).
Steering ratio: 3⅛-turns, lock-to-lock.
Fuel capacity: 8 gallons (Range: 200 miles).
Wheelbase: 8 ft. 2½ in.
Track: Front, 4 ft. 3½ in.; rear, 4 ft. 2½ in.
Dimensions: 13 ft. 10 in. × 5 ft. 2½ in. × 4 ft. 7 in. (high).
Price: £910 (£1,100 3s. 1d., inclusive of purchase tax).
Makers: Ford Motor Company Limited, Dagenham, Essex, England.

LOTUS-CORTINA ROAD-TEST

allowed to instal i.r.s. this tendency to weave, and transmission of noise from the road wheels, might have been eliminated. As it is, there is very little judder through the rigid Cortina body shell but the axle does build up some shudder or mild vibration, which releases a number of body rattles. Reverberations from the engine can be cured by using the two lower gears when pulling away from low speeds.

The clutch of the Lotus-Cortina is extremely heavy, but engages progressively. The short remote gear lever is splendidly placed, and has a neat wooden knob. It controls a gearbox with the most commendably closely spaced and high ratios I have used for a long time, bottom gear being as high as 9.75 to 1. Chapman has clearly designed this gearbox for enthusiasts and doesn't intend you to use a Lotus-Cortina for towing a caravan up Porlock.

The gear change is very quick and positive but the action is notchy and the synchromesh can be beaten if very rapid changes are attempted or the clutch not fully depressed. I rate this a good but not a superlative gear change. Reverse is easily engaged by lifting the lever beyond the 2nd gear position and the gears are quiet, but at certain speeds the lever rattles. The synchromesh bottom gear is as easy to engage as the rest of those in the box, which enables quick use to be made of the lowest ratio to keep the revs. up on sharp corners and steep hills.

The Girling brakes, 9½ in. disc at the front, 9 in. drums at the back, with a suction servo on the n/s of the engine, are just the job for a car with Lotus-Cortina urge. They are light to apply, yet not too light and never sudden, and stop the car very powerfully and progressively with no vices, except for a tendency to pull to the right under heavy applications, on the test car. The hand brake is a normal Ford pull-out and twist affair.

The combination of speed, acceleration particularly, road-clinging and powerful retardation possessed by this remarkable Ford enables 60 m.p.h. averages to be achieved on British roads effortlessly and safely, the Lotus-Cortina being easy to drive, no special techniques being called for, while its only notable disadvantages are some rather tiring engine noise and an uncomfortable back seat. However, the outstanding impression imparted by this excellent saloon car is of willing, purposeful acceleration, which goes on and on with no trace of hesitation or flat-spot. For this I feel quite certain the two twin-choke, side draught Weber

40DCOE18 carburetters deserve most of the credit. The performance does not come up to the publicity estimates, as our figures show, but even so the Lotus-Cortina is a very rapid vehicle by 1.6-litre standards, quite apart from the fact that it is a 4-seater saloon! Because bottom gear can be held to nearly 50 m.p.h. and because acceleration commences to be really effective from around 3,000 r.p.m., a snick into 2nd gear produces extremely useful acceleration that leaves loiterers far and cleanly behind! Especially when it is realised that the rev.-counter needle only just touches the red mark at 70 m.p.h. in this gear, or at over 90 in 3rd gear!

In spite of its racing-type engine this Ford is perfectly docile in traffic, although if you motor through the thick of the rush-hour it is seemly to use 1st and 2nd gears more frequently than the 3rd and top gears, the water temperature will rise to 90°C but will stay at that, and your clutch leg may get rather tired. Starting from cold presents no problems.

I have dealt with the performance and controllability aspects of the Lotus-Cortina first, instead of commencing, as I do usually, with details of controls, instruments and decor. This is because anyone contemplating this particular and so very acceptable version of the popular Ford Consul Cortina will regard these aspects as of major importance, and also because in general layout the car is like the normal, staid Cortina.

The separate front seats are comfortable and offer good support; they adjust in two planes, forward and upwards, in one movement. Upholstery is in matt black p.v.c., with a light roof lining. The dials are on a neat hooded panel before the driver, as on the latest Cortina GT models, but the instruments are better contrived, and in this case the background simulates metal instead of grained wood. The 110 m.p.h. speedometer has trip with decimal and total milometers, the tachometer is marked in red between 6,500 and 8,000 r.p.m., although the engine peaks at 5,500 r.p.m. The small fuel gauge is properly calibrated but shows a very definite zero some 30 miles or more before the 8-gallon tank empties. There is a combined oil-pressure gauge and water thermometer matching the fuel gauge in size; the oil pressure reading shows barely 40 lb./sq. in. at normal engine speeds, and falls to a depressing 5 lb./sq. in. at idling revs., although the green warning light does not show. In view of the fact that the twin-cam Harry Mundy-designed head has been grafted onto a standard Ford engine-base, this low pressure may prove disturbing to sensitive-minded engineers. No doubt proprietory oil-coolers will soon be offered to owners of these cars! Normal water temperature is 80°C. The two main dials are notable for steady-reading needles, white against a black background and moving in the same plane, which, with the steady-reading small dials and black interior trim, imparts an air of luxury, not found in lesser Fords. The usual Ford fixed r.h. stalk carries lamps and winker switches, the lamps control faired off, unlike that on other Cortina models. This makes it even less easy to use. That no lamps flasher is fitted is a serious omission;

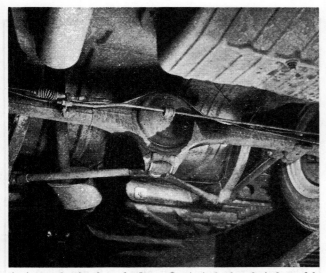

A picture showing how the Lotus-Cortina's back axle is located by side radius arms and an A-bracket. If the photographer had taken the trouble to clean it, the light-alloy differential housing might also have shown up!

IN ACTION!—Henry Taylor's Ford Lotus-Cortina on a night stage of last year's R.A.C. Rally.

the horn push on the wheel, which is inoperative, might well be employed as such, enabling the push on the stalk-extremity to be used as a lamps-flasher.

On this Ford the screen-washers knob is adjacent to the starter-key, and the wipers knob, on the other side of the dash, pulls out to start the single-speed wipers. There is the usual choke knob. The bonnet is opened from outside the car and has to be propped up, although the self-locking boot-lid is self-supporting. The bonnet opens to reveal the neat twin-cam engine, with those big Webers on the o/s and a 4-branch exhaust system dropping away efficiently on the n/s. The ignition distributor is inaccessible beneath the carburetters. The latter have a cold air box fed through a flexible pipe from a filter in the grille. The dip-stick is close to the dynamo bracket, but accessible. Blue cam-box covers signify the 105 b.h.p. version of this 1,558 c.c. Ford engine, but for competition purposes the "red" 140 b.h.p. engine is available.

This "blue" engine has a 9.5-to-1 c.r., so 100-octane petrol is called for. On a fast run from Hampshire to Somerset and back this was consumed at the rate of exactly 25 m.p.g. The absolute range on a tankful, which holds within 1/20th of a gallon what the makers specify, was 200 miles. The horizontal filler pipe is unsuited to refuelling from a can.

The Lucas 60/45 watt sealed-beam headlamps enable most of the Lotus-Cortina's performance to be used after dark and the illumination provided in the dipped position is to be highly commended. There is nothing else to mention that distinguishes the car from its less powerful brethren, except that the spare wheel lies on the boot floor, the battery and two strengthening struts are found in the boot, the boss of the 15 in. racing-type steering wheel and the gear-lever knob are endowed with Lotus badges, which are repeated on the radiator grille and on each rear quarter of the body, and that the 6 in.-section Dunlop tyres look imposing.

We obtained the following performance figures, two-up, using an electric speedometer on the test track (average of several runs, best time in parenthesis, best Cortina GT acceleration times within square brackets):—

0-30 m.p.h.:	4.0 sec.	(3.9 sec.)	[3.5 sec.]
0-40 m.p.h.:	5.4 sec.	(5.3 sec.)	[5.5 sec.]
0-50 m.p.h.:	8.8 sec.	(8.4 sec.)	[8.6 sec.]
0-60 m.p.h.:	11.0 sec.	(10.9 sec.)	[12.1 sec.]
0-70 m.p.h.:	15.0 sec.	(15.0 sec.)	[17.0 sec.]
0-80 m.p.h.:	21.0 sec.	(20.5 sec.)	[25.9 sec.]
s.s. ¼-mile:	18.0 sec.	(18.0 sec.)	[19.0 sec.]

Speeds in gears (6,500 r.p.m.): 1st., 45 m.p.h.; 2nd., 70 m.p.h.; 3rd., 92 m.p.h.; top, 105 m.p.h.

N.B.—These times were recorded on a wet track, but as it was impossible to induce wheelspin, they were unaffected. Lack of space prevented taking acceleration figures at speeds higher than 80 m.p.h. The speedometer was corrected for error; it was 2 m.p.h. optimistic at 60 m.p.h., 3 m.p.h. fast at 80 m.p.h. When regarding the ¼-mile times allowance should be made for the very high gearing. No doubt better times would be accomplished on the

optional 4.1 axle ratio. Carburation tuning will improve on these figures, but at the expense of m.p.g.

If these figures disappoint anyone, there is the Cheshunt-built 140 b.h.p. race-tuned 1,594 c.c. Lotus-Cortina to bring smiles of satisfaction—if you can afford £1,725 or get your hands on one of the 30 to be constructed! But for all practical purposes the ordinary Ford Lotus-Cortina (or the 125 b.h.p. Special Equipment version) should provide amply sufficient speed and acceleration and, with its good road manners, will soon be giving joy and rapid travel to many discerning sportsmen. It is a much better car than I had dared to hope and there is something very pleasing in the knowledge that Lotus racing "know-how" has been handed on to this outwardly sober Ford saloon, which goes so well, is such great fun and so safe to drive, and which enjoys the widespread Ford spares and servicing facilities. Under the circumstances this Ford Lotus-Cortina is a good car to buy for £1,100 3s. 1d., or £9 10s. extra if front-seat safety belts are specified. (Other extras are a 4.1 to 1 back axle and a reversing light).

Time will show just how reliable this combination of Ford and Lotus components proves but in 600 hard-driven miles the only failures were the Smiths tachometer, which just couldn't believe the engines high rev.-limit, and a loose bolt holding the carburetters intake box in place. The rubber fell off the clutch pedal. Twin-cam engines are sometimes thought to consume oil but none was used by the Lotus power unit in 600 miles.

In conclusion, I approve very strongly of Colin Chapman's idea of a British Giulietta, which Ford sells at a price poor men can afford! As for the race-tuned version . . . ! !—W. B.

The hall-mark of high-performance!

CONTINUED FROM PAGE 11

external spring-loaded adjuster. These parts are enclosed in a new one-piece diecast aluminium timing cover.

The five-bearing crankshaft, which is finely balanced to stand up to continued high rpm, has been prepared by Cosworth, and this firm also makes the high compression, flat top pistons. The normal camshaft is retained in the cylinder block so that it drives the distributor, oil pump, and fuel pump; but, of course, the tappet blocks are removed.

Performance figures at 6500 rpm quoted by the Ford Motor Company are very impressive and it will be interesting to see if production models live up to these: Top gear approx 115 mph, third gear 92 mph, second gear 69 mph, first gear 45 mph. Acceleration from 0-100 mph is quoted as around 30 secs.

Girling brakes are fitted, the system being vacuum servo-assisted and having 9½ in discs at the front and 9 in by 1¾ in drums at the rear. Lining materials which will stand up to the hardest possible use are fitted to the disc pads and brake shoes.

The centre of gravity of the car has been lowered by modifying the front suspension units. Springs having a 140 lb/in rate are fitted, the wheel camber has been reduced to zero and a firm ride is produced by using a stiffer 15/16 in diameter stabiliser bar. At the rear a solid axle still takes preference over an independent system, although why Ford did not use the Elan independent layout is a mystery. However, the company has compromised by letting Lotus designers work out a neat suspension incorporating two radius arms and an 'A' bracket to control the axle during braking, accelerating, and cornering. Coil springs are used, surrounding heavy duty rear telescopic shock absorbers with hard ride

settings. Unsprung axle weight is reduced by the removal of 'cart springs' and the use of a differential housing made from aluminium alloy.

A close-ratio gearbox is fitted, the drive being transmitted through an 8 in diaphragm Borg & Beck clutch. This type of clutch is used widely nowadays, having passed very stringent tests during experiments with racing cars.

Standard rear axle ratio is 3.9:1, but there are several alternatives, depending upon what the car is to be used for. These are 4.125, 4.429 and 3.77. Lightweight steel wheels with a wide rim section of 5½ inches are used and these serve to increase the track slightly and improve road holding.

Obviously, the British Motor Corporation's successful tie-up with John Cooper has set Sir Patrick Hennessey thinking and this is his answer to the fabulous Mini-Cooper. For several seasons now Fords have been providing mechanical units for leading Formula Junior and sports cars particularly Lotus and the success that they have achieved has undoubtedly led to this amalgamation of Ford, Lotus and Cosworth and their production of a fast, safe, saloon car.

A spokesman for the Lotus Company announced that it was the intention in the coming season to enter the Consul Cortina Special in major sedan car races in the UK and on the Continent. Drivers chosen for this task show just how seriously Ford and Lotus are going into this. They include Jim Clark, Trevor Taylor, and Peter Arundell.

The standard Cortina, when first announced, had a poor reception and its critics were many. Mid-way through January of this year the manufacturers altered the specification and made it available with the 1500 cc Classic engine, and now this high-powered version with the twin-cam engine should cause a few changes of mind. #

Facia features return of decent round instruments and wood-rimmed wheel, while interior also has twin front bucket seats, remote control gear-lever and crash-padding.

SCOTLAND FOR LUNCH?

By the high-road and LOTUS CORTINA it's

IT STARTED WHEN WE FOUND ourselves with holiday time on our hands, a red Vitesse convertible booked for test, an absence (for once) of any special urge to cross the Channel, a standing invitation to the Highlands and a distinct feeling that if we saw another traffic jam we'd take up *bombe plastique*. That was the slow way to Scotland—so slow we felt bound to find a contrast.

It came in the form of a tipsy wager; a pint of Red Barrel to a Pepsi-Cola we couldn't get to within piping distance of Edinburgh quicker than Jim Clark. Our conspirator reckoned a pal of his had told him he'd had it from his brother's uncle's father-in-law that Clark boasted a point-to-point time of 5½ hours by Lotus Cortina. Mature reflection convinced us it was all a load of old cobbler's; in fact we were on the point of calling it no contest and soiling our lips without a fight. But the advent of a road test Lotus Cortina put just enough temptation in our way. 'Why, it's just like Jim's . . .'

Neither trip went according to plan (if there ever was any plan) and what we managed to prove is debatable. At a wild guess it was that Scotland needn't be so much a means as an end, or that doing the journey with the handbrake on in one of Beeching's Best you may be diddling yourself of half the fun. Incidental points worth noting, though, are that England in 1964 isn't *quite* all smoky semi-ds and the A1 is no longer the Great North Nightmare of *Motocar* legend.

Let's look at the slow way first. As we indicated long ago in a piece about escape routes for summer touring, it's endemic to SMALL CAR's definition of fun on the road that there should be as complete an absence as possible of commercial traffic both heavy and light, of struggling tourist buses, of long frustrated queues of sweating families with roof-racks and birdcages and boots full of buckets and spades, of ugly ribbon development and of the kind of semi-industrial landscape dropsy that makes you think the world is one big London.

That kind of freedom is getting more elusive every day. Our object in taking to the little lanes which nobody follows has always been not so much to get there quickly as to keep ourselves on the right side of the sanity barrier in an atmosphere which suggests that before very long this country just won't be worth living in any more. Up to the week of this our slow trip to Scotland the SMALL CAR escape-route network extended throughout the home counties and as far north as Norwich, as far south as Poole, as far west as Bradford-on-Avon. All our original routes were in fact faster than the main roads: this time we would try sacrificing the time element altogether in an effort to keep it clean—to stay out of every city and town and to shy off man-made ugliness. The real object was amusement. Getting it would be hard work.

In fact the trip took two days up and, with harder driving and some route modification, a day and a half back. It paid off 100 per cent in sheer tonic effect. We got back feeling that perhaps this fair old grassy-green paradise we call home hadn't changed so much in 400 years after all.

Just think of it! Miles, even hours of brisk wind-in-the-hair driving with literally no other car anywhere. A lazy afternoon winding through parts of leafy southern Yorkshire that looked as if they'd just dropped out of an 18th-century engraving. Whole days without a single offensive building to groan over—no building at all, as often as not, later than 1830. Syllabubs like this are still there for the sipping: it's just that you have to reach to get at 'em.

Logic seemed to indicate a start on M1, which is still running well within capacity even at 10am on a sunny Saturday. Not that the sun made a lot of difference, except to the scenery: with the Vitesse's hood irretrievably stuffed away under a well battened-down half-tonneau we were soon chilled enough to initiate a swift detour up the Luton exit ramp for scarves and pullovers—oh, and for a stout thong to make fast my new flat-'at which showed every sign of following the last one *forwards* off my forehead and out.

Afterwards the car showed itself to be hardly in the Jaguar class (it vibrated like a Japanese wrestler over about 83) although it covered the ground quickly enough to induce in me the customary motorway mental palpitations. Should I stay here in the fast lane till I'm past that Vanguard or should I throw out the anchors and let his Nibs with all those headlamps get through? What happens to me if that Dormobile swings out from behind the lorry just as grandma in the Consul draws nigh? Why don't they keep eight-wheelers off the outside strip? You know it all. How I long for the day when these will be our only worries . . .

Up at the top end of M1 we switched right instead of left to a little place called Crick, where we joined the undulating, nicely surfaced minor road that was to carry us almost parallel with the appalling A5 as far as Barwell between

But wouldn't you rather take the low road, a

Hinckley and Leicester. Lunch-time led us to peep longingly at the picnic basket poking out from between the seats, and right on schedule the curtain of elm and beech up ahead parted to show us a charming little hump-back bridge over the infant Avon and a deserted farm-road with views through another little wood to historic Stanford Hall—complete with liveried attendant, incidentally, glowering at us because we looked to be dodging his 6d parking lot. Such is Century 20.

A new leg took us well up into the Potteries, where I already knew there's many a fine, steep back-road to be found if you've the patience to avoid the numerous unsignposted trap-junctions which so delight in luring you siren-fashion into the dreaded maws of Derby or Stoke-on-Trent. Our route worked out nicely, thank you, whisking us with minimum fuss by totally deserted lanes from Barwell, where we had to join the ugly A447 for a mile or two, through by Market Bosworth and Newton Burgoland to Barton under Needwood, from where we fled due north through Needwood Forest into the wide green haven of the Pennines without having seen so much as a single pottery-stack closer than a mile and a half.

Time for a Light Interlude, and just as we'd begun to get into the swing of those undulating, perfectly surfaced left-right-left-handers a particularly deft (ahem) bit of overtaking provoked an uncommonly skilful boy-racer type in a white Angular to giving first tongue and then chase. We'd got him on a downhill series of sweeping S-bends with wide views to the hills beyond, and by the time we'd reached the valley floor our friend had made up the distance his reaction time and vengeful gearchange had lost him. My navigator kept track of developments in the supplementary mirror: 'Look out, he's got no hubcaps on . . . strapped-down suspension, probably Konis . . . there's a girl in there with him . . . correction, it's his mother-in-law . . . coo, what a noise!'

We held him on acceleration, but obviously it was only our outland-ish tailwaggery that scared him into holding back on the corners. Would that count as baulking under SMALL CAR rules? Came a straight stretch and he was on our tail as we closed rapidly with a slow-moving Daimler. Did he have discs? Ob/nav was uncertain, so we let him through for fear of wearing him amongst the luggage and then gave equally spirited chase.

It was great for getting to know the Vitesse. We found we could take the tail fearfully wide with all that weight in the boot and still fetch it back on demand; right with him through that one, and again, and (oops) again—ah, now for a straight blast with nothing in sight for a mile. By tramping on the loud pedal in second after the last apex we managed to get enough initial urge to bring us level. The little six's torque as we snatched third helped to urge us past just as he was running out of steam. An exchange of grins and we were through. The last we heard was a muffled toot-toot as he disappeared into the evening, leaving him to turn off down towards Manchester. Friendly, these Midlanders.

Night fell just as we came down from the mountain and pushed on into the yellow-lit no man's land 'twixt Huddersfield, Dewsbury, Halifax and Bradford. To be honest, this was where our Great Escape broke down rather badly and it wasn't till days later when we'd spent another leisurely hour or two with the maps that we managed to dream up a way round for the return trip. In the meantime it was getting on for nine as we began to penetrate the hills once again, and at a little village-in-a valley on the fringe of the Dales we halted at the sign of the Hare and Hounds and begged sustenance.

No, they couldn't put us oop because they had relations but they'd see what they could do at the farm up the road. And if we cared to wait till 10 they'd be serving pie-an'-peas in the bar. We overheard the conversation as we downed our pints and tucked into our 1s 6d-worth: ''Ullo, Ethel—'Are an' 'Ounds 'ere . . .'

It was fun, that night. We wound up at Ethel's, which turned out to be one of those gloriously mellow 17th century hill-farms with a carved inscription over the door and a wood-oven full of muffins. In the morning we loafed over breakfast, then sauntered down to the sunny little stone village at Ethel's suggestion to marvel at England's second biggest water-wheel: 50 ft from side to side and so dank and still in its semi-derelict spillway you could feel the ghosts of the rioting machine-wreckers all across the years.

We wandered on. A sudden conviction that it would be both warm and deserted took us across now to the Lake District. It was, but it took time. Our return route was better this way, too: for the record it runs the other side of Bradford and Leeds, ruling out poor Ethel, and then sneaks up between Harrogate and York through some of the loveliest country in the whole world via

VITESSE CONVERTIBLE and two whole days?

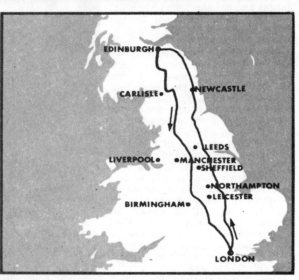

Leyburn and the Dales, Haltwhistle and Hadrian's Wall to wander finally through Selkirk and Peebleshire by Biggar and Forth to the hills. But by the time you get up this far you can't go wrong: you're 200 years back in history. Who's for the back-roads? Who's for the slow-roads now?

Obviously *we* weren't when it came to our far-famed attempt on Jim Clark's record. There had to be some rules: for example speed limits (inasmuch as there are any on A1 in its refurbished form) were for sticking-to, and we didn't want to end up in court on any dangerous driving charges either. But by and large it was to be about as hurried a trip as we could reasonably make on the public roads and for that we needed to stick for most of the way to the one road we knew would let us sustain the Lotus Cortina's natural cruising gait. That left two minor decisions—whether to start off again on M1 and then cross over from Northampton to Stamford, and whether to take off from Scotch Corner up the Roman road to A68 and Carter Bar.

We chose, wrongly as it turned out, to stick with A1 all the way. Just to make things easy we settled on a 2 am Saturday start which quickly became 4 and then 6 am as freezing weather threatened ice on the roads but promised sun to clear it at dawn. 'See you lunchtime' we wired gaily to friends in Edinburgh. We got up on schedule. The sun didn't.

Nevertheless the Lotus seemed to lap it all up as we called for petrol at the all-nighter behind Selfridges with the clock at exactly 6.30, headed out through Hampstead and Finchley with the other kind of clock on 40 and one eye on the mirror for prowlers—of which, be it known, we counted five between Swiss Cottage and Mill Hill. Who says the witching hour's a legend?

The roundabouts north of Hendon gave us plenty of warning of trials to come. Each one bore traces of ice, with matching evidence of graunch-marks and deep furrows in the emerald central sward and an occasional inverted A35 van for good measure. In fact one poor fellow had lost everything in such a big way he'd gone backwards clean through the middle of one of those vast red multiple-arrow signboards and taken a concrete lamp standard with him. Some people carry their racing-driver aspirations a little too far: we can't all be Paul Hawkins.

Stevenage bypass, that staccato bit of bracket-M-unbracket motorway just south of Letchworth, was clear of ice and traffic. It helped whisk us past Baldock by the time our first hour was up—50 miles and nothing but dual carriageway ahead for another hour.

At least that's the way it looked from where we sat. Then came frost: great thick gobs of it all over roof-tops and trees, making them look like Mr Softy with elephantitis, and occasional lakes of it in the middle of the road. The Lotus took it well, but there was worse to come. We hadn't dared use the screenwashers to get rid of filth from the inevitable convoys of naked-wheeled heavies for fear of getting a wall of frozen mud under the wipers. By the time we were halfway up Huntingdonshire and well into our second hour the mud was frozen before it got to us, and on the Grantham bypass (another miniature motorway: another poor joke) we met our first freezing fog.

Now freezing fog is one of those things you read about in rally reports and seldom ponder deeper. At the best of times and even in quite thin layers it can be a damned nuisance; when you strike a thick patch at perhaps 80 or 90 mph it's positively terrifying—in fact I rate the effect identical with what happens when your windscreen shatters, except that there's less you can do. The only remedy after we'd stopped to clear off the first dose was to switch the heater over to full defrost, turn on the head-lamps and press on at a subdued 60 with visibility at five catseyes.

Some of the side-effects were amusing. When we stopped for fuel in Newark (first and one of the few remaining holdup-towns on the route) at the beginning of Hour Three we found the whole car covered with a thin sheet of ice. We had to kick great saucers of the stuff off the headlamp glasses to convert our high beams from a mere glimmer to the real thing, and the wheel arches were so full we had icicles dripping out of them. Even the radio aerial had an inch-deep frozen strip on its leading edge. And this was a record trip?

Days later, we told them back at Bert's Bar it was the freezing fog that stopped us. Actually I doubt that we would have made it anyway. Keeping straight on at Scotch Corner turned out to be a major booboo because it landed us in Newcastle just in time for Saturday shopping; indeed Newcastle is the only real bottleneck left on the whole route, and the one that will probably remain for keeps.

What *was* our speed? We rolled into Edinburgh at precisely five minutes to four, giving a total journey time including fuel stops of seven hours 35 minutes. Knock off half an hour for Clark's 40-mile

saving through living south of the city and you get a lag of about an hour and a half. Counting the world champion's journey as 350 miles and ignoring the bit we did from there to Edinburgh you get an average speed discrepancy of nearly 14 mph—50 for us against just under 64 for Clark.

Well, we downed our wages of modesty and survived. Backstage they tried to work out what we'd achieved. The answer is nothing if you're thinking of driving ability or Lotus Cortina performance, since anybody in almost any car could have equalled our time on a clear day: although come to think of it *that's* something, since it makes a London to Edinburgh weekend a perfectly sensible proposition (thanks to all those bypasses) for the first time by road. We never thought to check with the man himself whether he really does go as quickly as rumour speculates. Maybe he goes quicker. That wasn't the point!

How does the Lotus shape up as a point-to-pointer? In the 100 or so fog-free miles granted us before the blanket dropped it occurred to us that here was a car one could usefully live with for keeps. It has plenty of little faults: ours rattled a lot, and you got a hefty clonk from the rear-end every time you planted the foot among all those Webers with any determination. Some of the detail equipment wasn't quite up to the total performance image—for example the wipers were weak even before they got frozen, and the headlamps might have been better. We would have felt safer at 100-plus on something stronger than Dunlop C41s.

But by and large you can forgive it a lot of shortcomings. It will carry two people economically in extreme comfort and four in something less than the other thing over vast distances very quickly indeed and remain just as much a pleasure to steer, stop and change gears in at the end as it was when you started. We learned to throw it about to the point where few roadsters could catch up in corners, and its acceleration is enough to shake off almost anything except another Lotus. The one thing that went wrong with ours in 1500 miles was that the oil filler cap (a nasty slippery thing) fell off and all the oil spewed over the engine compartment. Our only warning was the pressure light which began to come on under braking. We heeded it in time.

'It's the same one Clark used to win the world championship' we told the attendant who sold us a replacement. 'See, there's the supercharger.' He was thrilled.

Doing without hotels is a major back-road joy. This Yorkshire farmhouse (top left) made a splendid substitute, and the farmer's wife and woolly home help (centre left) asked only 15s a head. Weem Hotel near Aberfledy (above) is the sort of pub any budget will run to north of the border. Below, the Vitesse pauses beside a lonely Cumberland hill-shepherd's hut

You take the fast road and I'll take the slow road. You'll be in Scotland afore me, and so you ought with a Lotus Cortina under you. But using my modified escape route with its Manchester bypass (patent pending) I'll have seen parts of Britain on the way you just wouldn't believe were there. Anyone for Pepsi?

LOTUS CORTINA

A tiger among the puddycats—

THE FORD LOTUS Cortina is the result of a successful marriage between Colin Chapman's tiny Lotus factory and the vast English Ford operation. The purpose of the car is to give EnFo (the FoMoCo's English branch) a GT class winner with all the resulting publicity, and also to incorporate the Lotus name in a sporting version of a standard Ford product. By using the Lotus facilities to assemble the car, Ford has successfully avoided the disruption to its production lines entailed by any form of limited and specialized construction. At the same time, Lotus benefits from a steady income derived from the "mass production" of some 30 cars a week.

The result is one of the most exhilarating small sedans we have ever driven, and it seems unfortunate that there are no plans at present for marketing the car in America. It appears that the English market is able to absorb all the cars Lotus can produce, and it would be necessary to convert to left-hand drive for the American market, which would require considerable modification of this particular car. However, Rod Carveth of San Carlos, Calif., who has handled Lotus products for a long time, offered us his personal car for testing and we were very glad of the opportunity. As usual when testing cars in the San Francisco area, we were offered the use of Cotati Raceways, where the strong arm of the law can't reach us and where the drag strip is ideal for acceleration tests.

The main feature of the Lotus Cortina is the twin cam Lotus engine which produces 105 bhp at 5500 rpm from its 1558 cc. However, the remainder of the car has been tweaked by Chapman in many subtle ways so that the road holding, braking and general handling are the equal of the power output. Even the bodies are altered by the addition of aluminum doors, hood and trunk lid to compensate in part for the weight of the other Chapman modifications, although the resulting car still weighs about 150 lb more than the standard Cortina. On the other hand, the power output

LOTUS CORTINA

AT A GLANCE...

Price as tested	£910 ($2548)
Engine	4 cyl, dohc, 1558 cc, 105 bhp
Curb weight, lb	1930
Top speed, mph	106
Acceleration, 0–60 mph, sec	10.5
Passing test, 50–70 mph, sec	6.2
Overall fuel consumption, mpg	22

Competition version will exceed 130 mph.

LOTUS CORTINA

of the Lotus version is almost double that of the standard car.

The bodies are shipped from Ford to Lotus already painted white, and the aluminum parts are then added by Lotus after they have been painted. The result is that the potential customer can order his car in any color he chooses, provided it is white with a distinctive green flash along each side.

Surprisingly enough, the standard of fit and finish is very high indeed and this has not been a particularly notable feature of Lotus products in the past. However, it appears that the object of the car is to offer a degree of luxury not usually found in small sedans, in addition to the car's superlative performance. This is achieved by including such items as heavily-padded, competition-type front seats, a handsome instrument cluster, a gearshift knob with tiny Lotus crest and a wood-rimmed steering wheel.

The Lotus engine is based on the same power unit that swept the Formula Junior field and, with its five main bearings, short stroke and extremely rugged design, it can easily withstand the additional demands of the twin-cam head layout. The clutch is an 8-in. diameter unit with a diaphragm type cover assembly, and it is quite stiff and has a very positive engagement. However, any deficiencies in the clutch department are made up in full by the transmission, which is superlative.

Due to the high rear-axle gearing and the close gearbox ratios, the Lotus Cortina is definitely an open road car requiring intelligent use of the transmission to extract full per-

formance. In town the car is not at its best, and the clutch requires some practice before it can be operated smoothly, but here again the transmission, with its synchronized first gear, is a great asset because the car will achieve 45 mph in first. Thus, one is confined to first and second for city driving.

The suspension of the Lotus Cortina has undergone considerable modification. It is evident that the complete rear suspension of the stock Cortina was unacceptable to Chapman, as the conventional leaf springs have been thrown out and replaced with coil suspension units. These are retained by trailing radius arms on each side and a central A-frame.

Another modification is the aluminum differential housing to reduce unsprung weight, and two tubular strengthening struts inside the trunk. To improve the weight distribution and permit more room under the hood, the battery has been relocated in the trunk and the spare wheel lies flat on the floor of the trunk instead of being carried upright. Although the result of modifying the rear suspension is a great improvement in road holding, the whole layout seems to produce considerably more noise, and a loud clonking sound is evident if the clutch is engaged suddenly.

As part of the suspension modifications, the car is fitted with 6.00 x 13 tires mounted on special lightweight wheels with a rim section of 5.5 in. The recommended pressures are 22 lb front and 27 lb rear but, as is usual with English manufacturer's recommendations, better results are obtained if the pressures are increased; to 32 lb all around. The steering has a strong self-centering action and is comparatively stiff, although the stiffness disappears at higher speeds.

On the road, the Lotus Cortina is a revelation in what can be done for a small sedan through racing experience, provided it is driven in the manner required. It starts easily from cold and idles at 800 rpm, but prolonged idling in traffic tends to load up the plugs, so it is not ideal for short hauls to the supermarket. On the open road its ability to cover long distances effortlessly is remarkable. As we have mentioned before, the axle ratio is low and the transmission ratios are close so 70 mph is attainable in second and 90 mph in third. The power does not really come in until 3500 rpm is reached and a good shifting point under normal conditions is 5500 rpm. However, one can go as high as 6500 rpm if necessary, but the engine is starting to buzz rather alarmingly at that speed.

The whole car has an extremely firm feel and the road holding is at its best at high speeds. One can enter a fast bend and maintain a predetermined line without any sense of insecurity because the car is basically understeering, the wide tread on the 6.00 x 13 tires seems to glue the car to the road and the steering is very positive. In the event of an emergency, the brakes are much more than adequate for the car. ▶

All Lotus Cortinas are right-hand drive.

Spare is relocated horizontally in the trunk.

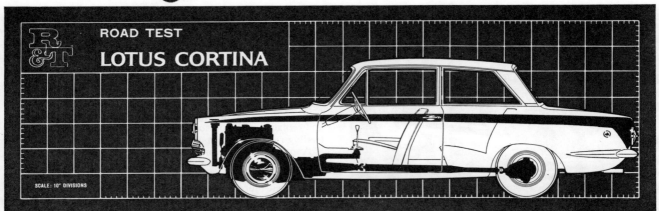

ROAD TEST
LOTUS CORTINA

SCALE: 10" DIVISIONS

PRICE

FOB Cheshunt,
England.........£910 ($2548)

ENGINE

Engine, no. cyl, type...4-cyl, dohc
Bore x stroke, in......3.25 x 2.86
Displacement, cc............1558
  Equivalent cu in..........95.06
Compression ratio..........9.5:1
Bhp @ rpm..........105 @ 5500
  Equivalent mph............95.5
Torque @ rpm, lb-ft..108 @ 4000
  Equivalent mph...........69.4
Carburetor, no., make....2 Weber
No. barrels—diameter..2-40 mm
Type fuel required......premium

DRIVE TRAIN

Clutch diameter & type: 8 in.,
  single plate diaphragm spring
Gear ratios, 4th (1.00)......3.90
  3rd (1.23)...............4.80
  2nd (1.64)...............6.40
  1st (2.50)...............9.75
Synchromesh........on all four
Differential ratio............3.90
Optional ratios.........4.10, 4.40

CHASSIS & SUSPENSION

Frame type: unit with body
Brake type f/r.........disc/drum
  Swept area, sq in.........282
Tire size & make..6.00 x 13 Dunlop
  Wheel revs/mi............890
Steering type....recirculating ball
  Overall ratio...........13.4:1
  Turns, lock to lock........3.0
  Turning circle, ft........34.0
Front suspension: independent
  with Macpherson struts, lower
  A-arms, coil springs
Rear suspension: live, located by
  A-arm & trailing radius arms,
  coil springs

ACCOMMODATION

Normal capacity, persons........5
Hip room, front, in......2 x 21.5
  Rear......................51
Head room, front............38
  Rear......................36
Seat back adjustment, deg...none
Entrance height, in...........51
Step-over height..........13.2
Floor height..............10.9
Door width, front/rear......32/0
Driver Comfort Rating:
  for driver 69-in. tall........95
  for driver 72-in. tall........85
  for driver 75-in. tall........80

GENERAL

Curb weight, lb............1930
Test weight................2245
Weight distribution with
  driver, percent..........52/48
Wheelbase, in.............98.4
Track, front/rear......51.6/50.2
Overall length............168
  Width..................62.5
  Height.................53.9
Frontal area, sq ft........18.7
Ground clearance, in........5.3
Overhang, front..........28.5
  Rear....................46
Departure angle, no load, deg..14.5
Usable trunk space, cu ft....11.6
Fuel tank capacity, gal......9.6

INSTRUMENTATION

Instruments: 140-mph speedometer, 8000-rpm tachometer, oil
pressure, water temperature,
fuel.
Warning lamps: high beam, ignition, turn signals, oil pressure.

MISCELLANEOUS

Body styles available: 2-door sedan
as tested.

ACCESSORIES

Included in list price: heater, cigar
lighter, windshield washer.

CALCULATED DATA

Lb/hp (test wt)..............21.3
Cu ft/ton mi..............84.8
Mph/1000 rpm (4th)........17.3
Engine revs/mi............3460
Piston travel, ft/mi........1650
Rpm @ 2500 ft/min.......5230
  Equivalent mph..........90.5
R&T wear index.............57

MAINTENANCE

Crankcase capacity, qt........3.5
  Change interval, mi.......5000
Oil filter type...........full flow
  Change interval, mi.......5000
Lubrication grease points......10
  Lube interval, mi.........5000
Tire pressures, front/rear,
  psi...................22/27

ROAD TEST RESULTS

ACCELERATION

0–30 mph, sec.............4.0
0–40 mph.................5.7
0–50 mph.................7.8
0–60 mph................10.5
0–70 mph................14.1
0–80 mph................19.0
0–100 mph...............38.1
Passing test, 50–70 mph......6.2
Standing 1/4 mi, sec........17.5
  Speed at end, mph........77

TOP SPEEDS

High gear (6500), mph......106
3rd (6500)................90
2nd (6500)................68
1st (6500)................45

GRADE CLIMBING

(Tapley Data)

4th gear, max gradient, %.....10
  3rd......................14
  2nd......................20
  1st......................28
Total drag at 60 mph, lb......110

SPEEDOMETER ERROR

30 mph indicated.....actual 29.4
40 mph.................39.8
60 mph.................58.3
80 mph.................77.6
100 mph................96.8

FUEL CONSUMPTION

Normal range, mpg........18–24
Cruising range, mi.......170–230

ACCELERATION & COASTING

SS 1/4

4th
3rd
2nd
1st

ELAPSED TIME IN SECONDS
MPH   5   10   15   20   25   30   35   40   45

The Girling system employs 9.5-in. discs in front and 9 x 1.75 in. drums at the rear, with a vacuum booster to give the pedal a light but progressive feel.

The Ford Lotus Cortina comes in various stages of tune, and the ultimate is the 145-bhp model, produced specifically for competition. This has a maximum speed of 128 mph at 7000 rpm with the 3.9 axle ratio and is reputed to have achieved 140 mph on the banked circuit at Monza. It has been extremely successful in European GT racing but, by no stretch of the imagination, could it be called a road car. Apart from engine modifications to increase the power output, the car is gutted internally and comes equipped with Plexiglass instead of safety glass in the side windows, light-weight fiberglass seats and a higher ratio steering box, among other items.

Our test car appeared to be an excellent compromise between performance and comfort, and our assessment of the car is that it would find a small but ready market in America if it was offered for sale. It is the perfect answer for the sports car enthusiast who has a family, because its performance is as good as many sports cars (and better than some), while at the same time it offers the accommodation and comfort of a sedan. On the debit side, it is not very satisfactory around town because of its gearing and lack of torque at low speeds, but this is a small price to pay for the pleasure of driving the car on longer trips.

Arrangement of rear suspension.

Twin-cam engine with two Weber carburetors develops 105 bhp.

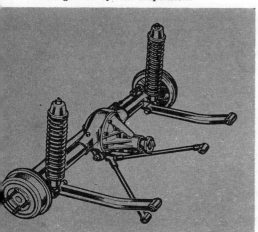

LOTUS-CORTINA

A letter recently arrived in our offices from a reader which suggested that we should propound our ideas for what the writer described as "the ideal family/touring car". A couple of years ago we would have been delighted to oblige. Our specification would have been based around a four-seater saloon body of compact dimensions, with a lively, punchy power unit of between 1½ and 2 litres, mated to a close-ratio, all-synchromesh four-speed gearbox. Light weight, assisting towards a high power/weight ratio, would be combined with high overall gearing to provide high-speed cruising and usable high maximum speeds in the lower gears. And so on.

Today, of course, we would be wasting our time, for a car which conforms almost exactly to the letter of this ideal specification is now produced—the Lotus-Cortina. Externally, the Lotus-Cortina is distinguishable from other two-door Cortinas only by its black-painted grille, white colour, with a Lotus-green flash at the waist, and its wood-rimmed steering wheel. The exterior, however, is virtually all that the two cars have in common Beneath the bonnet, the existing push-rod, four-cylinder engine has been replaced by a Lotus twin-cam unit. This is based on the Ford 1½-litre engine and, in fact, employs the same block. The stroke remains unchanged at 72.75 mm., but the bore has been increased to 82.55 mm. to give a total swept volume of 1,558 c.c. compared with the push-rod version's 1,498 c.c. Valves are operated by twin overhead camshafts in the alloy cylinder head and the compression ratio is raised from 8.3 to 9.5 : 1, the mixture is supplied to the combustion chambers by two twin-choke 40 DCOE 18 Weber carburettors and an A.C. mechanical fuel pump. This results in a net b.h.p. output of 105 at 5,500 r.p.m., while the torque figure is increased from 81.5 lb. ft. to 108 lb. ft. at 4,000 r.p.m.

The transmission is by a diaphragm spring clutch, in an aluminium housing, to an all-synchromesh four-speed gearbox: the top gear ratio remains unchanged, at 3.9 : 1, but the first, second, third and reverse gears have all been raised to take advantage of the increased torque available from the twin-cam engine. With ratios of 9.75, 6.39 and 4.79 : 1 (reverse is 10.95 : 1) in the Lotus model a considerable stepping-up is seen when compared with the standard ratios of 13.82, 9.34 and 5.5, with 15.5 : 1 for reverse. Translated into practical terms, this results in nearly 50 m.p.h. being available in bottom gear, with just under 70 in second and over 90 m.p.h. in third. The front suspension is unchanged, consisting of independent wishbones with coil springs and telescopic shock absorbers.

The rear end, however, is completely rebuilt and the existing longitudinal semi-elliptic leaf springs with lever-type shock absorbers are replaced by a live axle with trailing links and an "A" bracket, the suspension medium being coil spring/damper units. The whole car is lowered appreciably, and sits much closer to the ground.

On the front wheels 9½ in. disc brakes are fitted, with 9 in. drums at the rear; the standard Cortina has drum brakes on all four wheels, and with its rear drums of only 8 in. diameter, a considerable increase in braking surface is offered—which, in view of the tremendous performance offered by the Lotus-developed car, must be regarded as a matter of utmost importance.

The interior of the car is furnished on rather spartan lines in the interests (Chapman-style) of keeping excess weight to a minimum. There are no carpets, and the black leather seats, fully adjustable and specially designed for the car, look less comfortable than in fact they are. Instrumentation, of course, is more comprehensive than on standard Cortinas. A neat panel is mounted in front of the driver, incorporating an impressive 140 m.p.h. speedometer (unusually accurate on the test car) with trip and total mileage recorders, an 8,000 r.p.m. tachometer (red-lined at 6,500 r.p.m.), fuel contents, water temperature and oil pressure gauges. In addition to the latter, the speedometer dial includes an oil pressure warning light, as well as that for the flashing direction indicators; in the rev.-counter dial are warning lights for headlamp main beams and dynamo charge. With white figures on black faces, all these instruments have steady needles and are easy to read.

With such a specification and the hand of Colin Chapman, it is scarcely surprising that this is a car which fills the needs of the sporting motorist with a family. The relatively high state of tune of the power unit does not spoil its smoothness or tractability, and it is apparent that the five-bearing crank Ford engine is eminently suitable for this class of car. Throughout the test period it was an instantaneous starter, and idled smoothly whether hot or cold. The warm-up period was short, and the engine pulled well from cold and, while it is noiser than when in its less potent form, the noise level is not unpleasantly high for a car of this type. The power range is concentrated in the upper half of the speed range, and to get the best out of the car fairly frequent use of the gearbox is desirable, although this is scarcely a hardship for the prospective owner, and certainly no disadvantage on a car as well-equipped in this respect as the Lotus-Cortina.

The clutch is light to operate, and grips firmly and precisely, with not a trace of slip or spin. The gearbox has powerful synchromesh, and clean changes can be made with great speed and accuracy. On the test car an annoying, and at times very pronounced, gear-lever rattle was present, notably on the over-run. The lever is, however, light and precise to operate. The intermediate gears, as shown above, are fairly high ratios, and this accentuates the car's unwillingness to "trickle" in traffic in high gear. With a maximum speed in first of 48 m.p.h., however, slow-moving traffic can be dealt with by the engagement of this ratio without engine revolutions growing unpleasantly high. First gear, in fact, with such a high ratio becomes an extremely useful, and much-used gear, and within a few miles one finds oneself selecting it quite naturally for full acceleration out of roundabouts and tight corners.

The suspension provides a firm ride, and allows a good deal of road noise to penetrate the interior. On the credit side, however, it endows the car with road-holding of racing car standards, and if a high average speed is to be maintained this can be exploited to its splendid full potential. There is no trace of axle tramp, and wheel-spin is extremely rare unless the driver is clumsy with his feet; in the wet, some caution is needed when accelerating out of corners, but under all conditions the cornering power of the chassis is so high that one is unlikely to get into irrevocable diffi-

culties. As might be expected of a product bearing the Lotus name (and the test car bore the Lotus name in no fewer than eight places!) this is one of those cars of which the driver seems to become a part, and it is controlled by a flick of the wrists or a jab of the throttle rather than by any conscious movement of the driver's arms or legs.

A maximum speed of just over 107 m.p.h. permits a comfortable cruising speed in the nineties, although in fact it was driven rather harder than this during our test, yet despite sustained three-figure speeds the power unit showed no signs of distress. Assuming that the revs. are up around 4,000 r.p.m., top gear acceleration is generally sufficient for overtaking purposes, and the car springs quite vigorously from, say, 70 m.p.h. to 90 m.p.h. For real snap acceleration, however, the gear-lever can be snicked to third, which provides a maximum speed of 92 m.p.h. Second gear will encompass 69 m.p.h., and on consideration it is not surprising that average speeds of higher than 50 m.p.h. can be maintained over long distances with little conscious effort on the part of the driver.

Such performance, of course, requires reliable stopping power, and the generous disc-drum combination fitted to the Lotus-Cortina, aided by a powerful servo, provides this in full measure. The brakes are capable of dealing with the car's performance with room to spare, and throughout the test they continued to provide powerful, stright-line braking on wet and dry roads. The hand-brake, however, is a disappointment. It is sufficiently effective, but is operated by a pull-out "T"-lever mounted beneath the dashboard, where it is difficult to reach and altogether out of keeping with a car of this type.

The Lotus-Cortina's principal disadvantage, however—and it is indicative of the general high level of motoring it provides that this is our biggest complaint—lies in its fuel tank. The standard Cortina eight-gallon tank is retained, and while this is no doubt perfectly satisfactory on the standard Cortina, the Lotus-developed car's increased thirst demands a larger reservoir. Our overall fuel consumption for our test was exactly 21 m.p.g., which means a cruising range between refuelling stops of little more than 160 miles. In terms of Continental motor roads, this means a stop at, perhaps, two-hour intervals, which is scarcely satisfactory

Cars on Test

LOTUS-CORTINA

Engine: Four cylinders, 82.55 mm. × 72.75 mm. (1,558 c.c.); compression ratio 9.5 : 1; twin overhead camshafts; two Weber twin-choke carburetters; 105 b.h.p. at 5,500 r.p.m.

Transmission: Single dry-plate clutch; four-speed and reverse gearbox with synchromesh on all four forward speeds. Central remote-control gear lever.

Suspension: Front, independent, with wishbones and coil springs; rear, live axle with trailing links, "A"-bracket and coil springs. Telescopic dampers all round. Tyres: 6.00 × 13.

Brakes: Front, Girling 9½ in. discs; rear, 9 in. drums.

Dimensions: Overall length, 14 ft. 0¼ ins.; overall width, 5ft. 2½ ins.; overall height, 4 ft. 5¾ ins.; turning circle, 37 ft.; dry weight, 16½ cwt.

PERFORMANCE

	m.p.h.			secs.
MAXIMUM SPEED	— 107.2	ACCELERATION	0–30 —	3.4
(Mean of 2 ways)	— 107.1		0–40 —	4.5
			0–50 —	6.0
			0–60 —	8.5
SPEEDS IN GEARS First	— 48.0		0–70 —	11.3
			0–80 —	15.8
Second	— 69.0		0–90 —	19.6
Third	— 92.0	Standing quarter-mile		— 16.8

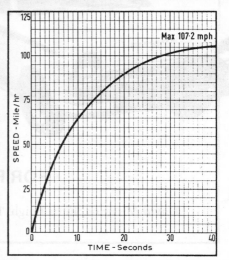

Manufacturers: Lotus Cars Ltd., Delamare Road, Cheshunt, Herts.
Price: £1,100 2s. 11d., including purchase tax.

LOTUS-CORTINA *continued*

for a car which must be considered as a Grand Touring machine.

Another, though perhaps lesser, criticism, lies in the fitting and furnishing of the interior. As it stands, the Lotus-Cortina is an enthusiast's car—splendid for the man who loves driving for driving's sake, but less so for his passengers. For a car in this price category, irrespective of its performance, one might reasonably expect a rather higher standard of interior trim and finish The test car, although admittedly a hard-worked example, possessed a number of anoying rattles and vibrations. The basic conception of the car is probably approaching the ideal for a small, fast compact car with comfortable room for four people; it is only in matters of detail that the finished product falls just a little short of this ideal.

CORTINA IN LOTUS-LAND

Continued from page 14

To be frank, the Lotus Cortina is noisy mechanically. The timing chains clatter, the gearbox sings, and the differential growls. Music to the red-blooded motorist who is a Stirling Moss at heart. Murder to the devotee of the whisper-quiet comfortmobiles. On the test car quite heavy vibration built up from 70 mph to a peak of 80, then vanished as the speed grew. Possibly this is the critical vibration period in the twin-cam engine, or it may have been an out-of-true tailshaft. I was assured that this was the first time the car had acted up.

With an engine that will spin away merrily past the danger point, there is a tendency to overlook things. So Lotus came up with a simple and effective way of preventing bent valves and untidy holes in the block. As the red zone is reached the rotor button automatically cuts out and the engine dies until a safe level is attained.

Suspension at the front is by modified McPherson struts and anti-roll bar, and at the back by trailing A-frames and telescopic coils hitched to the live axle.

The ride is firm and well controlled, with a minimum of pitching. Indeed, the system soaks up potholes and other rough going better than the mass-produced Cortina.

Cornering is flat with just the right shade of understeer for fine, precise handling. Bends can be taken on the limit with no fear of sudden tail breakaway or other unpleasantries. It is one of those rare cars that has the measure of most drivers while keeping a bit up its sleeve for emergencies.

Three-figure cruising is noisy, exhilarating and safe. The alloy doors flutter, the wind roars, and other drivers blink in astonishment as the squat, square-looking upstart rasps past. Brakes are most important on a high-speed car, and the Lotus has more than its fair share of stopping power. The front wheels carry 9¾ in discs and at the back there are 9 by 1¾ in drums. The servo assistance means that the pedal needs little more than a caress to stop the car with tyre-smoking force.

Acceleration tapered off above 60 mph, probably because of ratios in the standard Holden gearbox. A Jaguar box would undoubtedly improve this situation and generally make for better figures, especially in the high speed bracket. Over 80 mph I felt as though there should be another ratio. As a result 0 to 70 took 17.3 sec and the standing quarter was a disappointing 18.5. Speed at the end of the quarter was in excess of 75 mph. Top speed was timed as 112.53 mph.

General handling characteristics are good. The car corners firmly and does not give driver or passengers bad moments even when pressed hard. There is no body lean to speak of. With basic and pleasantly controllable understeering characteristics, the tail can be induced to hang out when thrown hard around a corner, but control is never lost. The plan to lower the rear end three inches should solve this problem.

Fuel consumption for within-the-limit-driving around town was a remarkable 24.1 mpg. However on the acceleration tests and high speed work I could only average between 8 and 10 mpg on a one-in-three methyl benzine mixture.

There is little scuttle shake and the general rigidity of the body is a tribute to Thompson's work. And he does have a unique car.   #

World champion Jim Clark, still fighting to retain his title, nevertheless found time to scoop the British Saloon Car Championship this year in a Cortina-Lotus.

BUT YOU'VE GOT TO FINISH TO WIN

In this special article, he looks at some of the differences between Grand Prix and saloon car racing.

FOR some years now, saloon car racing has been as popular with spectators as any other form of motor racing.

I think there are two main reasons for this. First, in saloon car racing the spectator can identify the cars with those used on the road—and can to a certain extent identify himself with the drivers. (Quite often there is a genuine partisanship displayed by spectators, who cheer on their own particular make of car.)

But the second—and main—reason for its popularity is the spectacular way in which the cars corner and perform.

Part of the excitement undoubtedly stems from the stringent regulations governing the modification of saloon racing cars, which keep them within their various classes at a relatively equal potential.

Another important point is the fact that, in most cases, the car reaches its limits before the driver reaches his. This is not so much the case in Grand Prix racing, where driver and car alike are driving on a finely balanced limit all the time.

I am often asked to compare saloon car racing with Formula I Grand Prix racing. This I always find difficult because, although in both cases the aim is to get the car around the circuit as quickly as possible, the techniques are very different.

With a FI car, everything is developed to the limit. Independent suspensions are used for roadholding, multi-speed gearboxes are the rule, high-revving engines with a narrow range are fitted, and so on.

The consequent margins for error are very small indeed, and one needs a very fine touch to guide a car, even with good roadholding, through a corner on the limit.

In a saloon car, however, with its comparatively reduced roadholding and brakes, it is easier for a driver to find the limit of the car. Although I firmly believe that a good driver will show up in any form of racing, I feel that the differences are not likely to be so great in a saloon car race as, say, in Formula I.

I have often watched saloon car races myself, of course, and like everyone else I have been thrilled—if not a little scared—at times. I don't mind saying I entered my first full season of saloon car racing with mixed feelings.

However, I think that in saloon car events—as, indeed, in all forms of racing—things look more dangerous from the grandstand than they do from the driving-seat.

Whether driving or watching saloon car races, I never cease to be amazed at the punishment and work these production cars will stand. Let's face it, there is very little one can alter on these cars to strengthen them for such severe tests.

YOU can never win a race without finishing, and in my first seven races which counted towards the 1964 saloon car championship I never had a moment's doubt about my car's ability to finish. The Cortina-Lotus is a first-class example of a production road car with the qualities which make a world-beating racing saloon.

For me, the acid test of this car's toughness and reliability was the 1964 Sebring 12-hour endurance race for sports and GT cars.

As I was in America at the time for preliminary tests at Indianapolis, I was invited to go to Sebring to drive a Cortina-Lotus in the 250-km saloon car race. After finishing third overall (first in the class) to a Galaxie and Falcon, and having had a tremendous dice with Dan Gurney (my Indianapolis team-mate) in another Cortina, we decided to enter the car in the 12-hour endurance race.

We had very little time to prepare the car, and our only practice consisted of the final night session. My co-driver for the event was our chief mechanic on Cortinas—Ray Parsons— who had done a bit of test-driving with the car in England.

On reflection, our chances of success in a GT race with a saloon car looked remote. In our class were four of the very fast new works GTZ Alfa Romeos, as well as the usual Porsche contingent. In the bigger classes, we were sharing the track with such cars as the 4-litre works Ferraris.

Despite one or two interesting incidents, the Cortina came in second in class behind one of the GTZs. This proved to me that the car not only had speed but stamina too, for during the race we never eased off.

Since that day I have had a great deal of respect for the Cortina . . . and this driver/car confidence is essential to success in any form of motor racing. With confidence in his car, the saloon racing driver can use his skill to the full without having to hold himself back.

With the Cortina, for example, I make full use of the car's astonishing ability to corner on three wheels—even at speeds in excess of 100 mph. This is a great advantage on certain corners where, knowing that the inside front wheel is off the ground, one can steal a few vital inches off the grass verge with absolute confidence.

The technique is one of many that are exclusive to saloon car racing, and which help to give it special excitement for both spectator and driver. If one were to try to apply the same techniques to Grand Prix racing, the effects might be spectacular but almost certainly slower!

For this reason, and the others I have mentioned, saloon car and Grand Prix racing are almost two different worlds. But without this difference, and the thrills and skills peculiar to each, motor racing as a sport would be distinctly poorer.

HOT

TRYING HARD in the wet, our man at Aintree lifts a wheel on the Longbacon Lotus-Cortina.

Left : The twin-cam head of the Longbacon Lotus-Cortina. Centre : Driving compartment of the Lotus, showing the driver's bucket seat. Right : The Taurus Austin 1100 looks very standard from the outside.

HOT cars are usually fun to drive and three hot cars of very different types have come my way in the last month or so. The first was so hot that it was virtually undrivable on the road and it was necessary to go to the wastes of industrial Liverpool to try the car on the deserted Aintree circuit, which seems fated to be lost to motor racing before long. The car in question was a racing Lotus-Cortina in Group 2 trim, owned by Longbacon Engineering, which had the distinction of finishing ninth overall in the Spa 24-Hour race out of 58 starters, was third in its class of 15 entrants, was the first Ford to finish, and, in fact, was the first British car to finish. Due to heavy business commitments the team was unable to do any more racing after the Spa race on July 25/26th, and when I tried the car last month it had not been touched since the race except to give it a wash.

The car was bought " over the counter " from Lotus and came in standard Group 2 trim, costing around £1,700. Various modifications were made by Longbacon mechanic Paul Kelly, including boring out by 1 mm. to 1,594 c.c., raising the compression ratio to 11 to 1, regrinding the camshafts and modifying the valve gear. The engine was also completely balanced, the oil pressure increased from the rather low standard pressure of around 30 p.s.i. to about 50 p.s.i., the carburetters were re-jetted, the fuel pumps were changed for Bendix pumps, and larger-bore fuel lines were fitted. The exhaust system was modified to protrude from the side of the car, an oil cooler was fitted, and a large amber oil-pressure warning light was fitted on the facia. The plugs were changed to Champion N58R and a spare Lucas sports coil and a spare condenser were also fitted.

Chassis modifications were also numerous and several suspension changes were made to improve the handling. These included modified springs all round, with adjustable dampers at the rear, a thicker front anti-roll bar, and a higher-geared steering box. The mountings of the rear " A "-bracket were also strengthened. The shields were removed from the brakes and Ferodo front pads and rear linings were fitted and the master cylinder was changed. One of the Hewland limited-slip differentials specially made for the Cortina was also fitted.

All this work brought the cost of the car over the £2,000 mark, but for the 24-hour race a good deal more work was necessary.

A 22-gallon long-range fuel tank was fitted in the boot and supplied with a reserve switch so that one gallon remained in reserve should the car run out of fuel on the course. A special racing bucket seat was fitted, together with Irvin full safety harness, and a leather-covered steering wheel replaced the wooden one. A high-capacity 2-speed wiper motor was fitted and Trico supplied a set of their special racing wiper blades, while a 1-gallon screen-washer tank was fitted inside the car behind the front seats. A pair of Lund long-range lamps were supplied by Ted Lund, who was to be one of the drivers, and a pair of identification lamps were fitted at the front so that the car could be easily identified as it passed the pits at night.

With the 3.9 axle and 5.50 × 13 in. Dunlop R6 tyres (£10 10s. each!) the car would reach 128.1 m.p.h. at 7,000 r.p.m., which would have been very useful on the straights at Spa, but the drivers, Paul Kelly, Bill Allen (of Team Elite fame) and Ted Lund (the Le Mans M.G. exponent) decided on a 6,200-r.p.m. rev.-limit. In the race they were soon left behind by many cars but, despite temptations, they kept to their limit except for the occasional indiscretion. This wise decision paid off eventually, for other cars began to drop out at regular intervals and number 305 moved up the lap chart. The Achilles' heel of the Lotus Cortina is the differential, which often lets its oil out under the strain put on it from the " A "-bracket, but the oil level and bolt tightness was checked at every pit stop and the axle gave no trouble at all. Two dynamos gave up under the strain and the first one drained the battery, so a new battery had to be fitted, but apart from this the car needed no attention at all, although as a precautionary measure the near-side rear wheel was changed and the gearbox oil level was checked. They need not have changed the wheel as it turned out, and at the end of the race the other three tyres had tread depths of 1.5 mm. and 1 mm. at the front and 2 mm. on the off-side rear, having started out with 5 mm. of tread. The car ran with 50 p.s.i. in the front tyres and 55 in the rears. The car ran on Esso Golden fuel and got through 145.83 gallons for a fuel consumption of approximately 14.5 m.p.g., and the engine used two gallons of Esso 40/50 oil. The car covered 242 laps of the Spa circuit, a distance of 2,119.92 miles, at an average speed of 88.11 m.p.h.

HEADS

ries a Racing Lotus-
uned Ford Cortina GT
uned Austin 1100

LOOKING OUTWARDLY like an ordinary Cortina GT, the Willment Sprint is a real wolf in sheep's clothing.

Left : The 42DCOE Weber sits comfortably behind the Taurus-converted Austin 1100 engine. Centre : New seats transform the driving position of the Willment Sprint. Right : Wide-base wheels and Dunlop SP tyres help the Willment Sprint to corner extremely well.

The team was encouraged by its first venture into International saloon-car racing as a change from GT racing, and plan to do a full season next year, but they felt that the reaction from the Press and from potential Trade sponsors was lukewarm in the extreme, both groups seeming to prefer the hares who didn't finish to the tortoises who did. And in long-distance racing it is usually the tortoises who get in the money.

The glorious summer failed us at Aintree and the circuit was drenched in torrential rain squalls every few minutes, but I got in a few laps during the odd dry spells. The bucket seat fits you like a glove and with the safety harness done up I felt almost as if I was screwed to the floor, which is most reassuring in a competition car; being a six-footer I would have preferred more rearwards movement on the seat runners to give me more leg room, but I was still able to heel-and-toe adequately.

The engine is the acme of intractability, which the extraordinarily high 1st gear does nothing to alleviate; the car will stall if there is less than 3,000 r.p.m. on the tachometer, and it really prefers something like 5,000 r.p.m. plus a good deal of clutch slipping to get away cleanly. Full-blooded racing starts with 6,000 r.p.m. on the clock resulted in a drop to 2,000 r.p.m. and a sort of kangaroo hopping before the engine picked up revs. When we took some performance figures, I found it best to use 5,000 r.p.m. and slip the clutch gently. There is precious little power below 4,000 r.p.m. and not much until 5,000 r.p.m. is reached, and one begins to wonder how Lotus-Cortinas go so quickly round circuits, until suddenly there is a noticeable kick in the back and the tachometer needle streaks round to 7,000 r.p.m., and the next gear has to be snatched very quickly indeed to avoid over-revving. As long as the revs are kept well up the car fairly streaks along, the close ratios helping the driver nicely in this respect, while the gearbox is delightful to use, having the same action as that of the normal Cortina. Using 6,500 r.p.m. as a change point the Group 2 car has speeds in the lower gears of 50, 72 and 95 m.p.h., while top would give a theoretical 120 m.p.h. at six-five. However, only the Club circuit was in use at Aintree, which left us not much more than two-thirds of the Railway straight, meaning that we could only reach 90 m.p.h. from a standstill, or a little over 100 m.p.h. while lapping. With a

hastily corrected speedometer we got performance figures from a standstill of 0-50 m.p.h. in 5.0 sec.; 0-60, 8.1 sec.; 0-70, 10.3 sec.; 0-80, 15.0 sec.; and 0-90, 19.5 sec.; still restricting ourselves to 6,500 r.p.m. and on a soaking-wet track!

My first introduction to the handling of a Lotus-Cortina was as shattering as it has been to most racing drivers, for (to use the kindest adjective I can think of) it feels atrocious. The car skitters about on the bumps, lacks directional stability, wanders in a side wind, and when cornering hard the inside front wheel lifts (as the picture shows), leaving the car poised on a few square inches of rubber on the off-side front wheel, at which point the steering feels decidedly odd to say the least. Despite all this the car can be cornered faster than any other saloon car you can name and even when skating through deep puddles with 50 p.s.i. in the tyres it sticks like a leech. It will break away of course, but juggling with throttle and steering soon saves the situation. In fact the car felt worse on the straights, when it would suddenly aquaplane through a puddle and the steering could be moved from lock to lock without causing the car to deviate appreciably from a straight line. Drivers tell me you soon learn to live with these odd characteristics, and since the Lotus-Cortina has virtually turned saloon-car racing into a one-model domination it can't be that bad. I'm no Jim Clark but a lap time of around 1 min. 23 sec. against the normal time of 1 min. 12.0 sec. or so in the dry shows that the handling must be pretty good in the wet. The brakes are first class and the steering would be a revelation to the driver of a normal Cortina for it is incredibly light.

I enjoyed my drive immensely and look forward to seeing this car in action next season, when, if it is driven as sensibly as it was at Spa, it should do well in the European Championship.

Willment Cortina GT Sprint

The next hot car I tried was a Willment Sprint GT, a considerably modified version of the Ford Cortina GT. The name of Willment needs no introduction to racing enthusiasts and they have been converting and racing Ford cars for 15 years or more, long before their current racing team hit the headlines. They have been tuning Cortinas for some time but these have invariably been on a one-off basis, according to the requirements of the customer, and already this year over 100 cars have been tuned. However, they have decided to market a standardised car called the Sprint GT which will sell as a new car for £910, although used cars can also be converted to this specification. The modifications are pretty extensive and cover most of the more criticised aspects of the Cortina GT. The list in the data panel gives the details and prices of the various modifications. The engine is only lightly modified, with re-worked cylinder head, inlet manifold and carburetter, and a new camshaft which raise the power output to over 90 b.h.p. The major part of the work concerns the suspension, which is lowered by the use of different springs, and shock-absorbers, and also uses a heavy-duty anti-roll bar and a set of 5½J wide-based wheels. The brakes have hard pads and linings and a Girling servo is fitted. A wooden steering wheel and a gear-lever knob are supplied, and extras above the cost of the Sprint kit are new seats, Britax reel-type safety belts, racing wing mirrors and a brake fluid level indicator.

The three most criticised features of the Cortina as far as the enthusiast is concerned are the road-holding (especially in the wet), the seating position (especially for the six-footer) and the gear ratios. Willment have sorted out the handling and the seating, but there is little they can do about the gear ratios at a reasonable price; the Lotus-Cortina gearbox is expensive and has a high 1st gear and other proprietary gear sets are meant for racing and rather noisy. What they may do in the future is to offer a 4.1-to-1 axle ratio instead of the present 3.9 to 1, which will make the car more tractable in 3rd and top gears, but still allow a 100 m.p.h. plus top speed.

On the road the ride is a revelation, for gone is the sloppy ride, axle hop and general untidiness that the Cortina is prone to over rough surfaces. The ride becomes firm and there is some bounciness at low speeds but once in the upper 80s, where the needle seems to spend most of its time, the Cortina covers rough roads most impressively. The test car was shod with Dunlop SPs (although Pirelli Cinturatos are offered as standard equipment on the Sprint GT) and it stuck to the road like a postage stamp, with none of the tail-happy tendencies which the normal Cortina develops. Roll is reduced and the car can really be flung around; the seats contribute to this for the tall driver can get away from the wheel and has plenty of room to play tunes on the pedals and to stretch his arms. These seats resemble the Lotus-Cortina seats but are made for Willments specially and are most comfortable to use, with a soft cushion and a back-rest which gives some lateral support. At £23 a pair on exchange they are excellent value.

The engine modifications only give themselves away at idling revs when the engine tends to be lumpy, but once the revs rise the engine becomes clean and from then on it will whistle straight off the clock, which is red-lined at 6,000 r.p.m. to 7,000 r.p.m. The noise level is no higher than standard as the exhaust system is unmodified. When taking performance figures we restrained ourselves to 6,000 r.p.m., but even so the figures in the data panel are more than satisfying and much better than those we obtained for the standard GT Cortina. From standstill to 60 m.p.h. in 10 sec. is excellent, while 80 m.p.h. can be achieved in 17.5 sec. Acceleration tails off a little after that but 100 m.p.h. will come up far more quickly than one has any right to expect from a 1½-litre family saloon, and at 6,000 r.p.m. in top the speed is 105 m.p.h. Willment's competitions manager Jeff Uren has seen 6,600 r.p.m. on the rev.-counter during development testing, which is around 117 m.p.h. At the lower end of the speed scale it is necessary to drop down through the gears to cope with traffic conditions otherwise there is considerable judder from the transmission; this is of course encountered on the standard GT Cortina. There is also some " hunting " when trickling through traffic at speeds under 15 m.p.h., even in 1st gear, and the clutch has to be dabbed to avoid jerky progress.

All in all, I thoroughly approve of Willment's mods to the Cortina and quite frankly if I were in the market for a car of this type and price I would by-pass the Lotus-Cortina with its fussy handling, vague steering, and its trick of spilling its rear axle oil, and go for the Willment car. I'm talking about road use, of course—racing is a different proposition.

Taurus Austin 1100

Taurus are one of the newest and smallest of the mushrooming band of tuning specialists but already they have garnered a lucrative corner of this booming market. Like so many others, they specialise in tuning B.M.C. products, and the car I recently tried was one of their versions of the Austin 1100. Perhaps the main criticism laid at the door of the Morris and Austin 1100 is lack of performance, although the M.G. 1100 is available for the more affluent, who have an extra £120 to spend.

The Taurus conversion is simple, but incorporates the fairly expensive Weber 42DCOE carburetter, thus accounting for much of the £74 9s. cost of the conversion on our test car. The cylinder head is modified to stage 1 tune for an exchange price of £24, the single twin-choke Weber is mounted on a suitable manifold and supplied with the necessary linkages, and an exhaust manifold is supplied by the R. J. V. company, who specialise in this commodity. A Servais silencer and large-bore pipe completes the ensemble.

As the performance figures in the data panel indicate, the Taurus 1100 makes the normal 1100 look extremely slow, knocking some 10 sec. off the 0-60 m.p.h. time of 25.6 sec., and is still comfortably 4 sec. quicker than the M.G. 1100 to the same speed. As far as top speed is concerned the car will just about hold 90 m.p.h. on a level road but it is best regarded as a happy 80-85-m.p.h. cruiser as the engine is turning over rather rapidly at 90 m.p.h. At the lower end of the scale the choke area of the Weber is obviously a little too much for the Austin engine and it is getting more petrol than it needs; this results in some gobbling noises from the engine, accompanied by occasional " hunting " if high gears are held onto at low speeds. It also helps the fuel consumption to depreciate to something like 25 m.p.g. if all the performance is used most of the time, but 28 m.p.g. can be had in exchange for a lighter throttle foot.

Having saved £120 by buying an Austin 1100 instead of an M.G. 1100 we have spent £75 of that on the Taurus conversion, still leaving us £45 in hand. I would spend some of that on assisting the brakes to stop the car a little better and a little more on a decent driver's seat. This would still leave some in hand to buy a wooden steering wheel, electric rev.-counter and all those other goodies so beloved by the performance enthusiasts.

Looked at in this light the Taurus conversion is astonishingly good value for money, which makes one wonder just how the factory can charge so much for the M.G. version of these extraordinarily fine cars.—M.L.T.

PERFORMANCE COMPARISONS

	Ford Cortina GT	Lotus-Cortina	Willment Sprint GT	Morris 1100	M.G. 1100	Taurus Austin 1100
0-30 m.p.h.	3.8 sec.	4.0 sec.	3.0 sec.	6.4 sec.	5.7 sec.	4.8 sec.
0-40 m.p.h.	6.4 ,,	5.4 ,,	5.2 ,,	10.3 ,,	8.8 ,,	7.0 ,,
0-50 m.p.h.	10.4 ,,	8.8 ,,	7.0 ,,	16.5 ,,	14.5 ,,	11.0 ,,
0-60 m.p.h.	14.0 ,,	11.0 ,,	10.0 ,,	25.6 ,,	19.2 ,,	15.5 ,,
0-70 m.p.h.	19.0 ,,	15.0 ,,	13.4 ,,	—	28.0 ,,	23.0 ,,
0-80 m.p.h.	27.6 ,,	21.0 ,,	17.5 ,,	—	—	—
0-90 m.p.h.	—	—	26.4 ,,	—	—	—
Date tested	July 1963	Jan. 1964	—	Dec. 1962	Dec. 1962	—

EQUIPMENT FITTED TO WILLMENT SPRINT GT

Modified Parts	Non-Exchange £ s. d.	Exchange £ s. d.	Labour Charges £ s. d.
Cylinder head	—	35 0 0	)
Inlet manifold.. ..	—	6 0 0	} 27 0 0
G.T.4 camshaft	—	11 0 0	)
Carburetter modifications	1 10 0	—	
Heavy-duty anti-roll bar	5 0 0	—	
Front suspension struts ..	—	6 0 0	)
Rear shock-absorbers ..	—	8 8 0	} 9 0 0
Modified rear springs ..	—	8 0 0	
Modified front coil-springs..	—	3 0 0	)
Anti-fade brake pads ..	3 12 0	—	)
Anti-fade rear linings ..	—	3 6 0	} 10 0 0
Girling brake servo ..	13 0 0	—	
Wood-rim steering wheel ..	5 17 6	—	
Wooden gear-lever knob ..	10 6	—	)
Set (5) 5½J rims, wide base ..	17 17 6	—	}
Set (5) Cinturato 165 × 13 tyres and tubes	43 5 0	—	} 3 0 0
(Allowance on existing tyres and wheels, £25 0s. 0d.)			

Extras to Sprint Specification

Modified front seats	—	23 0 0	
Britax reel-type safety belts ..	12 12 0	—	3 0 0
Racing-type wing mirrors ..	2 11 6	—	1 10 0
Sovy brake fluid level indicator	17 6	—	1 10 0

Complete car supplied new for £910 inc. purchase tax.

EQUIPMENT FITTED TO TAURUS AUSTIN 1100

	£ s. d.
Taurus Stage 1 cylinder head..	24 0 0
42DCOE Weber carburetter, inlet manifold, linkages, etc. ..	35 0 0
R. J. V. exhaust manifold	9 9 0
Servais silencer and large-bore pipe	6 0 0

0-100 IN 30 SECS!
110 M·P·H!

THE NEW HIGH POWERED
CONSUL
CORTINA

developed by
LOTUS

The eagerly awaited first joint production car of Ford and Lotus. Outstanding features include: Special Ford-based 1½ litre Lotus twin overhead cam engine producing 105 bhp. Two twin choke Weber carburettors. 4 speed close ratio gear box with remote control. Suspension developed for high speed motoring. Light-weight rear axle. Servo-assisted brakes, discs at front. Wide rimmed road wheels. Individual front seats. Full instrumentation including tachometer. For more information about Ford of Britain's fastest car contact your Ford dealer.

Now you can own the same exciting sedan Colin Chapman modifies for Jim Clark:

Ford's Cortina Lotus.

Until now there just weren't enough Cortina Lotus to go around. It takes time to build a car that is partially hand-crafted at the rate of only six per day for the entire world market. But now you can get immediate delivery on this exciting road car with a great racing record.

Cortina Lotus delivers all the luxury of the Cortina De-luxe Sedan, plus the performance only Colin Chapman could have added. The four-cylinder engine has double overhead cams, high compression head, intake manifold with two dual choke Webers, tuned exhaust, and a

heavy-duty crankshaft. The diaphragm clutch connects the engine to a four-speed all-synchromesh transmission. There are front disc brakes and rear drumbrakes. A racer's wooden steering wheel, ammeter and tachometer. And the suspension has been modified so that Cortina Lotus handles as well as she goes.

But you really have to drive this bomb to believe it. Test a Cortina Lotus for yourself at your nearest Ford's Cortina dealer. For his name, write: Imported Vehicles, Ford Division, 3000 Schaefer Road, Dearborn, Michigan.

Road impressions by PATRICK McNALLY of two cars modified by—

A leaf-spring converted Lotus Cortina...

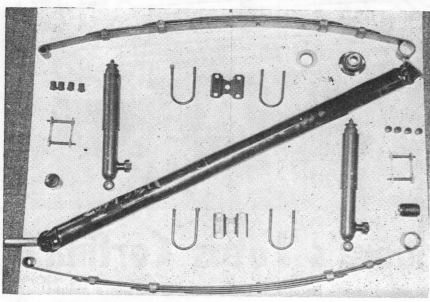

ALL THE NECESSARY BITS that go to convert a coil-spring Lotus Cortina to leaf-spring specification. The modification is not as difficult as one might first envisage, as the chassis already has the mounting points for the springs.

IT is no secret that the big problem associated with pre-1965 Lotus Cortinas is the rear end—the differential is forever working loose and depositing its contents on the road. This is due to the design of the rear suspension, for the axle is located by an A-bracket which is attached to the axle at the base of the differential. When the car is subjected to heavy stresses, for instance under really hard acceleration and enthusiastic cornering, the axle tends to twist, and the locating arm, operating as it does on the bottom of the differential unit, transmits some of the loads on the differential housing. This usually results in the nose-piece working loose in its banjo housing and permitting the oil to seep out. Then the inevitable happens—running low or without oil the crown wheel and pinion devour each other and everything comes to a grinding halt. Remember the Six-Hours at Brands Hatch when the leading Cortina had trouble in the last half hour with just such a failure?

Having at one time owned an A-bracket-type Lotus Cortina which spent a great deal of time at Cheshunt for this very reason (fortunately under guarantee!), I was in a good position to comment on Ian Walker's conversion which brings early Lotus Cortinas up to latest design with leaf springs and single-piece prop-shaft.

Last year's times around the circuits with leaf-spring-suspended Lotuses were considerably better than with the old layout, particularly at the Nürburgring, where, predictably, handling is of utmost importance. From this it is safe to assume the leaf-spring set-up is as good, if not better.

But perhaps most important of all, especially where road cars are concerned, the converted rear end gives no trouble. During the entire test there was never a trace of oil from the differential housing. Full throttle acceleration and vicious cornering caused the rear end not the least concern. Although the car was set up for the road, in my opinion the road-holding was better than both the A-bracket cars I had previously driven. The acceleration times were unaffected, and the performance figures on Ian Walker's converted car were if anything better than standard.

What exactly is entailed in making the change-over? Not a great deal. The whole rear axle is removed from the car complete with A-bracket and coil springs. The coil springs are discarded and leaf springs substituted. Fortunately the Cortina body chassis unit is already equipped with all the right spring mounts, so the leaf springs go straight in. The two-piece prop-shaft is replaced by a single-piece shaft, and a new rear axle pinion flange is fitted. The shock absorbers are replaced by Armstrong Firmarides. It's a pretty straightforward modification and Ian Walker's can do the job in a day. However, as can be seen from the accompanying photograph, there are lots of little bits necessary, like shackle pins, etc.

If I were doing the job myself, while I was about it I would fit a substantial Panhard rod to cut out any tendency towards rear-wheel steering and improve the high-speed stability of the car. The car I tested had a nasty tendency of moving across the road for no apparent reason when being driven quickly. However, this may well have been due to the fact that the car had been shunted previously, and Cortinas always feel a bit odd after they have had a good knock.

The complete conversion, including labour, is reasonably priced at £50, which must be considered cheap if only for your own peace of mind. No longer need you drive with one ear permanently tuned to the hum of the diff.

John Whitmore's Lotus Cortina

Track test and technical description of the European Saloon Car Champion's mount

By PATRICK McNALLY

ONE car stood out among all others during the qualifying rounds of the European Touring Car Championship—the red and gold Lotus Cortina entered and prepared by Alan Mann Racing and driven with enormous skill and verve by Sir John Whitmore. The only time the car didn't win was the first round at Monza when Alfa Romeo scored a home victory when the two Alan Mann cars blew up spectacularly. These, however, were 1964 cars with the very first of the B.R.M.-prepared Ford twin-cam power units. From then on, using 1965 leaf spring suspended Lotus Cortinas, the Alan Mann team were triumphant with Whitmore winning everywhere he went.

AUTOSPORT went down to Goodwood to see just how fast these cars are, how they behave, and try to determine what makes them go so well. With the wide open stretches of the Sussex track before us, the car did not seem at all quick—that is until we arrived at Madgwick, when a very strange sensation was experienced, the steering feeling extremely odd and the car appearing to weave about without any apparent reason. It takes a few laps before one gets acclimatize oneself to this before one gets

down to driving the car. As there is relatively little power available (152 b.h.p.) it has to be set up so it is easy to induce oversteer, as there is not enough power to drift through corners in the conventional manner. It is not a vicious, unpredictable oversteer, but rather the type that is easily induced by throwing the car sideways well before the apex and then driving through on full power. This has been found to be the fastest way of getting these machines through bends although it appears very dramatic. The front end is so stiff the front wheel has to lift, and in certain circumstances so does the rear inside wheel. When a rear anti-roll bar is fitted as on the team Lotus cars this effectively stiffens up the rear suspension and there is even more of a tendency for a rear wheel to come off the ground.

As can be seen from these observations, the Lotus Cortina handles in a spectacular manner and to go really quickly demands a great deal of a driver, as he spends the majority of the time on three or even two wheels. It is possible for a mediocre driver to go reasonably quickly and get within a second or so of a highly skilled, experienced Lotus Cortina driver, but the

last fractions of a second—the ones that count—sort out the men from the boys, because they demand perfect co-ordination and timing.

Graham Hill was once down at Goodwood when Alan Mann and John Whitmore were testing. Hill tried John's Cortina, did a couple of laps, and came in sure something was about to fall off it, remarking it could not possibly handle like that normally. He would not be reassured by Alan Mann that the car was perfectly allright, and a wager was laid that John Whitmore could not equal the lap record in the car. Almost needless to say, it was Graham who had to pay for the lunch that day. Later on in the afternoon he did a few more laps and got very close to Whitmore's times. Jackie Stewart's comments are also worth a mention here. When asked what he thought of racing Lotus Cortinas he is reported as replying "They're such a laugh, ye can nae take them serious."

The power does not have to be used with any great degree of caution, and there is plenty available between 5,000 and 7,800 r.p.m. The close ratio Lotus Cortina gearbox enables one to keep the revs. up in this region, the gearbox itself being extremely fast, with first-rate synchromesh and a very small movement across the gate.

The location of the back axle appears to be extremely good, and there was no question of any tramp, even with full power on fairly rough surfaces—for instance on the second part of St. Mary's. Although the car I drove had a Hewland limited-slip differential it had done many racing miles and was not operating as efficiently as it might. Going through Madgwick, as soon as the inside rear wheel lifted we lost some traction, and this naturally slowed our progress, as well as making the car momentarily unstable.

One of the nicest features of the car are the brakes. These are absolutely fade-free, extremely light in operation, and imparted unto the driver great confidence. Whether when used really hard, on a circuit like Brands, they would give trouble, I do not know, but around Goodwood they gave me not a moment's worry—unlike those of Mustangs and Galaxies. The stability at high speed appeared to be good, as soon as one became used to the odd feeling of the steering.

It is important in a car such as this for the driver to be very firmly located in his seat, and the bucket seats fitted to the car were really ideal, giving plenty of lateral location, with good back and thigh support. A steering wheel 14 ins. in diameter covered in leather replaces the standard, rather spidery wooden object and has a much nicer feel to it. All the other controls are unaltered—even the accelerator pedal needs no modification to make "heel-and-toe" possible. There are no additional gauges to frighten the driver, as the standard instrumentation is more than adequate, with the rev. counter right in front of the driver. A Britax full-shoulder harness holds you firmly in place and there is a fire extinguisher reassuringly at hand.

What has been done to this Lotus Cortina to make it such a great performer? Not a great deal, because the car has to conform to appendix J group 2, which forbids all but the most scanty modifications. The engine is a 1,558 c.c. Lotus Ford twin-cam unit bored out to the maximum permissible size of 1,595 c.c. Not every block will rebore and they have to be selected to find ones with adequate meat in the cylinders. All engine modifications are done by either Cosworth or B.R.M.s; the engine in our car was a phase 2 prepared by the latter. In order that the rods will take over 7,000 r.p.m. these are replaced by the optional steel ones with special pistons.

The camshaft gives 10.42 mm. lift and is timed at: inlet opens 54 degrees B.T.D.C., closes 82 degrees A.B.D.C., exhaust opens 72 degrees B.B.D.C., closes 54 degrees A.T.D.C. The combustion chambers match out at 40 c.c. which gives a compression ratio of 9.8 : 1. Maximum power is said to be just over 150 b.h.p. at 7,800 r.p.m. A pair of Weber 40DCOE carburetters with 115 main jets and 30 mm. chokes meter the fuel through the cast alloy inlet manifold cast integral with the cylinder head. The seal between the carburetter and manifold is by a rubber O-ring. The mechanical fuel pump is discarded in favour of a high pressure Bendix Blue Top. Conventional Lucas coil and distributor ignition is employed along with Autolite spark plugs. The throttle cable is specially made up to give minimum friction, and a more progressive opening.

A Borg and Beck diaphragm single-plate clutch with hydraulic operation conveys the power to the Ford four-speed all-synchromesh gearbox. This has a centrally mounted floor change and ratios of 2.51, 1.64, 1.23 and 1 to 1. The propshaft is of the two-piece variety with a central

bearing and both parts of it are carefully balanced. For British circuits, 4.7 and 4.1 Hypoid differentials are used, fitted with Hewland limited slips. These limited slips work on the ZF cam and plunger principle and have a life of approximately 12 racing hours. Castrol 29/59 is used in the back axle, whilst the engine runs on R.

The rear suspension is by semi-elliptic leaf springs with a pair of radius rods locating the axle. The back-end is made as soft as possible, by removing some of the leaves and relocating the eyes which effectively lowers the car. The front suspension is stiffened up and lowered by the use of a 15/16 roll-bar and shorter, stronger springs in the MacPherson struts. No doubt there are several other detailed ameliorations! Armstrong AT9 shock absorbers are used, these being of the adjustable variety at the rear. Girling disc brakes are used on the

front with Ferodo D.S.11 pads. The back plates of the rear drum brakes are perforated to improve cooling for the VG95 linings.

The racing Cortinas all have aluminium doors, bonnet and boot and the gearbox extension and differential housings are also made of an alloy. The fuel pipes are re-routed through the car rather than underneath it, and all the electrics are secured rather more permanently.

Credit for the splendid preparation of the Alan Mann Cortinas goes to Bob Hadlington and Norman Still who built the cars to group 2 and maintained them all season under the guidance of chief mechanic Ted Woodley. The very distinctive paintwork is the work of Dennis McNiff, of Antomac Autos, Shoreham, who, incidentally, is responsible for the very high standard of body finishing and spraying of all the Alan Mann team cars.

MOTOR week ending May 14 1966

Outwardly, there is little change from the original on this 1965 Lotus Cortina apart from the Aeroflow outlet vents on the rear quarters and a different grille, but underneath . . .

A diary of development

The Ford Lotus Cortina

by Michael Bowler

THERE is a thin dividing line between the incorporation of running changes and the announcement of a Mk.II variant. As long ago as the last racing and rally season works Lotus Cortinas were running around with leaf-sprung back axles apart from other less major changes from the original specification. but the announcement of a new model never came. The original Lotus brief was to produce a Cortina capable of winning the saloon car championships—European or B.R.S.C.C.—and of course, they did win. When the "Consul Cortina Sports Special" first appeared in January, 1963, it was the ultimate in saloon car conversions: just about everything had been modified. except the overall shape.

It s interesting to follow the changes from a standard Cortina. Apart from the well known Cosworth developed twin-cam engine. the majority of these affected the suspension. Although the final weight of the Lotus Cortina was much the same as

that of a standard 1200. the extra weight of the engine (with larger carburetters) and much heavier tyres had to be compensated by astute use of aluminium. The bonnet. boot lid and doors were replaced with aluminium panels: the clutch housing. gearbox extension and remote control were alloy castings. Unsprung weight was reduced with an alloy differential nose piece and coil springs replaced semi-elliptics.

Obviously cost had to come into the design consideration and so the rear axle location linkages used the original leaf spring mounting points. where strength was already built in. Two links trailed from the forward spring mounting to brackets welded to the forward side of the axle casing. and sideways location was provided by a trailing A-bracket with a base almost as wide as the track: each forward mounting was a bracket welded underneath the original spring mounting and. at the apex. a rubber bush was housed in

another bracket welded under the axle casing: a threaded bearing allowed the A-bracket to pivot freely.

Coil spring and damper units picked up on the original damper mountings and struts from both ends of the rear leaf spring mounting to this point braced the bodywork. That this arrangement was not really strong enough for hard use is shown on some cars by ripples along the rear panel.

The rear axle design was really the Achilles heel of the whole car and almost entirely responsible for its rather poor reliability record. With the original design. braking and driving forces were absorbed in leaf spring wind-up. but in the Lotus version the loads are taken by the trailing arms and the A-bracket. Since the vertical separation of these is relatively very much smaller than the radius of the tyre. the fore and aft forces were greatly magnified. With the lower link operating on the centre of the axle casing and the trailing links at each end, the casing was also subjected to a bending moment which it was never designed to resist. With a cast-iron nose-piece, there is a reasonable hope that the seal between it and the casing might be retained, but the aluminium housing warped, loosening the retaining nuts and allowing the oil to escape—which is what happened in the *Motor* six-hour race of 1964 when the winner kept stopping to do up the nuts and add oil.

At the front end, the springs were shortened, lowering the car, and the dampers were stiffened; a forged lower link, longer than the standard pressing, reduced the camber angle, and the stiffer anti-roll bar had its trailing arms slightly longer than standard, which decreased the castor angle to zero, but the increased self aligning torque of 6.00–13 tyres on 5½J rims gave an overall increase in self-centring action. Shorter and parallel steering arms gave higher gearing to increase the feel still further.

The gearbox had a delightful set of ratios in the standard Ford casing giving ideal performance once you were moving, but first was a shade high for frequent traffic creeping sessions. A set of Lotus instruments looked very nice and the front seats were specially built for the car. The total cost was a few shillings over £1,100 so, compared with the basic 1200, the conversion cost £527, giving a car of completely different character.

Once 1,000 cars had been built to the homologated specification, the design was rationalized to use standard Ford components where possible and, from June, 1964, the aluminium panels were gradually replaced by steel ones, some cars having a mixture during the changeover period. At the same time the alloy castings, including the differential nose-piece, were replaced with standard bits—incidentally, the original specification offered a 3.7:1 final drive but this was never quantity produced —and a split prop-shaft was introduced to remove the torsional vibration period between 55 and 70 m.p.h. in top. Although it was obviously a sensible decision for a road car the exchanging of the delightful close ratio box for a standard Cortina one with uprated second gear was a pity. In the back axle department, the A-bracket threaded bearing was replaced by longer lasting polyurethane bushes.

At the 1964 Motor Show, the Lotus Cortina adopted the Aeroflow ventilation of the new Cortina range together with a revised instrument panel. After this rationalization with an increased number of standard parts, the price came down to £992 and there were few cars which could match the combination of performance, space and cost.

Up to this point Ford had not dared to rally the Lotus Cortina for fear of leaving the A-bracket behind on a boulder; they had to use Cortina GTs, homologated with twin Webers for Group 3. Other people, including Willment, had been experimenting on the new 1965 Cortina GTs with leaf springs and upper radius arms and

Unchanged; the 105 b.h.p. Lotus twin-cam Cortina engine.

Inside the boot of the A-bracket Cortinas, you can see the stiffening struts reinforcing the bodywork.

found the handling every bit as good and in some cases better than the A-bracket layout. This was no reflection on Chapman's original design which made best use of the currently available mounting points—the GT brackets, welded under the rear seat pan were not fitted to the original Cortina. It is possible, but difficult, to change an A-bracket location to a radius-arm one.

In July, 1965, the Lotus Cortinas started to roll off the lines with leaf springs and radius arms, thus removing the main trouble spot; the front suspension and the gearbox remained the same. Meanwhile Lotus were, and still are, offering their Special Equipment car with 115 b.h.p. SP41s, safety belts and adjustable shock absorbers. In theory the rear roll centre of the new layout is slightly higher than before but different springing will probably nullify this. A trial run in a well used example suggested that although the roadholding is probably as good as before the handling is not so reassuringly firm.

At the 1965 Motor Show the gear ratios were changed again for the close ratio ones used in the Corsair V-4 GT; this should give a nice compromise between easy take-off and sporting use. Other changes were new front brakes with the caliper at the front of the disc, self adjusting rear drum brakes, and Cortina GT front seats.

Perhaps the best proof that the back axle is capable of withstanding the hardest use, apart from its increased reliability shown in rallies, is the way it stands up to police work. According to Lotus the police trick when in a hurry is to keep the foot flat on the accelerator when changing gear, secure in the knowledge that the ignition cut-out prevents over-revving. Far be it from us to suggest better ways for the police to drive (apart from increased wear and tear on transmission, the resulting clutch slip could well reduce acceleration) but this does prove the reliability.

And that is where the story ends—for the moment.

Continued on the next page

A diary of development
continued

The distinctive green flash and rear panel on a white car is the Lotus hallmark. Boot, bonnet and doors are no longer aluminium panelled.

Modern Lotus Cortina with radius arms since July 1965. Roll centre height is virtually the same as with the A-bracket layout.

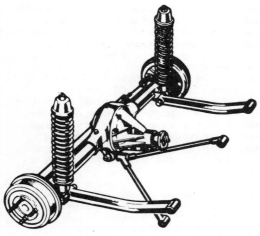

Although the original Lotus rear suspension design appeared to be very well located it produced greatly magnified stresses in the back axle casing, the main cause of unreliability.

Interior of the early cars was a revamped version of the standard Cortina 1200. Comfortable seats were built up on standard frames.

Gear ratio changes

The gear ratio story really starts with the Lotus Elan announced in October, 1962; it was introduced fitted with standard Ford Cortina ratios, but by the time it arrived on the market it had the delightful close ratio set which was subsequently adopted for the Lotus Cortina. In the first rationalization period, the Lotus Cortina ratios went back to those of the standard Cortina with an uprated second gear; these lasted until the Corsair GT V-4 appeared with much higher first, and slightly higher second and third gear ratios and these are now standard for the Lotus Cortina.

Meanwhile, back on the Elan . . . The original close ratios were still fitted to the S2 until February, 1966, but now the standard set up is with a 3.77:1 final drive and the Corsair GT ratios with the close ratio gears costing £35 extra as the quantity required is too small for mass production. On the S2 special equipment the 3.545 final drive is fitted. Now on the coupé you can have the 3.77:1 final drive with close ratios or the 3.545 with Corsair GT ratios. All the final drive ratios are interchangeable so you could get a 3.77 for your Lotus Cortina. **M**

	Ford Cortina 1st Lotus Elan	Production Elan 1st Lotus Cortina	Lotus Cortina interim ratios	Lotus Cortina Elan coupé Ford Corsair GT
Top	1.0	1.0	1.0	1.0
Third	1.412	1.23	1.412	1.397
Second	2.396	1.64	2.04	2.010
First	3.543	2.50	3.543	2.972
Reverse	3.96	2.80	3.96	3.324
Final drive	3.90	3.90	3.90	3.90 Lotus Cortina
				3.77 Elan Coupé. S2 and Corsair
				3.545 Elans optional

All final drive ratios are interchangeable.

Cortina LOTUS

A REIGNING champion will come to the United States with the introduction of the Cortina Lotus in English Ford line dealerships.

Holder of the European Touring Car Championship and numerous competition records and awards, the Cortina Lotus is well-known to American motorsports fans through its victories at Sebring, Fla., and elsewhere.

The Cortina Lotus is the result of the combined efforts of Ford of Britain, builder of the Cortina, and Colin Chapman, designer of the World Championship and Indianapolis 500 Lotus racing cars.

The Cortina Lotus is available only in two-door sedans distinguished by a small Lotus medallion attached to the grille and by a white color in combination with a green side trim. Inside, the Cortina Lotus has black vinyl trim with bucket seats in front and a bench seat in the rear.

But the three-spoke combination steering wheel with its Lotus crest and the full instrument panel behind it leave no doubt that the Cortina Lotus is a purposeful machine. Aircraft-type white on black instruments include a tachometer, fuel gauge, oil pressure gauge, ammeter, temperature gauge, and 140-mile-an-hour speedometer.

Under the hood, the knowledgeable find final confirmation that the Cortina Lotus is an enthusiast's automobile. Double-overhead camshafts crown a four-cylinder engine. With dual two-choke Weber carburetors, this engine is basically the Lotus-modified high performance power plant that won the Formula II Championship in open-wheeled racing cars.

Developing 115 hp, the Lotus-modified engine is

combined with Lotus chassis modifications to the Cortina. The front and rear suspensions have been lowered and stiffened. Radius rods have been added to the rear. A large-diameter drive shaft and heavy-duty shock absorbers and anti-roll bar have been added with 6.00 x 13-inch 4-ply rating nylon tires.

The gear ratios of the four-speed manual transmission have been carefully tailored to the output of the Lotus-modified engine and, to complement the outstanding performance, disc brakes are fitted to the front wheels.

Although the Cortina Lotus is small — only 168.3 inches long, 62.5 inches wide, and weighing only 1857 pounds — the many accomplishments of the Cortina Lotus in open competition are evidence of the car's performance. But the Cortina Lotus is equally at home on road or track.

Combined with sedan size and seating for four, the Cortina Lotus offers such comfort features as flow-through ventilation with fresh-air heater and defroster. Other standard equipment includes electric windshield wipers, bumper guards, padded sun visors, padded instrument panel, padded door armrests, interior light with courtesy switches, center console and ash tray, rear compartment ash tray, and a unique European feature — a full-width parcel tray underneath the dash.

Optional equipment includes a radio, white sidewall tires, cigar lighter, heavy duty battery, and full-width carpeting.

Combining the economy and practicality of a European sedan with the handling and performance of a sports car, the Cortina Lotus adds a new dimension to the Ford vehicle lineup for 1966. ∎

FORD CORTINA-LOTUS

ONCE INDIANAPOLIS made Lotus-Ford into a household word, an appropriate climate to plant hybrid passenger cars bearing that hyphenated nameplate thereby was created. The car had been available before that, but word of its delights had seldom reached more than a handful of colonials. It was the exact converse of the race car, to be sure, being a Lotus engine in a Ford chassis, but an opportune marketing entrepreneur could ignore that so long as that name was there.

Among the domestic motorsporting minority, a great deal of interest existed in this sedan that dominated overseas "saloon" racing. Transplantation of the Cosworth-developed double overhead camshaft adaptation of the English Ford engine into a void under the English Ford Cortina hood had been a happy step. Unhappily, however, examples of the car were all too rare in this country —despite an expansion of production by EnFoCo to meet homologation minimums.

Now Lotus-Ford Cortinas are reaching these shores, in the aftermath of the Lotus & Clark/Ford & dohc victory at Indianapolis. A subsequent reassignment of English Ford marketing programs to domestic Ford Division dealers helps their distribution. They arrive somewhat modified: The expected Chapmanesque coil-sprung rear suspension, radial ply tires and lightweight aluminum doors and hood and deck lid have been lost somewhere in shipment. What does arrive is virtually the Cortina GT variant fitted with the steel-blue Lotus dohc engine and a thoroughly instrumented, brushed aluminum dash panel.

Starting life as the 116E EnFoCo 4-cyl. block, the engine has undergone a transformation at the hands of a talented engineering team composed of Mike Costin and Keith Duckworth (hence Cosworth Engineering). Both had been early architects in the burgeoning Lotus empire of Colin Chapman during the late '50s, but an extra moonlight engineering enterprise of their own soon became a prime supplier for Lotus. With the explosive popularity created in the wake of Lotus-Cortina competition successes, they have been forced to concentrate efforts on production of this engine.

An initial slight overbore from the stock 3.1875 in. increases displacement from 90.1 to 95.1 cu. in. (1558 cc). Special lightweight high-crown pistons are carefully fitted into the larger bore. Together with the special dohc cylinder head, this brings compression ratio up to 9.5:1. The light alloy head casting, subcontracted to the highly-regard J. A. Prestwich firm of JAP motorcycle engine fame, carries the twin camshafts in four bearings each. The cams are driven by a roller chain, which also operates

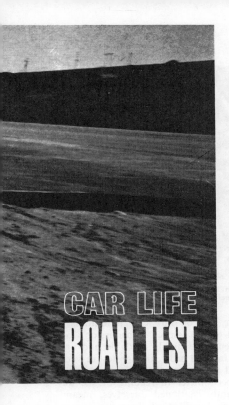

CAR LIFE ROAD TEST

in the valley between the cam covers and offset 0.87 in. from each cylinder center, are the spark plugs. Valves are angled 27° from the vertical and their broad faces comprise much of the hemispherical chamber surface. Because the diameter of the combustion chamber across the face is 2.5 in., more than a quarter inch of overlap remains around the cylinder bore, which promotes combustion-enhancing squish. Tangential delivery of the fuel/air charge, moreover, adds to chamber turbulence to further improve performance.

The engine's exceptional breathing and the reduction in reciprocating mass inherent in the overhead camshafts mean this diminutive Street Hemi cranks up frightful revs as a matter of course. The tachometer is red-lined at 6500 and a 400-rpm safety factor was discovered in the test car's instrument, but inadvertent over-revs beyond such prudent limits are of little consequence.

While the engine's free-revving capacity insured sprightly performance, there

was some compromise evident in the choice of final gearing. The selected ratio provided a freeway cruising speed that kept the engine speed near 4000 rpm. Acceleration in that area was not quite up to expectation. Going up through the gears, however, was pure exhilaration; an engine which rips effortlessly and without strain up to 6000 before the shift, three times in quick succession, somehow stirs blood through the driver's veins at a similar velocity.

The engine has some difficulty in achieving a smooth idle, turning over quite roughly and tending to rapidly foul spark plugs. Blipping the foot throttle is the best technique for preventing plug failure. Warm-up is rapid and the car moves off from rest very smoothly, thanks to the hydraulic clutch operation. During the test period, maximum performance starts were hampered by excessive fuel loading, which reflects in the data panel times. Normal driving, however, revealed no such problem with ▶

Amazing Performance From a Demure Package

the distributor and oil pump drives located lower in the block. Sufficient sturdiness to handle increased engine operating stresses is provided by the standard 5-main bearing lower end, although a carefully counterbalanced crankshaft is substituted during assembly.

Carburetion is by a brace of dual-throat Weber 40-DCOE-18 units, drawing through a silencer box over inlet horns. On the opposite side, an extractor-like manifold collects and routes the exhaust down and out through a low restriction resonator and muffler. When the engine was first applied to the Cortina, it had a rating of 105 bhp at 5500 rpm. However, something—perhaps better grade fuels—has increased that rating on imported versions to 115 bhp at 5700 rpm. In any event, premium grade fuel is necessary.

Ports in this head are short, direct and generous. Centered between them,

GENE BOOTH PHOTOS

FORD CORTINA-LOTUS

MATCHED PAIR of Weber twin-choke carburetors and steel-blue cam covers are inspiring sight.

the fuel metering abilities of the Webers.

As a setting for this engine, the Cortina makes obvious those virtues that first attracted sedan class racers to the car. It is a solid unitized body structure that could well have been designed for racing sedan service and later adapted to passenger car use. Suspension modifications in the Cortina-Lotus have lowered the riding height slightly and, while one feels disappointed at getting the regular steel doors, there certainly is no loss of structural integrity with their retention.

Few production automobiles place the driver so thoroughly in command as does the Cortina-Lotus. Seats are chair high (front) with good back support, providing the average-size driver with exceptional visibility—as close as 6 ft. over the short, downswept hood and exact position of all four corners. Switches, knobs and minor controls all are less than an arm-reach away. Foot pedals are well placed and can be operated with deft dabs of the toe. The remote control shift lever is faultlessly linked to the 4-speed transmission. Instruments are highly readable and arrayed in good order, though test drivers tended to confuse the tachometer with the speedometer (a reading of 40, we constantly cautioned ourselves, meant 70 mph road speed because it was indicating 4000 rpm). It was a thoroughly inviting car to drive, to drive briskly.

The pity of it all was that there is so little opportunity left in this country to

1966 FORD
CORTINA-LOTUS SEDAN

DIMENSIONS

Wheelbase, in.	98.0
Track, f/r, in.	51.5/50.5
Overall length, in.	168.3
width	62.5
height	53.4
Front seat hip room, in.	2 x 21
shoulder room	n. a.
head room	37.7
pedal-seatback, max.	42.0
Rear seat hip room, in.	52.0
shoulder room	n. a.
leg room	35.0
head room	37.4
Door opening width, in.	40.5
Floor to ground height, in.	10.25
Ground clearance, in.	5.3

PRICES

List, fob factory	$3481
Equipped as tested	3528

Options included: Floor carpets, seat belts, outside mirror, emergency flashers.

CAPACITIES

No. of passengers	5
Luggage space, cu. ft.	11.6
Fuel tank, gal.	9.6
Crankcase, qt.	4.2
Transmission/diff., pt.	2.15/2.4
Radiator coolant, qt.	9.3

CHASSIS/SUSPENSION

Frame type	unitized
Front suspension type: Independent with Macpherson strut and lower A-arm, coil springs; telescopic shock absorbers; anti-roll bar.	
ride rate at wheel, lb./in.	n. a.
anti-roll bar dia., in.	n. a.
Rear suspension type: Hotchkiss drive with longitudinal semi-elliptic leaf springs; longitudinal radius arms; telescopic shock absorbers.	
ride rate at wheel, lb./in.	n. a.
Steering system: Recirculating ball-nut, transverse tie rods.	
gear ratio	n. a.
overall ratio	15.1
turns, lock to lock	3.5
turning circle, ft. curb-curb.	37.25
Curb weight, lb.	2060
Test weight	2450
Weight distribution, % f/r.	51.1/48.9

BRAKES

Type: Single-line hydraulic with front caliper discs and rear duo-servo shoes in cast-iron drums.	
Front disc, dia. x width, in.	9.625 x n. a.
Rear drum, dia. x width	9.0 x 1.75
total swept area, sq. in.	281.6
Power assist: vacuum servo	
line psi @ 100 lb. pedal.	n. a.

WHEELS/TIRES

Wheel size	13 x 5.5J
optional size available	none
bolt no./circle dia., in.	n. a.
Tire brand	Dunlop Gold Seal C-41
size	6.00-13
recommended inflation, psi.	24
capacity rating, total lb.	2920

ENGINE

Type, no. cyl.	IL-4, dohc
Bore x stroke, in.	3.25 x 2.86
Displacement, cu. in.	95.06
Compression ratio	9.5
Rated bhp @ rpm	115 @ 5700
equivalent mph	100
Rated torque @ rpm	108 @ 4000
equivalent mph	70
Carburetion	Weber, 2x2
barrel dia., pri./sec.	1.60
Valve operation: Chain-driven camshafts, inverted cup followers.	
valve dia., int./exh.	n. a.
lift, int./exh.	n. a.
timing, deg.	n. a.
duration, int./exh.	n. a.
opening overlap	n. a.
Exhaust system: Single, reverse flow muffler.	
pipe dia., exh./tail.	n. a.
Lubrication pump type.	n. a.
normal press. @ rpm	n. a.
Electrical supply	generator
ampere rating	22
Battery, plates/amp. rating.	n. a./51

DRIVE-TRAIN

Clutch type .single dry plate hydraulic.	
dia., in.	n. a.
Transmission type: 4-speed manual shift.	
Gear ratio 4th (1.00) overall	4.125
3rd (1.39)	5.763
2nd (2.02)	8.29
1st (2.97)	12.26
synchronous meshing?	all
Shift lever location	console
Differential type: Hypoid.	
axle ratio	4.125

GREEN FLASH along sides distinguishes those Cortinas which have received Chapman touch.

INSIDE TRUNK, which is of ample capacity, Cortina-Lotus carries relocated battery to improve weight distribution.

take advantage of a car designed for bashing down meandering, narrow British roads. Even in such near-stock form, the suspension could cope with any strained situation which opportunity did present. Its modification includes a slight lowering of riding height and the inclusion of wide-footprint tires which help considerably in cornering precision. Steering, though slightly heavy at lower speeds, is so positive and precise at higher speeds that one could overlook any other problem

which the car could conceivably develop. In like manner, the brakes are near perfect in operation (though somewhat under expectation in effectiveness) without any bad manners to anticipate. Only the ride, which tends to be a bit choppy, and the noise level, which is somewhat high, even though of a delightfully melodious, happily mechanical variety, would be considered drawbacks by most American buyers.

It is remarkable that Ford, a name so synonymous with the masses, and

Lotus, most often coupled with the Elite, have combined to produce such a delightful and desirable automobile. Its price, obviously, is a bit steep for a car of its size, but its value can be measured by more than dollars. Undoubtedly the Cosworth 'cammer will share some of the maintenance bothers so characteristic of highly tuned small engines. Yet, it's all worth it to have that teenie yellow polka dot with the green guitar pick on it, mounted on the grille and flank. ∎

CAR LIFE ROAD TEST

ACCELERATION & COASTING

MPH — ELAPSED TIME IN SECONDS

(graph axes: MPH 0–120 vertical; ELAPSED TIME IN SECONDS 5–45 horizontal; curves labeled 1st, 2nd, 3rd, 4th, SS ¼)

CALCULATED DATA

Lb./bhp (test weight)	21.3
Cu.ft./ton mile	78.4
Mph/1000 rpm (high gear)	17.5
Engine revs/mile (60 mph)	2610
Piston travel, ft./mile	1720
Car Life wear index	62.1
Frontal area, sq. ft.	18.5
Box volume, cu. ft.	324.4

SPEEDOMETER ERROR

30 mph, actual	29.5
40 mph	37.2
50 mph	48.7
60 mph	59.2
70 mph	69.1
80 mph	79.3
90 mph	87.4

MAINTENANCE INTERVALS

Oil change, engine, miles	n. a.
transmission/differential	n. a.
Oil filter change	n. a.
Air cleaner service, mo.	n. a.
Chassis lubrication	n. a.
Wheelbearing re-packing	n. a.
Universal joint service	n. a.
Coolant change, mo.	n. a.

TUNE-UP DATA

Spark plugs	n. a.
gap, in.	n. a.
Spark setting, deg./idle rpm	n. a.
cent. max. advance, deg./rpm	n. a.
vac. max. adv., deg./in. Hg	n. a.
Breaker gap, in.	n. a.
cam dwell angle	n. a.
arm tension, oz.	n. a.
Tappet clearance, int./exh.	n. a.
Fuel pump pressure, psi	n. a.
Radiator cap relief press., psi	n. a.

PERFORMANCE

Top speed (5700), mph	100
Shifts (rpm) @ mph	
3rd to 4th (6100)	77
2nd to 3rd (6100)	51
1st to 2nd (6100)	33

ACCELERATION

0-30 mph, sec.	3.8
0-40 mph	5.3
0-50 mph	7.2
0-60 mph	9.7
0-70 mph	12.9
0-80 mph	17.8
0-90 mph	29.9
0-100 mph	
Standing ¼-mile, sec.	17.6
speed at end, mph	80
Passing, 30-70 mph, sec.	9.1

BRAKING

(Maximum deceleration rate achieved from 80 mph)

1st stop, ft./sec./sec.	24
fade evident?	none
2nd stop, ft./sec./sec.	26
fade evident?	slight

FUEL CONSUMPTION

Test conditions, mpg	17.7
Normal range, mpg	16.5-18.5
Cruising range, miles	158-177

GRADABILITY

4th, % grade @ mph	7 @ 62
3rd	14 @ 55
2nd	23 @ 48
1st	29 @ 33

DRAG FACTOR

Total drag @ 60 mph, lb.	100

I.W.R. Cortina-Lotus

Extra wide-rimmed mag wheels fitted with oversize Pirelli Cinturatos are not standard. The car is a 1964 model

AS our regular readers will know, Peter Garnier took delivery of one of the very first Cortina-Lotuses to be built and the back axle and suspension gave a great deal of trouble in the next 29,000 miles. That story began in May 1963 and two years later the rear suspension reverted to leaf springs along with many other development changes during the period. In the meantime over 1,000 cars had been built with Chapman coil-spring rear suspension and an A-bracket for lateral location.

After reading Peter Garnier's article in our issue of 9 September. Ian Walker offered us one of his converted cars as a comparison. The test car was an earlier Cortina-Lotus with the suspension modified back to leaf springs, but without the radius rods fitted on the latest cars, and a stage III engine conversion. It also had the later gearbox with Cortina GT ratios including up-rated second gear, instead of the original very high close-ratio set.

From an engineering standpoint the switch back to leaf springs is not too difficult. Anchor points for the trailing arms in the coil spring set-up are the same as the leaf spring eye mounts, and the Walker modifications involve changing the aluminium alloy axle nose piece (which always gave trouble with its joint to the cast-iron banjo) for a standard cast-iron one, discarding the entire A-bracket. coil spring and damper

assemblies and trailing arms, and changing the two-piece propeller shaft for a single-piece one. The cost including fitting is £50 plus £2 10s if adjustable dampers are required, or £7 10s extra if Armstrong Selectaride units are specified. The test car also had magnesium alloy wheels shod with oversize Pirelli Cinturato tyres.

Handling

The result on the handling of the car is quite marked, with a definite improvement in road-holding and, of course, much greater reliability. As we tried the car, it was set up for rallying, with rather a "nervous" response to the steering. All Lotus versions of the Cortina have higher-geared steering in any case, and the greater self-centring action of the wider tyre sections and the different king-pin offset make the steering quite heavy. Even so, the Walker Cortina reacts immediately the wheel is tweaked and initially there seems to be some rather sudden oversteer. As soon as the car has taken up its attitude in the corner, however, this changes to stable understeer and one soon learns to set the car up very early rather like with an Alfa Romeo or some of the finely-balanced works cars we have tried.

The much lower gearbox ratios rather spoil the great "seven-league boots" character of the old Cortina-Lotus as we knew it, but the acceleration is

obviously much improved and the car is more tractable in traffic. One of the old bug-bears, petrol consumption, seems to be improved with the Walker engine modifications and we recorded 23.4 m.p.g. over 351 miles of really rally-style driving. The other shortcoming of the Lotus twin o.h.c. engine, oil consumption, is as bad as ever and we barely managed 100 miles without having to put a pint of oil in the sump and when taking off after a spell at idling great clouds of blue smoke billowed out behind.

In many ways the test car showed its age and the obvious way it had been hard used. On the second-hand market today a Cortina-Lotus of the 1963 to 1965 period should carry about a £500 to £600 price tag. Walker suspension modifications (which can include inspection of the crown-wheel and differential unit for little extra cost) add £50 and if one then wants to go all the way and have a stage III engine conversion, another £140 must be added. However, this work involves a complete strip and balancing, new camshafts and refitting in the car. For only about £750 therefore (the price of a new Cortina GT) one can obtain a very competitive genuine 110 m.p.h. four-seater saloon with good rallying or club speed event potential.

Ian Walker Racing are at 236 Woodhouse Road, London, N.12. Telephone ENTerprise 6281. ∎

CORTINA LOTUS
OR
LOTUS CORTINA

If you prefer it!

A COUPLE of years ago we reckoned that the Lotus-Cortina was close approaching an ideal sort of combination car—in standard form fine for the family, for fast touring (except for a funny little petrol tank) and not-too-serious competition. Since then the car has undergone a number of changes, of which the most radical has been the reversion to leaf springs instead of the coil-spring—"A"-bracket and trailing-arm rear suspension set-up of the first cars. It was given Aeroflow ventilation equipment at the same time as the Cortinas got it (the 1964 Motor Show, to be exact) and at last year's show the gearbox was filled with the close-ratio ones from the V4 Corsair GT. All of which has improved the machine as a basic motor-car, and at the same time has somewhat changed its personality.

But before we get on about that, let's get it straight about the car. It isn't to begin with, supposed to be a racer, or even for that matter a rally machine despite a very successful record in the first bracket and a pretty satisfactory one in the rally field since the introduction of leaf-springs at the back: one of the only real snags to the "A"-bracket cars was the tendency for the thing to break up, which rather put it out of court for serious rallying in case the major part of the rear suspension had to be left by a Greek roadside. Then what the hell is it? Well, it's a sort of motor which is creeping up on us these days—a sort of fast touring shopping car which you can thrash up Prescott or round the Silverstone club circuit—probably without actually winning anything, but on the other hand not disgracing yourself either. Unless, of course, you can't drive a nail in a wall. The best description is probably a sports saloon—a two-seater with four seats, if you follow us.

And so what's it got that the Cortina GT hasn't got—apart from a three-figure top speed and the ability to lumber itself from nothing to the legal limit in round about twelve seconds? Stand up that boy who said twin overhead camshafts and move up to the next class. The twin-cam engine is a development of the five-bearing crankshaft 1500 Ford engine; the stroke is unchanged at 72·75 mm. but the bore goes up to 82·55 mm. to give a total capacity of 1,558 c.c. An alloy cylinder head provides a home for valves and twin camshafts to push them up and down; the compression ratio is 9·5 to 1 and attached to the business end of the manifold is a pair of 40 DCOE 18 Webers. The whole thing churns out 105 b.h.p. at five-five, and maximum torque is 108 lb. ft. at four thousand.

A diaphragm spring clutch which seems capable of withstanding the harshest treatment links all this to the gearbox, already mentioned, the new ratios giving considerably less dramatic maximum speeds in the gears than the old ones

but, on the other hand, making the car a bit nicer to drive in traffic. Nearly fifty in bottom gear had its points, but was hell on earth when it came to crawling along in the going-home-time rush hour, but with the new cogs giving 39, 55 and 79 m.p.h. in the gears the car still needn't hang about. Suspension still involves shorter front springs, stiffer dampers and reduced camber angle at the front, along with a huskier anti-roll bar. Shorter, parallel steering arms give higher-geared steering than on the normal Cortina, the castor angle is reduced to zero and, at both ends of the cars, 600 x 13 tyres are fitted on 5½J in. rims. At the back, the dreaded "A"-bracket stuff have been replaced by semi-elliptic cart springs and radius arms. Roadholding probably hasn't really suffered at all, but somehow the roadholding *felt* a lot better in the old days. The car doesn't feel quite so firm and all-of-a-piece with the leaf-spring set-up, and we did occasionally experience the dreaded axle tramp which the "A"-brackets were supposed to have eliminated.

The first Lotus-Cortina (or, if you prefer it, Cortina-Lotus) we tried was pretty stark inside when you came to look closely at it, and the modern ones seem to be a bit better off in terms of creature comforts. There are carpets nowadays and things like wireless sets, ash-trays and even a cigar-lighter. But the very smart, very functional Lotus instruments still nestle away in front of the driver telling him all the things he wants (or would prefer not) to know. You get Cortina GT front seats, which are very comfortable but which, like all Fords, put you a bit on the close side to the wheel and there's no scope for Jim Clark stuff with out re-mounting the runners (and eliminating most of the leg-room in the back). All the controls are light; the gearbox is pretty well faultless, of course, and the higher-geared steering is a Good Thing. The brakes (from last year the fronts have new-type discs with the calipers on the leading side, and

the rear drums are self-adjusting) work splendidly through a vacuum servo, but we simply could not get enthusiastic about the revolting hand-brake lever—a ghastly chrome umbrella handle under the dash which feels as though it will come out by the roots at any moment.

As we said before, the handling is by no means as firm as it was, and while the new gear ratios are undoubtly a more practical proposition, the two things together, plus the added luxury, have transformed it from a sort of instant racer (which it was never really supposed to be) into a much more civilised sort of vehicle which, frankly, we found less exhilerating. Not that it doesn't still go like a bat out of hell—it ruddy well does, and it takes a strong old car to match the average speeds you can set up with one of these little tools. But it doesn't feel so hard, so taut or so fast as it did—that's the first reaction that strikes you. But the added reliability is probably worth it and it's still a car we quickly got very fond of. Despite its more gentlemanly nature, it still handles beautifully—there's no other word for it, and you can take the most hideous liberties and get away with it. For reasons outside our control we once had to brake rather hard when two-thirds of the way round a roundabout, which we were negotiating somewhat briskly. The tail started to slide, as you might expect, but half-a-turn or so of lock was enough to put it straight and apart from protesting noises from the tyres (and the passenger) nothing else took place to indicate that anything untoward had taken place. A nice secure

feeling, this sort of thing gives you. The car is at its best, as all sporting carriages should be, on fast twisty roads, where the thing can be hammered along mostly in top but occasionally in third. It isn't as much fun as it used to be on tight corners because the maximum speeds in the gears aren't so high, and tight hairpins, where you used to be able to slot it down to bottom gear and then accelerate like hell, with nearly fifty coming up before you snatched second, aren't the same any more.

But for all that it has a useable maximum speed (on the continent, we hasten to add) of 106 m.p.h., which is just about the red line on the tachometer and which will appear on quite short straights. In terms of sheer acceleration, traction is still good enough in the dry to reach sixty in under ten seconds from a standing start, but the back wheels aren't quite so secure in the wet, or at least not as secure as we remember them from the "A"-bracket days. It's still not a car which hangs about though, and as we said you can cover the ground in a pretty lively manner with one of these. You could probably make even higher average speeds with an Elan, but there isn't much else that will do better on give-and-take roads, where the car's combination of above-average acceleration, first-class roadholding and excellent brakes add up to what it's all about.

We did over a thousand miles in the car, and the only snag which cropped up was the sudden departure from its home of the rear core-plug in the block, which put a lot of water where no water ought to have been. Luckily the gap was plugged with a certain amount of simplicity by a piece of wooden chair which a chum happened to have handy: we have been given to understand by a number of owners that this sort of thing isn't unusual, so you might like to keep a spare kitchen chair in the boot. Or something.

The only real criticism—and one we made before—lies in the size of the fuel tank, which only holds eight gallons. Bearing in mind that, while you can get 24 m.p.g. from the car, you are more likely to get about twenty, this is a bit of a bind, and the thing always seems to get low on go-juice when the last filling station was miles back and there isn't another for a further fifty. That's life, we suppose, and the answer is to carry a can or fit a supplementary tank, of which there are plenty about.

Cars on Test

FORD CORTINA-LOTUS

Engine: Four cylinder, twin-overhead camshafts; 82·55 mm. x 72·75 mm., 1,558 c.c.; twin 40 DCOE 18 Webers; 105 b.h.p. at 5,500 r.p.m.; max torque, 108 lb. foot at 4,000 r.p.m.

Transmission: Diaphragm-spring clutch; four-speed and reverse gearbox with synchromesh on all forward gears.

Suspension: Front, independent with coil springs, anti-roll bar; rear, semi-elliptic leaf springs and radius arms. Telescopic dampers all round.

Brakes: Front, 9½ in. discs; rear, 9¾ in. drums, with vacuum servo.

Dimensions: Overall length, 14 ft. 1 in.; overall width, 5 ft. 2½ in.; overall height, 4 ft. 6 in.; turning circle, 37 ft.; ground clearance, 5¼ in.; weight, 21 cwt.

PERFORMANCE

	m.p.h.			secs.
MAXIMUM SPEED	107	ACCELERATION	0–30—	3·2
Mean of 2 ways	106		0–40—	4·6
			0–50—	6·8
SPEEDS IN GEARS	First—39		0–60—	9·4
	Second—55		0–70—	12·8
	Third—79		0–80—	16·2
			0–90—	22·0

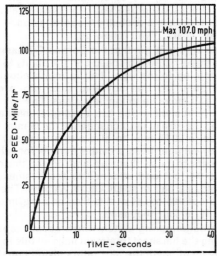

Max 107.0 mph

SPEED - Mile/hr

TIME - Seconds

Price: £1,010

Supplement to Motor road test No 5/64

MOTOR TESTED

Ford Lotus Cortina

. . . so firm and well mannered . . . good compromise for a keen driver (with family) . . . acceleration most impressive

THERE are not many cars into which we can jump and drive fast with complete confidence; if we can it is probably because the performance and handling characteristics are so mundane and soggily safe that we have met them all before. But the Lotus Cortina is rather different. You feel at home as if in a personally tailored car from the moment you get in, but the acceleration is far from mundane and the car feels so firm—too firm on poor roads—and well mannered that you can exploit most of it after very little familiarization. The initial impression is one of accelerative performance—sufficient to leave many sports cars behind—and the freedom from temperament and comfortable fast cruising increase one's liking for a car which is a good compromise for a keen driver who has to remember that the family must sit somewhere.

We told the Lotus Cortina development story in *Motor* issue May 14, 1966 and it is necessary now only to recapitulate the design differences between this test car and the one we road tested originally. Basically the car has moved further away from the original Lotus Cortina and nearer to the current Cortina GT; the old A-bracket and coil spring rear suspension has been replaced by the leaf spring upper radius arm layout of the GT,

and the close ratio gearbox has given way to the current Corsair GT set—still close but not very close. Aeroflow ventilation, as on current Cortinas, is a useful bonus of production rationalization but the special aluminium body panels formerly fitted to the Lotus Cortina have all been replaced by standard steel parts. The extra hundredweight has offset any advantage in acceleration that might have accrued from the lower intermediate ratios.

It is very much a matter of personal preference, but we think the handling has suffered from the rationalization rather than just undergone a change of character. Where previously the understeer was so great that one navigated fast corners (on a test track) with a considerable excess of lock over direction, now on the same corners oversteer sets in and the inside rear wheel spins as on any other modified Cortina on the limit, although at rather higher speeds. In short the original Lotus Cortina touch has gone, but the new layout should be more reliable and it is still a delightful motor car, at its best on roads which are not long and straight.

Considered objectively as a touring saloon, it is a four/five seater capable of speeds comfortably over 100 m.p.h. with acceleration times to match; fuel consumption will be between 20 and 30 m.p.g. depending on which country's speed limits you happen to be obeying. Roadholding is good but the suspension design has been biased to suit the handling rather than the ride which is very firm. In fact, it is a spendid carriage for the enthusiast who still enjoys fast safe motoring.

PRICE: £836 plus £191 11s. 8d. tax equals £1,027 11s. 8d.

Continued on the next page

Ford-Lotus Cortina

Continued

From the rear it could be an original Lotus Cortina except that the observant could spot the A-bracket on the earlier cars.

Well planned facia is easy to use and tells a lot. The comfortable seats give good support and seem to offer a commanding view over the bonnet to all sizes. Unsporting pull-out handbrake.

Performance and economy

Although early Lotus Cortinas had a slightly chequered reliability history, the power unit has never given trouble and is still exactly the same in specification, with the Lotus twin cam version of the five bearing Ford engine giving 105 b.h.p. at 5,500 r.p.m. This unit is remarkably smooth and quiet running considering the output; the only sign of any temperament is a slight tendency to soot the plugs in prolonged town running but this clears as soon as you get the chance to accelerate hard in, say, second. Oil consumption during our 2,000-mile test worked out at 350 miles per pint, which is reasonable for a well developed power unit, particularly for one with over 11,000 miles on the clock.

Any change in performance is due to the change in gear ratios and the increase in weight, but 0–50 m.p.h. in 7.4 sec. is fast by any standards and slightly better than before; beyond 60 m.p.h. the greater weight and the wider ratios have a bigger effect and the latest car drops progressively further behind the original. It is possible that some minor difference in the outputs of the two nominally identical engines might be magnifying the effect of the changes, but however great the difference may appear from the stopwatch times, it is hardly noticeable on the road and the acceleration is most impressive. Its performance is in the category which makes it so much safer to join into traffic streams from side roads without getting in anyone's way.

It is worth recalling that the Weber carburetters make the engine very sensitive to starting techniques; the right one is fool-proof. When starting from cold it needs full choke and *no* throttle or you might flood the plugs with a squirt from the accelerator pumps; once the engine has fired and run for a few seconds the choke can be pushed in. Similarly when the engine is warm, it is again better not to touch the throttle until it has fired.

With fuel being consumed at the rate of around 25 m.p.g. or less, the 8-gallon tank gets emptied depressingly quickly as the miles go by so fast and it would be a great advantage to have at least four more gallons.

Transmission

Although the new mass production gearbox does not have the same delightfully close ratios in which first was half way between the current first and second, it is probably a better general compromise for town and country work. It still has the same hot-knife-through-butter feel of extremely smooth lightness, and it is easy to make shock-free changes despite the drive line feeling almost as rigid as before; the upper radius arms seem to eliminate cushioning by spring wind up particularly on take-off, when it was impossible to get wheelspin on our abrasive test track. As we let the clutch in sharply at around 5,000 r.p.m., the excessive shock load applied to the transmission resulted in rather noisy axle tramp and an immediate drop to 2,000 r.p.m.—which on two occasions produced a failure in the transmission line. Although this is far removed from normal road techniques, the weekend sprinter will have to treat his back axle with respect. Controlled clutch slip produced no faster take-offs. This obviously affected our standing start figures and it would probably have been faster off the line with

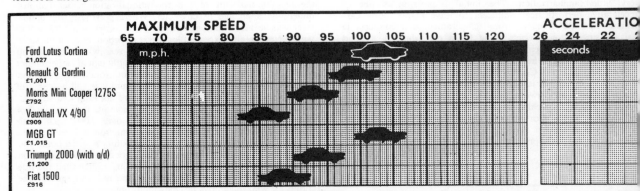

	MAXIMUM SPEED												ACCELERATIO
	65	70	75	80	85	90	95	100	105	110	115	120	26 24 22
Ford Lotus Cortina £1,027													seconds
Renault 8 Gordini £1,001													
Morris Mini Cooper 1275S £792													
Vauxhall VX 4/90 £909													
MGB GT £1,015													
Triumph 2000 (with o/d) £1,200													
Fiat 1500 £916													

standard tyres on narrow wheels and an ordinary Cortina rear axle which would have allowed some wheelspin; as it was, the Dunlop C41s on 5½J rims gripped very well, particularly when doing fast take-offs on wet roads.

Handling and brakes

This is the department in which the biggest change has taken place. The front suspension is still as originally set up by Lotus, but the rear suspension is borrowed from the Cortina GT whose rates are apparently stiffer. Admittedly the original Lotus Cortina spent most of its time on the bump stops when laden with more than two people and luggage, but the car now handles almost like any other Cortina except that the wide tyres and different front suspension make everthing happen at rather higher cornering forces and with rather less roll than, say, a Cortina GT.

Near neutral handling which covers most of the range before final oversteer sets in is possibly a better all-round compromise than the previous permanent strong understeer. A natural tightening of the line as the tail moves out is often useful and always controllable. Another by-product of the increased rear spring stiffness is an increased sensitivity to side winds, not to anywhere near an alarming level, but the car does notice them; this, together with a tendency for the front tyres to climb sideways up any longitudinal ridges in the road surface, makes the car restless in a straight line.

Bumpy roads decrease the cornering power but on most roads it goes round fast bends very well and you would have to be trying hard on a familiar road to reach the oversteer condition, unless you provoke it at lower speeds with power. On wet roads you have to be rather more careful as power carelessly applied has to be caught quickly, but steering, which is sensitive, and not entirely free from kickback, keeps you well informed of what is happening at the wheels. But much as we enjoyed driving the car, there is just a tinge of regret that the handling has changed so much; somewhere between the previous and the present models there would have been an ideal.

Comfort and interior fittings

With the introduction of the Aeroflow Cortinas in October 1964, the interior of the Lotus Cortina also underwent a change which gave the facia a much more professional air rather than being an apparent after-thought. All the necessary instruments are there and the switches are well placed; we still do not like the umbrella handbrake, which is displaced from the transmission tunnel by a central armrest and locker.

Of all the Ford Aeroflow installations, that on the Cortina is the most versatile and could be a model for some other manufacturers: with this face level ventilation there is less need for opening quarter lights and the Lotus has fixed panes which eliminates a potential source of wind noise; the car is surprisingly quiet when cruising at a steady 85 m.p.h. or so—no wind noise and just a distant hum from the engine which is scarcely enough to require an increase in radio volume.

Those more interested in comfort than roadholding will find the ride a bit firm and rather lively on poor surfaces, but for such a car where roadholding is the prime design requisite, this is a small sacrifice.

MAKE: Ford MODEL: Lotus Cortina MAKERS: Ford Motor Co. Ltd., Dagenham, Essex/Lotus Cars Ltd., Delamare Road, Cheshunt, Herts.

Performance

Conditions

Weather: Overcast 0-15 m.p.h. wind.
Temperature 58°-62°F. Barometer 29.28 in. Hg.
Surface: Concrete and tarmacadam, damp in places
Fuel: Premium 98-octane (R.M.)

Maximum speeds

	m.p.h.
Mean of opposite runs	107
3rd gear)	81
2nd gear) "cut-out" designed for 6,500 r.p.m.	56
1st gear)	38
"Maximile" speed: (Timed quarter mile after 1 mile accelerating from rest)	
Mean	104.7
Best	105.9

Acceleration times

m.p.h.	sec.
0-30	3.5
0-40	5.2
0-50	7.4
0-60	10.4
0-70	13.8
0-80	19.5
0-90	28.9
Standing quarter mile	17.8

m.p.h.	Top sec.	3rd sec.
10-30	—	6.6
20-40	9.2	5.8
30-50	9.2	5.6
40-60	9.3	6.1
50-70	10.3	6.9
60-80	12.2	—
70-90	15.7	—

Fuel consumption

Touring (consumption midway between 30 m.p.h. and maximum less 5% allowance for acceleration) . . . . 21.2 m.p.g.
Overall . . . . 21.7 m.p.g.
(= 13.0 litres/100 km.)
Total test distance . . . . 2.170 miles
Tank capacity (maker's figure) . . . . 8 gal.

Weight

Kerb weight (unladen with fuel for approximately 50 miles) . . . . 17.4 cwt.
Front/rear distribution 54/46
Weight laden as tested . . . . 20.1 cwt.

Specification

Engine

Cylinders	4
Bore and stroke	82.55 mm. x 72.75 mm.
Cubic capacity	1.558 c.c.
Valves	D.o.h.c.
Compression ratio	9.5:1
Carburetters	Twin double-choke Webers. 40DCOE
Fuel pump	A.C. mechanical
Oil filter	full flow
Max. power (net)	105 b.h.p. at 5,500 r.p.m.
Max. torque (net)	108 lb. ft. at 4,000 r.p.m.

Transmission

Clutch	8 in. dia. s.d.p.
Top gear (s/m)	1.000
3rd gear (s/m)	1.397
2nd gear (s/m)	2.010
1st gear (s/m)	2.972
Reverse	3.324
Final drive	Hypoid bevel 3.90:1
M.p.h. at 1,000 r.p.m. in:—	
Top gear	17.4
3rd gear	12.4
2nd gear	8.7
1st gear	5.9
Tyres	6.00-13. Dunlop C41
Rim size	5½J-13

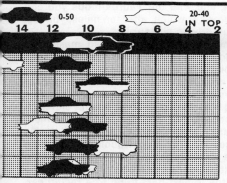

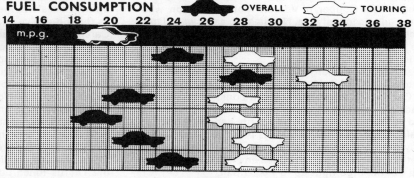

FUEL CONSUMPTION
m.p.g.

A LOTUS-CORTINA

TAURUS-TUNED!

116 M.P.H.
0-60 IN 7.0 SECONDS

WHEN the Lotus-Cortina first came out it was a sort of answer to a young man's prayer—an answer to namby-pamby sports cars which differ from family saloons only in the number of seats they have: it was a rough, tough motor-car which had real performance and road-holding which opened your eyes again. Unfortunately it wasn't all that tough really, and revealed a few spots of unreliability which obviously had to be ironed out. The big snag was that in ironing them out they also took away a lot of its rugged character, and the modern Lotus-Cortina, although still a high-performance sporting saloon, just doesn't seem to have the hard edge to it that the old coil-spring and "A" bracket cars seemed to have. It doesn't beg and plead to be hurled about like the old one; it hasn't got the fierce, snarling performance and, to be frank, is much more of a gentleman.

This makes it a better car, of course, but every now and again we lust after the more primitive animal that was the Lotus-Cortina of yesterday—a sort of Super Seven with a roof on. And the other day (to get to the point at long last) The Man at Taurus rang up and asked if we'd like to have a go at just such an animal. In this case, a 1963 Lotus-Cortina ("A"-brackets, coil springs, high bottom gear and all) belonging to Mike Cooper, of Venture Motors, Clacton, who are Taurus agents in that area. Needless to say it was also a car which Taurus had been giving a bit of the treatment to, with the idea of making it even more of a competition car just having a rest between events.

To this end they had enlarged the bore to 83.5 mm, bringing the capacity up to a full 1600 c.c. On to this they had put a Taurus Continental conversion, which consists of a modified head, with an 11 to 1 compression ratio but retaining standard valves (which are already pretty generous in size) and a pair of high-lift camshafts. This plus the usual careful assembly put up the power to around 135–140 b.h.p., and along with close-ratio gears provides an engine which really punches out the urge right up to 7,000 r.p.m.

It was just like old times when we collected the car from Taurus at Hammersmith and commenced the drag home. A bottom gear high enough to make you slip the clutch in slow traffic—and what a clutch: in/out, or sudden death, isn't in it, and it's hell in traffic and close to the ideal on the open road when you really start snapping the gears through. A harsh, jerky ride at low speed which smooths out into a glue-pot in each wheel when the going gets excitingly fast, and steering so precise you can steer it between a row of matches at sixty if you want to. This is what Lotus-Cortina motoring is all about, and with the Taurus mods you end up with a real live motor-car which, after ten miles, you feel as though you've been driving all your life.

Careful assembly and treatment of the head makes the power unit a lot smoother than normal, and also improves the flexibility to a point where, despite high-lift cams, the car is in fact more tractable than it used to be in standard form. The high bottom gear apart, this is a car which auntie could drive if her leg was strong enough for the clutch. It starts flawlessly, and showed no sign of temperament throughout our tenancy despite some pretty evil traffic hold-ups—no over-heating, no plug trouble, no nothing nasty at all. But once on what passes for the open road in these overcrowded little islands and it all starts to happen—the Taurus-tuned Lotus is next best thing to a racing car,

CONTINUED ON PAGE 64

'67 FORD CORTINA-LOTUS

NEW Ford Cortina-Lotus based on the revised Cortina GT first introduced last October. Previous special-equipment engine now standardized, but several formerly exclusive items discontinued. Car now to be Ford-built rather than Lotus-built, on the Dagenham assembly lines. Impressive list of optional extras for competition use, including Tecalemit fuel injection. Small price increase.'

PREDICTABLY, after the revised Ford Cortina had been released at the last Earls Court show, a revised Cortina-Lotus was expected, but although the old model Cortina-Lotus was discontinued, the new car took some time to complete its development. It is released this week, and should be seen in Ford showrooms shortly.

Compared with the 1966 version of the Cortina-Lotus, there are several important changes. The new one is being assembled on the Dagenham production lines, dovetailed in among the Cortinas and Cortina GTs without discrimination, whereas the earlier models were assembled by the Lotus factory at Cheshunt (before the lines were moved to Norfolk). The previous "Special Equipment" engine is now standard, and there is no longer a distinctive facia or steering wheel. Unlike the previous model, there is a full range of colours, including the familiar white with a green stripe. Drag-strips along the sills are optional extras, and further identification points include the black mesh grille, Lotus badges and the very wide-rimmed wheels and radial tyres.

To understand the engineering of the new car, it is really necessary to trace the basic development of the old model. When announced in January, 1963, the Cortina-Lotus had the twin-cam engine, ultra-close gear ratios, light alloy body panels and a Chapman inspired trailing-arm-and-coil-spring rear suspension. The facia design was new, and special seats and trim details were included. As time went by there were big changes, and the ultimate 1966 version had lost its aluminium panels, its ultra-close gear-ratios, and its special rear suspension. To all intents and purposes the 1966 car was a Cortina GT with the twin-cam engine and a few trim changes.

The 1967 Cortina-Lotus is very closely based on the new Cortina GT, perhaps even more so than before, but there is a really impressive list of optional extras, which includes a racing version of the Tecalemit fuel injection system. All engineering extras will be supplied after assembly, to the customer, from the Ford Competition Department at Boreham, near Chelmsford.

Basically, the well-known Lotus-inspired twin o.h.c. engine—itself a conversion of the Cortina GT unit—is unchanged, but the Special Equipment tune, previously a costly extra item, has been standardized.

Theoretically, power output is only increased from 105 b.h.p. at 5,500 r.p.m. to 109 b.h.p. at 6,000 r.p.m., but Ford engineers reckon the improvements to be more marked than this, as the old figures were supplied by Lotus and never verified by Ford. The latest engine has been further developed by Ford engineers and refined in several ways. Principal changes have been to camshaft timing and valve lift, the compression ratio being unchanged. The new valve timing is: 26-66-66-26deg, the figures having their usual meaning, whereas the old engine timing was: 22-62-62-22deg. An aid to refinement is the large air silencer-air cleaner which lies across the top of the cylinder head and is connected to the two twin-choke Weber carburettors by fat trunking. There has been a lot of detailed development in the engine, particularly to stop oil leaks.

The standard gearbox is identical with that fitted to the Corsair 2000E and, since January this year, to the Cortina GT; it was also fitted to the 1966 Cortina-Lotus. In the new car it has the revised linkage first found on the 1967 Cortina GT, with reverse alongside top gear and improved reverse-stop arrangements. The Lotus ultra-close-ratio box (very suitable for competition work, but not for road use) is optional. Unlike on the new Cortina GT, a split prop-shaft is fitted. If a single, long, shaft had been used it would have had to be at least 3.5in. diameter. This would in any case have been too heavy, and posed serious clearance problems under the body. The rear axle ratio is 3.77 to 1, like the Corsair 2000E and higher than the previous car, which was 3.9 to 1. Many optional ratios are available.

No brake changes have been necessary from the 1966 car, on which the system was the same as the Cortina GT and Corsair GT and 2000E. Its 9in. rear brakes are self-adjusting. A Girling vacuum brake servo is retained, under the bonnet on the near side of the car. This, and the bulky Weber carburettors have meant that the battery must remain in the boot, neatly stowed in the tool well, but accessible.

Wheels are 5.5in. rimmed, as before, but radial ply tyres—either Pirelli Cinturato or Goodyear G800—are standard. Their size is 165—13in., a size less than Ford rally cars have been using for some time now. Because the revised Cortina had a wider track than before, with a better turning circle, it has not been necessary to restrict the lock on the new car; partly due to this, and partly because the new car has normal Ackermann effects, the lock is a very creditable 30ft. In fact, the Cortina-Lotus track, front and rear, is an inch wider than is ▶

'67

FORD CORTINA-LOTUS

used on the basic Cortina and Cortina GT.

Suspension geometry is not changed, and the rear suspension radius arms are retained, as on the Cortina GT. Suspension spring rates and damper settings have been revised, though the new car is little stiffer than the Cortina GT. The suspension has been lowered by approximately 1in. all round.

Even the 1966 Cortina-Lotus had a unique and very attractive special facia design and the slim-spoked Lotus wood-rimmed steering wheel, but the new car's facia is almost identical with that of the Cortina GT, and the seats *are* the same. The speedometer reads to 140 m.p.h., and the electronic rev-counter to 8,000 r.p.m. Normally there will be no chance of the engine reaching such r.p.m. as there is an ignition cut-out in the distributor which begins to operate at 6,500 r.p.m.; this is to protect the engine, which might fail mechanically if 6,500 was exceeded regularly. Ford seat belts are standard for front-seat occupants.

Externally, the Cortina-Lotus is almost identical with the Cortina GT. The familiar Cortina-Lotus front quarter bumpers have been abandoned, though the black-mesh radiator grille is retained. Lotus badges are on each rear quarter, but not on the grille. Happily, there is now a full choice of body colours, and the Lotus trade mark of a green flash on the all-white body can be supplied. Present plans are that this will be a self-adhesive stripe, not painted as before.

To the purist, the rationalization of the Cortina-Lotus is disappointing, but there can be no doubt that the 1967 car will be the best engineered and most reliable yet. The car will be sold through all Ford main dealers, with the full Dagenham guarantee. The special equipment engine alone justifies a price increase, which has been kept down to only £61. The new Cortina-Lotus is to retail at £1,068 2s 11d, and potential competition drivers can then begin to add approved Ford competition parts to the car. ∎

Above: The familiar Lotus green flash is only available on white cars. The door-sill drag strips are extras too. The black grille, and very wide-rimmed wheels are obvious recognition points

Cortina-Lotus racing and rallying equipment.
Optionally available only from Ford Competition Department.
Tecalemit fuel-injection equipment
Modified exhaust system
Connecting rods, pistons, camshafts, valves, oil pump
Oil cooler
Close ratio gearbox
Optional axle ratios—3·9, 4·1, 4·4 and 4·7 to 1
Limited slip differential
Light alloy diff. casing, clutch housing and gearbox extension
High ratio steering box
Heavy duty front suspension
Adjustable rear dampers
Racing brake pads and linings
Cast electron racing wheels
Light alloy body panels—doors, bonnet and boot lid
Auxiliary fuel tank
Replacement long range fuel tank
Fuel tank skid shield
Sump shield
Competition front seats

Right: A large AC air-cleaner has been fitted to reduce intake noise from the Weber carburettors. The brake servo is standard. The battery is in the boot. Left: The new Cortina-Lotus facia panel and interior trim is almost identical with the 1967 Cortina GT. The rev counter reads up to 8,000 r.p.m. and the speedometer to 140 m.p.h. Front seat belts are standard, but the radio fitted here is extra

SPECIFICATION

ENGINE

Cylinders	4, in line
Cooling system	Water; pump, fan and thermostat
Bore	82.55mm (3.25in)
Stroke	72.75 mm (2.86in)
Displacement	1,558 c.c. (95 cu.in.)
Valve gear	Twin overhead camshafts, bucket tappets
Compression ratio	9.5-to-1
Carburettors	2 Twin-choke Weber 40DCOE
Fuel pump	AC Mechanical
Oil filter	Full flow, renewable element
Max. power	109 b.h.p. (net) 6,000 r.p.m.
Max. torque	106 lb ft (net) at 4,500 r.p.m.
Max. b.m.e.p.	168 p.s.i. at 4,500 r.p.m.

TRANSMISSION

Clutch	Borg and Beck, diaphragm spring, 8.0 in dia.
Gearbox	4-speed, all synchromesh
Gear ratios	Top 1.0, Third 1.397, Second 2.01, First 2.972, Reverse 3.324
Final drive	Hypoid bevel, 3·77-to-1

CHASSIS AND BODY

Construction	Integral, with steel body

SUSPENSION

Front	Independent, MacPherson struts, coil springs, wishbones, anti-roll bar, telescopic dampers
Rear	Live axle, half-elliptic leaf springs, twin radius arms, telescopic dampers

STEERING

Type	Recirculating ball Wheel dia. 15.5in.

BRAKES

	Girling, disc front, drum rear
Servo	Girling vacuum
Dimensions	F, 9.62in. dia. R, 9.0in. dia. 1.75in. wide shoes
Swept area	F, 189.5 sq.in., R, 96.1 sq. in. Total 285.6 sq. in.

WHEELS

Type	Pressed steel disc, four stud fixing. 5.5in. wide rim
Tyres	Radial ply, G800 Goodyear or Pirelli Cinturato tubeless size 16.5—13in.

EQUIPMENT

Battery	12-volt, 38-amp. hr.
Generator	Lucas 22 amp d.c.
Headlamps	Lucas sealed beam 60/45-watt
Reversing lamp	None
Electric fuses	2
Screen wipers	Single-speed, self-parking
Screen washer	Manual plunger standard
Interior heater	Standard, fresh air
Safety belts	Standard
Interior trim	Pvc seats, pvc headlining
Floor covering	Carpet
Starting handle	No provision
Jack	Scissor type
Jacking points	4, under body sills, near wheels
Windscreen	Zone toughened, laminated optional
Underbody protection	Anti-corrosive treatment
Other bodies	None

MAINTENANCE

Fuel tank	10 Imp. gallons (no reserve) (45 litres)
Cooling system	12.5 pints (including heater) (7.0 litres)
Engine sump	7.2 pints (4.0 litres) SAE 10W/30. Change oil every 2,500 miles; change filter element every 2,500 miles
Gearbox	1.8 pints SAE 80. Change oil after first 5,000 miles only
Final drive	2 pints SAE 90. No oil change needed
Grease	None required
Tyre pressures	F, 24; R, 24 p.s.i. (normal driving)

DIMENSIONS

Wheelbase	8ft 2in. (249cm)
Track: front	4ft 5.5in (136cm)
Track: rear	4ft 4in (132cm)
Overall length	14ft 0in. (427cm)
Overall width	5ft 4.9in. (165cm)
Overall height (unladen)	4ft 7.7in. (140.5cm)
Ground clearance (laden)	6.3in. (16cm)
Turning circle	30ft 0in. (9.1m)
Kerb weight	2,027lb (964kg)

PERFORMANCE DATA

Top gear m.p.h. per 1,000 r.p.m. 17.8
Mean piston speed at max. power 2,860ft/min

PRICES	£	s	d
Ford Cortina-Lotus	869	0	0
Purchase Tax	199	2	11
(Total in G.B.)	1,068	2	11

CONTINUED FROM PAGE **60**

and shows it in every response. The roadholding is practically flawless—O.K., it picks up a wheel now and again. So what? Master Clark regards it as a plus point—says it shortens every lap!

On a twisty road—a really twisty road, we mean—a car like this becomes a sort of extension of yourself. It seems to respond to your very thoughts. Bottom gear, for instance, will give you close on fifty miles an hour, which makes it just the job for the really tight ones. Second gear is good for seventy, and she'll do 94 in third, which isn't hanging about (assuming you go somewhere that Auntie Barbara doesn't say it's naughty to do more than seventy). And with 60 coming up from rest in exactly seven seconds, and the legal (Auntie Babs again) limit appearing on the lock in under ten seconds—well, there isn't a lot that can stay with you. The 0–70 acceleration, for instance, is two-tenths of a second better than we got from the 4.2 "E"-type! By the time Taurus have finished with it, this is a pretty rapid machine, and the acceleration graph goes more or less straight up!

It keeps on going up for quite a long way, too—we got a maximum speed, both ways, of 116 m.p.h. compared with a top whack of 106 from the current standard model, with leaf-spring rear suspension. The acceleration makes interesting comparisons, too—compared with the standard leaf-spring product currently produced, the Taurus version is two-and-a-half seconds quicker to sixty, three seconds faster to seventy, and the same amount gets knocked off the 0–80 time, too. In fact, the Taurus car has got to seventy less than half-a-second after the standard product reaches sixty! And you don't do all this at fantastic cost in fuel. We got 24 m.p.g. overall—by a coincidence we had both cars for the same length of time and covered almost an identical mileage in each—out of both standard model and tuned version, about which there ought to be no complaints especially when you think in terms of the performance you've got on tap.

We've always had a bit of a hankering after the old-style Lotus-Cortina. We know all about its disadvantages, its snags and its faults. But this was the sort of car that motoring—our sort of motoring—is all about, when the machine responds to every thought and even seems to be able to do a bit of thinking on its own. The Taurus version reminded us of this, and since this car did it all and then some, we hankered even more strongly. We kept Mike Cooper apart from his car for some time—but we liked it so much that he was lucky to get it back at all!

 **Cars on Test**

TAURUS LOTUS-CORTINA

Figures in brackets relate to standard car

Engine: As standard Lotus Cortina except: bore increased to 83.5 mm; capacity 1,600 c.c.; modified cylinder head; compression ratio 11 to 1; high-lift camshafts; 135-140 b.h.p.

Transmission: As standard Lotus-Cortina except close-ratio gears.

Suspension: As standard Lotus Cortina ("A" bracket/coil spring rear end).

Brakes: As standard Lotus Cortina.

Dimensions: As standard Lotus-Cortina.

PERFORMANCE

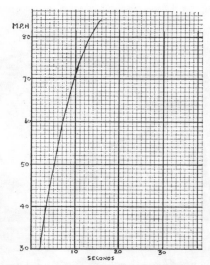

	m.p.h.			secs.
MAXIMUM SPEED	116 (106)	ACCELERATION	0–30	2.0 (3.2)
Mean of two ways			0–40	3.4 (4.6)
SPEEDS IN GEARS	First 48 (39)		0–50	5.2 (6.8)
	Second 71 (55)		0–60	7.0 (9.4)
	Third 94 (79)		0–70	9.8 (12.8)
Fuel consumption: 24 m.p.h. (24)			0–80	13.2 (16.2)

Cost of conversion: Head and cams, £75; boring and pistons, £75; balancing, £13 10s; labour and fitting charges, £50; total cost £213 10s.

Car converted by: Taurus Performance Tuning Ltd., Childs Place, Earls Court Road, London S.W.5

Cortina-Lotus
The Trophy Trail

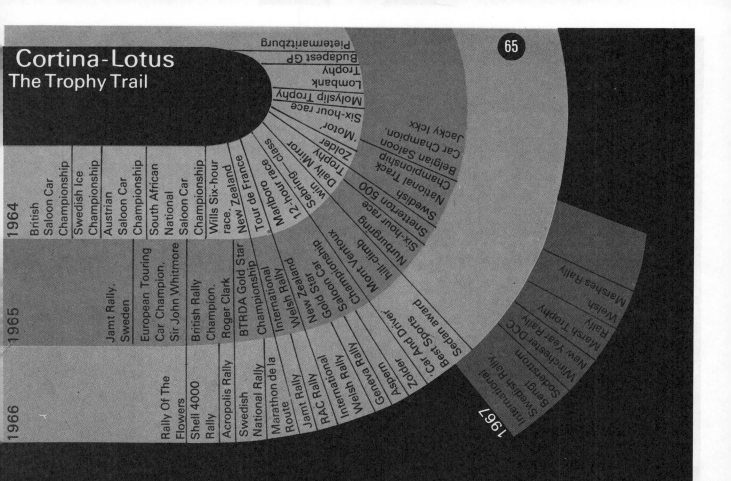

CORTINA+LOTUS '67/THE GO-FASTER FORMULA

The Cortina-Lotus success list is formidable. From 1963 to 1967, from one side of the world to the other, motor sport's top names have taken the car from glory to glory. Now, after an 18-month test programme, the '67 Cortina-Lotus bows in —constructed almost entirely on Ford production lines and powered by an engine developed by Ford, Lotus and Cosworth to produce 115 bhp at 6,000 rpm in standard form. Subject to the same stringent quality checks applied to all vehicles that come out of Ford's British plants, the new Cortina-Lotus appears externally similar to the 1967 Cortina GT. Its two-door body is available in the *full* range of Cortina trim/body colour combinations; but 'sidewinder' stripes like those of Ford GT40s will be sold as accessories and white

THE GO-FASTER FORMULA *continued*

models can be supplied with the familiar green side flashes. Other identifying features include a matt black radiator grille, Lotus badges—and performance that takes the car up to 108 mph and from rest to 60 mph in ten seconds.

The power unit is based on the famous 1,500 cc Ford five-bearing block, its alloy twin overhead camshaft cylinder head and twin-choke Weber 40DCOE carburettors more than doubling the output of the original production engine. A special cut-out device incorporated in the distributor limits crankshaft revs to 6,500 rpm, ensuring long life and reliability. The suspension is stiffened and lowered; 165—13 radial-ply tyres on 13 in 5½J wheels are standard. Power is transmitted through an 8 in diaphragm spring clutch to an all-synchromesh close-ratio gearbox, a heavy-duty divided propeller shaft driving a rear axle located by leaf springs and twin radius arms. Competition-proved front disc brakes and self-adjusting rear drums are servo-assisted.

Inside the car, the comprehensive instrumentation is basically that of the Cortina GT. The speedometer is calibrated to 140 mph, the tachometer to 8,000 rpm; ammeter, oil pressure, water temperature and fuel gauges are mounted in the centre of the facia; front seat belts are standard; Aeroflow changes the air inside the vehicle once every 34 seconds.

A host of high performance extras are available from Ford's Performance Centre: fuel injection, ultra-close-ratio gears, modified suspension units, lightweight touring seats, alloy body panels, limited-slip differentials.

Car price, including PT and delivery: £1,068 2s 11d.

Glory-chaser 1967-style . . . and Ford begat it

THE GO-FASTER FORMULA / JOE LOWREY WRITES

'Really good breathing is the vital secret of the Cortina-Lotus engine ... providing 77 per cent more power than a normal Cortina 1500 and 37 per cent more than a Cortina GT.'

PICTURES: JOHN WRIGHT AND KEN SHIPTON

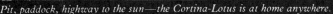

Pit, paddock, highway to the sun—the Cortina-Lotus is at home anywhere.

Making a spacious and comforta[ble] production saloon go quite abn[or]mally fast involves widespr[ead] design changes. For example[, it] requires about 33 per cent m[ore] power to increase a car's top sp[eed] by 10 per cent . . . and this po[wer] has to be applied usefully to [the] wheels, which must cling to [the] road and have good brakes beh[ind] them. Then, since potential cus[to]mers are likely to be exception[ally] fussy about such things as g[ood] seating, precise gearshifting [and] adequate instrumentation, g[reat] care has to be taken to provide [?] the right 'package' around [the] power plant.

It is remarkable, therefore, [?] how much of the 'normal' Cor[tina] saloon has been found suita[ble] for inclusion in the latest h[igh] performance Lotus variant . . .

As has been pointed out, po[wer] for the new Cortina-Lotus co[mes] from an engine based on prod[uc]tion Ford components—the 1,[?] cc five-bearing unit. Lotus [en]gineers were attracted to [it] about five years ago. Sturdi[ness] combined with low weight, [a] five-bearing crankshaft and [an] over-square stroke-to-bore [?] seemed to offer a promi[sing] foundation on which to bui[ld a] double overhead camshaft cylin[der] head. And sure enough, when [the] conversion was built and teste[d it] proved effective enough to [win] races in single-seater cars as [well] as form an excellent power [unit] for Lotus sports two-seaters.

The Lotus factory has been [fit]ting the twin overhead cams[haft] engine into Cortina saloons s[ince] 1962. And what was at fir[st a] saloon modified for racing [has] gradually become reliable in [town] and road use, quiet and powe[rful.] The Lotus engine is being built [into] 1967 saloons at Dagenham, h[ow]ever, development having ena[bled] it to pass the stringent accepta[nce] tests to which Ford engineers [sub]ject all new designs.

Really good breathing is the [?] secret of Cortina-Lotus en[gine] performance. A separate air su[pply] to each cylinder, through [the] choke tube of a Weber carbu[re]tor to the inclined inlet va[lve] provides 77 per cent more po[wer] than a normal Cortina 1500 [and] 37 per cent more than a Cortina [GT.] More about that in 'Joe's P[age'] on page 28. Let it just be said [here] that the engine breathes so f[reely] that a safety limit of 6,500 rp[m]

▶ had to be set by a cut-out in the ignition system.

The introduction of a diaphragm clutch has given the normal Cortina the advantage of light pedal pressure. The faster-revving Lotus engine's 8 in diaphragm spring clutch has the further advantage in that, unlike a set of coil springs, it is untroubled by centrifugal effects.

In the latest Ford gearbox for Lotus and GT variants, progressive ratio spacing provides a $32\frac{1}{2}$ per cent drop in engine rpm from first to second gear, a $30\frac{1}{2}$ per cent drop from second to third and a $28\frac{1}{2}$ per cent drop from third to top. For racing, ultra-close-ratio gears can be obtained from Ford's Performance Centre, or there is a five-speed Hewland box. As catalogued, the ratios give good overtaking performance yet provide a low enough bottom gear to cope with city traffic congestion.

Despite pulling an extra-high top gear, the Cortina-Lotus can spin its propeller shaft faster than normal-engined models. So to eliminate harmful vibration, the shaft is divided into two and supported by a rubber-mounted central bearing behind which is an extra universal joint.

When Lotus first converted Cortinas to twin overhead camshafts the rear suspension was altered from leaf to coil spring, axle move-

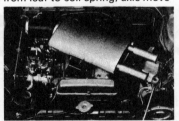

Powerhouse, Cortina-Lotus '67

ment being controlled by radius arms and an A-bracket. Roadholding with this design was good, but stresses on the axle and body structure were great. When Ford engineers evolved an equally efficient combination of radius arms and leaf rear springs which *prevented* stress, Lotus switched to the layout.

Much the same arrangement of radius arms, with the improved 1967 rear spring geometry, is found on the new Cortina-Lotus. In comparison with the latest Cortina GT, slightly stiffer and lower rear springs are controlled by more powerful shock absorbers. Ford apply their rear radius arms

so that they do not absolutely prevent axle twist on the rear leaf springs some 'Hotchkiss drive' cushioning of the transmission being retained. By preventing fore-and-aft axle movement, however, the radius arms inhibit axle tramp which gearbox-multiplied torque from a 115 hp engine might otherwise generate.

Higher maximum speed does not mean that a car's brakes must be able to exert greater forces, ability to lock the wheels being the maximum effort ever required. More frequent and more sustained braking does, however, require increased ability to dissipate kinetic energy as heat.

The self-adjusting brakes of the latest Cortina—discs at the front and drums at the rear—are large enough to cope with Lotus performance and are given extra-hard linings to guard against fade at high working temperatures. A vacuum servo is added to the hydraulic operating system to maintain pedal effort at an acceptable level. (Moving the battery from the engine compartment to the boot makes room for the servo and, incidentally, puts extra weight on the driving wheels to assist acceleration on greasy roads.)

Road grip, as modern racing cars have demonstrated, depends on having as much rubber as possible touching the road, and conspicuously 'fat' tyres are fitted to the Cortina-Lotus—radial-ply casings of 165-13 mounted on rims $5\frac{1}{2}$ in wide. Buyers of the model are assumed to value precise controllability above the utmost in ride smoothness.

Much toughening-up of the original Cortina-Lotus design has been done by the Performance Centre: it was a twin overhead camshaft Cortina from the workshops there which won last autumn's tough RAC Rally in the hands of Bengt Soderstrom and Gunnar Palm. And already there is a long list of special competition extras which can be ordered for the new variant. Some, such as cast electron wheels, are conspicuous; others, such as weight-saving aluminium castings and body panels, are not. Some—fuel injection to replace the carburettors, for example—are aimed at giving yet *more* power; others offer extra resistance to tough racing or rallying conditions. Ford Times will publish a selection soon.

Do you define a sport a high-powered engine costing at least £2000

Then here's one that seats five, does 108 mph and costs only £1068. (We even give it a racy Italian name.)

Some people define the new Cortina Lotus as a racing car disguised as a family saloon. Others say it's the other way round. Both definitions fit it exactly. With New Cortina Lotus you get a family-size saloon which gives rally-car performance. It's been built that way—for the driver who wants comfort and space combined with that dash of flair and extra power that lifts motoring out of the everyday. And the delivered price is geared well towards the medium-sized budget, too! Power! Top speed of 108 mph . . . 1558 cc twin overhead camshaft engine with two twin-choke Weber carburettors . . . acceleration of 0-60 in 10·4 seconds . . . these are only three of the exciting, racy engine features of New Cortina Lotus. Handling! And to handle this power-package: radial ply tyres on $5\frac{1}{2}$ J rims for sure, supple roadholding on all surfaces . . . servo-assisted

brakes all round . . . anti-roll bar, radius arms a lowered suspension . . . all-synchromesh gearb with floor-mounted remote gear lever for f smooth changes. Looks! Upholstery and trim Cirrus 200. Door-to-door fitted deep-pile carpeti Stylish trim exterior, too—flowing body lines fo really distinctive look. Comfort! 'Aeroflow' vent tion for a complete change of air every 40 secon Front contoured bucket seats. Spacious back se Room to breathe, room to move. Extra Bonus—is wide range of special Cortina Lotus racing rally equipment available from the Ford Competiti Department. Recommended delivered pr including purchase tax £1068. And this mea exactly what it says—with Ford there is no ex charge for delivery. (This price does not apply Ireland.)

ar as having two seats,
a racy Italian name and

New Cortina Lotus

LINE OF IMPROVEMENT

The Ford Cortina-Lotus, developed for the public by the Competitions Department

WHEN the 1967 Cortina-Lotus was introduced, perhaps rather quietly by Ford's standards, there was a general feeling that this was a toned-down version of a car which had earned so many competition successes, and perhaps much of the character had been removed.

But the proof of the pudding is in the eating. On paper the specification has been improved, driving the car underlines its superiority, and detailed investigation shows that nine months of rigorous development, in the right hands, has made it a vastly better product. Much of the groundwork experience was put into the Cortina GTs taking part in the Safari Rally, and their mechanical reliability was such that, presuming Ford take part again next year, there will be virtually no specification changes other than running with the Lotus twin-cam engines.

Towards the end of the GT's proving trials last April two new cars were fitted with Special Equipment Lotus engines developing 115 b.h.p. gross and handed over to Henry Taylor's Competitions Department at Boreham Airfield, Essex. Under the supervision of Bill Meade, the Rally Engineer, two mechanics commenced a punishing programme of development to eliminate the faults of the previous Lotus version.

First of all the cars, one with left-hand drive, were lowered by one inch front and rear and fitted with wide-rim wheels and Goodyear or Pirelli radial-ply tyres. Early testing consisted of high-speed runs over a " rally route " at Bagshot Heath to prove the strength, and the selected drivers, Ken Wiltshire and Mick Jones, put in favourable reports about the improved suspension, finding it particularly good through a trough which could break the front struts of the old cars. Heavy-duty export bodyshells are used exclusively for the Lotus versions, having stronger welds around the suspension mountings.

During the summer and right through to January testing continued at Bagshot, at the Motor Industry Research Association proving ground, and at Lommel, a Belgian proving ground. Each car covered up to 25,000 miles in this time, including 5,000 miles on corrugations and pavé, 4,000 miles at maximum speed and 2,000 miles testing engine durability.

It took five weeks at Lommel to select the damper settings, the suspension going into production with higher spring rates. Compared

Responsible for Cortina-Lotus development were Henry Taylor and Bill Meade (foreground), seen here with test drivers Ken Wiltshire and Mick Jones. George Baggs, Special Vehicle Manager, was responsible for the programme.

with the previous model, the new car has forged top camber arms, angled front springs and specially treated bushes to reduce " stiction " and offset the side loading. Rear suspension geometry has been altered so with the wider track and lower centre of gravity the handling has been altogether transformed, eliminating the " lurch " that preceded roll previously.

Mechanical changes are more far-reaching than we imagined, partly because the Lotus version has been specially developed by rally engineers and partly because it is now in production on Ford's own production lines at Dagenham and Halewood, subject to an extremely strict quality control which demanded at least a dozen improvements straight away. Engine durability testing revealed piston failure, which has been cured by a new specification, and the throttle linkage has been made heavier and stronger. Thicker gauge metal in the exhaust manifold has cured a resonance and the system is suspended in O-rings instead of straps. It was also found possible to incorporate two mufflers in the system instead of three.

Noise level was a major consideration and it took several months to evolve a new, large AC air cleaner which has cut induction noise to a minimum. Such is the size of the unit that the battery had to be moved to the boot, incidentally improving the car's weight balance. Ignition timing has been altered, again in the interest of durability, and the dynamo has been made more reliable with thicker field wire. Trouble on the Safari Rally, incidentally, was caused by dust entering the generator and should not therefore be a problem in normal use.

A hydrostatic (self-adjusting) 8-in. clutch is incorporated with much lighter pedal pressure, 30 pounds instead of 50, and the gearbox is improved. The box, similar to the one used latterly on the old version and now fitted to the 2-litre Corsair, has a better shift integral with the extension housing which cuts out the " fizz," and it will be noted that reverse is located right-and-back instead of left-and-back. The driveshaft is now split and jointed, eliminating whip which occurred at high speeds, and with competitions in mind it will cope with speeds up to 8,000 r.p.m. in top gear, possibly over 130 m.p.h. depending on gearing. Also new is the 3.77 ratio axle, exclusive to Lotus versions and much stronger than previously; having high-tensile nuts and bolts on the differential carrier, it is known to cope with up to 140 b.h.p. in competition use.

Brakes, with servo assistance, are the same as those used on the Corsair 2000 and a dual system has also been developed for the American market. Handbrake efficiency is improved, while all markets share a benefit of better crankcase emission control demanded by U.S. regulations. Finally, a 10-gallon petrol tank replaces the 8-gallon tank fitted previously, increasing the range to approximately 250 miles.

With pride, Ken Wiltshire and Mick Jones claim that the ride is better than on the GT even though the car is an inch lower, using the same spring rates but higher damper settings. There is no export specification now since the suspension was developed mainly on the Continent and is considered suitable for all territories except possibly darkest Africa, so far as the customer is concerned. It was with new respect that we drove the test car back to London from Boreham appreciating that it certainly handles better than the old Lotus.

It took several months to evolve the most efficient air-cleaner, substantially reducing induction noise, and the battery was moved to the boot.

Although the ride is slightly firmer than that of the GT we soon ceased to worry about running over potholes, because the anticipated shock is not transferred through the car. Most of the testing was done on Pirellis, which are fitted to about half the production cars, but the test car was shod with Goodyear tyres which have a new rubber mix, perfectly adequate on the wide rims to cope with wet weather conditions. The only complaint about the car is that rain gathers at the bottom of the screen at high speed and is forced upwards, proving too much of a task for the single-speed wipers.

Without the pronounced induction noise the "C-range" Lotus is not the boy-racer some people expect, being quiet, comfortable and refined—it needs a stopwatch to prove that it is quicker, the extra horsepower rating having overcome a small weight disadvantage. All the controls are very light, the clutch particularly so, and right up to maximum speed the car is smooth and restful to drive.

Clearly there is a ready market for "performance-plus" cars, since a sixth of the 1,500 Cortinas manufactured every day are GT or Lotus versions. Whereas in the past difficulty may have been experienced in obtaining modified parts for competitions, dealers should now be ready, willing and able to supply a car modified practically up to the specification of the works cars raced and rallied. We say practically because on April 29th Graham Hill was due to drive a Cortina-Lotus at Silverstone equipped with the new Ford-Cosworth 16-valve Formula Two engine, and there is a long waiting list for this power plant! Among the performance items which can be supplied are Jackson-Tecalemit petrol injection (£60), alloy door panels (£13 10s. each) or bonnet and boot-lid (£12 10s. each), a limited slip differential £(25), close-ratio gearbox (£60), sump-shield (£12 10s.), high-ratio steering box (£11 19s. 6d.), engine modifications and a good many more items listed in a catalogue.

As we started off by remarking, there is a good deal more to the new car than meets the eye.—M. L. C.

" Go and test the cars in rally conditions," they said. The best drivers make mistakes sometimes but this car suffered little damage, and the doors remained shut.

On the road the Cortina-Lotus, although the most exciting of the C-range of Ford cars, accomplishes extremely well what Dagenham intends it to do, namely constitute a saloon of exceptional performance (see table) so docile and well-mannered that it will be bought by family men, whether for prestige purposes or because it will appeal to the older members of a household while offering the competition flavour younger drivers desire.

The test car was in 2-door form, carrying the Lotus badges and "speed flashes" along the body-sides. This twin-cam Cortina is nicely finished within, with comfortable seats, although long-legged drivers will probably prefer to reverse the brackets of the driver's seat, so as to raise the cushion when the seat is in the fully-back location. The full instrumentation of the push-rod Cortina GT, the "Aeroflow" ventilation and Weber 40DCOE carburation, are amongst the car's best features. Indeed, until it is driven hard this Cortina-Lotus feels and sounds almost like the Cortina GT, except for faintly more cam-noise from under the bonnet. The ride is not too bad, and the old understeer and weaving tendency have been eliminated. Indeed, there is a tendency for basic oversteer to make the nose dive inwards on corners, even on a light throttle opening, and in the wet power oversteer can be provoked, although normally the wide-base Goodyear G800 tyres hold satisfactorily. The servo brakes are powerful and progressive; cornering normally quite neutral, with little roll. The steering ratio is the same as on the GT (3½ turns lock-to-lock, plus sponge), the action light and precise.

Gone are the heavy clutch, high bottom gear and notchy close-ratio box of the first exciting Cortina-Lotus I enjoyed so much in 1963. The 1967 Ford-built version has an *extremely* light clutch and well-chosen gear ratios, with a sensible bottom gear. It is a far more refined car than Chapman's version, or even the version I tried last year, but I am delighted that it is back in the Ford catalogue. The Ford/Lotus/Cosworth engine now gives 108(net) b.h.p. at 6,000 r.p.m. (it is governed to a maximum of 6,500) and in spite of slight misfiring at high revs., the test car would hold a sustained speed of nearly 100 m.p.h. without anxiety. In catalogue trim, costing £1,068 2s. 11d., this is a fascinating, easy-to-drive, dual-purpose car for which there are available a host of enthralling extras, like *durable* magnesium wheels, for instance. Fuel consumption of 100-octane petrol averaged 24.6 m.p.g. and after 600 miles sump level had scarcely dropped. The "racing-engined" Cortina is now a very nice, fast saloon; the only version of similar urge and even more effortless functioning is the Pirelli-shod car Henry Taylor commutes in. This has the 3-litre V6 Ford engine mated to a Corsair gearbox, in a two-door Cortina body shell. But this one is *not* in the Ford catalogue !—W. B.

THE FORD CORTINA-LOTUS
TWO-DOOR SALOON

Engine : Four cylinders, 82.5 × 72.75 mm. (1,558 c.c.). Inclined overhead valves operated by twin overhead camshafts, 9.5 to 1 c.r. 108(net) b.h.p. at 6,000 r.p.m.

Gear ratios : First, 11.2 to 1; second, 7.57 to 1; third, 5.27 to 1; top, 3.77 to 1.

Tyres : 165 × 13 Goodyear G800, on bolt-on steel disc wheels.

Weight : 18 cwt.

Steering ratio : 3½ turns, lock-to-lock.

Fuel capacity : 10 gallons. (Range approx. 250 miles).

Wheelbase : 8 ft. 2½ in.

Track : Front, 4 ft. 3½ in.; rear, 4 ft. 2½ in.

Dimensions : 14 ft. ¼ in. × 5 ft. 2½ in. × 4 ft. 5¾ in. (high).

Price : £869 (£1,068 2s. 11d., inclusive of p.t.).

Makers : Ford Motor Company Ltd., Dagenham, Essex, England.

Performance figures

0-30 m.p.h.	.. ..	..	4.0 sec.
0-40 ,,	.. ..	..	5.75 ,,
0-50 ,,	.. ..	..	7.8 ,,
0-60 ,,	.. ..	..	11.0 ,,
0-70 ,,	.. ..	..	14.8 ,,
0-80 ,,	.. ..	..	20.2 ,,
Standing-start quarter mile		17.6 ,,	

Speed in gears :

1st	.. ..	..	37 m.p.h.
2nd	.. ..	..	55 ,,
3rd	.. ..	..	78 ,,
4th	.. ..	..	105 ,,

Fuel consumption : 24.6 m.p.g.

first report
FORD
CORTINA
LOTUS

By John Blunsden

Ford is trying to win On yet another battlefront!

THE ANTICIPATED, NEW FORD CORTINA LOTUS resembles the Cortina GT much more than its predecessor did. Inside the car, you have to look at the speedometer and tachometer calibrations to tell the difference. Outside, the main identification features of the Lotus are the matte-black grille, different badges on the rear quarters and trunk lid, and 5½J instead of 4½J wheels.

The rationalization is part of Ford of Britain's policy to expand the market for the Cortina Lotus. Also, it fits in with the company's decision to take over the car's manufacture from Lotus, and to promote it more thoroughly through Ford dealerships.

Only minor detail modifications have been made to the 1.6-liter, twin-overhead-cam engine, which retains its cylinder dimensions of 82.55 mm bore and 72.75 mm stroke to give a displacement of 1558 cc. Maximum power (gross) is 115 bhp at 6000 rpm, and maximum torque is 106 pounds/feet at 4500 rpm. To make room for the engine in the new Cortina body-unit, the battery has been moved from the engine bay into the trunk.

An eight-inch diaphragm clutch takes the drive through to a close-ratio gearbox (ratios: 1.0, 1.4, 2.01, and 2.97 to 1, with 3.32 to 1 reverse). The standard axle ratio is 3.77 to 1.

Compared with the Cortina GT, the suspension has been lowered almost an inch all around. Spring rates have been altered considerably; those at the front have gone up from around 110 to 140 pounds, and those at the rear have been dropped from 107 to 85 pounds. The normal GT front anti-sway bar is retained, as

is the trailing-link set-up at the rear. The wider wheels, of course, have had the effect of increasing front and rear tracks by an inch. Normal tire equipment will be Goodyear G8000 165 x 13 radial-plies, although Pirelli Cinturatos will be optional.

Once again the Cortina Lotus will only be marketed as a two-door sedan, and those hunting in the specifications for a visible status symbol will be relieved to know that the traditional green Lotus flash along the body sides will be available on cars finished in white. However, a full range of other colors and trims will be available without the flash. The stick-on styling flashes running along the bottom of the side panels are an item of extra equipment. Shelby really started something when he put them on his GT 350 — it's the latest craze in Europe, from Minis upward!

Evidence of Ford of Britain's intention to get the new Cortina Lotus into the winner's circle is to be found in an initial list of twenty-one 'per-formance' items being marketed for the car by Competitions Department, most of which will presumably be featured on the car's homologation sheets in due course. The list reads as follows: ventilated, cast-alloy, high-performance wheels; long-distance touring seats; close-ratio gearbox; sump shield; fuel-tank protective shield; auxiliary touring fuel-tank; extra long-range fuel-tank; alternative axle ratios (3.9, 4.1, 4.4, and 4.7 to 1); limited-slip differential; lightweight differential-casing; lightweight clutch-housing; lightweight gearbox-extensions; high-ratio steering box; heavy-duty front suspension; adjustable rear shock absorbers; high-performance brake pads and linings; oil-cooler kit; high-performance exhaust system; fuel injection; high-perform-ance connecting rods, pistons, camshafts, valves, oil pump; light-weight-alloy body-panels for doors, hood, and trunk lid.

Not bad for a start!

The 1967 Ford Cortina Lotus appears similar to Cortina GT, but has a 1500-cc twin cam Lotus 115 bhp engine with two twin-choke Weber carbs. Tach and speedometer are finished in a matte black, go to 8000 and 140 respectively.

On the Road with products from Ford

Exploring Pre-War Trials' Routes in the Latest Cortina-Lotus

IMPASSABLE.—The approach to Cusop Dingle Hill, used in trials in the 1930s, as it appears today, unclimbable even by a Ford Cortina-Lotus.

I HAVE a very high opinion of the Ford Cortina as a useful, reliable, economical value-for-money saloon of sensible passenger-carrying and luggage-containing proportions. I have previously given my reasons for holding these views, based on considerable experience of the C-series Ford in GT form.

When it was first introduced, in 1962, as Colin Chapman's conception of what a 1½-litre competition saloon should be, the Cortina-Lotus was great fun to drive but hardly every family's idea of how saloon-car motoring should be. Since then a development programme has been completed, aimed at softening up, and building reliability into, the high-performance version of the Cortina, without spoiling its appeal to the average enthusiast. All this we covered at some length last February, including brief road impressions of a car I regard as constituting the " third-phase " in Cortina-Lotus history.

But when the opportunity arose for me to acquire further experience of this useful Ford I accepted towns eagerly, for I could thereby establish a sound idea of the reliability factor of the 105-m.p.h. Ford and its suitability or otherwise for all kinds of hard usage.

The car I was allocated—CTC 25E—had already had a strenuous life, having been used for road-test purposes by several motor journals. It came to me with 8,718 miles on the odometer, being collected by a member of my family, who promptly vanished into the London traffic with it, using it for town commuting. It was later brought home to me with the comment " Why is there a red light showing all the time ? " This referred to the dynamo warning light, but Vick Bros. of Aldershot went into action after some female persuasion, replacing a faulty voltage-regulator, and since then all has been well.

The Cortina-Lotus' next assignment was to have a very heavy load of roof slates stacked in its capacious boot and be driven fast for a distance exceeding 300 miles. This it accomplished without complaint, the rear-end load making little, if any, change to the car's almost-neutral cornering characteristics or troubling the servo-assisted Girling disc/drum brakes, although the weight was sufficient to take the sharp edge off the normally-outstanding acceleration (s.s. ¼-mile in 18.0 sec.).

This sort of treatment underlines rather nicely, I think, the purpose behind the present Cortina-Lotus, which, apart from those Lotus badges and wide-base wheels, resembles bread-and-butter Cortinas in appearance. There are not, perhaps, many £1,000 twin-cam cars one would find so suitable for use as hack transport—indeed there are not many £1,000 twin-cam saloons! But the Cortina-Lotus, which is in effect an Elan-powered family model, is rugged, capacious and uncomplaining, yet is also an extremely effective high-performance

car. A good deal of glamour and fastidious rumour surrounds twin-overhead-camshaft engines, and rightly so. Ford, who now manufacture this engine in its entirety, have therein a completely docile, untemperamental 109-b.h.p. power unit, which idles quietly, burns 99-octane fuel (although 100-octane is recommended), and runs so smoothly and unobtrusively that, unless one detects the subdued " fizz " of the timing gear from outside the car, as when standing in front of it, it can easily be mistaken for the push-rod engine of the Cortina GT.

Except, that is, when the throttles of the dual-choke 40DCOE31 Webers are opened wide, when there is a very useful increase in performance, in terms both of pick-up and speed—83 m.p.h. in 3rd gear, for instance, from an engine which goes up to 6,500 r.p.m. before the ignition cuts out, but which has good top-gear pulling power from a speed as low as 1,500 r.p.m. This encompasses such diverse performance factors as picking up smoothly from 27 m.p.h. in the 3.78-to-1 top gear and cruising along the Motorways of civilised countries at an effortless 90 m.p.h. The previously-recounted load-carrying experiment (a necessity, really, if rain was to be kept out of my ancient Welsh hide-out!) proved that the slight weaving of early Cortina-Lotuses, which some drivers found disconcerting, has been entirely eradicated by the adoption of Cortina GT rear suspension (½-elliptic leaf springs with radius-arms) of the now-normal back axle, although the presence on the car about which I am writing of Pirelli Cinturato (13 in.) tyres may have contributed to this straight-line running, while the rough-road ride, if by no means irreproachable, has definitely improved.

I think choice between the GT or Lotus version of this excellent C-model Ford depends mainly on whether you regard the considerably greater performance and "willingness" of the t.o.h.c. engine over that of the push-rod power unit to justify the somewhat heavier petrol thirst and greater craving for oil of the Lotus version. That is, if reliability and freedom from petty faults are comparable between the two cars—about which, together with further comment on the matters of fuel and oil consumption, I cannot pass judgment until I have covered a greater mileage.

The next chore to which CTC 25E was subjected was a run to mid-Wales *via* a pre-war trials' route. Which trial this route applies to is lost in the mists of antiquity. It so happened that, when we were in process of moving the MOTOR SPORT offices, some ancient route cards fell, almost literally, into my lap. Most of these applied to M.C.C. Exeter and Land's End Trials of the mid-1930s, and there

Optional Extras for the Cortina-Lotus, available from the Competitions Department of the Ford Motor Company

1. Ventilated cast electron high performance wheels.
2. Long-distance touring seats.
3. Close-ratio gearbox.
4. Sump shield.
5. Fuel tank protective shield.
6. Auxiliary touring fuel tank.
7. Extra long-range fuel tank.
8. Alternative axle ratios : 3.9 : 1, 4.1 : 1, 4.4 : 1, 4.7 : 1.
9. Limited slip differential.
10. Lightweight differential casing.
11. Lightweight clutch housing.
12. Lightweight gearbox extensions.
13. High-ratio steering box.
14. Heavy-duty front suspension.
15. Adjustable rear shock-absorbers.
16. High-performance brake pads and linings.
17. Oil cooler unit.
18. High-performance exhaust system.
19. Fuel injection.
20. High-performance connecting rods, pistons, camshafts, valves, oil pump.
21. Lightweight alloy body panels for doors, bonnet and boot lid.

was a card covering the S.U.N.B.A.C. Colmore Trophy Trial of 1935—of which, more later.

But a single card covering part of a long-forgotten trial (they were " reliability trials " not " rallies " in those days, although the latter were held as well) caught my eye and as the route embraced Hereford, through which city we intended to travel, it seemed logical to put the Cortina-Lotus to this inadvertently-acquired test. In fact, the route did not *start* from Hereford, because the sheet I was looking at is numbered " 2," and it is therefore apparent that many miles and several " observed sections " had been covered by those trials drivers of long ago before they had reached this part of the competition. The time of departure from Hereford is given simply as " 6.0," so whether there had been a breakfast-stop there, or whether these intrepid but to date unidentified drivers had taken tea in this fine city, there is no means of knowing. The thing finished, at " 9.26," assuming you were in car No. 1, at the Forest Rest House outside Ross-on-Wye. Was this then, a nice, simple afternoon and evening affair, starting as well as finishing in Wales ? Or could it have been a Gloucester Trial, commencing, maybe, in Gloucestershire and terminating at Ross ? Memory is weak and, unless I do some research, I shall never know. . . .

But old trials' routes are pleasant to drive over, since they usually take in beautiful scenery seen from little-frequented roads without the necessity for map-reading or even carrying a map. For this reason we (my wife and I) agreed to discover where following this route card, almost certainly over 30 years old, would take us. It may have routed tough competition for trials-specials such as abbreviated Ford V8s and Allards, or it could have been a jaunt for ordinary cars, like Morris Ten/Fours, Austin Sixteens and Ford Populars. Whatever it was (and possibly some trials expert will be able to name it), how sad to reflect that such fun-and-games have been banished from the motor sporting scene, simply because the Police objected to the amount of mud " comp "-tyres, with their knobbly treads, brought onto ordinary roads from the muddy acclivities that constituted the " observed sections "! And, unless they were shod with tyres of this kind, ordinary cars became too pathetic to contemplate in competitions of this sort. . . .

Thus the Cortina-Lotus again found itself heavily loaded, this time with conventional luggage, but its strong springs inspire confidence, so off we went. Finding Peterchurch from Hereford was troublesome on account of modern one-way roads and the fact that A463 seems to have become B4348 since this aged route card was printed. But, making our way across country through fine pastoral scenery in the mid-afternoon sunshine, we eventually reached this point, where we partook of a splendid tea in the immaculate garden of a " bed and breakfast " cottage, served by a pleasant-natured old lady. Then it was right turn at the Cross Ways and on to Dorstone Hill, stopping on the way to look at what appeared to be a windmill converted into cylindrical, one-windowed living-quarters, and now for sale.

Had the clock gone back, converting us, perhaps, into wind-swept competitors crouching behind aero-screens, we should have soon taken an Acceleration Test. As it was, the Cortina-Lotus climbed Dorstone disdainfully, up past the ancient monument, Arthur's Stone, although needing bottom gear momentarily. Its ability to go from 0 to 60 m.p.h. in 10 seconds would probably have given us high marks in this timed test of yesteryear! After the 1-in-4 descent we got a bit lost, for Dorstone level-crossing apparently went with, or before, Beeching. . . .

Our next objective was Ponty Weston Hill. A girl cyclist, asked where it was, regarded us as if we were lunatics, but the farmer past whose farm we were directed remembered 160 or so trials cars coming to climb it in the early mornings of long ago but advised against trying in 1967, because, he said, the water has since played havoc with it and nothing has used it for years. I have, perhaps, reached the age

of discretion in these matters, having been stuck in my time for so many hours in so many different cars. . . .

So it was back up Watery Lane, now tarmac, but apparently a stony running torrent in the times to which we had endeavoured to project ourselves. After this, things continued to fall apart, even though the Ford just went on and on uncomplainingly, fed with Shell 4-star and a quart of Castrolite.

Turning towards Cusop just outside the drab, seemingly deserted town of Hay, we sought our next " observed section," Cusop Dingle Hill. The approach was remote, beyond a stone house bearing a " For Sale " notice and a " Dangerous Corner " sign lying, disregarded, in the ditch. A young man working on a Mini directed us, but told us the hill was now quite impassable to cars, adding " I once got a few feet up in a 1932 Austin 7." He was absolutely right! The gated lane is overgrown, the water splash at the hill's approach so steep that it would frighten a Land-Rover. We reversed out, and retreated. . . .

Evening had by now come down, as we set off again from Hay, where a late-closing shop had supplied provender and a Pothus Miracle can-opener which subsequently fell to pieces and nearly resulted in the motoring dog going without her supper. The route now lay over narrow, winding deserted lanes, entirely devoid of traffic, except that, immediately after I had remarked that I doubted whether, even in Ireland, greater desolation would be experienced, we narrowly missed another Cortina coming from the opposite direction. Later, a farm lad on a motorcycle, encountered at one of the many blind corners, obviated disaster by putting his machine into a broadside slide to kill its speed and then skilfully resuming the upright position, to shoot through what little space I had managed to provide for him. . . . We were bound, our route card told us, for Craswell, which time, or it may have been a misprint, now renders as Craswall. At last the remote " Bull's Head " Inn was reached and we were trying to find " S.O. to Farm buildings, Llanvynoe." A young couple were baffled but an old man standing at a farm entrance knew at once, telling us how to wind round towards Black Hill, another observed section and no doubt a very fine one, approached *via* a muddy gated hill-track. But again prudence made us turn back at Up and Over Hill, before getting to the real gradient. On the descent we had to wait while an old Ford Popular with a puncture was reversed down to a place where its ruined tyre could be changed before the youngsters in it proceeded to their evening picnic. . . . .

As we had been motoring for over eight hours without stopping for food we decided not to look for the last observed-section, Hill Lane near Long Town, which might well have been as elusive or impassable as the others. So, in the gathering dusk, it was back *via* Hay, Three Cocks, dinner, Builth Wells and home. It was now noticeable that the outcrop of simply enormous road signs has spread to rural Wales. Huge reflecting signs are all very well when one is travelling at 100 m.p.h. or more on a Motorway but are a terrible waste of money— yours and mine!—in a country where we are not supposed to drive at more than 70 m.p.h. and may soon be held to 60 m.p.h.—and they look quite absurd beside quiet country roads. Contrastingly an Aveling & Porter 10-ton steam-roller, an old friend of mine, is still working on the Doldowlod–Rhayader road.

The Cortina-Lotus has served since this expedition as a country-house hack, coping with such varied chores as taking elderly ladies to church, meeting trains, carting dustbins round the farm (that big boot !)—but also going to the Crystal Palace for the B.A.R.C. Race Meeting. Its Lotus engine makes no complaints about operating comparatively low down on the tachometer-scale, in spite of its rally and saloon-car-racing pedigree. To date I have used it for 2,150 miles, during which it has averaged roughly 27 m.p.g. and 1,400 m.p.g. of oil. It is proving a very useful, satisfying and reliable car, about which I hope to make further comment when it has built up an appreciable mileage. The only troubles since the voltage regulator was replaced have been a piece of beading loose on the n/s door and failure of the Tudor screen-washers. It is finished, incidentally, in a nice shade of slate-blue.

The extras on this particular Cortina comprise Triplex laminated windscreen, a small Springall competition steering wheel (the pliable sponge-rubber rim of which I find less pleasing than a leather-gaitered ordinary wheel) and a Ford push-button radio. This brings the total price, inclusive of purchase tax, to £1,117 17s. 10d.

* * *

Cortina victory *in the third*

International London

Gulf Rally by Colin Taylor

A TITANIC tussle ended in victory for the speedy Swede Ove Andersson and Britisher John Davenport, piloting a works Lotus Cortina, the car having been taken from the North American export line, was left-hand drive and had a twin braking system. Last year's winner Ake Andersson and co-driver Sven-Olof Svedberg looked all set to win, until the final stages, when a broken driveshaft on their Group 2 Porsche 911 resulted in the maximum penalty of 500 marks on stage 45, which put them down to fourth place. They drove furiously for the remaining part of the rally, but could only pull back one place. Bjorn Waldergäärd moved up one on his last year's placing, finishing in second spot in another 911 Porsche. The International London Gulf Rally lived up to its tough reputation, with just over 40 competitors finishing out of 120 starters.

On Tuesday, June 27, the star studded entry assembled at the Excelsior Hotel, Manchester Airport. A look through the list of competitors gave one the impression of quality, with a strong flavour of over-seas challenge. In fact, no less than 47 crews were from other shores, with the Swedish contingent greatest in number and apparent ability. The plot was laid by the organizers of the event, the London Motor Club, and stirred by Clerk of the Course, David Seigle-Morris. The ingredients of 1,350 road miles and 460 miles of special tests on tortuous Forestry Commission tracks, to be consumed in three days and nights. The incentives being supplied by the sponsors, Gulf Oil, to the tune of over £3,000 with a tasty £1,000 first prize.

At 9 p.m. on Tuesday, actress Miss Susan Hampshire started the first car away, and Ake Andersson/Sven-Olof Svedberg sped the Porsche down the ramp, soon to be followed by the rest of the field. The route wound its way to the first real test of the rally, the Welsh special stages. All having been calculated at a 50 m.p.h. average, competitors needed to fly, and this they did. On the very first, Clocaenog—Ake

Andersson set the pace with the Porsche, being 10 seconds faster than Bengt Söderström/Gunnar Palm, in the works fuel-injected Lotus Cortina, said to develop 152 b.h.p. with a BRM camshaft. Bjorn Waldergäärd, Porsche and Ove Andersson equalled Söderström's time, followed closely by the Finn, Simo Lampinen and Erik Carlsson both driving V4 Saabs. Tony Fall in the works Cooper S was only one second farther back. Already disaster struck the Swedish pair, Ulf Björkman and Sören Andersson, retiring their Volvo 122S. On the second Clocaenog stage Norwegians Jan Nielsen and Sverre Bryde rolled their two stroke Saab. By the third stage Ake Andersson had increased his lead, and beat the other Porsche of Bjorn Waldergäärd by 10 seconds on this stage. Ove Andersson, Carl Orrenius/Gustav Schröderheim, V4 Saab, and Simo Lampinen were next fastest. Moving towards Bettws-y-Coed, stage 6 saw the retirement of one of the Rally's potential winners Vic Elford and Terry Harriman running out of track, and wedging the Porsche 911S on a stony shelf, after the car had jumped out of gear due to broken gear selector mechanism.

At the end of stage 7 the positions showed that Ake Andersson was still in the lead, but Tony Fall had pulled up to second place in the Cooper S due to some hectically fast motoring. This elevation was short lived when his Mini left the track, losing over five minutes. Bjorn Waldegäärd, Porsche, Carl Orrenius, Saab V4, Ove Andersson, Lotus Cortina, Erik Carlsson, Saab V4, Bengt Söderström, Lotus Cortina were next in line, tailed by the two V4 Saab's of Simo Lampinen and Häkan Lindberg, with Roger Clark in 10th overall position. Mrs. Pat Carlsson running under the Moss family number of seven, was well placed, despite the inconvenience of getting a puncture on a stage.

By the time the infamous Dovey stage was reached, mist gave an added hazard for the competitors. The rough going was taking its toll and past winner of this event

Roger Clark retired with noisy ends, after a broken oil pipe had drained the engine dry on the works fuel-injected Lotus Cortina. Barry Williams and Tommy Thompson rolled their Rally Imp although they managed to get it going again, and finally finished second in their class.

Dyffryn Castell was a time control, and a refuelling point with petrol pumped from a tanker into barrels to conform with the many regulations. However, before this point was reached the Bill Mellis/David Michael, Cortina GT, had run out of petrol on a stage and retired. This was sur-prising, as the petrol is supplied free, making the London Gulf the least expensive of the Internationals, all being covered by the £25 entry fee. The rally route squeezed out of the southern end of Wales towards Glou-cester. The Welsh stages had been tough as expected. Roy Fidler had experienced a damaging roll in the Triumph 2000 and made the remark that "It leaned over a bit too far". However, he and co-driver Barry Hughes carried on, and retained a high position. The two fast Renaults of Jean-Francois Piot, and Stig-Sune Hallstrom had their rear screens pop out; a generous help-ing of masking tape remedied the problem. Many of the cars were showing scars, and by the time the last one reached Oulton Park, 30 of the original 120 were missing.

Oulton Park was not used because of its circuit, but as a three-hour rest period. Grouped under their banners, the various service crews worked like Trojans. Gearboxes and trans-axles appeared to be most sought after, halfshafts, engine mount-ings, springs and shockers were replaced in great numbers, and the welding torch was being used to zip up a variety of holes and loose ends. New tyres were being fitted as though they cost the price of horse shoes, although the more private runners were less extravagant. The eventual winning Lotus Cortina had a new gearbox fitted, looking rather precarious propped up by two sets of wheels.

Continued on page 80

Glimpse of the winner, the Ove Andersson/John Davenport Lotus Cortina.

Hard cornering during one of the special stages by the Stig Blomqvist/Ulf Osterman Saab which finished eighth in general category and first in class one.

Slightly dented as a result of a roll during the Welsh stages, the Roy Fidler/Barry Hughes Triumph 2000 motored on, finishing sixth in general category and third in class.

Amongst the papers handed to the crews when they re-started for the Wednesday night session were up-to-date computer-calculated positions of competitors. This information spurred many on, and resulted in a hotter pace being set by the top crews, especially those who found themselves farther down the chart than expected, and in the end probably spelt their undoing. The official placings at this juncture, including 20 special stages, showed the Porsche of Ake Andersson comfortably in the lead with 1,151 penalty marks, followed by his team mate Bjorn Waldergäärd on 1,408. The other leading runners being Carl Orrenius/Gustav Schröderheim, Saab V4, 1,456; Ove Andersson/Lotus Cortina, 1,486; Erik Carlsson/David Stone, Saab V4, 1,537; Simo Lampinen/Torsten Palm, Saab V4, 1,598; Lars Ytterbring/Lars Persson, Cooper S, 1,603; Häkan Lindberg/Bo Ohlsson, Saab V4 and Bengt Söderström, Lotus Cortina, 1,797.

The rally route followed the A6 to the Scottish Border, for the next series of stages, west of Dumfries. A familiar Scotch-like drizzle made the going more difficult, and lost marks became more common. The leading positions after six more stages saw only two changes. Erik Carlsson dropping two places and Lars Ytterbring moving up to take over. The fast and successful Frenchman Jean-Francois Piot wedged his Renault out of sight on the "Greystoke Stage," so he and his Paris-based co-driver John Brown had ended their fight. The other Renault of Stig-Sune Hallstrom soon followed when the stub axle gave up. Tony Fall and Mike Wood

ended their Cooper S challenge in a tree on stage 29 "Dalbeattie". The seeded entry of the rally organisers was proving more reliable than the Wimbledon selection, but the cars were behaving with less consistency than the rackets, and with the pressure on, retirements became more evident. The bigger V4 engines were taking more out of the Saab gearboxes, and in consequence were proving more vulnerable than the older two-stroke version. The Opel Kadett of Jon Flom smashed a wheel and lost its brake fluid. Ronald Larsson also retired after an excursion that damaged the Volvo's radiator.

The rally route travelled from east to west during Thursday, and moved on to the exciting "Wauchope" (stage 43) west of Hawick. Wauchope was a fast stage of 4.03 miles with a bogey time of 4.50 minutes. The two Porsches of Bjorn Waldergäärd and Ake Andersson were fastest in 4.26 and 4.28 minutes respectively, they were also leading the rally. Third fastest on this stage in 4.29 minutes was the Lotus Cortina of Ove Andersson, who had moved up to third place, and was closing the gap on the second Porsche. Retirements up to this point included the remaining fuel-injected works Lotus Cortina of Bengt Söderström and the Häkan Lindberg, V4 Saab, although another V4 Saab of Olav Bromark was improving. Soon to join the list of casualties were the two V4 Saabs of Erik Carlsson/David Stone and Mrs. Pat Moss Carlsson/Liz Nystrom and the Lars Ytterbring Cooper S, resulting in some new faces appearing in the Top Ten. Roy Fidler was still there, and despite various

problems Tony Chappell/Hywel Hughes had their Lotus Cortina well placed.

The lead dramatically changed when the leader broke down, and was towed out of stage 45, "Bewshaugh". Although Ake Andersson pushed the repaired Porsche he was unable to re-establish his lead; and the second Porsche of Bjorn Waldergäärd went off tune and lost oil. The Ove Andersson/John Davenport Lotus Cortina took the lead, knowing they would not suffer the halfshaft trouble of Söderström, with two new ones fitted. The North England stages were smooth and fast, working through Yorkshire to Croft where a "Rally cross" course ended the special stages, and a gentle belt to the finish at Manchester Airport brought the London Gulf Rally to an end on Friday morning. Ⓜ

Provisional results

General category: 1 Ove Andersson/John Davenport, Lotus Cortina, 2,880 penalty marks; **2** Bjorn Waldergäärd/Lars Helmer, Porsche 911, 2,989; **3** Ake Andersson/Sven-Olof Svedberg, Porsche 911, 3,009; **4** Carl Orrenius/Gustav Schröderheim, Saab V4, 3,078; **5** Simo Lampinen/Torsten Palm, Saab V4, 3,801; **6** Roy Fidler/Barry Hughes, Triumph 2000, 4,497; **7** Tony Chappell/Hywel Hughes Lotus Cortina, 4,947; **8** Stig Blomqvist/Ulf Osterman, Saab, 5,076; **9** Olov Bromark/Rolf Eriksson, Saab V4, 5,276; **10** Bob Bean/Brian Marchant, Cortina GT, 5,559.

Class winners: Class 1: 1 Stig Blomqvist/Ulf Osterman, Saab, 5,076; **2** Leslie Cowan/Arnold Price, Morris Mini, 11,343; **3** Graham Rood/Roger Palethorpe, Cooper S, 12,817. **Class 2: 1** Gunnar Blomqvist/Mrs. Ingelov Blomqvist, Cooper S, 6,337; **2** Robert Murray/Ronald Palmer, Cooper S, 6,805; **3** Bob Freeborough/L. F. Harris, Cooper S, 8,745. **Class 3: 1** Ove Andersson/John Davenport, Lotus Cortina, 2,880; **2** Carl Orrenius/Gustav Schröderheim, Saab V4, 3,078; **3** Hakan Lindberg/Bo Ohlsson, Saab V4, 3,801. **Class 4: 1** Bjorn Waldergäärd/Lars Helmer, Porsche 911, 2,989; **2** Ake Andersson/Sven-Olof Svedberg, Porsche 911, 3,009; **3** Roy Fidler/Barry Hughes, Triumph 2000, 4,497. **Class 5: 1** John Sprinzel/Gerry Ryan, M.G. Midget, 7,129; **2** Barry Williams/Tommy Thompson, Rally Imp, 9,531; **3** John Woodward/Alex. Jardine, M.G. Midget, 11,758. **Classes 6 and 7: 1** Bob Bean/Brian Marchant, Cortina GT, 5,559; **2** David Pollard/David Fawcett, Rally Imp, 6,913; **3** Gerry McNamara/Brian Cusack, Cortina GT, 6,937.

Ford Cortina-Lotus 1,560 c.c.

AT A GLANCE: Eager, tireless performance from very smooth and free-revving twin-cam engine. Road-holding, steering and brakes all in sports car category. Ride a little joggy when laden, levels out at speed. Fuel consumption good in relation to performance. All controls light and positive.

MANUFACTURER
Ford Motor Co. Ltd. Warley, Brentwood, Essex.

PRICES

Basic ..	..	..	£869 0s 0d
Purchase Tax ..		..	£199 2s 11d
Total (in G.B.) .			£1,068 2s 11d

EXTRAS (inc. P.T.)

Laminated windscreen..			£15 19s 7d
Competition steering wheel	..	..	£7 0s 0d
Radio ..	..	..	£26 15s 4d

PERFORMANCE SUMMARY

Mean maximum speed	104 m.p.h.
Standing start ¼-mile ..	18·2 sec
0–60 m.p.h. ..	11·0 sec
30–70 m.p.h. (through gears)	11·3 sec
Fuel consumption ..	24 m.p.g.
Miles per tankful ..	240

OCCASIONALLY there comes a new model which is so different from, and superior to, the one it replaces, that we regret the continuation of the same name. With the latest product of Ford's association with Lotus, the Cortina retains much of its dynamic performance, yet is so much more refined than the earlier car that there is scarcely any comparison between them. It is immensely better, and is now a thoroughly satisfying high-performance car.

In basic make-up, the Lotus version of the Cortina is the two-door GT saloon fitted with the same 110 b.h.p. engine as is used in the Lotus Elan. This is evolved from the in-line four-cylinder 1½-litre unit, with bores enlarged from 81mm to 82.6mm to give 1,560 c.c.; and it has a cylinder head with two chain-driven overhead camshafts and twin Weber 40 DCOE side-draught carburettors. The transformation which this engine brings about is remarkable, and serves as very impressive proof of the old saying that the engine is the heart of a car.

Excellent smoothness, with even torque from as little as 10 m.p.h. in top, and really forceful acceleration at almost any speed and in any gear, are combined with low noise level and complete absence of fuss or temperament. A faint hum can be heard all the time from the camshaft drive chains, but this is a pleasant sound and there is barely any more noise or vibration right up to maximum revs. At a cruising speed of 90 m.p.h., which the Cortina-Lotus keeps up very easily indeed, the rev counter reveals that the engine is turning over at 5,000 r.p.m., but to the driver's ear it sounds much less; and there is no impression that the engine is working too hard or that an overdrive or higher gearing are needed.

Compared with the previous model, the new car has a higher top gear (3.78 instead of 3.90 to 1) yet is bigger and weighs 1½ cwt more. Its mean maximum speed of 104 m.p.h. is 3 m.p.h. slower than before, but because of a gearbox change the standing start acceleration figures are not much affected at the lower speeds. The new car reaches 30 m.p.h. in 3.6sec—a fraction quicker than before —but from rest to 100 m.p.h. it is nearly 10sec slower, at 44sec.

The Cortina-Lotus is still a very fast car, and as there are no external signs to distinguish it from a plain 1300 model except three tiny Lotus badges on the tail and rear quarter ▶

Autocar road test number 2146

Make: Ford
Type: Cortina-Lotus 1,560 c.c.

TEST CONDITIONS
Weather: Fine, sunny.
Wind: 15-20 m.p.h.
Temperature: 29 deg.C. (84 deg.F.)
Barometer: 29·40in. Hg.
Humidity: 30 per cent.
Surfaces: Dry, concrete and asphalt.
Figures taken at 7,500 miles by our own staff at the Motor Industry Research Association proving ground at Nuneaton.

WEIGHT
Kerb weight 17·9cwt (2,009lb-912kg) (with oil, water and half-full fuel tank)
Distribution, per cent F, 52·6; R, 47·4
Laden as tested: 21·4cwt (2,394lb-1,087kg)

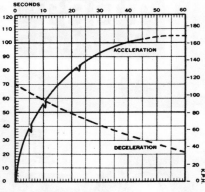

MAXIMUM SPEEDS

Gear	m.p.h.	k.p.h.	r.p.m.
Top (mean)	104	167	5,850
(best)	105	169	5,900
3rd	83	138	6,500
2nd	58	93	6,500
1st	39	63	6,500

Standing ¼-Mile 18·2 sec 76 m.p.h.
Standing Kilometre 32·2 sec 92 m.p.h.

TIME IN SECONDS	3·6	5·6	7·9	11·0	14·9	20·1	30·9	44·0
TRUE SPEED M.P.H.	30	40	50	60	70	80	90	100
INDICATED SPEED	32	42	52	63	73	84	94	105

Mileage recorder 3·2 per cent over-reading.   Test distance 2,152 miles.

Speed range, gear ratios and time in seconds

m.p.h.	Top (3·78)	3rd (5·28)	2nd (8·86)	1st (11·21)
10— 30	10·0	7·7	4·4	3·0
20— 40	10·0	6·7	4·1	—
30— 50	9·8	6·3	4·5	—
40— 60	10·6	6·4	—	—
50— 70	12·4	6·9	—	—
60— 80	15·4	8·8	—	—
70— 90	18·7	—	—	—
80—100	23·2	—	—	—

FUEL CONSUMPTION

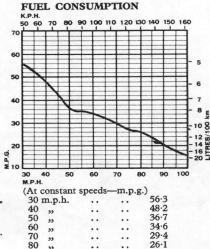

(At constant speeds—m.p.g.)

30 m.p.h.			56·3
40 „			48·2
50 „			36·7
60 „			34·6
70 „			29·4
80 „			26·1
90 „			20·5
100 „			16·1

Typical m.p.g. 24 (11·8 litres/100km)
Calculated (DIN) m.p.g. 26·7 (10·6 litres/100km)
Overall m.p.g. 22·2 (12·7 litres/100km)
Grade of fuel, Premium, 4-star (min 97RM)

OIL CONSUMPTION
Miles per pint (SAE 10W/30) .. 350

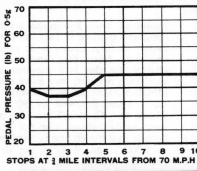

STOPS AT ¼ MILE INTERVALS FROM 70 M.P.H.

BRAKES (from 30 m.p.h. in neutral)

Load	g	Distance
25 lb.	0·36	84 ft
50 „	0·78	39 „
75 „	0·95	31·7 „
100 „	1·01	29·8 „

Handbrake 0·35   86 „
  Max. Gradient, 1 in 3
Clutch Pedal: 20lb and 5in.

TURNING CIRCLES
Between kerbs L, 30ft 8in.; R, 29ft 6in.
Between walls L, 33ft 1in.; R, 31ft 11in.
Steering wheel turns, lock to lock   4·3

HOW THE CAR COMPARES:
MAXIMUM SPEED (mean) M.P.H.

70   80   90   100   110
- Ford Cortina-Lotus
- Alfa Romeo Giulia Super
- Auto Union Audi 90 2 door
- Ford Corsair 2000E
- Renault 8 Gordini 1300

0-60 M.P.H. (sec)

20   10   0
- Ford Cortina-Lotus
- Alfa Romeo Giulia Super
- Auto Union Audi 90 2 door
- Ford Corsair 2000E
- Renault 8 Gordini 1300

STANDING START ¼-MILE (sec.)

30   20   10
- Ford Cortina-Lotus
- Alfa Romeo Giulia Super
- Auto Union Audi 90 2 door
- Ford Corsair 2000E
- Renault 8 Gordini 1300

M.P.G. OVERALL

10   20   30
- Ford Cortina-Lotus
- Alfa Romeo Giulia Super
- Auto Union Audi 90 2 door
- Ford Corsair 2000E
- Renault 8 Gordini 1300

PRICES

Ford Cortina Lotus	£1,068
Alfa Romeo Giulia Super	£1,499
Auto Union Audi 90 2-door	£1,147
Ford Corsair 2000E	£1,008
Renault Gordini 1300	£1,231

Left: With dark upholstery the multi-pleated door trim does not look too fussy. Tufted carpets, with rubber heel insert for the driver, are standard but the padded wheel is an extra. Right: The front seats tip forward for access to the rear, but the short end of the safety belt tends to get jammed between the seat and the central glove-box-cum-armrest

panels, many drivers of fast cars are left behind looking somewhat surprised.

This really sporting performance and response to the throttle come easily and make the car a real pleasure to drive on today's crowded and restricted roads. The very even torque curve spreads over an unusually wide rev range starting from below 1,000 r.p.m. and extending to 6,500 r.p.m. At this speed, which is the start of the red sector on the rev counter, an ignition cut-out operates. When taking the performance figures it was important always to change up at about 6,300 r.p.m. so that the break in ignition and momentary pause in performance were avoided.

A very "soft" clutch is fitted, and the rear wheel grip is so good that it is impossible to spin the wheels on a dry surface even if the clutch is let in abruptly at about 5,000 r.p.m. For best getaway, the clutch has to be held slipping until the car is well under way. With its high maximum of nearly 40 m.p.h., bottom gear is really useful, yet with care and enough controlled clutch slip it was just possible to get away, two-up, on a 1-in-3 gradient.

The Ford gearbox has been praised many times before for its positive, light and fairly short-travel change which can be whisked from one gear to the next without any synchromesh delay or gear crash. Some gear whine is audible in the indirect ratios; one could never forget to change up and stay in third by mistake.

Although the final drive ratio is a shade higher, raising top gear speed per 1,000 r.p.m. from 17.4 to 17.8, the indirect ratios are all appreciably lower than before, answering criticisms that the previous car was too high geared in its indirects. The gears now seem better spaced as well, and the maxima of 39 for bottom gear, 58 in second and 83 m.p.h. for third

gear show that the Cortina-Lotus is still a high-geared car. The diminutive wooden gear lever knob of the earlier car is now replaced by a more conventional round one which is more comfortable to the hand. Instead of having to lift and move the lever to the left for reverse, the driver now simply knocks it to the right and back parallel with top.

Fuel consumption, with an overall figure of 22 m.p.g. was better than with the previous car, but a larger fuel tank is needed. With capacity of only 10 gallons, and rather vague fuel gauge, the tendency is to refuel when there are still three gallons left, so the effective range becomes about 160 miles. At first, no specific recommendation about fuel grade was found in the handbook, so premium fuel (97-octane, four-star) was used satisfactorily for the whole test mileage, which is commendable in view of the 9.5-to-1 compression ratio. More detailed study later revealed that Ford prefer to play safe and recommend Super (5-star) in the specification.

In warm summer weather throughout the test, it was never necessary to use the choke for the first start of the day; the engine always fired and pulled strongly at once, with just a touch of throttle. Occasionally, starting when hot gave problems; the twin Weber carburettors can be flooded easily.

Coil spring rear suspension with A-bracket location proved unreliable on the first few hundred Cortina-Lotuses so this layout was abandoned in production in favour of the standard GT arrangement of half elliptic leaf springs with trailing radius arms to prevent axle wind-up. Pirelli Cinturato or Goodyear G800 tyres are standard (we had Pirellis on the test car), and the cornering adhesion on both wet and dry roads is exceptional. It is basically an understeering car, though the balance is not far off neutral, and with so much torque available it is very easy to kick the tail round on sharp corners giving almost an oversteering effect and calling for opposite lock to correct the tail swing. When power is used in a

The under bonnet layout looks tidy, but access is nowhere particularly good. However, the air cleaner box is quite easily unbolted for access to the sparking plugs

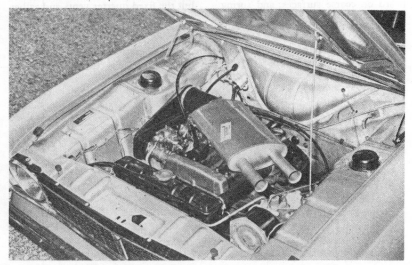

In this view only the wide rim wheels and small Lotus badges (one matching the fuel filler cap, and one on each side near the tail lamps) identify the Cortina-Lotus; but it also has a matt radiator grille in place of the bright one of the Cortina 1300

low gear on corners in the wet, the beginnings of some axle tramp can be felt but this is well restrained.

Recirculating ball steering gives light and accurate control, and it is much higher geared than its 4·3 turns from lock to lock suggest; the compact 30ft turning circles account for this, and with light steering as well, the Cortina is a very easy car to manoeuvre. Wide-rimmed wheels and fat tyres increase the king-pin offset and decrease the self-centring effect slightly compared with a standard Cortina. Over the last half turn to the straight-ahead position the steering does not self-centre at all. The car does not wander in side winds, yet it never feels quite as directionally stable at high speed as it should. The wood-rimmed Lotus steering wheel is no longer fitted and we had a neat pvc-covered one on the test car; it costs £7 extra, the normal Cortina wheel being standard.

Initial travel of the suspension is very soft, and the front dips noticeably under quite gentle braking. With three or four people on board this softness is taken up by the extra weight, and the ride is a little hard and choppy over irregularities and not as comfortable as when only one or two are in the car. Regardless of load, however, the ride levels down very well at speed. No road roar is heard on coarse surfaces, and spring movements are well damped.

Girling front disc brakes with drums at the rear and strong servo assistance are standard. Retardation increases progressively in almost direct proportion to extra pedal load, up to 75lb. Hard braking (100lb pedal load) gives a little extra, to an excellent maximum of over 1g. Fade tests had hardly any effect on the brakes at all. A pull-out umbrella handle control under the facia for the handbrake is a little out of keeping, but it works very well; a strong pull holds securely on 1-in-3, and the handbrake is above average in giving a 0·35g stop at 30 m.p.h.

The light pedal loads needed on the brakes in ordinary swift driving are in keeping with the rest of the car's controls; steering, gearchange, and particularly the clutch (with operating load of only 20lb) are all very light. Many drivers were also happy with the pedal layout, but not with the driving position. Here one's leg length is critical because of the poor design of the seat adjustment. As the seat is pushed rearwards, its whole angle alters, and from being about right for small drivers the seat backrest becomes much too upright from about halfway back on its rearward adjustment. The seats are otherwise comfortable both front and rear, with ample cushion length and, as they are fairly softly upholstered, occupants tend to sink into them to be well-located on corners. Legroom in the rear is adequate even with the front seat well back.

Visibility is quite good; the top of the steering wheel does not intrude, but the fixed quarter vents and rather thick screen pillars obstruct vision to some extent. The wipers clear the screen effectively, but work at only one fairly vigorous rate. The twist knob for the wipers is also pressed in to work the washers. Tiny switches beside the main instruments control the panel lamps and side and headlamps. There are separate green telltales for the indicators on each side, and the switch has multiple functions as is becoming more and more popular on British cars today; it flashes or dips the headlamps and sounds the horn. In emergency it may not always be easy to push the lever in to sound the horns, and the frail "beep" which results is in any case inadequate at high speeds.

In the showroom, the minor instruments would appear very well positioned, on an extension of the facia capping, centrally above the heater controls. In practice, however, they are liable to be obscured by reflections, and are not too visible to the driver unless he takes his eyes off the road to look straight at them. During the test we became rather instrument-conscious, as the dynamo often went on strike, leaving the battery occasionally too weak to start, and towards the end of the test a heater hose repeatedly blew off.

Trouble was also experienced with the oil filler cap occasionally coming undone even after careful tightening; the same trouble has been experienced with this engine in the Elan, and it seems time for this aspect of the design to be improved.

With Ford's splendid Aeroflow ventilation, rear seat passengers, as well as those in the front, benefit from the good exchange of air through the car, and even in hot weather it is excusable that the rear side windows are fixed. Front quarter vents are also fixed but even this does not completely cure the problem of wind whistle at speed, which gets progressively worse from about 75 m.p.h. onwards.

Both front seats tip forward for access to the rear, and there are no safety catches to hold them upright in event of an accident. The Lotus version is not available in four-door form. Locking arrangements of the doors leave room for some improvement, as there is no outside key-

An elastic strap secures the toolkit beside the spare wheel. The ignition key has to be used every time to open the boot, as the lid is self locking

lock for the passenger door.
Care is needed when opening the bonnet. As the upper part of the central C motif in the grille is pressed, it tends to move sideways towards the left of the car. If the thumb is pressed on it to work the catch, there is danger of catching the nail on the side of the grille; but happily we do not speak from experience. The lid then lifts, after releasing the safety catch, and reveals a very clean and purposeful under-bonnet layout.

It is not until routine maintenance is contemplated that the snags are apparent. Then it is seen that the air filter must be unbolted and removed for access to the plugs, and that the distributor—whose position was dictated by the original engine design—and the coil are completely obscured by the carburettors. It is even a fiddly job to remove the dipstick.

Buyers will no doubt have to ponder hard to make up their minds

between the Ford Corsair 2000E, which comes complete with radio, four doors and reclining seats as standard in a total price some £60 lower, and the Cortina Lotus which looks outwardly so similar to a £700 Cortina 1300. It is a car in which a test drive would be essential before deciding to buy, and then the man who values a real driver's car—a four-seater with sports car performance and handling—will have no difficulty in making up his mind.

SPECIFICATION: FORD CORTINA-LOTUS (FRONT ENGINE, REAR-WHEEL DRIVE)

ENGINE
Cylinders .. .. 4, in line
Cooling system .. Water; pump, fan and thermostat
Bore .. .. 82·6mm (3·25in.)
Stroke .. .. 72·8mm (2·87in.)
Displacement .. 1,560 c.c. (95·17 cu. in.)
Valve gear .. Twin overhead camshafts
Compression ratio 9·5-to-1: Min. octane rating: 100
Carburettors .. Two Weber 40 DCOE
Fuel pump .. AC mechanical
Oil filter .. .. Full flow
Max. power .. 109·5 b.h.p. (net) at 6,000 r.p.m.
Max. torque .. 106·5 lb. ft. (net) at 4,500 r.p.m.

TRANSMISSION
Clutch .. .. Borg and Beck diaphragm spring 8·0in. dia.
Gearbox .. .. 4-speed all-synchromesh
Gear ratios .. Top, 1·0; Third, 1·40; Second, 2·01; First, 2·97; Reverse 3·32
Final drive .. Hypoid bevel, 3·78-to-1

CHASSIS and BODY
Construction .. Integral with steel body

SUSPENSION
Front .. .. Independent, MacPherson strut, coil springs, telescopic dampers, anti-roll bar

Rear .. .. Live axle half-elliptic leaf springs, telescopic dampers, radius arms

STEERING
Type .. .. Burman re-circulating ball
Wheel dia. .. 15·5in.

BRAKES
Make and type .. Girling discs front, drums rear
Servo .. .. Girling vacuum
Dimensions .. F, 9·62in. dia. R, 9·00in. dia. 1·75in. wide shoes
Swept area .. F, 189·5 sq. in. R, 96·1 sq. in. Total 285·6 sq. in. (267 sq. in./ ton laden)

WHEELS
Type .. .. Pressed steel disc 5·5in. wide rim
Tyres—make .. Pirelli or Goodyear
—type .. Cinturato or G800 radial-ply tubeless
—size .. 165-13in.

EQUIPMENT
Battery .. .. 12-volt 38-amp. hr.
Generator .. Lucas C40 22 amp. d.c.
Headlamps .. Lucas sealed beam 120/90-watt (total)
Reversing lamp .. Extra
Electric fuses .. None
Screen wipers .. Single speed, self-parking
Screen washer .. Standard, manual plunger
Interior heater .. Air blending type

Heated backlight .. Not available
Safety belts .. Standard (static type)
Interior trim .. Pvc seats, pvc headlining
Floor covering .. Carpet
Starting handle .. No provision
Jack .. .. Screw pillar
Jacking points .. 2 each side under sills
Windscreen .. Zone toughened (standard); laminated on test car (extra)
Underbody protection .. Phosphate treatment prior to painting

MAINTENANCE
Fuel tank .. .. 10 Imp. gallons (no reserve) (45·5 litres)
Cooling system .. 12·5 pints (including heater) (7·1 litres)
Engine sump .. 7·5 pints (4·3 litres) SAE 10W/30. Change oil ever 2,500 miles; change filter element every 2,500 miles
Gearbox .. .. 1·75 pints SAE 80. Change oil only at first 2,500 miles
Final drive .. 2·0 pints SAE 90EP. No change needed
Grease .. .. 1 point every 2,500 miles
Tyre pressures .. F, 24; R, 24 p.s.i. (normal driving). F, 24; R, 30 p.s.i. (full load)

PERFORMANCE
Top gear m.p.h. per 1,000 r.p.m.   17·8
Mean piston speed at max. power   2,867ft/min
B.h.p. per ton laden   104·7

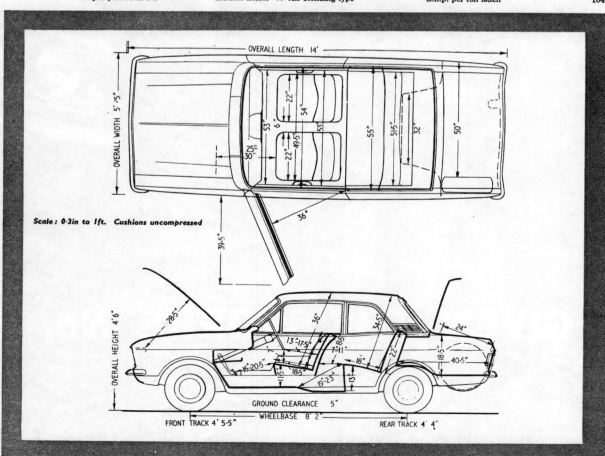

Scale: 0·3in to 1ft. Cushions uncompressed

OVERALL LENGTH 14'
OVERALL WIDTH 5'5"
OVERALL HEIGHT 4'6"
GROUND CLEARANCE 5"
FRONT TRACK 4' 5·5"
WHEELBASE 8' 2"
REAR TRACK 4' 4"

GIVEN THE WORKS No. 8/

IT'S the old model really, with the square front and back, that one associates most with international rallies. Jim Clark shooting off into the trees on last year's RAC is typical of the way the white and green-striped machines hit the headlines. And while the big names were having their excursions, the invincible Swedish drivers were quietly taking away all the prizes. The success story of the Cortina-Lotus is as long as any arm and longer. The name of Roger Clark seems almost synonymous, yet it was Bengt Soderstrom who won the RAC and Swedish Rallies in a Cortina-Lotus.

For a couple of seasons now we have been putting gentle pressure on Ford's competition department to let us try one of the "real" rally cars. The truth of the matter is that there just has not been a car to spare. This year, after the new model was announced in March, a Saluki bronze car was built for Soderstrom to drive on the Acropolis rally and he came third. Without any further preparation he took the same car to Sweden for the Jant Rally and then after a quick check at Boreham it went on the London Rally in the hands of Ove Andersson, who won. Immediately after that event we had a call from Ford to say we could collect this car and keep it a week.

It was a hot and sticky day when I arrived at the seclusion of Boreham airfield where the test track and competition department are housed. The car was left-hand drive and exactly as it finished the rally, except for a quick wash. No real rev limit (but *please* don't burst the engine) and watch out for the odd characteristics of the limited-slip diff.

The seat is strictly tailored to Soderstrom's stern and is hard. It doesn't adjust and hugs the buttocks firmly. Of course, if you are bigger or smaller than Soderstrom, then you will bounce or jam. All the interior has been treated with matt black paint making it look like a war-time fighter plane and there is the usual collection of special circuits, switches, Halda and watches.

We were surprised to find only lap-strap seat belts. Apparently a lot of the Swedish drivers prefer it this way because they are afraid of whip-lash neck injuries if they impact with something solid ("roadside furniture," the quaint M.o.T. call it) and they always brace themselves pretty hard. The navigator usually grips the roof handle, with his other arm round the back of the driver's seat.

Ove Andersson was the outright winner of this year's Gulf London Rally in the works Cortina-Lotus which Autocar has been testing (left). Above: Apart from wheels and tyres, and the elastic to keep the boot lid secure, it looks much like any other Cortina-Lotus.

The degree of engine tune is not very high and I was surprised how tractable and untemperamental was the Cortina. Most of the rorty throb came from the air intakes of the Webers, naked as the Italians intended, and the exhaust was really quite tolerable. Several minutes of stop-start crawling through the City of London in heavy traffic caused no plug fouling nor any rise in temperature. Idling was smooth at about 1,000 r.p.m. but there was a tendency for everything to die for no reason unless one gave it the occasional blip to clear its throat.

It is possible to potter along at only 1,800 r.p.m. quite quietly at dead of night, but opening up from this speed causes a deep and very vibrant growl, which suddenly switches to full noise from 4,800 onwards. At 5,600 all the torque comes in as well and for really rapid progress the rev counter must be kept swinging between 4,500 and 7,500 r.p.m., which we took as the limit. The crescendo of mechanical whine, throb and beat as the revs build up, drop momentarily when gears are switched and then continue in a different key is something which has to be experienced. An American magazine once described it as something to make a grown man scream with ecstasy and I can't think of a better way of putting it, although I just become flushed and tingle inside.

This car was built for rough going, with sump guard and big knobbly radial-ply tyres. The whole of the underside had been rippled by tobogganing over rough tracks and ▶

WORKS CORTINA-LOTUS

Impressive lamp array and the sump guard for " Scandinavian skiers."
Right: Special midships stowage for a spare, extra petrol tankage and
other boot furniture for rallying

What rallying can do to a car; damage to the floor from rocks has destined
this body for scrap. Below: Soderstrom's tailored driving seat is said to be
quite comfortable if you are the same size as him; it's a pea in a pod fit

Lack of air cleaners on the twin Webers is the chief source of noise when
the Cortina-Lotus is motored hard; there seems to be an awful lot
of plumbing and wiring to keep in order

apparently this body shell was now fit only for scrap. The tyres sang on smooth surfaces like a police siren but really gripped, even on loose gravel.

The limited slip differential was deliberately slack to give some flexibility and insulation from vicious torque reversals. It made the most alarming crunch each time it freed, like someone standing on a wine glass. Each time the car moved off from rest the tail gave a tiny wiggle on its suspension as one side pushed before the other. At speed it had a kind of self-twitching effect which immediately set the car up automatically at a slight angle of drift. On smooth, good-friction surfaces the car under-steered as both rear wheels worked together, but on the rough stuff it seemed all too easy to emulate that dynamic style of the professionals, provided one had enough nerve.

One thing was most impressive above all else (and we have noticed this on most other rally cars). The whole car felt extremely sensitive to the steering, almost nervous, so that there was no reaction delay at all before it changed direction, often before the driver was conscious of moving the steering wheel. This is a characterstic the drivers demand. Any lack of immediate response could mean the difference between winning and crashing through the trees now that no reconnaissance to make pace notes for the special stages is allowed.

Taking the acceleration figures was a difficult task because there was too much grip to get the car away from rest quickly. This shows in the comparison with the standard car, which was 0·1 sec faster from 0 to 30 m.p.h. because it was possible to get some wheelspin. With its perfect close-ratio gearbox the works car reached 7,000 r.p.m. in top before the quarter-mile post and we had to back off the thottle before the kilometre to prevent over-revving.

Of the works cars we have now tested, this Ford is by far the most civilized and comfortable. It probably therefore takes less from the driver, or conversely the driver can put more into it for longer; which may be a reason for its success. It is certainly extremely exciting and the kind of machine that one can never leave standing; it just has to be driven

G. P. H. ■

Figures in brackets are for the Ford Cortina-Lotus tested in Autocar of 17 August, 1967.

Acceleration times (mean): *Speed range, gear ratios and time in seconds:*

m.p.h.	Top (4·70)	3rd (6·01)	2nd (7·87)	1st (10·79)
10–30	— (10·0)	7·9 (7·7)	5·4 (4·4)	3·5 (3·0)
20–40	9·4 (10·0)	6/2 (6·7)	3·9 (4·1)	2·9 (—)
30–50	7·7 (9·8)	5·6 (6·3)	3·9 (4·5)	—
40–60	7·8 (10·6)	5·3 (6·4)	—	—
50–70	7·5 (12·4)	5·4 (6·9)	—	—
69–80	7·5 (15·4)	— (8·8)	—	—
70–90	8·7 (18·7)	—	—	—
80–100	— (23·2)	—	—	—

From rest through gears to:

30 m.p.h.	..	..	3·7 sec (3·6 sec)
40 ,,	..	..	5·0 ,, (5·6 ,,)
50 ,,	..	..	6·9 ,, (7·9 ,,)
60 ,,	..	..	9·4 ,, (11·0 ,,)
70 ,,	..	..	12·1 ,, (14·9 ,,)
80 ,,	..	..	16·3 ,, (20·1 ,,)
90 ,,	..	..	21·1 ,, (30·9 ,,)
100 ,,	..	..	— ,, (44·0 ,,)

Standing quarter-mile 17·1 sec (18·2 sec)
Standing kilometre 32·1 sec (32·2 sec)

Maximum speeds in gears:

				m.p.h.	k.p.h.	r.p.m.
Top (mean)	...	...	...	97 (104)	156 (167)	7,500 (5,850)
(best)	..	..	..	97 (105)	156 (169)	7,500 (5,900)
3rd	..	..	..	75 (83)	120 (138)	7,500 (6,500)
2nd	..	..	..	57 (58)	92 (93)	7,500 (6,500)
1st	..	..	..	42 (39)	67 (63)	7,500 (6,500)

Overall fuel consumption for 630 miles:
23·3 m.p.g.; 12·0 litres/100km
(22·2 m.p.g.; 12·7 litres/100km)

REFINED RACER

The boys' racer grows up and gets civilised

THE NEW CORTINA LOTUS

QUITE a lot has happened to the Lotus-Cortina since it started life. In the old days it was a Cortina in body-shell alone, and all the works, from engine to rear suspension, were pure Lotus—and not too far removed from the racing Lotuses at that. It was taut, tough and very quick, and the nearest thing to an instant competition car that ever came out of a motor-factory.

Since then things have changed a bit. It now goes under the name of the Cortina-Lotus, and it's more of a Ford than a Lotus—in other words, it is more of a fast car for the family man than a roofed-in racer. It is quieter, more docile, more comfortable and more civilised: it has even lost such standard recognition-points as a wood-rim steering wheel and the white-with-green-side-flash colour finish that was officially exclusive to the Lotus-Cortina but which was aped by an awful lot of people without mechanical claim to the title (we once saw this colour scheme on an old Vauxhall Victor, so there!). The only way you can tell it apart from a Cortina GT without looking underneath nowadays is because the little badge says "Lotus" and not "GT".

For all this it hasn't actually lost very much, and is still one of the most sporting four-seaters around the place. The process of evolution is a pretty logical one. It just isn't necessary any more—not even as much as it was, say, five or six years ago—to associate high performance and good handling with harshness and discomfort. In fact, with a monster boot, comfortable seats, decent interior trim, full instrumentation and plenty of space inside for odds and sods PLUS the most sophisticated ventilation system outside the millionaire class it is a pretty sound investment for the chap who wants a car he can live in with the wife and kids as well as one which provides him with above the average in terms of go. It has a top speed of comfortably over the ton, gets from 0-60 in under ten seconds, and from 0-100 in not too much over the half-minute; maximum power arrives on the scale at six thousand revs; maximum torque is achieved at four-five, but this doesn't mean that it is inflexible. It is, in fact, very flexible, and the way the urge comes bounding in all the way from a thousand revs and upwards combines with a really first-class gearbox and excellent road-holding to give a sporting little old motor (as they say where the Ed. comes from) which is hard to beat when it comes to carting four bods about the place for exactly a thousand smackers or so.

The power comes from the latest version of the twin-cam Ford engine. The bore and stroke are 82·57 mm x 72·82 mm to give a total capacity of 1560 c.c.: the last time we came across the Lotus-Cortina they were 82·6 mm. x 72·75 mm., and the total cylinder capacity was 1,588 c.c. This is probably not particularly significant—what is important is that because the new-style body weighs more than the old one and is aerodynamically less efficient, Mr. Ford has re-jetted the twin Weber 40 DCOE carbs and fitted as standard the camshaft which used in the old days to be that fitted to the Special Equipment model. This gives an increase according to the book of four horse-power, putting the total figure up to 109·5 at 6,000 revs., while maximum torque is realised at 500 revs. further up the scale.

The gearbox is mated to the engine by a diaphragm-spring clutch and is similar to that fitted to the Corsair V4 GT—now the 2000E. It has well-spaced ratios giving 37, 57 and 82 miles an hour in the bottom three cogs—all four forward gears have decent synchromesh, and the gearlever is one of the nicest to use on any medium-sized car. The clutch is very light and although you have to move the pedal rather a long way up and down is nevertheless a lot easier on the tootsies than it used to be on the hairy models. The final drive gear is very slightly higher than it used to be and gives 17·6 m.p.h. per thousand revs in top compared with 17·4.

As usual there are 9½ in. Girling discs on the front and 9 in. drums behind, with a servo to give lighter pedal pressures. Suspension has gone back to basic Ford instead of basic Lotus, as it was in the beginning but isn't now, to coin a phrase. At the front there are the usual Ford McPherson struts and coil springs, and semi-elliptic leaf springs and trailing arms at the back; 165 x 13 radial-ply tyres (standard options are Cinturatos or Goodyear G800s) are fitted to 5½J rims so that you get plenty of rubber on the road—and man alive, those tyres really look fat and businesslike.

The interior is very refined, really, considering how the Lotus-Cortina started life. The seats are more comfortable, the trim is better, there are carpets and a very well laid-out instrument panel, with an ammeter, oil pressure gauge, water temperature and fuel gauges in a little row on top of

Properly caged with the rest of the fierce ones.

the centre part of the facia; immediately in front of the driver are the speedometer and rev-counter, neatly matched and all pretty with white figures on black dials in the approved fashion. Aeroflow ventilation is built-in, naturally, the seats provide comfortable support—although most people would still like them to be adjustable further away from the wheel—and the steering wheel is pleasant to hold even if it isn't wood-rimmed any more, and at four turns from lock to lock you don't exactly get your fingers in a knot, although it could be slightly more highly-geared with some advantage in high-speed control.

So much for what it is—what about what it does? It does pretty nearly everything it ever used to, only it does it more quietly, more peacefully and in a more civilised manner. The boys' racer has, in fact, grown up into a pleasant high-speed touring machine which without much imagination can be turned out on to the hockey-stick at the local hill-climb and assuming that the pilot presses the loud pedal at the right moments it will not necessarily finish last in its class. The ride is pretty firm and you can feel the irregularities in the road surface, but this is a fairly small price to pay for first-class handling which is, to be honest, well up to any Lotus standards. The gearchange is fast, light and accurate, the synchromesh unbeatable but not an impediment to fast changes, and the roadholding is of the sort we like best—when the car can be made to slide predictably and controllably if you are really hanging it on, but if you're not in that much hurry (or if you pay for your own tyres!) it can be got round the bends very quickly indeed without so much as a squeal from the tyres. The pedals are well-placed for heel-and-toe operation, and the urge from the twin-cam engine is got on to the road without anything much in the way of fuss from the transmission— the wheels can be made to spin but axle tramp and wheel-hop is kept down very well indeed.

A cut-out is fitted to the ignition which operates at 6,500 r.p.m., thus preventing over-revving. This is no more than a very useful safety factor which in a missed change could save you from an expensive sort of bang: in normal driving is doesn't really show up and certainly isn't the kill-joy fitting which it might sound like in theory. In practice, you tend to change up at 6,000 because that's where maximum power is—we say maximum, although in fact this engine is so splendidly smooth and punchy nowadays that good solid urge flows through in an unbroken stream from a thousand revs upwards. You get some revs on and whack in the old clutch and fifty miles an hour shows up in just under seven seconds; sixty arrives in just under ten and in well under a quarter-minute you have reached the legal maximum (cries of "Shame"!) Assuming you can hop across to the continong and find a more enlightened transport ministry, or assuming that you have access to some of the small remaining areas of private land still left in this once-sceptred isle, you can try the fascinating and daredevil experiment of going up into the unexplored regions of eighty and even (whisper it) ninety miles an hour: it won't take long, come to that, because you can get to eighty in just four seconds longer than it takes to get to seventy and ninety shows up on the 140 m.p.h. speedo in a total of 25 seconds; keep it going just a little longer and you reach the ton in 38 seconds, which isn't at all bad for a weighty, chunky 1½-litre saloon, turning the scales in ready-for-the-road trim at comfortably over a ton.

So far as cruising speeds are concerned, it simply depends on the Government and how many borders you've crossed. Our legal limit is almost exactly four thousand on the rev-counter, so you can keep that up all day without even noticing. At five thousand you are doing just under ninety, and restrictions apart this would be a comfortable cruising speed. If only . . . !

If all this sounds lyrical, don't think there aren't snags. For a start we have only slightly gone into the seating. We said they're comfortable and provide good support—well, they are and they do. But the adjustment is just like it always used to be, and suffers from exactly the same things. You cannot get it far enough away from the wheel for comfort for most drivers; add to this the fact that the slides are angled so that the further back the cushion goes the more upright becomes the backrest, and you end up bent double in the middle—and still unable to get a decent driving position. Then there's the fittings—damn near de luxe in most respects, but spoiled by the proverbial ha'porth of tar in that there are only single-speed screen wipers, a terribly noisy heater fan, and rather poor washers. And so on. After all, this little old buggy cost over a grand these days and for this sort of money one might have been entitled to expect little points like this to have been attended to. After all, the 2000E Corsair is much better in most of these respects and costs less money.

CORTINA-LOTUS

ENGINE: Four cylinders, 82·57mm. x 72·82mm.; 1,560 c.c.; twin o.h.c.; compression ratio 9·5 to 1; twin 40 DCOE Webers; 109·5 b.h.p. at 6,000 r.p.m.

Transmission: Diaphragm spring clutch; four-speed and reverse gearbox with synchromesh on all four forward gears.

Suspension: Front, independent with coil springs and McPherson struts, anti-roll bar; rear, semi-elliptic leaf springs and trailing radius arms.

Brakes: Front, 9½ in. discs; rear, 9 in. drums, with servo assistance.

Dimensions: Overall length, 14 ft.; overall width, 5 ft. 5½ in.; overall height, 4 ft. 8 in.; ground clearance 5 in.; weight, 21¾ cwt.

PERFORMANCE
MAXIMUM SPEED 109 m.p.h.
Mean of 2 ways 105

Speeds in gears: First 37
Second 57
Third 82

ACCELERATION	m.p.h.	secs.
	0-30	3·5
	0-40	5·1
	0-50	6·8
	0-60	9·8
	0-70	13·3
	0-80	17·6
	0-90	25·0
	0-100	38·8

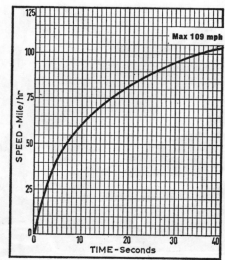

Manufacturers: Ford Motor Co. Ltd., Dagenham, Essex.
Price in U.K.: £1,068 including purchase tax.

LOTUS-

CTC 17E

CORTINA

MODERN MOTOR road REPORT

Under-statement at 105 mph

Under honest Ford bonnet, some new Chapman wizardry. Harold Dvoretsky reports from London

STATUS symbols just aren't what they used to be. At one time, if you owned a status symbol —by way of a souped-up version of the standard model owned by the bloke next door—you wanted the manufacturer to blazen it with symbols and stripes and beading down the side.

At least it had to be offered to you in a different color combination and preferably with a contrasting strip of color; like Ford's Falcon GT in Australia for instance.

In this way you could suitably impress not only the bloke next door, but also the peasants at the traffic lights who might have the same body shape (and it's cars, I mean, not the passengers in them).

But, ah, in this new world of changing fashions, this psychedelic era we live in, the status symbol's appearance has changed also. The reasons are pretty simple.

For a few bucks today, the kid down the street can blazen his car with go-faster striping, GT badges and chequered transfers to an extent that makes the old-type status symbol look perfectly dowdy.

Underside the kid mightn't have anything extra, but for his few bucks he has made his buggy look as expensive as any of those versions that once cost several hundreds more than the standard variety.

A change had to come about, I guess. To be with-it today requires more subtlety. Flamboyancy is on the way out. To make an impression with your expensive, higher-powered version, you need just understatement.

You need just enough to let the real enthusiast know you've got a car to beat his—and the clot who wouldn't know the difference doesn't really matter, anyway.

This all came to me—in a flash you might say—when I took myself out to Alf Belson's press car set up near London's suburb of Chiswick. It's here that Alf keeps the Ford press fleet, and tries to hammer them out

in record time after the world's motoring scribes have brought them back in varying degrees of shambles. Here, too, come the rally cars, the special event cars. It's a busy little workshop in a London backwater.

I'd gone out to collect the new Lotus-Cortina. Alf ushered me to a red Cortina shape—all plain bright red with just a green badge on the rear wing where they used to put the GT badge.

"Can't be," I said. "Only an expert would realise by the wide-based 5½ in. rims with low profile tyres, that there's a twin-cam donk beneath the bonnet". (You can imagine me saying it.)

But Alf was adamant. "You going to Zandvoort or aren't you going to Zandvoort?" he queried. I said I was, and departed.

The new Lotus-Cortina looks identical with the two-door GT version of the new Cortina range.

Internally there is the same well-laid-out interior with two big dials—

one speedo, the other tacho—right in front of the driver, and the four smaller dials centre-top of the dashboard for fuel, temperature, amps and oil pressure.

The only difference in instruments is that the speedo goes up to 140 mph and the tacho to 8,000 rpm.

There's the same solid gear lever connected to a delightful and well-spaced box (the new ratio box with the higher second gear used on the new GT version and the 2000E series Corsair).

Externally, the only difference apart from those I've already mentioned is the black mesh grille treatment. For those not wishing to be *avec*, as they say (or those requiring a little more

psychedelic treatment), you can still have the green stripe down the side on the white versions. You can also have Ford sidewinder striping along the lower body sill, and pretty bloody awful it looks, too.

Under the bonnet

But, anyway, it's not the body shape that attracts one to a Lotus-Cortina, it's what's under the bonnet. And there the twin cam engine is now supplied in slightly more powerful form than the original, which came out in 1963.

In those days the engine produced by Colin Chapman's Lotus concern at Cheshunt gave about 105 bhp net at 5,500 rpm. Today the engine is

tweaked at Ford's own factory and the car literally comes off the line.

Despite this semi-mass production method, the new twin cam gives 115 bhp gross (109 bhp nett) at 6,000 rpm.

The up-rating has meant refinement, and refinement has meant a much quieter sound from inside the cabin. The twin-choke Webers are now silenced with a huge, specially developed, air cleaner instead of the pancake variety.

Throat roar is something I can do without and this silencer — ungainly though it may be—does a very good job in the decibel department.

Continued on page 97

SPECIFICATIONS

Manufacturer: Ford Motor Co., Dagenham, G.B.
Test car supplied by them.
Price: £Stg. 1068 inc. tax.

ENGINE
Water cooled, 4 cylinders in line. Cast-iron block, five main bearings.
Bore x stroke .... 82.55 x 72.75 mm.
Capacity .... 1558 cc.
Compression .... 9.5 to 1
Carburettor .... 2 Weber 40 DCOE
Fuel pump .... mechanical
Fuel tank .... 10 gallons
Fuel recommended .... Super
Valve Gear .... dohc
Max. power (gross) ...... 115 bhp at 6000 rpm
Max. torque ...... 106 lb. ft. at 4500 rpm
Electrical system .... 12v.

TRANSMISSION
Four speed manual all synchro gearbox. Single dry plate 8in. clutch.

Gear	Ratio	Overall	Max. mph.
Rev.	3.324	12.555	—
1st	2.972	11.225	38
2nd	2.010	7.592	55
3rd	1.397	5.276	78
4th	1.00	3.777	105
Final drive ratio			3.77 to 1

CHASSIS
Wheelbase .... 8ft. 2in.
Track front .... 4ft. 5½in.
Track rear .... 4ft. 4in.
Length .... 14ft.
Width .... 5ft. 5in.
Height .... 4ft. 6in.
Clearance .... 6.3in.
Kerb weight .... 19 cwt.

SUSPENSION
Front: Independent by McPherson struts, coils and anti-roll bar.
Rear: Rigid axle, semi elliptics, trailing links, telescopic shock absorbers.

Brakes: Disc/drum, servo assisted; 285.6 sq. in. of swept area.

Steering .... Recirculating ball
Turning circle .... 30ft.

Wheels: Steel 5½J disc with 165 by 13 radial ply tyres.

PERFORMANCE

Top speed .... 105 mph
Standing quarter mile .... 17.5 sec.

Acceleration Zero to	seconds
30 mph	3.5
40 mph	5.1
50 mph	7.5
60 mph	10.1
70 mph	14.4
80 mph	20.9
90 mph	30.7

Consumption: 26.5 mpg.

VERY much one of the newer names in the tuning business is Westune, which have their home in a small garage in Bolton and have been in existence just four years. Their slogan is *Not the biggest name in tuning—so we try that bit harder*, and their record this year certainly bears that out.

Peter West, managing director of Westune, is a cheerful, burly 33-year-old who started his career as a qualified aircraft engineer in Cambridge. Not far from where he worked was Don Moore's workshop, and one day Peter decided that playing with motor cars might be more satisfying than playing with aeroplanes and he joined Moore, spending over four years with him during the era of the University team of A35s, Doc Shepherd's famous A40 and John Whitmore's original Mini.

Peter left Don Moore to move north and, after a period running a race preparation business in a disused stable in Bolton, Westune were launched in 1964. In a very short time they have built up a fine reputation for competition preparation, and this has provided most of Westune's business, although the firm is now expanding to cater for quality servicing of specialist cars and road conversions, there is a spares and accessory shop, and the staff has swollen to nine.

The competition side is still growing, too, for among the cars prepared by Westune are the pushrod Anglia of John Myerscough, which has been very successful in northern circuit events and was third in its class in the Redex Championship despite competing in none of the Brands Hatch rounds; on the hillclimb front, John Butterworth's supercharged Brabham BT14, Tom Warburton's Mini-Cooper S and John McCartney's 4WD Felday-BRM; and, in the world of rallying, Jimmy Bullough's Lotus Cortina.

Jimmy's record in British events last year has been astonishing. In fact he has been competing in rallies since before the TR2 days, and has nine Montes under his belt. In 1966 he was runner-up in the *Motoring News* Championship; last year his best ten results comprise five wins, four seconds and a third, winning both the RAC Rally Championship and the *Motoring News* Championship by a handsome margin. The basis of this consistent success —apart from 17 years' rallying experience and the ability to cover special stages really quickly, and the skill of his navigator, Don Barrow—is a Lotus Cortina which Westune have developed into a very potent weapon for special stage motoring.

Bullough bought the car new in 1967 and, after it had done several events in fairly standard form, it was completely stripped and rebuilt by Westune. The engine was bored to 1599 cc, and the head was extensively reworked. Reprofiled CL2 cams were fitted, but the bottom end remained more or less standard so that the car could still be run in Group 1 form in international events. The unit is fully balanced; an oil cooler and uprated oil pump are used, and the sump baffles and pick-up are modified.

Transmission is via a standard gearbox to a 4.4 rear axle with limited-slip diff. Naturally much work has been done to the suspension: "forest" springs and subtle strengthening front and rear cope with the yumpiest of stages, and the ground clearance is visibly increased. A special front cross-member supplied by Ford's Competitions Dept was further strengthened, and the engine mountings are modified for extra strength and to raise the engine slightly; the sump guard is of ¾-in dural plate.

Again to enable the car to be run in Group 1 in internationals without radical remodification, all brake and fuel lines remain outside the bodywork, although they are scrupulously encased to protect them from damage by flying stones. The steel wheels are usually shod with Dunlop SP44s. Twin fuel tanks give a total capacity of 17 gallons. The braking system is servo-assisted, with heavy duty front pads and harder rear linings, and the rear drums have been converted back to manual adjustment.

Lighting is by Cibié, the Type 22 headlights being supplemented by a battery of four Oscars. Inside there is a hefty rollover bar, and the purposeful dash layout includes a Halda Twinmaster, an eight-day clock with stop mechanism and a separate stop-watch. The whole car shows evidence of meticulous preparation, with careful attention to detail; for example, the throttle linkage has been redesigned to help the 40DCOE Webers to open more progressively, and a spare throttle spring is fixed to the linkage bracket in case of need. All ancillaries and wiring are carefully taped down; in front of the navigator there's a neat row of spare fuses, with an open fusebox on the transmission tunnel by his right knee.

The Westune Lotus Cortina is now on show at Autospeed 68, deservedly taking its place among the cars of the other 1967 championships. Immediately before it went on show Jimmy Bullough kindly offered the car to AUTOSPORT, and Rally Editor John Davenport and I spent a pleasant morning exploring the yellows and whites of Buckinghamshire in it.

Despite its reprofiled CL2s, the Westune Cortina appeals instantly as a smooth, flexible road car. The biggest chokes available are installed in the Webers, and naturally if one is careless with the throttle at very low revs the car hesitates, but from 2000 rpm onwards there is lots of torque and acceleration is very brisk indeed. But it is when the revs get above 5000 rpm that the car reveals its true character in a great surge of power, and the tachometer needle swings round the dial in a very convincing manner. Out of respect for Mr Bullough's machinery we kept the needle out of the red, but on Westune's rolling road dynamometer figures of 132 bhp at the back wheels

at 7200 rpm have been recorded.

There was no opportunity to take any standing-start figures, but we did try a start on loose surface; with plenty of revs, the limited-slip and the SP44s simply hurl the car off the mark. The handling on smooth surfaces naturally feels very different from the standard Lotus Cortina, mainly because of the raised suspension, but on patchily damp roads the car always felt very predictable, with strong understeer which could be counteracted with a dab of throttle. The overall impression was one of smooth, useful power and great sure-footedness, and it must surely be these two ingredients, plus an excellent reliability record, which contribute most to the recipe of the successful special stage car.

Certainly a lot more will be heard of Westune. On the circuits, watch out this season for John Myerscough in the ex-Alan Peer twin-cam Anglia with a new Westune 1762 cc motor. If you want to jump the queue, they're at 164 Tonge Moor Rd, Bolton, Lancs (Bolton 25888).

JIMMY AND DON in the Cortina on last year's Nutcracker—they finished second (top).

THE OFFICE: all additional wiring is accessible, and the Twinmaster and eight-day clock are mounted on the transmission tunnel, with the extra fusebox on their left (below).

JIMMY BULLOUGH'S WESTUNE LOTUS CORTINA

By SIMON TAYLOR

TWIN CAM BOTTOM END GEN

IF THE engine is intended for serious competition work where very high revs are going to be used, then considerable attention will be required on the lower half of the engine. The cheapest way to increase the rpm potential is to have the crank and rods tuftrided. If you send your own crank and rods to V. W. Derrington at Kingston-on-Thames, they will perform this service at a very reasonable cost. Before any toughening is carried out, establish that the crank is in perfect condition and has never at any time been bent. The same goes for the rods. If any of these components have had to be straightened, then the toughening operation will cause them to revert back to their bent state. All items must then be crack tested.

When the crank and rods have been toughened, a coating is formed on the surface. This must be removed from the bearing surfaces of the crank and from the bearing shell-locating surfaces of the rods. The tuftriding process also causes the little-end bushes to be eroded away, so these will have to be replaced. Having been toughened, the crank and rods must be checked for any signs of distortion. Any balancing operations must be carried out on the rotating and reciprocating components of the engine after the toughening has been done.

If you find a new crank is necessary, then a special tuftrided crank is available through Fords, having the part number CD 7901/3C/1/6303. It would appear, however, that there are two types of cranks available under this part number, one being for the early engines as used in the Mk. I Lotus-Cortina, which has the impregnated-rope type oil-seal on the flywheel end of the crank. The second is for the later engines from 1967 on, as used in the Mk. II Cortina-Lotus, which uses a neoprene oil-seal mounted in a housing secured to the block. The later crankshaft can be used in the earlier engine if the later-type oil-seal housing is used in conjunction with the later sump.

Apart from this, the only other change necessary is to turn down the gearbox input-shaft bearing from the early crank to fit the later one. The later crank seems to be a little stronger, so if high revs are envisaged

Who should be kerbing the works Lotus-Cortina round Brands in this shot but Graham Hill, closely pursued by John Miles. Photo: Dave Gray.

and a new crank is needed, it may well be worth the little extra trouble to fit this type. A second advantage in fitting the later crank is that the neoprene oil-seal functions better than the earlier type.

Steel mains-caps must be fitted to the block. These are available from Fords Rallye Sport Dealers under the part number CD 6000/1. Having acquired these, they must be inline-bored to 0.015 in. oversize to accommodate the Vandervell competition bearings. The purpose of the steel main-caps is to reduce bearing distortion and crankshaft whip at high revs. This leads to a reduction in the superfluous vibrations that reduce reliability at high revs. A bottom-end prepared thus is safe to 7500 rpm continuous, and 7800 in short bursts.

The weakest points

The weakest part of the bottom-end is the rods. Another way around this problem, apart from tuftriding the standard rods, is to obtain some

stronger forged-steel ones. Here again Fords can supply a stronger con-rod under the part number CD 125E 6200C. You may find, if you are using the Mk. II Lotus or Twin-cam Escort engine, that it is already fitted with these rods; so check the part forging number before ordering any more.

These stronger rods can be made even more reliable by replacing the big-end bolts with special high-tensile ones available from Cosworth Engineering. The weak point with these rods is the corner formed by the bolts locating-face and the square boss, on the big-end cap. Failure of these rods is caused by cracking from the corner through to the big-end bore. The possibility of a crack forming can be considerably reduced by polishing the rod at this point.

When a polishing operation is performed on these rods in this way, it is imperative to leave the area upon which the head of the big-end bolt sits untouched. If this area is not flat, or is

TWIN CAM BOTTOM END GEN

out of square due to the polishing operation, then one of two things can occur. The big-end bolt will either work itself loose or, due to uneven flexing because it's out of square, the big-end bolt will fail. None of these faults will occur immediately the engine is taken up to high revs. More than likely nothing will appear amiss until a reasonable number of hours running at high rpm have been amassed. At some stage the bolt or the rod (if the polishing has not been done) will finally fail. The first indication you will have will be a large hole in the side of the crankcase!

as mentioned earlier.

Use of the steel crank in conjunction with the Cosworth rods and the steel mains-caps will enable revs as high as 8500 to be used. Another firm which can supply a steel crank and rods is Vegantune. Again, like the Ford equivalent, the crank is to suit the later-type twin-cam motors, and the necessary changes will have to be made for use in earlier engines. The Vegantune crank is made of EN 40B steel, which is nitrided to give it a hard surface finish. This crank seems to be lighter than most steel cranks, due to a different counterbalance design. No gain in power will be found by this, but a useful drop in rotating mass, giving the effect of a lighter flywheel, is brought about. Vegantune can supply two types of crankshaft. One having an extended nose to enable a special alternator to be fitted directly into the crank, thus completely doing away with a V-belt-driven alternator.

The water pump, however, still needs to be driven, and this is carried

There seems little point in fitting the early type as one is still left with an inferior type of oil seal.

By replacing the standard crank and rods, and changing the main bearing caps with equivalent items of far greater strength, the possibility of failure in this area has been reduced to an absolute minimum. If your intention is to build a motor from which it is hoped to achieve a power output in excess of 170 bhp and sustain revs in excess of 8000 rpm for significantly long periods, then another problem can arise in connection with the bottom end. Above this particular output and at these sustained high revs, there is a real possibility of failure around the piston gudgeon-pin bores. Both the pistons and gudgeon-pins are likely to expire due to fatigue. The thickness of the material around the gudgeon-pin bores seems to have the greatest bearing on the life of the component at high revs.

If, due to manufacturing tolerances, the thickness of the gudgeon-pin boss is on top limit, then a reasonable life may be realised. If this is not the case, then in all probability it is due to a thinner section at the gudgeon-pin bosses. The only way around this problem is to fit pistons and con-rods which will accept 1 in. dia. gudgeon-pins as opposed to the standard $\frac{13}{16}$ in. dia. items.

Special pistons and rods having 1 in. dia. pins are available from Vegantune. The pistons are 83.5 mm dia. which, on a standard stroke, give a capacity of 1594 cc (the class limit for which they were designed being 1600 cc).

With engines which have had the blocks overbored considerably — ie 1650 blocks — another failure point can arise. The main-bearings, especially the centre main, can start to part company from the block. A crack can be propagated around the housing and continue up the bore. On an unlinered 1650 block this would not probably be noticed until it was found that water was leaking into one or another of the cylinders. With a linered 1650 block, which incidentally has a greater possibility of going, the first signs that trouble is afoot would be loss of oil pressure due to the bearing in the housing at fault being unsupported. If the mains have cracked in this fashion the engine will not run for very long before some spectacular catastrophy occurs. If you are bent on extracting as much capacity, horsepower and rpm from the engine as possible, then the problem of mains unwillingly parting company from the block can arise although it is by no means a certainty.

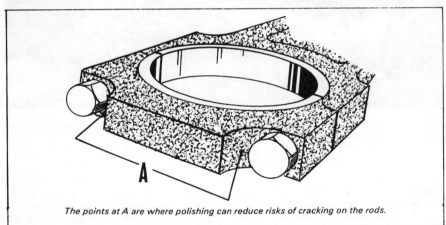

The points at A are where polishing can reduce risks of cracking on the rods.

Cosworth Engineering can also supply a conrod to withstand extremely high revs. This rod is slightly longer than the standard rod and brings the pistons flush with the top of the bore. This has the effect of slightly increasing the compression ratio.

Forged steel cranks and rods

For an all-out competition motor, the ideal solution to the problem of bottom-end strength is the use of a forged-steel crank and rods. The forged-steel crank is an expensive outlay but, if revs in the order of 8000 or more are envisaged, then it is an absolute must. Steel cranks are available from Fords under the part number CD 7901/3C/1-175. These cranks are made to suit the later-type Cortina and if they are intended for use in an engine prior to 1967, then the sump, oil-seal, etc., will have to be changed

out by means of a small cogged belt from the alternator to the water pump. Their second crank differs in as much as it does not have the extended nose and is meant for use with a normal crankshaft pulley. Talking of crankshaft pulleys, the standard pressed-steel one is decidedly unsafe over 7000 revs, so replace it with the Cosworth cast-iron one. Vegantune can supply an adaptor to convert the ordinary-style crank into the extended-nose variety so that a crank-mounted alternator can be used. To use this type of alternator a different front cover is required, having bosses cast on it for drilling and tapping the fixing points for the alternator.

Apart from forged steel rods, Cosworth Engineering also supply cranks to suit both early and late engines.

The limits for such a failure to occur, assuming a standard stroke, would appear to be a power output in excess of 170 bhp, a bore 85 mm or larger and revs over 8000-8500. This situation can be further aggravated if the stroke is lengthened, thereby increasing the peak inertia loads with which the main-bearings are expected to cope. If the stroke is shortened, and the block bored to restore the original capacity then, within limits, the reduction in block strength is compensated for by the reduced inertia loading. **DV**

In typical Clark cornering attitude — it's Roger and Jim on the Fermyn stage of last year's RAC Photo: Dave Gray.

LOTUS-CORTINA

Continued from page 93

Thanks to Britain's Mrs. "B" Castle (the non-driving Minister of Transport) and her 70 mph speed limit, the only place to test cars properly is on the Continent.

The Grand Prix "circus" takes us to delightful places and most are now connected by fast motorways or still relatively deserted minor and major roads. In among these are the rougher patches of roadway and cobbles which help bring out the best (and worst) in handling.

And so I was off to Zandvoort for the Dutch Grand Prix on my own—so I thought. My gourmet mate, Douglas Armstrong (who you will remember took over as Modern Motor's London editor for the four years I sunshined back home, and who has now lost three stone and can't stop talking about it), decided at the last minute he wanted to come with me.

He said it was the motor race, but he, like me, is a bit keen on the Rizstafl they serve at the Bali restaurant at The Hague seaside town of Scheveningen. It's out of this world—33 spicy dishes all on the table at once. But I digress.

Armstrong appeared at my North London home at 7.30 and less than two hours later we'd negotiated the countryside of Herts and Essex, and made Harwich, where the Lotus-Cortina was hoisted aboard by crane.

(Next year the Zeeland Shipping Company will introduce fast and luxurious drive-on-drive-off ferries on the seven-hour crossing to the Hook.)

The north route to Harwich via Hatfield, Baintree and Colchester is over some very twisty and narrow roads. The Cortina, by this time reasonably well-loaded, purred happily as the rev. limit came up through each gear change. You can't exceed this limit because of the distributor cut-out, similar to that used on Ford's GP engine.

Occasionally some citizen who thought he had a Cortina behind him was mighty staggered to find a purring red flash go by.

With 0-60 mph coming up in 10 sec., the Lotus-Cortina has plenty of that old-fashioned zing to make even the psychedelics take notice.

Once offloaded at the Hook it took but 15 minutes before hitting the motorway en route to Haarlem and Zandvoort.

With no speed limit to hinder our way and the bulk of the Neddielanders not cluttering their motorway system, I gave a little on the loud pedal.

The Lotus answered rapidly. With 90 mph coming up in under 30 sec. (and 100 mph genuine—103 on the clock—available if you really like to roll), we covered the next 20 miles before turning off the motorway in 16 minutes flat.

Torque-wise the twin-cam has nothing to be ashamed of. Even with a full load she will pull away in top at surprisingly low speeds without snatch or shudder.

Coming off the motorway, still rather in a hurry, we struck a few of the twisty bends around the Tulip beds. The Lotus's leaf springing at the rear with the axle located by a couple of transverse arms, took most of them well.

But if you do press too hard, the back-end, particularly on a bumpy corner, is inclined to tramp and flutter around a little. Not even the Pirelli Cinturatos could hold her down.

Get too adventurous and you find oversteer comes in with a wow—nothing to worry about on the normal dry roadway—but in the wet it became a little busy in the cockpit at times.

I spoke earlier of the distributor cut-out which stops the revs going over the top end without robbing you of maximum power in the gears.

The Lotus-Fords in which Jim Clark and Graham Hill tear around also work the same way. It's from an idea by designer Mike Costin and developed by Lucas.

There is a little screw, I understand, that can be turned and the revs can be altered to go up or down. (They tell me there is one man in the Lotus team who goes around with a per-

petual grin on his face—he is the only one who knows which screw to turn to get the revs up in the Lotus racers.

I looked around the Lotus-Cortina for it—without success. For my money this is one of the best ideas in years.

Rapid trips around Holland—some with four up—convinced me this is a delightful car in the old GT tradition. It can carry four people and their luggage quickly, quietly and efficiently at cruise speeds in the upper 90s or even the "ton".

My top speed worked out around 105 mph (speedo showed 109, Ford claim a maximum of 108 mph).

Fuel consumption worked out at 25.5 mpg over 1500 miles. Oil consumption was not quite a quart for a similar distance—and remember this car was taken close to its maximum virtually throughout the run.

The brakes, 9.6in. discs at the front and 9in. drums at the rear, are servo-assisted and for the most part can't be faulted.

Under full load conditions (four up and luggage) and pulling up from very high speeds (90-100 mph) there is some judder and weight transference.

The rears can lock up under these conditions, but the car continues to steer well.

If I've got to have a hate about this car (which at £869 stg basic is £168 stg. basic dearer than the GT in Britain), it would be aimed at the umbrella handbrake and the dished plastic steering wheel. Time for a flat wood-and-alloy job, I reckon, and another inch could be lopped off the already-shortened steering column.

Otherwise I reckon this is still a smooth performer. The motor is delightful, and I think the Ford Cortina-developed-by-Lotus (as Ford puts it) would fit my garage fairly well.

The performance figures for the 1558cc twin cam, coupled with the car's space and silence, low-rev torque characteristics and its docility, make it a car for getting smartly around town and for long distance cruising . . . and mum can drive it, too, with the kids. ●

Classic choice

Cortina Lotus

Jonathan Wood reports

The early 'sixties saw a world wide transformation in the image of the Ford Motor Company. For market research initiated by Ford's American headquarters in Dearborn demanded a corporate involvement in motor sport and the ripples of this decision were not long in reaching Dagenham. Therefore an intensive and highly professional rallying programme was launched of which the appearance of the Cortina Lotus of 1963 represents a significant starting point.

IT was in 1962 that Ford approached Lotus's Colin Chapman with an exciting proposition. Lotus had already decided to fit a twin overhead camshaft engine based on the five bearing crankshaft 116E Ford unit in their Elan sports cars which was due to appear at that year's Motor Show. Ford suggested, and Lotus agreed, that it also be used in their new Consul Cortina bodyshell which was also due to go into production later in the year. The idea was to build 1000 thus qualifying the car for Group 2 homologation.

While Lotus were to be responsible for suspension and chassis work, the engine side of the project was entrusted to Cosworth Engineering with production being assigned to J. A. Prestwich, well known for their JAP V twins of yore. In fact when the engine first appeared in the Elan its cubic capacity was 1498cc but increasing the bore size produced 1558cc as the Group 2 saloon car racing requirement stood at 1600cc.

Engine development was undertaken in a left hand drive Anglia which must have given other drivers a few shocks and in January 1963, the Lotus type 28 was released or, in other words "Cortina developed by Lotus". In fact the two door Cortina looked remarkably standard, the white bodywork carrying a distinctive green stripe along the side and two small Lotus badges on the rear wings and radiator grille. However, the doors, bonnet and boot lid were aluminium (no doubt contributing to an impressive kerb weight of 16·25 cwt) and 5½ J wheels were fitted. The principal suspension modifications included zero front wheel camber and an uprated anti-roll bar while the rear leaf spring suspension was replaced by a Chapman-designed layout incorporating coil springs with the axle located by A-brackets and radius arms. This was one area destined for radical alteration for the loading on the aluminium differential housing resulted in excessive oil leakage. The lube found its way on to the A bracket mounting

rubbers triggering off a chain of events that led to the collapse of the suspension. From September 1965 the cars reverted to a conventional leaf spring layout though five leaves instead of the customary four were used. Under the bonnet, the Lotus twin cam engine was producing 105 bhp, giving the car a top speed of 108 mph.

By November of 1963 *The Autocar* was able to report that cars were coming off the production line at Lotus's Cheshunt factory at the rate of five a day and homologation for Group 2 racing had been achieved. The cars arrived at the Hertfordshire works ready trimmed and in shell form, there being fitted with suspension and engine/transmission units, completed examples being road tested on the nearby A10!

The following year a fully race prepared Cortina Lotus was offered for sale, featuring prominently on the company's stand at the Racing Car Show and by then boasting a slightly larger 1593cc engine which developed 140 bhp and costing £1725 which was over £600 more than the "standard" model. By this time the cars were really race worthy, Sir John Whitmore becoming European Touring Car Championship at the wheel of a Cortina Lotus. In 1965 a Special Equipment variant was announced boasting a throaty 117 bhp engine, though the following year was to be the final one of production at the Lotus factory, the assembly line being shut down in the summer of 1966 and the company moving to larger premises at Hethel, Norfolk at the end of the year.

Production figures from the Cheshunt factory are as follows:—

Year	Production
1964	567
1965	1118
1966	986

In any event the Mark 1 Cortina was phased out in the Autumn of 1966 and it wasn't until February 1967 that the Mark 2 Cortina Lotus appeared which by this time was a totally Ford project, the Lotus name tag later being dropped in 1970 (the last year of production) and the model being designated Twin Cam, a la Escort.

Having, we hope, briefly spelt out the evolution of the Cortina Lotus, let us now consider points to look for when contemplating the purchase of a second hand example. The first thing to establish is that you really are buying one which isn't as daft as it sounds! This is because the GT version of the Cortina was, in many ways similar, and you don't want to be landed with a tarted up version of that. Obviously the aluminium panels are a real giveaway but these were only fitted

Above, the Cortina Lotus twin cam engine, not leaving room for much else! Below, where it belonged, an example on the race track, pictured during the model's heyday.

Above, two examples owned by Clark and Saxon of Theydon Bois, Essex, ex works 1965 car on left and 1963 example on right. The separate sidelights on the earlier car are a dating feature. Far left '63 dashboard, left '65 interior and 1965 BRM assembled engine.

until July 1964 being replaced by steel ones. There will be no battery tray fitted under the bonnet while the Lotus badges on the exterior of the car had a two pin mounting, the GT ones had a three, so if you've any doubts about the ancestry of the vehicle under inspection keep an eye open for a blanked off hole. Obviously a number of the shortcomings are also common to the Mark 1 Cortina and this applies particularly to the condition of the bodywork.

Bodywork

The Cortina Lotus suffers from all the usual areas of body rot found in the conventional Mark 1 and a few more besides. First port of call should be the top of the MacPherson strut mountings that you'll find at the top of each wing under the bonnet. These mounting points have a bit of a rough time being bombarded by mud thrown up from the wheels which tends to encourage corrosion plus the fact that the immediate area is under stress anyway. Keep an eye open for signs of bodged repairs and the fact that plates have been welded on to the mounts does not necessarily mean that all is well underneath! Another bad rust area is that immediately around the headlights and when this really has got a grip it can infect the reflector as well. Also the bottom of the front wing immediately adjoining the door is another trouble spot and may be a pointer to trouble with the aforementioned strut support.

Cortina Lotus

Moving backwards down the car, the outrigger/jacking points have a habit of rusting badly but this shortcoming may well be more prevalent on the nearside of the car. Then the rear wing valances have a habit of breaking out in unsightly rust patches. This is accelerated by the fact that the boot floor is a source of corrosion. On the nearside is the spare wheel well (which, in fact, doesn't contain the spare because the Cortina Lotus uses 5½J wheels and it won't fit) but it is a trap for water. On the other side is the battery tray. The standard Mark 1 had the battery under the bonnet but there isn't room for it with the twin cam engine in place so it was relegated to the boot. And we all know how corroded metal can get immediately around a battery! While you're scouting around in the boot check the rear suspension turrets which project into the floor. Rust can corrupt the turret walls, so beware.

If you are contemplating the purchase of an example built with aluminium panels you won't face a corrosion problem with the doors, bonnet and boot lid. But the metal was very thin and tended to dent easily. "One learns to close the boot and bonnet by allowing their lids to drop, rather than pressing them down" reported *The Autocar*'s tester.

Engine and transmission

The engine fitted in the Cortina Lotus was, as we have seen, virtually identical to that used in the Lotus Elan. These engines are, on the whole, reliable enough and don't be disturbed if they smoke a little under power. This is quite normal. One of the engine's most likely shortcomings is a comparative minor one, however, for a worn water pump is by no means uncommon on these motors, a state of affairs that can be exacerbated by an overtightened fan belt. You can tell whether the pump is suspect by grasping the fan blades (or the boss if it is a plastic one) and feeling for movement. If it is anything more than ¼ inch it will require replacement.

Timing chain noises will be a fairly good indicator as to whether the engine has received regular maintenance as it requires adjustment every 5000 miles. If it rattles then this shows that the long chain is on the loose side but a whirring sound indicates too much tension. Seek out the chain adjustment nut and examine the prominence of the threads. If there is about ½ inch exposed then it can be reckoned that the chain is in good condition but if all the threads have been taken up then you're going to need a new one. An oil consumption rate of 250 to 400 miles to the pint is by no means unusual and an acceptable oil pressure figure is 40 psi at 3000 rpm when the engine is hot. A 60 psi figure may indicate that a Cosworth high pressure cut out has been fitted. These twin cams are tolerably oil tight but when they do leak it is usually from the camboxes at the back of the engine. If you've never had an under bonnet look at one of these power units, don't be alarmed by the fact that the carburettors appear to be wobbly. The twin Weber DCOEs are supposed to move on their rubber O rings and should not be prevented from doing so.

The close ratio gearbox with its smart remote control lever shouldn't present any major problems and it is worth recounting that some of the early cars have aluminium bell housings and gearbox tail shafts. From July 1964 a two piece propeller shaft was fitted in place of the one piece unit.

Suspension, steering and brakes

It is worth remembering that most of the Cortina Lotus's suspension parts were peculiar to the car. This goes for the MacPherson struts, the track control arms, anti roll bar and bushes, steering drag link steering arm and ball joint. Some early cars had high ratio steering boxes. The Burman re-circulating ball unit shouldn't give much trouble though it does have a habit of suffering oil seal failure with the attendant loss of lubricant. As already mentioned, trouble was experienced with the original A bracket rear suspension but it can be made to work properly and the appropriate parts are still available. Many of the A bracket cars were converted to the leaf spring layout by Ian Walker Racing, however. Brake parts are still obtainable, P16 callipers being fitted to the discs at the front while 8 inch drums were used on the rear, as opposed to 7½ inch on the Cortina GT.

Interior

The cars were nicely finished inside having special front seats originally finished in Ermine White with green strips which echoed the car's exterior. The original black faced instruments were mounted on a matt aluminium panel but the later cars had more comprehensive dials and larger panel. From 1965 onwards the cars were fitted with the Ford Aeroflow ventilation and heating system, which is a definate plus. The Lotus monogrammed wooden gear lever knob was a nice touch (though all too often it has disappeared) and echoed the wood rimmed steering wheel.

How much?

You can expect to pay anything from £300 to £2000 for a Cortina Lotus depending on its condition with £800 to £900 providing an example in average condition. Potential buyers may care to note that the Lotus press cars were registered 164, 165, 166 FOO respectively. These had blueprinted, balanced engines (even down to the dynamos) and would certainly be well worth having today though it should be noted that 165 FOO did catch fire early in its career!

As far as spare parts are concerned, many of the parts are common to the conventional Mark 1s and such vital items like front wings are still available if you are prepared to ferret them out. A number of specialist firms will undertake work on the twin cam Lotus engines, just two being Ian Walker Service Ltd., of 236 Woodhouse Road, London N.12 and Vegantune of Cradge Bank, Scalding, Lincolnshire.

Membership of Club Lotus is a must if you have one of these cars. Write to the secretary at 107 Brandon Road, Watton, Norfolk. They have recently established a register of Cortina Lotuses and the registrar is Phil Baskerville of 217 Argyle Avenue, Hounslow, Middlesex.

My grateful thanks to Graham Arnold and Phil Baskerville for their help in preparing this feature.●

Left, the original A bracket rear end and above rear suspension turret check points.

Below, commodious boot, note battery box on right and, right MacPherson strut check point.

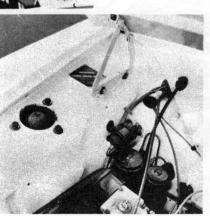

BROOKLANDS BOOKS

Part 2

CONTENTS

LOTUS-MODIFIED FORD CORTINA

A ravening wolf in slightly sheepish clothing

IT's happened. Lotus and Cosworth, who first tuned the Ford Anglia engine until it dominated Formula Junior races all over the world, and then put a twin overhead camshaft cylinder-head on the 1½-litre Ford Classic engine to get even more remarkable performance, have persuaded the Ford Motor Company to let them re-design the light and roomy Cortina saloon. With two overhead camshafts, two Weber double-choke carburetters, a special transmission, a new suspension system with coil springs all round, lots of light-alloy parts, and disc front brakes, the car which Ford dealers can now sell as the Consul Cortina Sports Special should be one of the liveliest four-seater saloons that money can buy. Road-going models of 105 b.h.p. rating are to be built at the rate of five per day in an extension of the Lotus factory—there will also be a handful of extra-special cars, with full Cosworth tuning producing an extra 40 b.h.p., in which the drivers of Team Lotus expect to win saloon car races outright as distinct from merely collecting class victories. Phew!

Nobody will doubt the ability of Lotus and Cosworth to make the Cortina go phenomenally fast. The greatest interest is in how they have modified this inexpensive saloon so that the power can be used, and whilst the modifications have been worked out in surprisingly few months they include complete re-design of the rigid-axle rear suspension to use coil springs and radius arms instead of leaf springs.

Road holding begins where the tyres touch the road, and normal wear for the special Cortina will be Dunlop C41 nylon cord tubeless tyres, of 6.00-13 size on 5½J rims which, since handling precision rather than comfort is the object of the operation, are a full inch wider than the normal rims for this tyre section. Behind the special wheels there are Girling brakes borrowed from a much heavier Ford model, 9¾-inch discs at the front and 9-inch by 1¾-inch drums at the rear with a vacuum servo of 2.04/1 ratio boosting the driver's effort.

Subtle but important changes have been made to the Macpherson strut I.F.S., which has lowered springs and stiffer damper settings. The track control arm (a forging instead of a pressing) is fractionally longer to eliminate wheel camber, and the anti-roll torsion bar which forms part of the lower wishbone has been extended by half an inch each end to reduce castor; it is also stiffer than the normal stabilizer. Shorter steering arms on the front hubs give effectively higher gearing and they have also been re-shaped to reduce the Ackermann angle—the traditional arrangement by which the inner wheel steers at a greater angle than the outer. A 15-inch steering wheel, with lightweight wood rim of low inertia, is not merely decorative but gives substantially quicker response.

Semi-elliptic rear suspension has been abandoned completely in favour of a design using coil springs. These new rear springs are mounted on larger-bore replacements for the normal Cortina's vertical telescopic shock absorbers, and to transfer the car's weight from its floor longerons to the top of these springs, extra tubular members at each side of the luggage locker link the damper tops to the former rear spring shackle mountings. Because of these extra body stiffening tubes, the spare wheel has to lie on the luggage locker floor instead of standing up inside one rear wing.

The main rear axle locating member is a tubular A-bracket (of which the base is almost as wide as the car) swinging on rubber bushes below the former leaf spring pivots. Apart from the welded-on box-section brackets which carry these bushes, the

The major mechanical changes

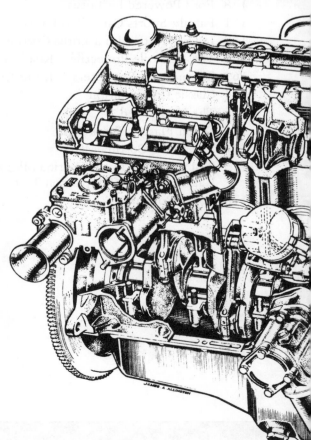

steel body shell is modified to provide extra clearance for a lowered suspension which, although very firmly damped, is not appreciably less flexible than the one which it replaces. Where the apex of the A-bracket is linked to the rear axle, just below the differential, a transverse rubber bush is combined with a fore-and-aft threaded bearing which prevents unwanted roll stiffness being added to the rear suspension. The low mounting of this A-bracket provides a roll centre about six inches above ground level, but not so high as to cause the directional hesitancy on bumpy straights which some cars with A-brackets above the axle have shown.

To complete the rear suspension linkage there are two pressed steel trailing links of top-hat section, rather above the A-bracket and connecting the former front spring mountings on the hull to the existing shock absorber mountings on the axle. A slightly nose-down attitude of the axle, which with a positive linkage cannot "wind up" as it does when torque reaction is taken by leaf springs, has avoided any need for extra clearance above the propeller shaft despite lowering of the car.

With this rear axle locating linkage, much of the accelerating thrust or braking drag is taken from the axle to the car at one point via the central A-bracket instead of at two points via springs bolted to each end of the axle. Thus horizontal forces impose substantially greater bending loads upon the axle tubes in this than in a normal Cortina, but whereas testing showed a need for reinforcement in the overhung body tail no weakness has become apparent at the axle.

J. A. Prestwich Industries Ltd. (known for J.A.P. motorcycle engines) are building engines for this high-performance Cortina and for the Lotus Elan two-seater, using the 1½-litre Ford engine as a starting point. The stroke is unchanged but the bores have been enlarged by 1/16th inch to give 1,558 c.c., the pistons are special and a five-bearing crankshaft with heavier counterbalance weights is used. Cosworth Engineering Ltd. developed the light-alloy twin-overhead-camshaft conversion cylinder head for this engine from a design by Harry Mundy, and will prepare engines for racing, but they do not handle routine production. An extension of the existing timing chain beyond the normal camshaft (which remains in the cylinder block to drive fuel and oil pumps and the ignition contact-breaker) goes to the overhead camshafts.

Two Weber double-choke horizontal carburetters are used in this Cortina, taking cold air from a filter ahead of the radiator. A tuned exhaust system has equal-length pipes connecting the outer and the inner pairs of cylinders to twin pipes, which in turn join up beneath the car in a single silencing system. An extra-tall radiator honeycomb, with more airflow to it through a simplified grille, provides cooling for this very much more powerful engine. The Ford Cortina all-synchromesh four-speed gearbox is used, but with closer spacings between top and third gears, and between third and second, though to retain re-starting ability on steep gradients the gap between second and bottom gears is widened. A diaphragm-spring clutch is used, of 8 in. instead of 7½ in. plate diameter, and the normal top gear is 3.9/1 giving approximately 103 m.p.h. at 6,000 r.p.m. though higher or lower ratios are also available.

Apart from the reduction in unsprung weight which comes from elimination of the half-elliptic rear springs, this car has an aluminium-alloy differential housing. Sprung weight is saved by use of light-alloy castings for the gearbox extension, remote control, and clutch housing, with aluminium panels for the doors, bonnet and boot lid. Transferring the battery to the boot

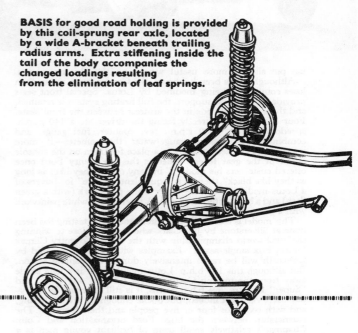

BASIS for good road holding is provided by this coil-sprung rear axle, located by a wide A-bracket beneath trailing radius arms. Extra stiffening inside the tail of the body accompanies the changed loadings resulting from the elimination of leaf springs.

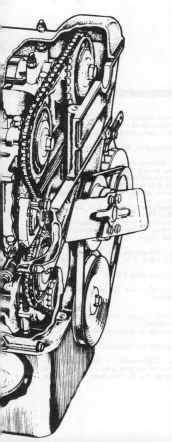

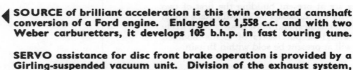

SOURCE of brilliant acceleration is this twin overhead camshaft conversion of a Ford engine. Enlarged to 1,558 c.c. and with two Weber carburetters, it develops 105 b.h.p. in fast touring tune.

SERVO assistance for disc front brake operation is provided by a Girling-suspended vacuum unit. Division of the exhaust system, and a cool air duct from the air filter to the carburetters, can also be seen below.

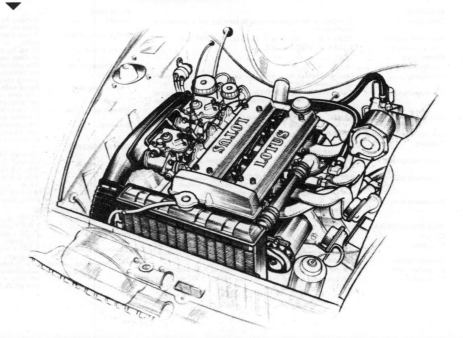

LOTUS...CORTINA

ON TEST by Jim Clark at Silverstone, a prototype of the Lotus-modified Cortina corners with very little roll on its lowered suspension and wide-rim wheels.

THE COCKPIT of the Cortina is modified by Lotus to have circular instrument dials, improved seating, a lightweight steering wheel and other sporting refinements.

has put slightly more useful weight on the driving wheels.

Although it has been lightened, the Cortina gains rather than loses comfort in being modified by Lotus. Special front seats provide more lateral support, the full heating system is retained, and there is a glove box in the armrest between the front seats. Four circular dials directly facing the driver are a 140 m.p.h. speedometer, an 8,000 r.p.m. rev. counter, fuel gauge, and combined oil pressure gauge/water thermometer—if more instruments are needed there is a place for them on the console ahead of the gear lever. Whereas the late Henry Ford once offered customers his model T in "any colour they like, as long as they like black" there is an equivalent "choice" for buyers of a Lotus-modified Cortina—either white paintwork (with a green flash) and a black interior, or a black interior and white paintwork with a green flash. . . .

This model is essentially race-bred, and much testing has been done at Silverstone by Jim Clark who came so close to winning the 1962 world championship with the Lotus-Coventry Climax Grand Prix single-seater. Examples with engines prepared by Cosworth will be raced intensively during the coming season. But although this 105 b.h.p. Lotus-modified car is a long stride away from the touring Cortina in its 1.2-litre, 48½ b.h.p. and "Super" 1.5-litre, 59¼ b.h.p. forms, it is still intended for every-day use. Very fast indeed, but docile enough for traffic driving, and with room for four or five people and their luggage. The partnership between the huge Ford organization and Colin Chapman's relatively small team of brilliant young men is a remarkable one (Lotus are at present building the first of two single-seater racing cars for the Indianapolis 500 Mile Race which will incorporate V-8 Ford engines) and Ford dealers seem likely to be besieged with would-be purchasers of Lotus-modified Cortinas, all of which will at present be sold within Britain.

Specification

ENGINE

Cylinders	4 in line with extra counterbalancing on a 5-bearing crankshaft.
Bore and stroke	82.55 mm. × 72.75 mm. (3.25 in. × 2.864 in.).
Cubic capacity	1,558 c.c. (95.06 cu. in.).
Piston area	33.15 sq. in.
Compression ratio	9.5/1.
Valvegear	Inclined valves operated by two chain-driven over-head camshafts.
Carburation	Two Weber 40 DCOE2 double-choke horizontal carburetters fed by mechanical pump from 8-gallon tank.
Ignition	12-volt coil, centrifugal and vacuum timing control, 14 mm. long-reach sparking plugs.
Lubrication	Full-flow filter and 6½-pint sump.
Cooling	Water cooling with pump, fan, thermostat, and oversize radiator.
Electrical system	12-volt 38 amp. hr. battery charged by 240-watt generator.
Maximum power	105 b.h.p. net at 5,500 r.p.m., equivalent to 159 lb./sq. in. b.m.e.p. at 2,625 ft./min. piston speed and 3.17 b.h.p. per sq. in. of piston area.
Maximum torque	108 lb. ft. net at 4,000 r.p.m., equivalent to 172 lb./sq. in. b.m.e.p. at 1,910 ft./min. piston speed.

TRANSMISSION

Clutch	8 in. single dry plate, diaphragm spring.
Gearbox	4-speed with direct drive on top; synchromesh on all forward ratios.
Overall ratios	3.9, 4.8, 6.4 and 9.75.
Propeller shaft	Single-piece open with central tube of 3 in. diameter.
Final drive	3.9/1 hypoid bevel (alternative ratios 3.77, 4.125 or 4.429).

CHASSIS

Brakes	Girling hydraulic with vacuum servo of 2.04/1 ratio, discs at front and drums at rear.
Brake dimensions	Front discs 9¾ in. dia.; rear drums 9 in. dia. × 1¾ in. wide.
Brake areas	81 sq. in. of lining working on 301.6 sq. in. rubbed area of discs and drums.
Front suspension	Macpherson strut independent with coil springs on telescopic damper struts, forged lower wishbones giving zero camber, and stiffened anti-roll torsion bar.
Rear suspension	Rigid axle located by A-bracket below propeller shaft and two trailing radius arms. Coil springs mounted on telescopic dampers.
Wheels and tyres	Bolt-on steel disc wheels with Dunlop C41 nylon cord tubeless tyres of 6.00-13 size on 5½J rims.
Steering	Recirculatory ball-bearing gear, lightweight wood-rim 15-in. steering wheel and modified steering arms to reduce Ackermann angle.

DIMENSIONS

Length	Overall 14 ft. 0.3 in.; wheelbase 8 ft. 2.4 in.
Width	Overall 5 ft. 2.5 in.; track 4 ft. 3.6 in. at front and 4 ft. 1.5 in. at rear.
Height	4 ft. 5.4 in.; ground clearance 5.3 in.
Turning circle	34 ft.
Kerb weight	Approx. 15 cwt. (without fuel but with oil, water, tools, spare wheel, etc.).

EFFECTIVE GEARING

Top gear ratio	17.15 m.p.h. at 1,000 r.p.m. and 35.9 m.p.h. at 1,000 ft./min. piston speed.
Maximum torque	4,000 r.p.m. corresponds to approx. 68-69 m.p.h. in top gear.
Maximum power	5,500 r.p.m. corresponds to approx. 94-95 m.p.h. in top gear.
Probable top gear pulling power	375 lb./ton. approx (Computed by The Motor from manufacturer's figures for torque, gear ratio and kerb weight, with allowances for 3½ cwt. load, 10% losses and 60 lb./ton drag.)

Distinguishing feature of Cortina-Lotus is contrasting color body stripe.

CORTINA-LOTUS

STORY AND PHOTOS BY DAVID PHIPPS

ON THE ROAD, the Cortina-Lotus (or whatever they finally decide to call it) more than comes up to expectations. The performance, for a 1.6-liter five-seater sedan, is very good —and so is the handling; the latter, in fact, is the car's most impressive feature, despite the live rear axle. The ride is very good too: a little on the firm side, but by no means harsh.

Thanks to the revised suspension layout and lowered center of gravity, there is virtually no roll during cornering, and this means that a surprising amount of power can be used in tight turns without upsetting the rear end; when the tail finally does break away it goes rather quickly, but the steering is geared just high enough to catch it.

Mechanically, the engine is remarkably quiet, and pulls strongly from about 1500 rpm. Exhaust noise is also reasonably subdued, but there is some resonance in the roof at steady high speeds; this will probably be overcome by redesign of the mufflers, a modification which is being actively pursued.

The only other snag is slight transmission roughness—a feature which is almost synonymous with positively located live rear axles. However, Colin Chapman says he can eliminate this.

The gear ratios are very close and seem rather high at first, until you realize that in town it is just as easy to use 1st and 2nd as 2nd and 3rd, thanks to the excellent gearshift and Ford's superb synchromesh.

The steering is very pleasant—light, positive and free from road shock— and the brakes do a good job with very moderate pedal pressure. The seats are comfortable and have a good range of adjustment, with the backrests becoming more upright as they are moved forward, and more reclining as they go back. The instruments are sensibly positioned and can be read at a glance.

Although only a prototype, the car we tried seemed very well finished in every respect. If the snags mentioned— exhaust resonance and transmission roughness—can be overcome, this will be a very fine motor car. It already puts most of Britain's other so-called sports saloons to shame.

The impact of this new alliance between Ford and Lotus has yet to be felt in production car racing in England, but felt it will be. No family-type car built in Europe has yet been able to match the 3.8 Jaguars in this type of racing, but expectations are that Jaguars will have met their match when a lightened and more modified version of the Cortina-Lotus hits the circuit— probably driven by Lotus team drivers Clark, Taylor and Arundell. If nothing else, it will further liven up the competition, which already provides some of the most exciting racing ever.

Lotus on the top, Ford on the bottom end and Cosworth in between.

Wood-rimmed wheel, floor shift.

FORD'S recent "marriage" with Britain's leading sports-car designer, Colin Chapman, has already produced its first offspring—an exciting 115 m.p.h. version of the Consul Cortina saloon.

This speedster was announced on January 23—only a few days after the release of the new Cortina Super 1500, described elsewhere in this issue.

Its official name is Ford Consul Cortina Special Sports, but everyone is calling it the Lotus-Cortina—a much more apt designation, since it uses a Lotus-developed Ford power unit, is put together at Chapman's Lotus factory and bears the Lotus emblem on its bonnet and on the steering-wheel horn button.

Specifications are calculated to make any enthusiast's mouth water:

A bored-out 1600c.c. version of the five-bearing Consul Classic engine; Lotus light-alloy, twin-overhead-camshaft cylinder head; twin double-choke Weber carburettors; close-ratio gearbox with snappy remote-controlled floor shift; servo-assisted disc front brakes; lowered suspension; lightened rear axle, suspended on coil springs and located by trailing arms and an A-bracket; full G.T. instrumentation, bucket seats and wide-base wheel rims.

Actually, the power unit is almost identical to the one that was introduced with the new Lotus Elan at the London Motor Show last October. It is based on the 1500c.c., twin o.h.c. engine which powered the Lotus 23—the amazingly fast little sports car which led the opening

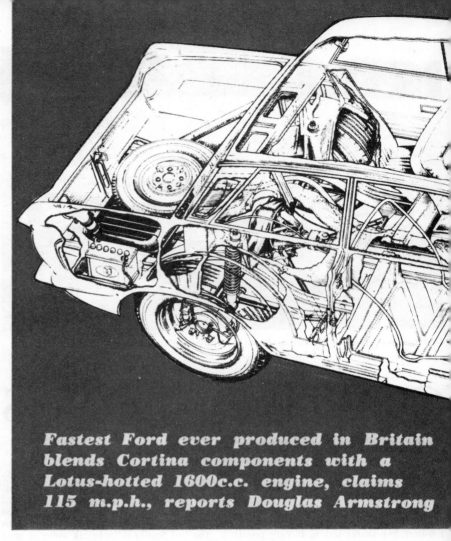

Fastest Ford ever produced in Britain blends Cortina components with a Lotus-hotted 1600c.c. engine, claims 115 m.p.h., reports Douglas Armstrong

LOTUS-CORTINA!

stages of last year's Nurburgring 1000-kilometre race until brake troubles and engine fumes got the better of driver Jim Clark.

With a compression ratio of 9.5:1, a special counterbalanced crankshaft and twin double-choke 40 DCOE2 Webers, the engine has a net output of 105 b.h.p. at 5500 r.p.m. and maximum torque of 108lb./ft. at 4000. The standard Ford Classic unit bore has been enlarged from 80.97mm to 82.55, but stroke remains at 72.75mm.

Although no weight figures have been quoted as yet, it is obvious that the car will scale considerably less than the 16½cwt. kerb weight of the two-door Cortina Super, since the outer body panels, doors, boot lid and bonnet are light-alloy pressings. The claimed acceleration figure of 0-100

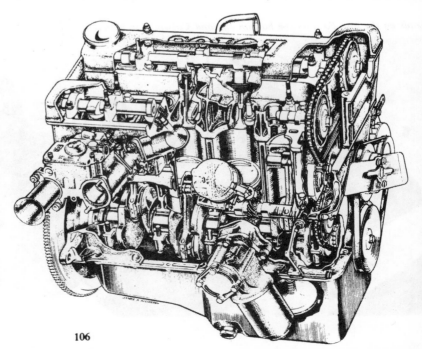

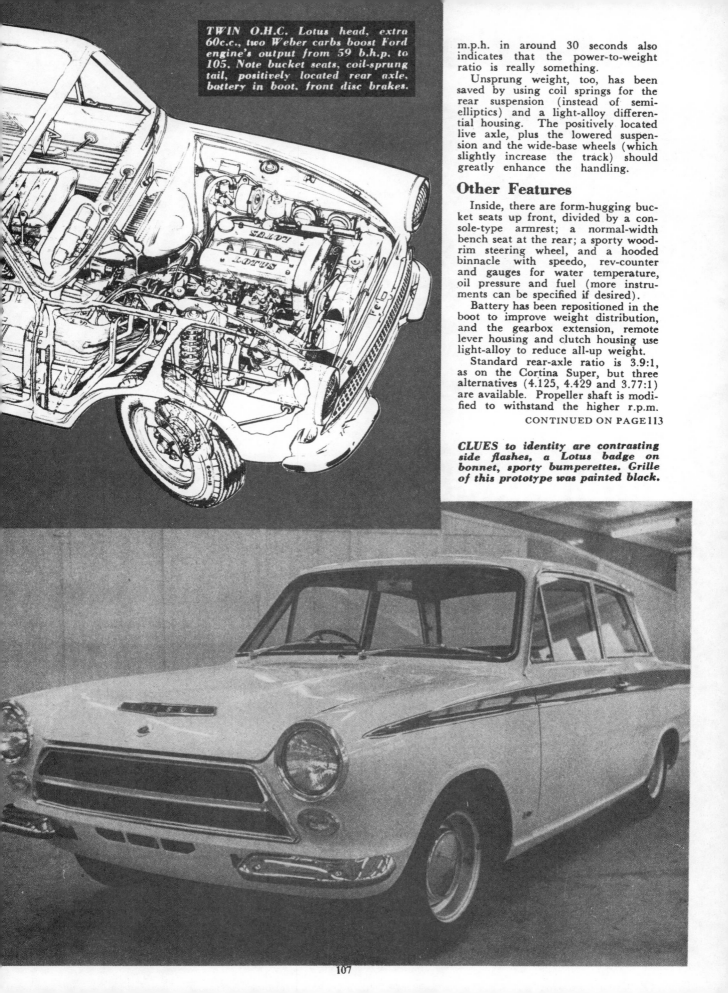

TWIN O.H.C. Lotus head, extra 60c.c., two Weber carbs boost Ford engine's output from 59 b.h.p. to 105. Note bucket seats, coil-sprung tail, positively located rear axle, battery in boot, front disc brakes.

m.p.h. in around 30 seconds also indicates that the power-to-weight ratio is really something.

Unsprung weight, too, has been saved by using coil springs for the rear suspension (instead of semi-elliptics) and a light-alloy differential housing. The positively located live axle, plus the lowered suspension and the wide-base wheels (which slightly increase the track) should greatly enhance the handling.

Other Features

Inside, there are form-hugging bucket seats up front, divided by a console-type armrest; a normal-width bench seat at the rear; a sporty wood-rim steering wheel, and a hooded binnacle with speedo, rev-counter and gauges for water temperature, oil pressure and fuel (more instruments can be specified if desired).

Battery has been repositioned in the boot to improve weight distribution, and the gearbox extension, remote lever housing and clutch housing use light-alloy to reduce all-up weight.

Standard rear-axle ratio is 3.9:1, as on the Cortina Super, but three alternatives (4.125, 4.429 and 3.77:1) are available. Propeller shaft is modified to withstand the higher r.p.m.

CONTINUED ON PAGE 113

CLUES to identity are contrasting side flashes, a Lotus badge on bonnet, sporty bumperettes. Grille of this prototype was painted black.

FORD CORTINA–LOTUS TWIN-CAM

Ford of Britain's Consul Cortina Sports Special, with a twin-cam Lotus engine, will undoubtedly be the most sensational British car of this year—and here's what John Blunsden, Peter Arundell and Jimmy Clark think of it.

THE WRITING WAS ON THE WALL on May 27, 1962. That was the day that Jim Clark climbed into a Lotus 23 sports car at the Nurburgring and proceeded to make a horde of Ferraris, Porsches and Maseratis look like so many old trucks as he led the 1000 Kilometers race with contemptuous ease. As we all know, the display came to an impromptu end when, half-asphixiated from an exhaust leak, Clark misjudged a turn and ended up with his car in a ditch.

Beneath the hood of his car was a new Lotus-developed twin overhead camshaft version of the eight-port Ford engine, with a capacity of 1½ liters. The car's performance had suggested that it was a highly tuned unit, but this was not so – a point which Clark was able to demonstrate by showing off the engine's exceptionally wide rev range and low-speed torque.

This was just a "cooking" touring-type engine, which, as keener observers noted, was a curious choice for an International sports car race, unless the event was simply being used as a development test for a unit planned for different applications.

Well, that's what it was, a development test. And, of course, the engine was planned primarily for Chapman's production cars. Subsequently it has been made available, in highly tuned form, for "over the counter" Lotus 23s, and in its mild form it has become the power unit of the exciting Lotus Elan. But now we have the third, and potentially the largest-selling application (also in the mild form) as the power unit for a high-performance version of the Ford Cortina.

With this new car, Chapman is jumping right into the touring car market, for his tie-up with Ford is considerably further reaching than is the BMC-Cooper bond. Unlike the Mini "bombs," the Cortina Lotus models are being assembled in a new factory at Cheshunt, although they are to be marketed through Ford outlets. And apart from the new engine, the car has been extensively modified and lightened, so that it is probably Britain's most promising article for sedan racing and rallying.

This has been quite a rush job, so much so, in fact, that when the car was announced to the British Press in January at London's Dorchester Hotel, only one "production" example had been built, and even that one didn't have the right size

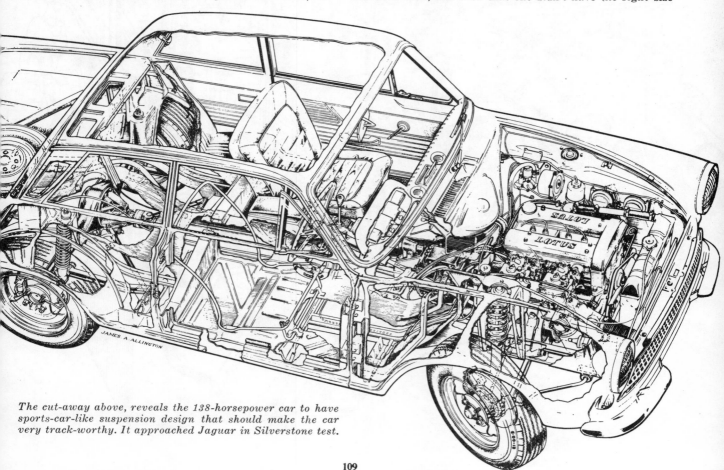

The cut-away above, reveals the 138-horsepower car to have sports-car-like suspension design that should make the car very track-worthy. It approached Jaguar in Silverstone test.

Modified bucket seats, good instrumentation, and flat steering wheel, above, aid controllability. At right the twin-cam head has Alfa-like appearance. Cutaway reveals good design.

PHOTOS: FORD OF BRITAIN

JAMES. A. ALLINGTON

of engine. Previously, several development cars had been built, but every one of them was non-standard in one or more respects. Consequently, although occasionally some performance figures were taken, none of these related to the car as it is now being turned out, although a pretty accurate assessment of stopwatch figures can be made.

In "production" form, the engine will have a bore of 3.25 inches (82.55mm) and a stroke of 2.864 inches (72.746mm), giving a displacement of 95.06 cubic inches (1,558 cc). It is to be operated on a compression ratio of 9.5 to 1, the fuel being fed through two twin-choke Weber 40 DCOE2 carburetors; maximum output is given as 105 horsepower (nett) at 5,500 rpm, and maximum torque as 108 pounds feet at 4,000 rpm (also nett).

But in addition, a strictly limited number of cars are to be built, modified to the CSI's Group 2 regulations. A team of three of these are to be run throughout 1963 by Team Lotus, the drivers being Jim Clark, Trevor Taylor, and Peter Arundell. A full International program is scheduled. Also, similar cars are to be built by Lotus for use by the Ford works International rally team. In both fields of endeavor, the Cortina Lotus is a real threat, but Ford Competitions Manager Syd Henson's chief worry at present is getting the car homologated as touring models. The CSI have laid down four dates on which homologation applications will be considered, the next date being April 25. This means that five important events will be missed, and Henson is now trying to persuade the CSI to convene an extra meeting, with all expenses paid.

The twin-cam engine, the original head design for which was done by Harry Mundy, is an ingenious blend of production and special components. The Ford cylinder head assembly and the front engine cover, with water pump casing, have been thrown away, but the standard cylinder block, with most of its ancillaries, have been retained, including the side-mounted camshaft, which continues to drive the distributor and oil pump.

The overhead camshafts in the light-alloy head are driven by the same single chain, each of the shafts running in four bearings. The valves are operated, at the comparatively narrow included angle of 54 degrees, by inverted bucket-type tappetts enclosing double valve springs, the head and throat diameters being 1.53 inches and 1.30 inches, respectively, for the inlet valves, and 1.45 inches and 1.20 inches for the exhaust valves. The 14 mm long-reach plugs are located vertically in the head, but are offset 0.87 inch from the centerline of the cylinders. The firing order is 1, 3, 4, 2.

The camshaft drive is enclosed in a new timing cover, which also incorporates the bearing for the fan and water pump, water inlet passages. All the timing and drive sprockets, and "V" belt pulleys are standard Ford components.

The inlet ports are extended from the head to form a direct mounting for the Weber carburetors, while the exhaust system incorporates four matched pipes, which blend into pairs, ending in a single pipe connecting to the reasonator box and muffler.

To withstand the increased rpm, there is an improved crankshaft, giving a greater degree of counterbalance (having five main bearings, of course) and although it had originally been intended to use standard Ford pistons, the units will, in fact, be fitted with pistons specified by Cosworth Engineering (who are co-operating closely on the venture). The pistons have two compression and one oil control ring.

A good engine is no use without a good transmission and chassis to go with it, and Chapman's staff have put in quite a lot of work on the rest of the car. There is a special close-ratio gearbox, giving the following ratios: 1st 2.50 to 1;

2nd 1.64 to 1; 3rd 1.23 to 1; 4th 1.00 to 1. The standard axle ratio will be 3.90 to 1, so this will result in overall ratios of: 1st 9.750 to 1; 2nd 6.396 to 1; 3rd 4.797 to 1; 4th 3.90 to 1. Three alternative axle ratios are also listed — 3.77, 4.13 and 4.41 to 1, and obviously the choice of ratio will have a considerable bearing on performance figures.

Considerable weight saving has taken place on the transmission, where light aluminum alloy has been used for the gearbox extension, the remote gearshift (which has a wood knob), the clutch housing, and the differential housing. There is a modified propellor shaft, three inches in diameter, swaged at each end to fit the standard production universal joints, and the latest-type diaphragm clutch, eight inches in diameter is used to deal with the increased rpm.

Chapman tried really hard to get the Ford chiefs to agree to an independent rear suspension, but in view of the rigor with which they defended their live axle on the standard Cortina when it was announced, it is hardly surprising that

Peter Arundell, shown here at Silverstone, had enthusiastic words for Ford/Lotus-developed car. Jimmy Clark agreed.

they have stood firm on this point. But the compromise is a great deal better than on the standard car. The leaf springs have been thrown away and replaced by coils mounted on hydraulic double acting telescopic shocks, the rear axle being located by radius arms and "A" bracket. At the front, the telescopic shocks are integral with the wheel spindle assembly, while the control arms are held in the fore-and-aft plane by a triangulated anti-sway bar.

Essential equipment on a car of this performance is a pair of disc brakes for the front wheels; these are 9.75 inches in diameter and carry DS5S pad material. The rear brakes are in drums, 9 inches x 1¾ inches, the leading and trailing shoes wearing DON24 linings. The hydraulic servo has a ratio of 2.04 to 1. The pressed steel 13-inch wheels have an unusually wide rim base of 5½ inches, to improve cornering power, and normally will carry 6.00 tires.

Lightening has also been carried out on the body, which in any case is a lighter-than-normal structure. Sheet aluminum has been used for the outer skins of the doors, the hood and the trunk lid. Inside the car there is an atmosphere of restrained luxury which is missing from the standard Cortina. The modified front seats are heavily padded for lateral support, and along with the body trim and crash pads, they are finished in black vynide. A non-dished, wood-rim steering wheel is fitted, and the steering ratio has been reduced to 13.4 to 1.

There is a new instrument binnacle, right ahead of the driver, carrying a 140 mph speedometer, with trip and total mileage recorders, a rev counter reading to 8,000 rpm, with the red line starting at 6,500 rpm. Supplementing these are the fuel, water temperature, and oil pressure gauges, and the usual collection of warning lamps. On the dashboard are the controls for the ignition-starter, wipers, washers, choke, and heater and fresh air unit, while the

FORD CORTINA

maxima of 45, 69 and 92 mph in the three indirect gears (all of which carry synchromesh), while the maximum speed has been put rather optimistically as "close to 115 mph." But as 6,000 rpm in top gear corresponds to 104 mph, with the 3.9 axle, I prefer Colin Chapman's personal estimate of about 108 mph, which is near enough to 6,250 rpm.

Acceleration from 0 to 60 mph should take approximately 10 seconds, and the car would be approaching 100 mph within half a minute of take-off. The standing-start quarter-mile should be covered in around 17 seconds. Fuel consumption, using best-quality gas, should better 25 mpg (US) in average use.

But with so much scope for variation by engine tuning or gearing, actual stopwatch figures are perhaps less significant than the car's handling qualities, and to get some of the background on this score I tackled Peter Arundell, who, with Clark and Taylor, has been doing the secret development work at Silverstone.

Understandably, more than half the driving there has been with the "hot" versions which the team plan to use this year. The Group 2 engine fitted for these tests was giving 138 horsepower, but the plan is to use 1,598 cc units in the team cars, and on the brake these have already given over 140 horsepower! But even with the "interim" engine, Clark has lapped the Silverstone Grand Prix circuit, under less than ideal conditions, in 1 minute 54.8 seconds, which is nudging the saloon car lap record currently held by a Group 2 Jaguar 3.8, while Arundell has been only 0.8 seconds slower at 1 minute 55.6 seconds.

Peter says the car is a revelation to drive in this form. Apparently Messrs Costin and Duckworth winced when told that he and his two colleagues had been using 7,000 rpm, but felt no ill effect seems to have been caused. But even with the 6,500 red line, the power curve is as wide as anyone would want it, and with the close ratio box it is naturally wise to move up a cog as soon as it will allow the rev counter to fall back on the peak torque figure of 4,000 rpm. From 3,500 rpm upwards there is a lot of really usable power, and the cornering power is governed not by engine output, but by the extent to which the inside rear wheel can be kept on the ground.

Arundell found that taking Silverstone's curves at full throttle meant that the one tire would lift just sufficiently to start spinning, causing the car to lose traction, while if he took the same curve at about three-quarters throttle he could keep all four corners in contact with the track, and, as a result, come out of the turns just that fraction faster.

Basically, it is an understeering car, but with so much power on tap there is no problem in converting this to over-steer whenever it is needed. But the cornering technique that pays off is not that one familiar to saloon car dicers, of sliding it sideways into a bend and pulling it through on opposite lock to kill the oversteer. The best technique on this car is to drive it as though it were on tramlines, feathering the throttle to maintain wheel grip, and generally driving the car tidily.

Apart from the engine modifications, alterations tried on the "hot" versions have included further retailoring of the suspension. This has been achieved by fitting softer coils at the back, and compensating this with stiffer dampers, and by stiffening up the front end, and fitting a thicker anti-sway bar up front. The steering ratio has also been raised again — up to 12 to 1, while the team cars may compete with steering as high as 10 to 1. Caster has been removed from the steering in order to compensate for the heavy feel, which makes some of the bends quite hard work!

Cosworth's design of sintered-plate clutch enables the car to be taken off the line at 4,500 to 5,000 rpm without losing "bite," and of course the gearshift is delightful, and the shift lever itself very well placed for the driver.

Even on the comparatively short Hangar Straight at Silverstone, the 138 horsepower Cortina has been timed at 122 mph, so on an ultra-fast circuit such as Reims, or on a Motorway, the maximum speed must be something not far short of a mile an hour for every horsepower!

Arundell has also tested the "production" type of Cortina Lotus to a considerable extent, and pronounces this as a real beauty. Due to the reduction of engine power, the rear-wheel hop just doesn't occur unless you "go crazy on some tight hairpin, just for the hell of it." And, of course, the car is even more tractable at the bottom end of the scale.

So there you are. The Cortina Lotus, or as Ford have styled it, the "Consul Cortina Sports Special." You will recognize it by the lower attitude of the body, the wide-rim wheels, by the green-colored flash along the body sides, the quarter bumper bars at the front, and the Lotus badge on the hood . . . And take warning: Don't lay down any speed challenges with your own sedan, because as like as not it'll show you a pair of spinning rear wheels, even if it is a production version, with that sleepy old 105 horsepower "cooking" engine!

AND A WORD OR TWO FROM JIM CLARK

The driver who came within a two-inch bolt and a missing locking washer of being the first Scottish World Champion racing driver recently wrote about his pre-production experiences with the twin-cam Cortina for *The Ford Times*, a British journal for Ford owners. Here are some of the highlights of his story:

"One gloomy day last winter I desperately needed a car to take a quick trip to my home in Scotland. After a few enquiries Colin Chapman said 'I know what we'll do, we'll lend you an Anglia.' I had up to that time been used to rather faster cars, like Porsches and Lotus Elites to do this journey very quickly. However, I had a look under the bonnet before I set out, and was amazed to find a twin-cam head with 'Lotus' written across the top.

"It was my first meeting with the engine which powers the Cortina Lotus. Once on the road I had a tremendous amount of fun. This Anglia had more acceleration than either the Porsche or the Elite. In place of the normal speedometer was one which read to 120 mph, and instead of being calibrated in tens of miles an hour this one swept up in fifteens!

"You can imagine the remarks of certain gentlemen in rather expensive cars when this secondhand-looking Anglia sailed past them on the motorway, with the speedometer flickering between 90 and 105 mph! I'm afraid the car did look a little second hand, having covered some 40,000 miles before coming to its destiny as a very mobile test bed at Lotus.

". . . When I heard that Colin was further developing the Cortina with this engine I was very keen to try it. This I did for the first time in October, when it was fitted with the first of the racing versions of the twin-cam engine, giving about 140 horsepower. I drove it part of the way up and I must say it gave me the same exhilaration as driving a Formula I car on the road.

"When I put my foot down to overtake it was as if someone had picked the car up and just thrown it past the car in front, and once past I kept easing my foot further and further off the accelerator, and yet the needle was still hovering round the 100 mph mark. On deceleration, the large servo-assisted disc/drum brakes really slowed me up with the minimum of fuss and effort — and most important, too, in a straight line.

"This might begin to sound too much of a fairy story if I said that everything went well all right at Snetterton, but in fact nothing went wrong, though we found several details which required altering, such as shock absorber settings, tire pressures, etc. When I went out, and took the engine up to its prescribed rev limits for the first time, I was amazed when I glanced at the speedo, reading as I changed gear: 2nd to 3rd gear, 75 to 80 mph; from 3rd to top at just over 100 mph, with the needle showing around 125 mph and still climbing by the time I braked at the end of the straight.

"When I stopped at the pits after a few laps it looked as if the front end

was on fire, but all it was, was that the anti-splash shrouds had been left on the brakes, and weren't letting enough air in to cool the discs under these conditions.

"Having removed these we had no more trouble. The track was never really dry that day, but we managed a lap in 1 minute 57 seconds, which was most encouraging as it was way below the record for that class.

"Colin Chapman took the car out just after a heavy shower, and after two or three fairly rapid laps everything suddenly went quiet. Fearing the worst, we all dived for our cars and raced around to the first corner past the pits, where we found Colin with the bonnet up, mumbling that the engine had just cut out on him. But as we got near him I had noticed faint criss-cross marks, slightly drier on the surface of the wet road, and when I suggested that perhaps the ignition lead that was loose had come off when he spun it, he

went slightly red, and said he wasn't sure which had happened first, much to the amusement of everyone there!

"Our next day's testing was at Silverstone, the day before I left England for the American Grand Prix, when, for the first time, the car was fitted with a neat remote-control gearchange, and a very pleasant facia panel, with all the usual array of dials to assure you that your engine is running normally.

"The weather was good, and it wasn't until then that I really appreciated the fantastic roadholding which had been achieved on the car. In fact, if anything, the front had too much grip, which tended to cock a back wheel and lose traction; only on taking Woodcote Corner really fast could one induce any real degree of drift.

"On a third day's testing, again at Silverstone, we tried a few alterations, such as a higher gear ratio, different linings on the rear brakes, different shock absorber settings, etc. Unfor-

tunately, it rained on and off all day, and the track was never really dry. But it did give us an idea of how controllable the Cortina was in the wet. It could be put into a drift at the beginning of a corner, and controlled completely on the throttle all the way through.

"At one point, while it was raining, Colin jumped into the back seat with the suggestion that it might help if we had some weight in the back. This, to the onlooker, if there had been any, would have looked quite frightening, with the two of us sitting discussing the various tendencies of the car as we splashed and slid our way around Silverstone in the 2 minutes 10 seconds region, in other words, around the lap times of a Zodiac in the dry!

"Anyhow, I now look forward with great interest to see how these fantastic little cars fare and add interest to an already spectacular and exciting form of motor racing."

COCKPIT has full instrumentation, wood-rim wheel with Lotus badge, remote-control shift, central console.

CONTINUED FROM PAGE 107

and uses three-inch tube, swaged at the ends to fit the standard-production universal joints. With the same idea in view, an 8in. diaphragm clutch has been standardised.

In addition to the lowered centre of gravity, front-wheel camber has been reduced to zero by means of modified MacPherson front suspension units and lowered track rods. Front springs are up to 140lb. per inch rate, and in conjunction with a stiffer 15/16in. anti-roll bar, almost roll-free high-speed cornering is possible.

Brakes are Girling, vacuum-servo-assisted, and comprise 9½in. discs on

the front wheels, and 9in by 1¾in. drums at the rear. "Hard" lining materials have been carefully selected for optimum performance and maximum toughness.

The "Cortina Special Sports" came into being mainly because Ford's recent successes in rallies, Formula Junior and sports-car racing events had led to a growing demand for a production sports car from Dagenham. Ford got together with Lotus and Cosworth Engineering, and this formidable model is the result.

The cars will be built at the Lotus factory at Cheshunt, in Hertfordshire,

which is being enlarged to cope with the expected demand. ("Already we are embarrassed by orders from many overseas markets," said Ford managing director Allen Barke at the car's official unveiling.)

Not Too Costly

Lotus will build their specialised components and fittings into Cortina shells and running gear supplied by the Ford Dagenham factory. At the time of writing no prices have been released, but it is forecast that the Lotus-Cortina will cost around £1200 stg. tax-paid in Britain — suggesting a figure close to £A2000 tax-paid in Australia, when (and if) the model is marketed "down under."

This wouldn't be excessive for a car that can reach 92 m.p.h. in third gear and 115 m.p.h. in top — the fastest Ford ever produced in Britain.

Ford have announced that they will enter both the Cortina Super and Lotus-Cortina in European rallies this season, while Lotus will race the twin-o.h.c. model in major saloon events, using their top drivers — Jim Clark, Trevor Taylor and Peter Arundell. I'll keep you posted on results! ● ●

Ford Cortina Lotus 1,558 c.c.

BEFORE going into the details of the Ford Cortina Lotus—the Consul Cortina developed by Lotus, with twin-overhead camshafts and much modified rear axle layout—it will help if we locate the car in the general motoring picture. Since its announcement last January many readers have asked whether it would meet their particular needs, ranging from pottering round the leafy lanes of Devon to hurtling round the racing circuits of Europe.

As tested, with the engine giving 105 b.h.p. net, it is by no means a "racer" and there is none of the temperament, intractability, plug-oiling and fervour that the name implies. But with the standard 3·9 to 1 rear axle fitted in conjunction with the Lotus close-ratio gearbox, it is very high-geared. Although quite practical for such mundane use as, say, daily commuting in London, this involves mainly first and second gear work with a bit of extra clutch-slipping. Even in first the top speed is 47 m.p.h. but, after a few miles, changing down into bottom becomes as natural and easy as into second on a lower-geared car, aided by the excellent Ford synchromesh. If ordering one of these cars it would be worth bearing in mind the optional 4·1 or 4·33 to 1 ratios, although the easy cruising speed in top, of course, would be lower.

Despite the reasonable tractability, the Cortina Lotus is essentially an open road car, and it would be a bit like putting a spirited hunter into the shafts of a coal cart to use the car mostly for domestic chores, particularly when such enormous fun can be had with it on fast give-and-take roads.

It was surprising to find that, while certain components (doors, boot and bonnet tops, gearbox extension and remote control casing, clutch housing and differential nose-piece) are of aluminium, the Lotus version at 16·25 cwt is still 28 lb heavier than the two-door Cortina 1200 we tested in September, 1962. The extra weight of the new cylinder head, two twin-choke Weber carburettors, rear end stiffening and suspension arms must more than make up for any saving. In terms of power-to-weight ratios, however, there is no comparison, for the Lotus figure is just over twice

PRICES		£	s	d
Two-door saloon		910	0	0
Purchase tax		190	3	1
	Total (in G.B.)	1,100	3	1
Extras (including P.T.)				
Seat belts, each		4	15	0

Make · FORD   Type · CORTINA LOTUS (1,558 c.c.)
(Front engine, rear-wheel drive)

Manufacturer : Ford Motor Co. Ltd., Dagenham, Essex

Test Conditions

Weather .... Wet, with 5-10 m.p.h. wind
Temperature .... 10·5 deg. C. (51 deg. F.)
Barometer .... 28·85in. Hg.
Wet concrete and tarmac surfaces.

Weight

Kerb weight (with oil, water and half-full fuel tank)
16·25cwt (1,820lb-825kg.)
Front-rear distribution, per cent F, 53·8; R, 46·2
Laden as tested .... 19·25cwt (2,156lb-978kg)

Turning Circles

Between kerbs .... L, 37ft 7in.; R, 37ft 6in.
Between walls .... L, 38ft 6in.; R, 38ft 5in.
Turns of steering wheel lock to lock 3

Performance Data

Top gear m.p.h. per 1,000 r.p.m. .... 17·4
Mean piston speed at max. power ... 2,620ft/min
Engine revs. at mean max. speed ...... 6,100 r.p.m.
B.h.p. per ton laden 109

FUEL AND OIL CONSUMPTION

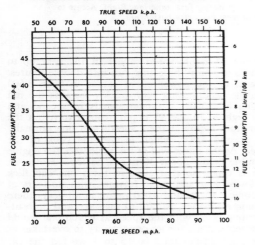

FUEL .... Super Premium Grade
(100-102 octane RM)

Test Distance	1,245 miles
Overall Consumption	20·8 m.p.g.
	(13·6 litres/100 km.)
Normal Range	18-25 m.p.g.
	(15·7-11·3 litres/100 km.)

OIL: S.A.E. 20W/30 Consumption 4,000 m.p.g.

MAXIMUM SPEEDS AND ACCELERATION TIMES

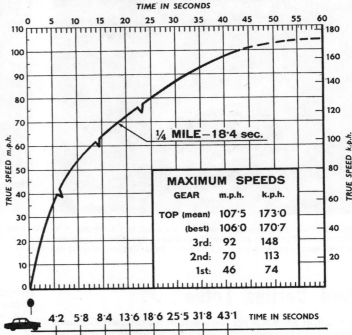

¼ MILE—18·4 sec.

MAXIMUM SPEEDS

GEAR	m.p.h.	k.p.h.
TOP (mean)	107·5	173·0
(best)	106·0	170·7
3rd:	92	148
2nd:	70	113
1st:	46	74

TIME IN SECONDS	4·2	5·8	8·4	13·6	18·6	25·5	31·8	43·1	
TRUE SPEED m.p.h.	30	40	50	60	70	80	90	100	
CAR SPEEDOMETER	31	41	51	61	71	81	91	101	

Speed range, gear ratios and time in seconds

m.p.h.	Top (3·90)	3rd (4·79)	2nd (6·40)	1st (9·75)
10— 30	—	—	5·3	3·0
20— 40	—	6·8	4·9	3·1
30— 50	9·0	7·0	4·8	—
40— 60	10·0	7·2	5·3	—
50— 70	8·9	8·1	6·4	—
60— 80	9·9	7·8	—	—
70— 90	12·5	11·2	—	—
80—100	11·3	—	—	—

BRAKES

(from 30 m.p.h. in neutral)

	Pedal load	Retardation	Equiv. distance
	25lb	0·29g	104ft
	50lb	0·61g	49ft
	75lb	0·80g	37·6ft
Handbrake		0·32g	94ft

CLUTCH

Pedal load and travel—45lb and 5·25in.

HILL CLIMBING AT STEADY SPEEDS

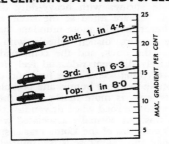

2nd: 1 in 4·4
3rd: 1 in 6·3
Top: 1 in 8·0

GEAR	Top	3rd	2nd
PULL (lb per ton)	275	350	500
Speed range (m.p.h.)	55–75	45–60	40–55

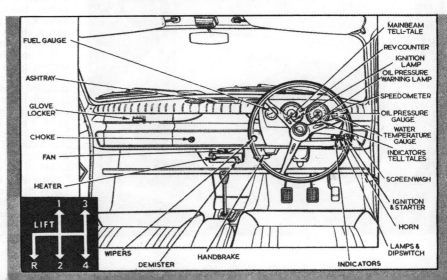

Left: One look at the interior shows this is no ordinary Cortina. A wooden gear lever knob (with tiny Lotus crest) matches the steering wheel which has rivet heads on its underside as finger-grips. Special front seats give excellent support during fast cornering. Right: Access to the back seat is rather hampered by the seat belts (optional extras) but there is room for at least two extra passengers

Ford Cortina Lotus . . .

as much, at 109 b.h.p. per ton laden, as the ordinary Cortina's mere 51. The aluminium panelling, incidentally, is a little flimsy and prone to denting, so one learns to close the boot and bonnet by allowing their lids to drop, rather than by pressing them down.

Because of the high axle ratio, acceleration from a standstill is initially a little disappointing, but once the car is rolling it becomes decidedly impressive, as the figures show.

With lightweight battery in the right flank, spare wheel bolted flat on the floor, and two strengthening struts the boot capacity is drastically reduced. The lid is made of soft aluminium so care is needed when shutting it

Indeed, for the 20 m.p.h. speed ranges in any gear up to 90 m.p.h. there are only three that run into double figures. The real meat of the power curve comes in from 3,500 r.p.m. when the needle soars very quickly towards the red sector starting at 6,500. Ultimate speeds in second and third are as high as 70 and 93 m.p.h. respectively, but the engine is far from happy at these speeds and one normally changes at around 5,500, which is also the peak of the power curve. At the lower end of the scale, too, the engine tends to rumble below about 30 m.p.h. in top. However, the exhaust is quiet, so that even in town one can flick down to a lower gear and surge forward with no fears of annoying people. At around 4,000 r.p.m. in all gears there was a booming resonance, painful to the ears, and unfortunately coinciding often with the speed at which one would hang back when waiting for an opportunity to overtake.

Since the compression ratio is 9·5 to 1 we fed the car on super premium fuel and there was never any pinking or running on. Starting from cold was always instantaneous and often without the choke which, if required, could be pushed home at once. The engine responded quickly and without hesitation immediately after a cold start and never stalled.

It is in the suspension and consequent general "sit" of the car on the road that the second Chapman influence is found. At the rear the half-elliptic leaf springs are replaced by vertical coil-spring-and-damper units with a trailing radius arm each side and a central A-bracket for lateral location. Higher rate springs with heavy-duty dampers and a stiffer anti-roll bar are fitted at the front and the car is an inch or so lower than its more mundane sisters.

To complete the set-up, dished wheels with wide-section tyres increase the track, and the combined effect gives the car an entirely different ride and feel from the standard product. Everything seems more firm and taut. It is much more susceptible to minor bumps and potholes, and the thumping of cats' eyes is more marked; on the other hand, it remains glued to the road when driven fast through bumpy corners in a way not normally associated with live rear axles. The only criticism of the Lotus rear suspension is in the way more road and axle noise is transmitted to the inside of the car through the extra attachment points.

Although basically an understeering car, the Cortina Lotus has sufficient power to produce the opposite effect. With a certain amount of skill one therefore has the best of both worlds, for the car holds its course at high speeds on the straight and its line through corners very well indeed. Should one feel boisterous, however, the tail can be hung

There is only one colour scheme available, white with a green flash each side that extends across the rear panel. Three Lotus badges are fitted, one on each rear quarter and another on the radiator grille

out by dexterous use of the throttle—steering corrections being easy and responsive.

Tyre pressure variations have an appreciable effect on the roadholding and handling generally. The makers recommend 20 p.s.i. all round for normal driving, with an increase to 22 p.s.i. front and 27 rear for fast driving. We found, however, that even with this increase the car still felt a little soggy through a succession of fast corners and we liked it better with 28 p.s.i. in the front and 34 in the rear, although this made the ride a little harsh.

Dual Role

In keeping with the dual role of the Cortina Lotus (at least of the "road" model—the 145 b.h.p. racing version is another story, see page 1026), the clutch is smooth and progressive. Being of the latest diaphragm-spring type it is no heavier in operation than normal but the final take-up is a shade quicker. Here again, there is nothing whatever of the "racer" about it and one's leg muscles never start to quiver when asked to hold it out for more than a few seconds at a time. It did not appear to suffer in any way, even after repeated and urgent standing starts. We were unsuccessful in getting away on a 1-in-4 hill with two up and test gear on board due to the high gearing.

An outstanding feature is the remote control gear change, ideally placed, and superbly smooth and precise in operation. Synchromesh is unbeatable and in all respects gear changing is above reproach—as befits a car with high close ratios there to be used regularly for the sheer fun of it.

The brakes, too, are of a very high standard with large front discs and vacuum-servo assistance. Pedal pressure is light and sensitive, giving great confidence at all speeds and for all surface conditions. There was never any fade or unevenness. During attempts to get an ultimate retardation figure, unfortunately during bad weather, the rear wheels locked first causing the car to slew on the damp surface, but quicker stops should be easy enough in the dry. The pull-and-twist handbrake is handy and held the car easily, facing up or down a 1-in-3 test hill. Competition drivers, however, would be happier with a pull-up lever beside the driving seat.

In a style associated with Grand Tourers, the entire interior decor (all save the roof) is in matt back Vynide. Separate, competition-type front seats are heavily padded at the sides and really do hold one in position, leaving the arms free to steer with instead of having to use the steering-wheel as a sort of grab-rail. Seat adjustment is in two planes at once, the runners being curved upwards towards the front so that when fully forward the seat is more tilted, and vice versa.

Though the oil pressure gauge is graduated up to 100 p.s.i., the pointer uses very little of this scale—the running pressure being between 35 and 40 p.s.i., dropping to around 5 or 6 p.s.i. at idling revs. Below this pressure a green warning lamp in the speedometer dial comes on.

Under the bonnet the cam covers are painted bright metallic blue. Accessibility of the fuel pump and distributor is obstructed by the two twin-choke Weber carburettors. The brake servo can be seen on the right

The screenwipers sweep a wide area right up to the pillar on the driver's side, but are of little use above 85 m.p.h. or so since they lift and leave a film of water rippling around on the glass. On a car with this performance (and price) one would expect two-speed wipers and anti-lift blades—and, incidentally, a much more commanding horn.

Stowage for parcels and maps is comprehensive, with a full-width shelf below the facia and a sizeable locker ahead of the passenger—the lid folding down to serve as a small tray. On the debit side, one needs to remove the ignition key (or carry a spare) to open the boot—a point that is invariably forgotten, especially when it is raining hard. And, on a car of this sort, which spends so much time overtaking others, a headlamp flasher is almost essential.

The Ford Cortina is well known for the size of its boot—though on the Lotus version this luggage space has been whittled down somewhat by the battery, the stiffening tubes running from the wheel arches to the rearward frame extensions on each side, and the fact that the left-hand of these encroaches on the space in which the spare wheel is normally stowed. The wheel now lies flat on the luggage locker floor, while its disused well appropriately filled with water in the case of the test car, easily drained by removing a rubber bung.

The fuel tank holds only eight gallons, which is scarcely enough at 20-odd m.p.g. The filler, beside the rear number plate, will take full-flow delivery—though it is impossible to fill up from a can without a cranked funnel or spout.

Except for an additional grease nipple at the axle housing end of the A-bracket, greasing points are the same as for the standard Cortina—eight requiring attention at 5,000-mile intervals. Unlike the Cortina, however, this car's engine oil and its filter element should be changed every 2,500 miles (5,000 miles on the Cortina)—when it is also advised to check the gearbox and rear axle oil levels. needs draining. On earlier examples of the Cortina Lotus, Gearbox oil is changed only once, after the first 5,000 miles, thereafter being simply topped up—and the rear axle never incidentally, the nuts holding the nosepiece of the axle casing to the banjo are liable to work loose so that these and the oil level should be checked frequently.

Except when the electrical cut-out stuck, and the battery went flat, the car gave no trouble during our 1,245-mile test. One must accept, though, that the extra performance and cornering power impose higher stresses on certain components than would apply to the standard product, so that one cannot expect quite the same trouble-free service and reliability normally associated with Ford cars.

As a high-performance car the Cortina Lotus is inconspicuous, and deceptive in its speed and acceleration. The neighbours would hardly be impressed, unless they were keenly informed, but the driver who knows his car can gain real satisfaction from driving it. On long journeys, distances seem less, and we averaged 63 m.p.h. on a Sunday from central London to Scotch Corner, at a fuel consumption of 22·4 m.p.g. To reach 100 m.p.h. from rest takes under three-quarters of a minute, so high speeds can often be used, and in this case they go hand-in-hand with a high standard of stability and braking power—the three criteria for a Grand Touring car.

Specification: Ford Cortina Lotus

Scale: 0·3in. to 1ft.

Cushions uncompressed.

ENGINE

Cylinders	...	4 in-line
Bore	...	82·55mm (3·25in.)
Stroke	...	72·75mm (2·86in.)
Displacement	...	1,558 c.c. (95·06 cu. in.)
Valve gear	...	Twin overhead camshafts
Compression ratio		9·5-to-1
Carburettor	...	Two double-choke side-draught Weber 40DCOE18
Fuel pump	...	AC mechanical
Oil filter	...	AC full-flow, renewable element
Max. power	...	105 b.h.p. (net) at 5,500 r.p.m.
Max. torque	...	108 lb. ft. at 4,000 r.p.m.

TRANSMISSION

Clutch	...	Single dry plate, 8in. dia., diaphragm spring
Gearbox	...	Four-speed, all-synchromesh
Overall ratios	...	Top 3·90, 3rd 4·79, 2nd 6·40, 1st 9·75, Reverse 10·96.
Final drive	...	Hypoid bevel 3·90 to 1

CHASSIS

Construction	...	Integral with steel body, aluminium doors, boot lid and bonnet

SUSPENSION

Front	...	MacPherson struts and wishbones, coil springs and anti-roll bar Armstrong telescopic dampers
Rear	...	Concentric telescopic dampers and coil springs, live rear axle located by A-bracket and radius arms
Steering	...	Burman recirculating ball
Wheel dia.	...	15in.

BRAKES

Type	...	Girling hydraulic, servo-assisted, discs front, drums rear
Dimensions	...	F, 9·5in. dia. discs; R, 9·0in. dia. drums, 1·75in. wide shoes
Swept area	...	F, 186 sq. in.; R, 96 sq. in. Total: 282 sq. in. (293 sq. in. per ton laden)

WHEELS

Type	...	Steel disc, 4-stud. 5·5in. wide rims
Tyres	...	6·00—13in. Dunlop C41 tubeless

EQUIPMENT

Battery	...	12-volt 38-amp. hr.
Headlamps	...	Lucas sealed beam 60/45-watt
Reversing lamp	...	Extra
Electric fuses	...	One
Screen wipers	...	Single-speed self-parking
Screen washer	...	Standard, manual plunger
Interior heater	...	Standard, fresh air
Safety belts	...	Extra
Interior trim	...	P.v.c. seats and roof-lining
Floor covering	...	Moulded rubber
Starting handle	...	No provision
Jack	...	Screw-type
Jacking points	...	2 on each side
Other bodies	...	None

MAINTENANCE

Fuel tank	...	8 Imp. gallons (no reserve)
Cooling system	...	10·5 pints (plus 2 pints for heater)
Engine sump	...	5·75 pints SAE 20W/30. Change oil every 2,500 miles; change filter element every 2,500 miles
Gearbox	...	1·75 pints SAE80. Change oil only after first 5,000 miles
Final drive	...	2 pints SAE 90. No provision for changing oil
Grease	...	9 points every 5,000 miles
Tyre pressures	...	F and R, 20 p.s.i. (normal driving); F, 22; R, 27 p.s.i. (fast driving); F, 28; R, 34 p.s.i. (see text)

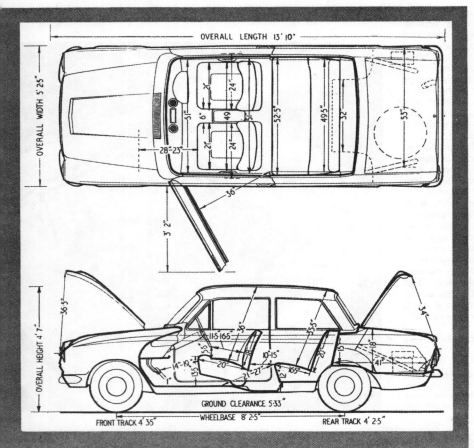

OVERALL LENGTH 13' 10"

OVERALL WIDTH 5' 2·5"

OVERALL HEIGHT 4' 7"

GROUND CLEARANCE 5·33"

FRONT TRACK 4' 3·5"   WHEELBASE 8' 2·5"   REAR TRACK 4' 2·5"

this is the LOTUS developed CORTINA

The magic of racing Lotus, educated to the elegance and indulgent comfort of the Ford Cortina. The pleasure of power, with a sense of family responsibility. Surge to 100 m.p.h. in under 30 secs. on 105 b.h.p. Chapman suspension, a lower, lighter body and trimmed by Lotus in quiet, perfect taste. Lotus developed Cortina—the best of all possible worlds—from £1100 inc. P.T. Lotus cars have won more races than any other marque—ever.

Normal part exchange, finance and insurance facilities available.

LOTUS RETAIL SALES DIVISION · DELAMARE RD · CHESHUNT · HERTS · WALTHAM CROSS 26181

FORD
CORTINA
LOTUS

There is a Ford Cortina to

At left, Blunsden smokes the well-behaved sedan around "The Hatch." Right, instrumentation includes a 140-mph speedo and 8000-rpm tach. Here Blunsden is flat out in 2nd gear in a Cortina.

suit every mood – this one is for them that likes it hot!

FORD OF BRITAIN has taken a leaf out of the book of the American parent company in marketing its Cortina, and as a result they have the best-selling British car of all time, as well as the top exported product. The policy has been "maximum variation on a common theme," and with options of three engine sizes, eight degrees of tune, different body styles, trim standards, transmission set-ups, and of course colors, the permutations run into several thousands. The end product ranges from the standard 1,200 cc two-door sedan — a sound but very unexciting motor car — through the highly popular GT range, to the specialized Lotus-built models, with twin-overhead-camshaft 1,558 cc power unit.

The Lotus Cortina should have hit the headlines early in 1963, when the European motor racing season opened, but homologation delays meant that it was well into the Fall before the car could make its impact in International racing. The Dagenham-built Cortina GT carried the Ford flag during the intervening months, and became so highly developed that, at the time of writing, in race trim it can still out-corner a track-modified Lotus Cortina! On the road, of course, and in production trim, the Lotus version has the edge, as is to be expected in view of the extensive modifications carried out at the rear of the car.

These include body stiffeners, the substitution of coil springs for the usual leaf springs, axle location by radius arms and an "A" bracket, and of course the use of special heavy-duty wide-rim wheels. The suspension has been stiffened up all round, and the result of all this is a car which is well able to make use of the considerable engine power.

Particularly noticeable is the way the back end sits down during cornering, even when the car is driven over rough patches. Body lean is checked firmly, so that the weight transfer becomes very predictable, and when a condition of rear-end breakaway is reached, the car remains most responsive to steering and throttle corrections. Driven more modestly, the car has slight understeering tendencies, and with a light steering mechanism, and at most times an ample reserve of engine power, this can be converted to neutral or oversteer without much difficulty.

The outstanding engine characteristic is its amazing smoothness all through the range. Although naturally it is an engine bred for comparatively high revs, it will pull from 1,500 rpm without protest, apart from a certain amount of vibration through the structure for the next 500 revs. The natural cruising speed seems to be in the region of 5,500 rpm, and there is a cut-out operative at 6,500 rpm (or 6,600 in the case of the car tested) to prevent inadvertent over-revving. The effect of the cut-out is to knock out one of the carbs and so starve two cylinders.

The twin-cam engine proved a good cold starter, and would warm up quickly at 2,000 rpm to a normal running temperature of between 80 and 85 degrees C. Fuel feed from the twin Webers was uneven for the first few seconds, but smoothed out as soon as the temperature began to rise. Using 100 octane fuel, there was no indication of pinking or running-on. The real "bite" of the power curve is felt from the top side of 3,000 rpm, but the engine could not be classified as in any way "lumpy." Both induction and exhaust noise were subdued, and although there was inevitably some top-end mechanical noise — to be expected from a high-efficiency power unit — this sounded pleasantly "taut."

The clutch action was quite faultless, the shift being well placed, and as light and positive in action as could possibly be expected. The special close-ratio indirect gears were rather noisy and there was some vibration through the shift lever around 6,000 rpm. Some slackness in the final-drive take-up was due either to an extensive program of testing, or to play in the "A" bracket mounting. By far the best acceleration times were obtained by using normal racing technique, letting the clutch in at 5,000 rpm, and controlling wheelspin.

Recommended tire pressures for fast driving are 22 psi front and 27 psi rear; raising front and rear tires by equal amounts can be recommended for really fast work when the road surface is good.

Inevitably, the low-speed ride is firm, and the Lotus Cortina cannot match the lower-priced versions' ability to iron out some of the pot holes and bumps. The body consequently has to absorb quite a few shocks, although this is felt mainly in the rear compartment. Road and final-drive noise is also higher than usual, but the body remained commendably rattle-free during the test, apart from occasional trouble from the window in the left-hand door.

The brakes are really excellent, and with a booster unit fitted as standard, the pedal pressure is light. It is just possible to lock a wheel in the wet, but altogether the brake efficiency is most reassuring. Slight unevenness when the discs were cold soon disappeared, and no fade could be induced during normal hard usage. The pull-and-twist handbrake is well placed, if not quite in keeping with the nature of this competition-bred car;

FORD CORTINA LOTUS

it was completely efficient.

Apart from the external distinguishing features of green side flashes on a light gray base color, and a black-painted grill (not to mention the Lotus badges) the interior of the car has also been given the 'works' by Lotus.

The special front seats are a great improvement on normal Cortina equipment, and offer adequate adjustment for most sizes of driver to find a comfortably relaxed position at the wheel. The seat cushion height also varies with the fore-and-aft adjustment, being at its highest at the mid-way position. Parcels accommodation includes a central box in a console behind the gear shift, a dashboard compartment and a tray beneath it, and a rear shelf. The trunk space has been reduced slightly by the twin body stiffening arms, the horizontal location of the spare wheel, and the relocation of the battery.

A special instrument panel incorporates matching speedo and tach, flanked by a fuel gauge and a combined water temperature and oil pressure gauge, all in round dials and easily read. The remaining controls are normal Cortina equipment, and all apart from the heater adjusters are easily reached with the driver's seat right back and the optional safety harness in use.

Serviceability is above average, oil and water fillers and dip stick being readily accessible, and plug changing being simplicity itself. Fluid reservoirs for the hydraulics, the coil and the distributor are also reasonably handily placed, but the fuel pump is hidden away below the rear of the twin Webers. The tool kit consists of a screw-type jack, to fit two lugs on each side of the body, and a wheelbrace.

In Britain, the Lotus Cortina costs nearly twice as much as the cheapest two-door Cortina, and consequently caters to only a specialized market. Nevertheless, enthusiasts who put a premium on a high power-to-weight ratio (in this case 130 horsepower per ton), a maximum speed of 108 mph, and an ability to cruise indefinitely at over 90 mph, will probably consider it excellent value, especially as the car is backed by the worldwide Ford sales and service facilities. — *John Blundsen*

FORD CORTINA LOTUS ROAD TEST 5/64

Vehicle	Ford Cortina Lotus
Price (as tested)	Approx. $3,100 in U.K.
Model	Two-door sedan
Options	Front seat belts

ENGINE:

Type	Four-cylinder, in-line, water-cooled
Head	Aluminum, detachable, with integral inlet manifold
Valves	Inclined, operated by twin overhead camshafts
Max. bhp	105 @ 5,500 rpm
Max. Torque	108 lbs. ft. @ 4,000 rpm
Bore	3.25 in. 82.55 mm.
Stroke	2.86 in. 72.75 mm.
Displacement	95.06 cu. in. 1558 cc.
Compression Ratio	9.5 to 1
Induction System	Two twin-choke Weber 40 DCOE 18 carburetors
Exhaust System	Dual two-branch manifolds into a single muffler
Electrical System	12 V. distributor ignition

CLUTCH:

Diameter	8 in.
Actuation	Diaphragm spring with hydraulic operation

TRANSMISSION:

Ratios:	
1st	2.50 to 1
2nd	1.64 to 1
3rd	1.23 to 1
4th	1.00 to 1

DIFFERENTIAL:

Ratio	3.9 to 1
Drive Axles (type) — Live axle with semi-floating shafts

STEERING:

Turns Lock to Lock	3
Turn Circle	38 ft.

BRAKES:

Drum and Disc Diameter	9½ in. disc, front, 9 in. drum, rear
Swept Area	282 sq. in.

CHASSIS:

Frame	Monocoque construction with integral steel body structure
Body	Steel with aluminum doors, trunk lid and hood
Front Suspension	Wishbones, coil springs, telescopic shocks, MacPherson struts and anti-sway bar
Rear Suspension	Coil springs, telescopic shocks, radius arms and A bracket
Tire Size & Type	600 x 13 Dunlop tubeless C 41

WEIGHTS AND MEASURES:

Wheelbase	98.5 in.	Ground Clearance	5.3 in.
Front Track	51.5 in.	Curb Weight	1,800 lbs.
Rear Track	50.5 in.	Test Weight	2,080 lbs.
Overall Height	55 in.	Crankcase	3 qts.
Overall Width	62.5 in.	Cooling System	6.25 qts.
Overall Length	166 in.	Gas Tank	9.5 gals.

PERFORMANCE:

0-30	3.6 sec.	0-70	12.8 sec.
0-40	5.2 sec.	0-80	17.2 sec.
0-50	7.0 sec.	0-90	23.0 sec.
0-60	9.4 sec.	0-100	sec.

Standing ¼ mile	16.8 sec. @ 78 mph
Top Speed (av. two-way run)	108 mph

Speed Error	30	40	50	60	70	80	90
Actual	30	40	50	59	67	78	88

Fuel Consumption:
		Recommended Shift Points:	
Test	18 mpg	Max. 1st	45 mph
Average	21 mpg	Max. 2nd	69 mph
		Max. 3rd	92 mph

RPM Red-line	6,500 rpm

Speed Ranges in gears:
1st	0 to 45 mph	3rd	21 to 92 mph
2nd	16 to 69 mph	4th	26 to 108 mph

Brake Test: 80 Average % G, over 10 stops. No fade encountered.

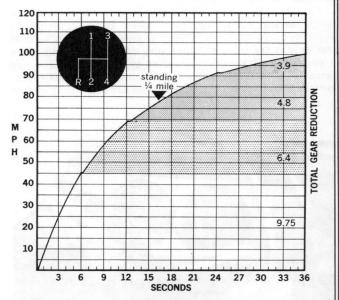

REFERENCE FACTORS:

Bhp. per Cubic Inch	1.1
Lbs. per bhp.	17.14
Piston Speed @ Peak rpm	51.6 ft./min.
Sq. In. Swept Brake area per Lb.	0.16

Autocar 1 OWNERS GUIDE SHEET

FORD CORTINA

September 1962, saw the introduction of the first Ford Consul Cortina; few models have met with such immediate success and the cars now offered in a number of forms continue to be top sellers. Yet when the details of the Cortina were first made known, many people were puzzled. Was it an Anglia replacement? Did it not overlap with the Classic, also prefixed with the name Consul—a name which was then associated more in peoples' minds with a car of the Zephyr 4 specification?

Eighteen months have passed and Ford's market researchers who had reported that this was the size and nature of family saloon likely to be in greatest demand, have been proved right; the Cortina has become a potent design in its own right, not directly replacing any other Ford model.

Seldom can there have been so many variants of one basic design. One may reflect that, as in this instance, successful families and ranges of car seem to depend greatly on, and be built-up-around, a good basic power unit. That of the Cortina (shared with Anglia and Corsair) is reliable, responsive, smooth and very amenable to tuning.

These are the variants on the four-cylinder Cortina theme in order of price: Cortina two-door, four-door, Cortina two-door de luxe, four-door de luxe, Cortina Super 1500 two-door, four-door, Cortina four-door de luxe estate car, Cortina 1500 G.T. two-door, four-door, Cortina Super 1500 Estate Car. The prices vary from £474 basic (total with tax £573 6s 3d) for the two-door Cortina, to £650 basic (total with tax £785 19s 7d) for the 1500 Super Estate Car. The Cortina-Lotus, a much modified special version costs £1,100 including tax.

A variety of options and extras may be had; examples with prices:	
1,500 c.c. engine in 1,200 c.c. models ...	£30
Heater (standard on Supers)	£15
Bench seat, column gearshift, panel brake lever (free choice on Supers) ...	£12 14s
Screenwasher	£1 15s
Overriders	£4 10s

FORD CORTINA

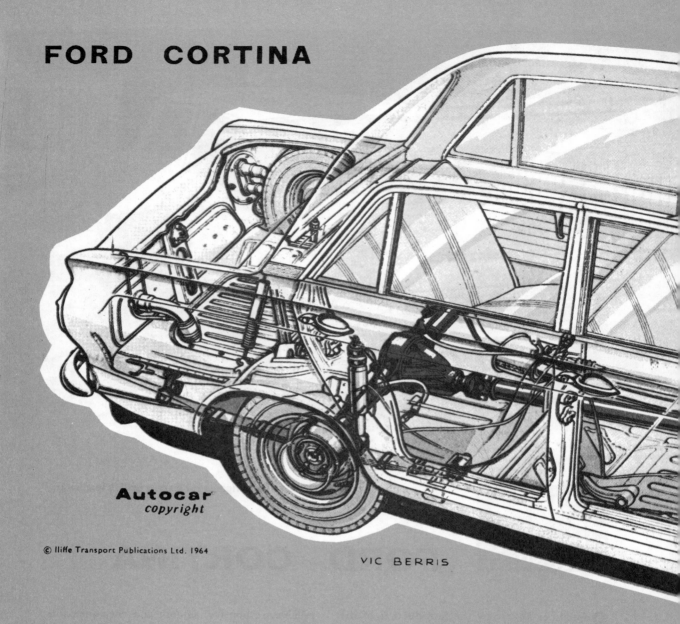

Autocar
copyright

© Iliffe Transport Publications Ltd. 1964

VIC BERRIS

BRIEF SPECIFICATION

Engine	1,198 c.c.	1,498 c.c.	G.T. 1,498 c.c.
Carburetter ...	1 Solex	1 Zenith	1 Weber
Compression ratio	8·7 : 1	8·3 : 1	9·0 : 1
Main Bearings ...	3	5	5
Max. power (net)	48·5	59·5	78·0
and r.p.m. ...	4,800	4,600	5,200
Max. torque lb ft	66·0	85·5	97·0
and r.p.m. ...	2,700	2,300	3,600

Suspension: Front: MacPherson struts, wishbones, coil springs, and anti-roll bar. Rear: Live axle, half-elliptic leaf springs. Armstrong telescopic dampers all round.

Transmission: Four-speed, all-synchromesh gearbox with option of column or central floor mounted levers. Hypoid bevel final drive.

Steering: Ford-Burman recirculating-ball.

Brakes: 1,198 c.c.—Girling 8 in. diameter drums front and rear.

1,498 c.c.—Girling 9·0 in. diameter drums front and 8·0 in. diameter drums rear.

G.T. 1,498 c.c.—Girling 9·5 in. diameter discs front and 9·00 in. diameter drums rear.

Tyres: 5·60-13 in. tubeless, Estate Cars 6·00-13 in.

AUTOCAR TESTERS' NOTES

Steering: Light, fairly high geared, adequate self-centering, good lock.

Handling: Crisp, safe and predictable, back end slides rather early in the wet.

Ride: Quite good, level, practically no pitch or roll.

Brakes: Light pedal load, good response, wheels lock rather easily.

Engine: Smooth at all speeds, noise never obtrusive.

Gear Change: Very good and precise, all four gears have effective synchromesh.

Noise: Wind noise appreciable at over 60 m.p.h.

Driver Comfort: Leg room limited. Steering wheel set rather high, seat fairly comfortable, not much sideways location.

Back Seat: Room for three on short journeys. Leg room limited, seat not very comfortable.

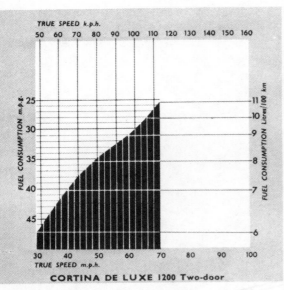

CORTINA DE LUXE 1200 Two-door

Autocar Test Results 28 September 1962 and 25 January 1963

   (i) CORTINA DE LUXE 1200 two-door

  (ii) CORTINA SUPER 1500 four-door

Speed and Acceleration

Max speed	(i)	77 m.p.h.
	(ii)	82 m.p.h.
Standing start ¼-mile	(i)	22·4 sec
	(ii)	20·8 sec
30–50 m.p.h. in top gear ...	(i)	13·1 sec
	(ii)	11·2 sec
Top gear m.p.h. per 1,000 r.p.m. ...	(i)	16·1 m.p.h.
	(ii)	17·4 m.p.h.

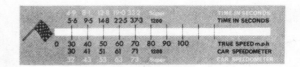

Petrol Consumption   Premium fuel 97 octane

Tank capacity   8 Imp. gal., 36 litres (no reserve)

Constant 50 m.p.h.—(i) 41·0 m.p.g. 6·9 litres/100 km
                (ii) 35·5 m.p.g. 8·0 ,,   ,,

Averages

Hard driving	(i)	25 m.p.g.	11·3	,, ,,
	(ii)	25 m.p.g.	11·3	,, ,,
Gentle driving	(i)	37 m.p.g.	7·6	,, ,,
	(ii)	36 m.p.g.	7·9	,, ,,
Overall test (1,430 miles)—				
	(i)	30·2 m.p.g.	9·4	,, ,,
Overall test (1,325 miles)—				
	(ii)	27·2 m.p.g.	10·4	,, ,,

Mean Turning Circle   Between kerbs: 34 ft 3 in.
                            Between walls: 36 ft 4 in.

Kerb weight ... (i) 16·0 cwt 1,792 lb 813 kg
               (ii) 16·4 cwt 1,842 lb 835 kg

Servicing ... ... 8 grease points every 5,000 miles

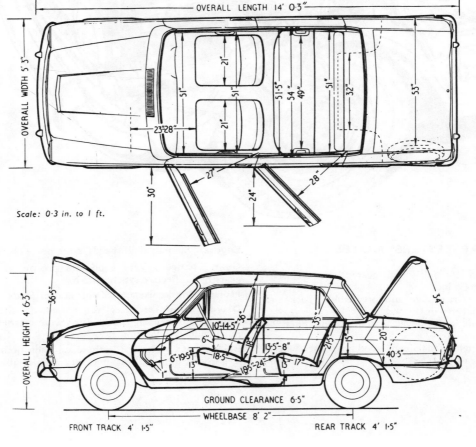

Scale: 0·3 in. to 1 ft.

Cortina-Lotus BEHAVIOUR AND PERFORMANCE

OF THE NEW SPECIAL EQUIPMENT VERSION

FOR the past year *Autocar* has had a Cortina Lotus in the staff fleet. To start with there were some troubles, but it has many attractive qualities and so our test staff were all anxious to try the new special equipment model from Lotus, which represents also the fruits of another year's development.

The main differences between the test car and the earlier standard Cortina Lotus are the divided propeller shaft, a different camshaft, "worked" cylinder heads and rear suspension modifications—including the fitting of Armstrong adjustable dampers and special coil springs. The cost difference is £95, new, making a total for the test vehicle with radio and other extras of £1,240 2s 11d. As an after-sale conversion for a low mileage car the extra is £135.

The ordinary Cortina or Cortina Lotus has a long, one-piece propeller shaft between its far-forward power unit and live rear axle. On all the latest Lotus Cortinas this is in two parts and the extra universal supported at about one-third of the length behind the gearbox. The two-piece shaft is less rigid, and the additional torsional "give" absorbs transmission snatch. In practice, this means that the clonks and jerks which are difficult to avoid when using the full performance of the earlier design have now virtually gone.

Modified cam profiles on the special camshafts are designed to improve low-speed tractability, at some slight sacrifice in torque, rather than increase out-and-out performance, but the figures obtained are also appreciably better at the top end. Usually the more highly tuned an engine is to start with, the less will be the return for additional time and money spent on it. Even so, in this case the improvement is considerable.

Pirelli Cinturato tyres were fitted on the test car. They have characteristic effects on handling and behaviour which can be summarized as excellent fore-and-aft grip, positive steering and a slight directional vagueness at high speeds in a straight line. On a wet road we set up front wheel slides and found that recovery in these conditions was rather slow.

Normal tyre pressures recommended in the instruction manual—20 p.s.i. all round—are too low for our liking and those for high-speed driving, 22 p.s.i. front and 27 p.s.i. rear,

are biased towards understeer. With the Pirellis fitted we used 28 p.s.i. front and 30 p.s.i. rear. The extra pressure in front reduced understeer but it probably accounted in part for the tendency to wander at high speeds on M roads.

We have nothing but praise for the handling of this much modified family four-seater; it corners very well and predictably up to very high speeds, and feels safe at all times. In our full road test of November last year we commented that the steering offers the best of both worlds. The car is basically a slight understeerer, which is considered a good thing for ordinary road use. This can be adjusted within limits by alterations of tyre pressures, front and rear. But there is plenty of power available and the car can be "laid" into and held through a corner with power on and tail out, as many will have noted in production car races.

An important difference in this special equipment model is the ability to carry four passengers and luggage without any bottoming on the rear suspension. (Racing Cortinas are usually sprung for carrying only the driver.) Rear seat passengers said the ride was better and quieter than that in front and very comfortable in a firm way—"Just right for a sporting grandmother" as one remarked. From the driver's point of view the car sits down better on the road and handles just as well with a load as when solo.

We thoroughly enjoyed measuring the performance figures because of the eager, free-revving nature of the engine and the crisp, precise gear-change. All the gears, of course, are synchronized and the box did not appear to object to the snatch changes which have to be made with cars on test, if one is to obtain the best acceleration figures through the gears. Towards the end of the two weeks of testing the change up into second had to be a bit slower, with careful double de-clutching to avoid a slight crunch. The clutch put up well with some hard use during standing-start accelerations and continued to work perfectly throughout.

The figures obtained with two up—one driving, one on the instruments—are very good indeed. In particular, we surprised ourselves with two 16·3sec. standing ¼-miles and a two-way mean of 16·5sec.

Figures in brackets are for the standard Cortina Lotus tested in Autocar *of 6 December, 1963*

Acceleration Times (mean): *Speed range, gear ratios and time in seconds:*

m.p.h.	Top (3·90)	Third (4·79)	Second (6·40)	First (9·75)
10–30	—	—	—	3·2 (3·2)
20–40	—	6·4 (6·9)	4·5 (4·9)	2·9 (2·9)
30–50	8·1 (8·6)	6·1 (6·8)	4·0 (4·5)	—
40–60	7·9 (8·8)	6·3 (6·6)	4·3 (4·9)	—
50–70	8·9 (9·5)	6·4 (7·2)	4·8 (5·9)	—
60–80	9·1 (10·5)	6·8 (8·2)	—	—
70–90	10·3 (12·0)	9·2 (12·2)	—	—
80–100	15·1 (19·4)	—	—	—

Standing quarter-mile 16·5 sec. (17·4 sec.)

Overall fuel consumption for 789 miles: 20 m.p.g. 14·1 litres/100 km
Typical fast journey average: 20·8 m.p.g. 13·6 litres/100 km.

From rest through gears to:

30 m.p.h.	.. .. ..	3·7 sec. (3·9 sec.)
40 ,, ..	.. ..	4·9 ,, (5·4 ,,)
50 ,, ..	.. ..	6·8 ,, (7·3 ,,)
60 ,, ..	.. ..	9·2 ,, (9·9 ,,)
70 ,, ..	.. ..	12·2 ,, (13·1 ,,)
80 ,, ..	.. ..	16·5 ,, (17·6 ,,)
90 ,, ..	.. ..	21·8 ,, (23·8 ,,)
100 ,, ..	.. ..	33·1 ,, (35·6 ,,)

Maximum speeds in gears:

	m.p.h.	k.p.h.
Top (mean)	111·0 (106·0)	178·6 (170·5)
(best)	113·0 (107·5)	181·8 (172·2)
3rd (at 7,000 r.p.m.)	96	154
2nd ,, ,, ,, ...	74	119
1st ,, ,, ,, ...	48	77

Low-speed pulling power is not very great—slightly less than with the standard Cortina-Lotus, in fact—although this is not normally apparent because the driver instinctively uses the gearbox freely. We found that to get the car away really quickly from standstill it was best to let the clutch in at about 6,000 r.p.m. and allow the minimum of slip. The revs did not then drop below 2,500 r.p.m. when the clutch was finally in and the times were good. Wheelspin on the dry tarmac was very slight and there was never a sign of axle hop.

In top gear the minimum even pulling speed was about 24 m.p.h.; this is with a 3·9 axle. The ratios are close and very well chosen, and first is as high as 9·75 to 1. This means that the minimum traffic speed without snatch or some clutch slipping is about 9 m.p.h., but the engine does not fuss in these conditions and picks up cleanly.

We were asked by Lotus to observe a 7,000 r.p.m. limit unless some particular figures were likely to be better if this figure was exceeded slightly. In the event there was no advantage and no gear changes could be saved. The engine was still pulling smoothly and had not run out of breath at 7,400 when we did a spot check at 100 m.p.h. in third, but we did not try to record third gear figures to 100 m.p.h. Owing to the Cinturato tyres, which have a smaller rolling radius than, say, the equivalent Dunlop C.41s, the speedometer reading was well out and showed about 110 m.p.h. at a true 100, reached in 33·1sec from rest. The highest true speed we saw on the level was 113 m.p.h. and the last three m.p.h. took a mile or so to build up. The water temperature rose over 90 deg after several high-speed runs on a fine warm day, but the oil pressure did not drop unduly. No oil cooler was fitted. The engine used only a quart of oil in 750 miles inclusive of the performance measurements.

We have a few detailed criticisms about matters that could easily be remedied. A tank of only eight gallons capacity with no reserve is irritating; a range of some 150 miles with the normal consumption of about 21 m.p.g. is not enough. Then there is the wire hook safety catch for the bonnet. This is easily damaged and readers have reported failures on early ordinary Cortinas. Ford now fit a more substantial catch which should certainly be adopted for the Lotus—possibly as a retrospective modification, too. A boot lid that will open only with the aid of the ignition key is rather inconvenient and the same is true of a bonnet top which has to be propped open with a wire stay. It is no fault of the car that the Ford radio sounds tinny, is prone to interference and fade, and has a very over-sensitive tuning control. The finish of the car is now pretty good inside and out, and the black interior trim is pleasing and restful.

From outside the car the exhaust starts quiet and builds up to no more than a subdued crackle to which no one would object. Inside there is very little engine, gearbox or exhaust noise for the type of car, just a moderate sound of work going on. The transmission and suspension clonks of some of the earlier cars have largely disappeared, and the performance as a whole is more refined.

The consensus of opinion is that this Cortina Lotus special equipment model is quite a step forward. At £1,200 it has some formidable competitors from home and abroad, but few can match its exhilarating performance or so easily interchange the competition crash helmet with the everyday cap as the desire and opportunities arise.

Looking aft. Left: Previous type of large diameter, one-piece propeller shaft. Right: Latest divided design of reduced diameter (with additional universal joint and centre bearing) for better torsional flexibility and reduced axle loadings

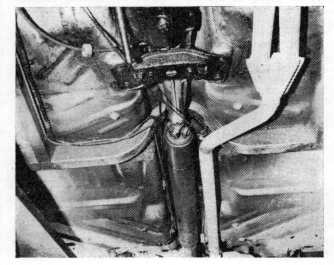
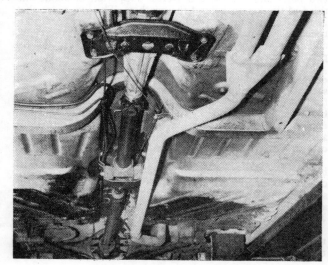

Ford Lotus-Cortinas made no mistake about winning England's classic saloon car race. They hit the front from the start.

LOTUS CORTINA WINS SIX HOUR

SUMMER in this exceedingly damp little island has arrived at last and motor racing here and all over Europe is in full swing. Next weekend is Le Mans, where a raging battle is anticipated between Ferrari and Ford, although raging battles on paper have a habit of falling flat in fact.

Disastrous Indianapolis 500

The disastrous Indianapolis 500-mile race is over, with those old-fashioned specialised American track cars supreme, in spite of all the pre-race ballyhoo over the British entries which were to have wiped the Offenhauser eye! It was unexpected tyre trouble that put the Lotus entries out and endangered the life of the reigning world champion.

Incidentally, another bitter disappointment after last year's fine showing at Le Mans is that there will be no Rover gas-turbine car there this year. Although this makes the race more of a sports car prototype event and less of a farce, it is sad that Rover do not feel able to compete on level terms with the piston-engined jobs with a gas-turbine vehicle. Nor do I see many of the new Rover 2000 cars on British roads to date.

The amount of motor racing we manage to pack in here is quite remarkable. Tomorrow, as I thrash this

out, there will be one of those club days at Silverstone and I see that the entries for this one meeting alone total 180. In sterner racing I get many letters of praise for Jack Brabham, who is doing so well with Grand Prix cars of his own make.

Racing Saloons for six hours

One race very difficult to report, but highly entertaining for spectors, is the Motor Six-Hour Race for Saloon Cars, which they run round and round the Brands Hatch circuit. This year everything went smoothly. No scrutineering troubles. No serious accidents. And enough rain to keep the worried tyre experts happy.

Ford Lotus-Cortinas finished first and second, although there was some anxiety about their back axles towards the end. When he designed light-alloy specially-located rear axles for these Fords, Colin Chapman said he was making the best of a bad job and would have preferred to have been allowed to use an independent system.

But it was a splendid tribute to Ford that these inexpensive saloons should vanquish the "works" Mercedes-Benz. Other cars which showed up well were the Lancia Flavias and a lone big Ford Galaxie. The lone BMW 1800 TI also went well until the clutch packed it in. The works BMC Minis rather disgraced themselves, and it was left to the Broadspeed Mini and a Don Moore-tuned Mini to bring home the bacon in the 1300 cc class.

LOTUS cortina

A potent little competitor, the Cortina Lotus has been making quite a name for itself in European sports car racing and rallying circles.

Nearly every American sports car enthusiast has been waiting for something like the Cortina Lotus, but now they will have to wait no longer. The Cortina Lotus has arrived on American soil and is being introduced across the country through English Ford dealers.

The Cortina Lotus rides and handles like a full fledged sports car, yet it has the luggage and passenger space of a compact sedan. It is a pert looking, well-constructed, exciting means of transportation. The Cortina Lotus weights in at approximately 1,900 lbs., and carries a live rear axle which contributes

to its responsive handling and firm ride.

British-American cooperation is very evident in the design and fabrication. It is the result of the combined efforts of Ford of Britain, builder of the Cortina, and Colin Chapman, designer of the World Championship and Indianapolis 500 Lotus racing cars.

The interior appointments carry everything necessary for passenger and driver comfort, both physically and mechanically. The bucket seats minimize road shock, while seat belts insure safety in an emergency. The easily readable instrument cluster containing speedometer, odometer, tripmeter, tachometer, ammeter and fuel, temperature and oil pressure gauges keep the driver in constant communica-

A healthy 1558cc, double-overhead camshaft, 4-cylinder Lotus engine equipped with dual Weber carburetors powers the Cortina.

The interior appointments carry everything necessary for passenger comfort, both physically and mechanically.

tion with his machine.

The power is supplied by a 1558cc, double-overhead camshaft, 4-cylinder Lotus engine. With dual two-choke Weber carburetors, this engine is basically the Lotus-modified high performance power plant that won the Formula II Championship in open wheeled racing cars. This engine delivers 115 h.p. at around 5700 r.p.m.

The front and rear suspensions have been lowered and stiffened, and radius rods have been added to the rear. A large-diameter drive shaft and heavy-duty shock absorbers contribute to the firm ride. The tires are 6.00 x 13-inch, 4-ply rating nylon...

Gear selection is supplied by a 4-speed all syncromesh gear box. The overall ratios are: first—12.260 to 1, second—8.291 to 1, third—5.763 to 1, and fourth—4.125 to 1. This transmission has been carefully tailored to the output of the Lotus-modified engine to insure outstanding performance.

Although the Corinta is small, only 168.3 in. long and 62.5 in. wide, the many accomplishments of the car in open competition are evidence of the car's performance. But the Cortina is equally at home on the road or track.

Combined with sedan size and seating for four, the Cortina Lotus offers such comfort features as flow-through ventilation with fresh-air heater and defroster. Other standard equipment includes electric windshield wipers, bumper guards, padded sun visors, padded instrument panel, padded door armrests, interior light with courtesy switches, center console and ash tray, rear compartment ash tray, and a unique European feature — a full width parcel tray underneath the dash.

Optional equipment includes a radio, white side-wall tires, cigar lighter, heavy duty battery, and full width carpeting.

Combine the economy and practicality of a European sedan with the handling and performance of a sports car and you have the Cortina Lotus. ■

The Cortina Lotus rides and handles like a full fledged sports car, yet it has the luggage and pasenger space of a compact sedan.

The potent little sedan weighs in at 1,900 lbs., and carries a live rear axle which contributes to its responsive handling and firm ride.

CORTINA DEVELOPED BY LOTUS
MINIMUM EQUIPMENT

BODY SPECIFICATION
Basic Data

Two Door Sedan —
Color — Ermine White, Green Side Flash
Black Vinyl Interior Trim
Laminated Windshield
Individual Bucket Type Seats
Front Seat Belt Anchorage Points (For Pillar and/or Floor Mounting)
Full Width Bumpers & Bumper Guards

Controls

Dished Three Spoke Woodrimmed Steering Wheel
Remote Floor Mounted Type Gearshift
Dash Mounted Handbrake
Combined Key Operated Ignition/Starter Switch
Choke Dash Mounted
Windshield Wiper/Washer
Instrument Panel Light Switch
Side and Headlight Switch
Steering Column Antenna Controlling —
— Horns
— Self-Cancelling Direction Indicators
Floor Mounted Headlamp Dimmer
Aero Flow Ventilation and Air Extraction

Instruments — Dash Mounted

Speedometer, Odometer, Tripmeter
Tachometer
Fuel Gauge, Temperature Gauge
Oil Pressure Gauge, Ammeter
Warning Lights for: — Generator
                      Oil Pressure
                      Main Beam
                      Turn Indicator

Fittings

Door Pull Armrests
Zero Torque Door Locks
Opening Front Quarter Vents
Crash Pad
Interior Sun Visors
Interior Rear View Mirror
Interior Light with Door Operated Courtesy Switches
Center Console Incorporating Glove Box, Arm Rest with Front and Rear Compartment Ashtrays
Package Tray with Padded Edge
Glove Compartment with Door
High Output Heater and Defroster

CHASSIS SPECIFICATION

Engine Type — 1558c.c., 4 Cylinder O.H.C.

(For use with fuel of 100 octane rating or over)

Compression Ratio .... 9.5 : 1
Max. Gross B.H.P. .... 115 at 5700 r.p.m.
Max. Net Torque .... 108 lbs. ft. at 4000 r.p.m.
Bore .... 3.25 ins.
Stroke .... 2.864 ins.
Light Alloy Cylinder Head
Chain Driven Twin Overhead Camshaft
Five Bearing Crankshaft
Crankcase Emission Control Device

Engine Lubrication

Externally Mounted Oil Pump
Capacity of System .... 8.4 Pints

Fuel System

Fuel Pump: Mechanical actuated by Eccentric on Distributor and Oil Pump Driving Shaft
Carburetor: Two Twin Choke Weber 40 DCOE 18
Air Cleaner — Paper Element
Tank Capacity .... 9.6 Gallons

Cooling System

Pressurized Pump Assisted
Capacity .... 18.6 Pints
Fan .... Two Blade 11.0 ins.

Transmission

Split Drive Shaft
Gearbox .... 4 Speeds All Synchromesh
Overall Ratios: 1st .... 12.260 : 1
               2nd .... 8.291 : 1
               3rd .... 5.763 : 1
               4th .... 4.125 : 1
Clutch: Hydraulic Single Plate (Diaphragm type)
Aluminum Clutch Housing

Axle Ratio .... 4.125 : 1

Capacity .... 2.4 Pints

Electrical

Battery .... 51 Ampere Hour
Battery Dimension .... 9.25 x 7.9 x 5.19 ins.
Generator .... 22 Amp
Horn Dual Tone
Windshield Wipers
Headlights: Sealed Beam

Suspension

Front: Independent Coil Springs and Hydraulic Double Acting Telescopic Shock Absorbers
Rear: Leaf Springs with Hydraulic Double Acting Telescopic Shock Absorbers and Radius Arms

Steering Gear

Recirculatory Ball Type
Ratio .... 15.1 : 1
Turning Circle .... 37.25 ft.
Control .... Left Hand Drive

Brakes

Front Disc Type .... 9.75 ins.
Rear Drum Type .... 9.0 ins
Front Pad Area (Swept) .... 182.60 sq. ins.
Rear Lining Area (Swept) .... 99.00 sq. ins.

Wheels

Widebased Pressed Steel Rims .... 13 x 5.5 J

Tires

6.00 x 13 4-Ply Rating Nylon

Tools

Jack, Wheelbrace

Instruction Book

In English

LOTUS CORTINA

By Jerry Titus

This little Ford went to Cheshunt, For more than just green stripes!

IT WAS ROUGHLY A YEAR AGO (September, 1965, to be exact) that SCG tested the Ford Cortina GT for its readers. We concluded it was a spunky, trim, but somewhat austere little vehicle (little in exterior dimensions only) that added up to an impressive bargain at $2116 POE Los Angeles. If you take the same basic package and add roughly $1400 to it in creating another version, the evaluation has to change ... by a whole lot. Thus, our first impressions of the Lotus-Cortina were viewed through a jaundiced eye. We were thinking that maybe it took a lot of guts to ask that kind of money for it. Gradually, the impression changed and grew to respect, the respect to enthusiasm.

Engine modifications make the biggest difference. Lotus bores the 116E in additional 0.0625-inches, to increase the displacement some 40 cubic centimeters. The twin-cam head conversion, with a pair of 40DCOE Webers, contributes to the increase in horsepower from 85 to 115. This is doubly significant in the light chassis (1860 pounds), as it improves its horsepower/weight ratio from 22.3-to-1 to an impressive 16.1-to-1 and, in terms of easily recognized performance, lowers its zero-60-mph acceleration time almost two full seconds. Gearbox and final-drive ratios remain identical to the GT.

There's no doubt about the Lotus-Cortina being quick, but this impression is considerably enhanced by excellent changes in suspension, tires, and wheels. For example, rim width is increased to 5.5 inches and 6.00 x 13 Dunlop SP's are mounted to them. The car is lowered a full inch via shorter, stiffer springs. It is further snubbed and roll-stiffened by heavy-duty shocks and a sturdy front anti-sway bar. Naturally, the ride is firmer

Airborne is an attitude which bothers the energetic sports sedan not at all, as SCG's Kovacik proves by taking it over a camelback at speed.

Stern view of the green-trimmed car quickly shows it to be lower than the production GT. Flat cornering and wider tires are some clues.

Clean front end has only a small Lotus medallion in the upper-right corner of the blocked-out grille to distinguish it as a special breed.

LOTUS CORTINA TWO-DOOR SEDAN ROAD TEST 9/66

Vehicle	Lotus Cortina
Model	Two-door Sedan
Price (as tested)	$3,528.44 POELA
Options	Cigarette lighter, full-length carpeting, white walls, heavy-duty battery

ENGINE:
Type	1558cc, 4-cylinder, dohc
Head	Alloy, removable
Valves	Direct acting, dohc
Max. bhp	115 @ 5700 rpm
Max. Torque	108 lbs. ft. @ 4000 rpm
Bore	3.25 in. 82.6 mm.
Stroke	2.864 in. 72.8 mm.
Displacement	95.03 cu. in. 1558 cc.
Compression Ratio	9.5 to 1
Induction System	Dual, 2-choke Weber Carburetors
Exhaust System	Headers, 4-into-2-into-1
Electrical System	12-volt, distributor ignition

CLUTCH:
Single plate (diaphragm type)
| Diameter | N.A. |
| Actuation | Hydraulic |

TRANSMISSION:
Four-speed, all-synchromesh
Ratios: 1st	2.97 to 1
2nd	2.01 to 1
3rd	1.39 to 1
4th	1.0 to 1

DIFFERENTIAL: Live, hypoid
| Ratio | 4.125 to 1 |
| Drive Axles (type) | Enclosed, Semi-floating |

STEERING:
| Turns Lock to Lock | 4⅛ |
| Turn Circle | 37.25 ft. |

BRAKES: (Servo-Assisted)
Disc Diameter	Front disc 9.75 in.
	Rear drum 9.0 in.
Swept Area	281.6 sq. in.

CHASSIS:
Frame	Unit-constructed, sub-assemblies
Body	Steel, unit.
Front Suspension	Independent Coil Springs; hydraulic, double-act, telescopic shocks
Rear Suspension	Leaf springs, hydraulic double-act telescopic shocks and radius arms
Tire Size & Type	6.00 x 13, 4-ply rating nylon

WEIGHTS AND MEASURES
Wheelbase	98.0 in.	Ground Clearance	5.3 in.
Front Track	51.5 in.	Curb Weight	1,857 lbs.
Rear Track	50.5 in.	Test Weight	2,092 lbs.
Overall Height	53.4 in.	Crankcase	8.4 pts.
Overall Width	62.5 in.	Cooling System	18.6 pts.
Overall Length	168.3 in.	Gas Tank	9.6 gals.

PERFORMANCE:
0-30	3.1 sec.	0-70	13.7 sec.
0-40	4.8 sec.	0-80	17.5 sec.
0-50	7.4 sec.	0-90	24.0 sec.
0-60	10.2 sec.	0-100	35.8 sec.

Standing ¼ mile .... 17.0 sec. @ 79 mph
Top Speed (av. two-way run) .... 107 indicated mph

| Speed Error | 30 | 40 | 50 | 60 | 70 | 80 | 90 |
| Actual | 30 | 39 | 49 | 59 | 69 | 78 | 88 |

Fuel Consumption
Test .... 19 mpg   Average .... 22 mpg

Recommended Shift Points
| Max. 1st | 40-36 mph | Max. 3rd | 78-76 mph |
| Max. 2nd | 55-54 mph | | |

RPM Red-line .... 6,500 rpm

Speed Ranges in gears:
| 1st | 0 to 36 mph | 3rd | 15 to 76 mph |
| 2nd | 5 to 54 mph | 4th | 25 to 107 mph |

Brake Test: 73 Average % G, over 10 stops.
Slight fade encountered on eighth stop.

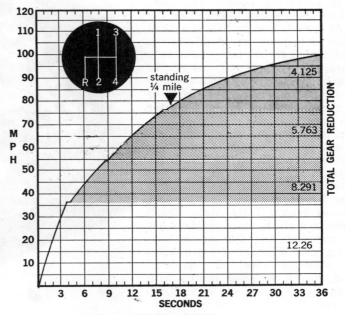

REFERENCE FACTORS:
1.21 bhp. per Cubic Inch	16.1 Lbs. per bhp
Piston Speed @ Peak rpm	2721 ft./min.
0.151 Sq. In. Swept Brake area per Lb.	

LOTUS CORTINA

Twisting mountain roads are a snap for Lotus-Cortinas with their power and maneuverability.

than the standard GT, but the harshness is reduced by the wider tire cross-section. There are noticeable improvements in sure-footedness, steering response, and, most definitely, in cornering power. The now-famous chassis flex that causes the inside front wheel to lift in a hard corner is present, but it affects the handling naught. In fact, you're only aware of it when you see photos showing the lift. We didn't measure the front disc brakes, but the specs list them at 9.75 inches; one-quarter inch larger than the Cortina GT. Stopping power and stability are improved, even though these were far from weak points in the non-Lotus models.

Helping to justify the additional price is a more deluxe interior that includes bucket front seats upholstered in a plush, black vinyl, as are the rear seats and door panels. Carpeting, also black, is of top quality. The steering wheel, of simulated wood, has a recessed center with brushed alloy spokes — a very attractive unit. Behind it is full instrumentation in the form of round, legible, and color-coded gauges, including a 7000-rpm tach and a row of water temperature, oil pressure, fuel, and

ammeter gauges. On the center tunnel, also more padded, is a small crest that attests to the fact that Chapman's talented elves have reworked this unit, as does the green body stripe.

Considering a trip as the acid test, we used it to transport ourselves to the Las Vegas USRRC, reported in last month's SCG. Four adults proved to be quite comfortable in it for the four-hour journey, the two in back sleeping like babes on the way back despite a rather ... ah ... crisp cruising speed. It passed many a Detroiter on the steep grades, all gauges reading normal. Average for the tour was just over twenty miles per gallon. It also passed the test as far as cop-attraction is concerned: they never gave it a second glance. A lot of mo-

torists knew what it was, howeve and wanted to play games — th single annoyance of the trip. In N vada, one chose to tag us until we above the century mark before deci ing this was indeed an unusual litt funny car, and may be best left alon

In summing up the Lotus-Cortin we have to conclude that it's a fi machine. Its breeding really come through. Every inch a little tiger, manages to achieve this charact without sacrifice in comfort, econ omy, or even in the noise-level depar ments. In today's competitive spor sedan market, it is very well-place and, we have to conclude, fair priced. If you're looking for som thing in this category — and it's great one because of the have-you cake-&-eat-it-too aspects — don overlook the Lotus Cortina.

A look beneath the hood tells much of the story, reveals the twin-cam conversion to the push-rod engine, the two Webers fed by a cold-air box, and the flowing exhaust headers opposite.

Interior manages to be plush without being a bit garish. Instrumentation is complete, located directly in front of the driver behind the three-spoke, deep-dished steering wheel.

Jim Adams, top contender for B-Sedan points, takes his fully race-prepared version through the famous corkscrew at Laguna Seca. Lap times often equal those of good E-Prod. sports cars.

EVEN WITH FULL knowledge of its awesome reputation in saloon (the British name for sedan) racing, it's still difficult to approach the Cortina Lotus with much credulity. The green stripes and Lotus emblems may warn insiders, but its overall appearance announces that as far as its original designers were concerned, carrying four of the Queen's loyal subjects and some of their personal effects would be about the most arduous task the Cortina would ever be called upon to perform.

But in spite of its upbringing, the Cortina soon fell in with the likes of Colin Chapman and his Lotus organization and, suitably modified, took to saloon brawling. It has since emerged victor in more than 300 races and rallies all over the world. One of its more recent important performances was taking 1st, 3rd and 9th places in the rugged Shell

Plaque on transmission hump commemorates Jimmy Clark's feat in different Lotus.

4000 Rally, run over Canadian roads whose surfaces ranged from snow to mud.

Built in a left-hand-drive version and introduced into this country late in 1965, it's now beginning to appear on the streets as well as the race courses, and is making its mark in both places.

The Cortina Lotus gets its racing legs from lowered and stiffened front and rear suspension, heavy-duty shock absorbers, added radius rods at the rear, and a stiff anti-roll bar at the front. Larger 6.00 x 13 nylon tires on wide rims complete the modifications. While the ride is definitely firm, it's not harsh. And, of course, the handling is first rate.

When driven at racing speeds, the car is a final over-steerer but feels quite neutral up to the point where the front end starts to plow. There's no sudden breakaway — just a gradual drifting outward

LOTUS CORTINA: SEDAN FOR SPORT!

WIDE WHEELS PRESENT REVERSED RIM APPEARANCE, PROVED THEIR SURE-FOOTEDNESS HERE ON UNEVEN, DRIZZLE-WETTED ASPHALT PAVEMENT.

as the maximum cornering force is exceeded. This predictable and forgiving behavior makes fast driving easy, and almost anyone can look like an expert in the Lotus Cortina.

The powerplant for the Cortina Lotus was developed by Lotus and consists primarily of a double-overhead-camshaft aluminum cylinder head of their own design mated to the Ford pushrod block. It breathes through a pair of Weber 2-barrel side-draft carbs and exhausts through 4-into-2-into-1 headers. It's the same engine used in the Lotus Elan sports car.

Racing versions of this engine are modified by Cosworth Engineering, an English racing engine building firm, to give around 150 hp. It has proved to be very reliable in this form and has chalked up many victories in sports and formula cars as well as in Cortina Lotuses.

The stock engine in our test car had some surprises in store for us. Since it displaces only 95 cubic inches (1558-cc), we had expected the 115 horses at 5700 rpm to be rather peaky. This turned out to be not the case at all. Rather than suddenly coming to life at a certain rpm, it pulled well at any speed between 2000 rpm and red-line. The 108 pounds-feet maximum torque occurs at 4000 rpm but, except for a sort

Test Cortina Lotus couldn't be made to lift inside front wheel under flat-out cornering.

of hammering sensation from the power pulses, isn't particularly noticeable because of the broad torque range.

All four throttle blades of the two 2-barrel Webers operate simultaneously by direct mechanical connection to the accelerator pedal. In other words, there is no staging action or vacuum-operated secondaries. This setup works very well, too. The engine comes to life instantaneously, with no stumble or lag, from the 650-rpm idle when you stab the throttle — quite a trick with the large

venturi area of the Weber carburetors.

This excellent throttle response can be attributed to two things. First, the idle mixture is calibrated rich — so rich that the exhaust emits black smoke at idle. Thus the inrush of air when the throttle is cracked moves the mixture toward the optimum instead of leaning it out. And second, the Weber instruments have small auxiliary venturis at the centers of the main ones which supply some fuel spray at low intake veloc-

continued

EXOTIC CHAIN-DRIVEN, DOUBLE-OVERHEAD-CAM POWERPLANT STARTED LIFE AS LOWLY BUT EXTREMELY WELL DESIGNED 54-HP PUSHROD ENGINE.

SIDE VIEW REVEALS FINNED BACK, SQUARED-OFF REAR WINDOW LINE, STRONG DEARBORN STYLING STUDIO INFLUENCE OF EARLY-'60S FORDS.

LOTUS CORTINA *continued*

DRIVESCRIPTION

ities, smoothing the transition from idle to part throttle.

Starting on cool mornings after the car had stood outside overnight proved to be no problem at all. One yank on the enrichening knob (no chokes are used) was all that was ever required to start the engine.

The Cortina is quite light for its size, which is part of the secret why the rather small engine pushes it to such good per-formance. Acceleration times with two aboard plus test equipment and a full tank for 0-30, -50 and -60 mph were 4.0, 8.1 and 11.5 seconds, respectively, with 17.8 seconds and 78 mph for the quar-ter-mile. This — in a sedan that com-fortably seats four, has good luggage capacity, and never gives less than 20 mpg — is something to brag about.

We've dwelled at length on the engine and handling of the car because they are the main features. But the Cortina has other virtues, too. Among them are: front discs that really stop the car, a full set of legible and accurate instruments, full vinyl upholstery, and a really supe-rior heating and ventilating system.

All switches on the instrument panel are of the toggle variety and have long, thin plastic knobs. While very handy to use, we feel they'll prove to be a bit fragile in service, as one was broken when we received the car.

Compared to other cars, the list of accessories isn't large for the Cortina Lotus; just about everything its particu-lar type of buyer would be looking for is standard equipment. Including the extra-cost cigar lighter, full-length car-peting, and heavy-duty battery, the price of our test car came to $3528.44 plus local taxes. If you're interested, have a chat with your local English Ford dealer.

— *John Ethridge*

PHOTOS BY DARRYL NORENBERG

Interior aspect affords much better clue to sporting nature of Cortina Lotus than does the rather plain, sedate exterior.

Deceivingly large trunk of Cortina swallowed all our test equip-ment and begged for more—a plus feature on this small sedan.

Cortina Lotus '67

The current body in its most sporting guise

AFTER four years of joint production by Ford and Lotus of the "Cortina-developed-by-Lotus" the responsibility has now passed fully to Ford. Development of the road cars is also Ford's project and it is only on the track that the Lotus hand is still evident; accordingly there is a long list of homologated extra parts which are available from the Ford competition department.

The new cars have the familiar twin o.h.c. Lotus developed engine, lower front and rear suspension settings, wide-rim 5½J wheels now with radials as standard, and a higher final drive ratio. The 1967 body is ¾-cwt heavier than before so the engine has been slightly uprated with Lotus Special Equipment cams and jets to maintain the same performance as the car we last tested. The effect of this is to raise the power from a doubtful 105 b.h.p. at 5,500 r.p.m. to a true 108 at 6,000; maximum torque has been raised 2lb. ft to 106 at 4,500 r.p.m.—500 r.p.m. higher than before.

The power increase on its own should increase the maximum speed but also on the credit side are a final drive raised from 3.90 to 3.777 (the old maximum speed was beyond the 5,500 r.p.m.

A very large air-cleaner conceals a lot of the engine but most parts are easy to reach.

Below: Workmanlike interior with round dials and deeply dished steering wheel.

power peak) and 165-13 radial ply tyres of lower rolling resistance than the standard crossply tyres on the 1966 models. The drag coefficient is 1½% higher than before so Ford's estimated maximum of 108 m.p.h. at 6,000 r.p.m. (gearing as with Dunlop SP41s) is not as big an improvement as might be expected. The gear ratios are those developed for the Corsair GT V-4 and as used on the previous Lotus Cortina.

Various changes have been made to the suspension. At the front, the total roll stiffness is much the same as before—342 lb.ft./deg. now against 368—but this is achieved by using stiffer springs and a smaller antiroll bar, following effectively the Cortina GT layout. In fact the spring rate is 140 lb./in., or 125 lb./in. at the wheel, giving a periodicity of 89 c.p.m. which is pleasantly firm.

At the rear, the suspension is softer than before, increasing front weight transference and hence understeer. The wheel rate is now 90½ lb./in. instead of 109 lb./in., or 76 c.p.m. As on all Cortinas the forward rear spring mounting has been lowered 1⅔ in. to give roll understeer where the earlier arrangement had the spring trailing downwards from the eye, giving roll oversteer. The Lotus divided propshaft is retained.

In the boot there is now room for the wide spare wheel to sit vertically in the well on the nearside while the battery occupies the other one. The interior and instrumentation are almost identical with that on the Cortina GT: the differences are a 8,000 r.p.m. tachometer—there is still a distributor cut-out at 6,500 r.p.m.—and a 140 m.p.h. speedometer with a trip mileage recorder. The familiar central arm-rest houses a useful locker. The handbrake is still under the facia. Other features are the same as in the GT.

Racing and rally extras

Ventilated cast electron high performance wheels; long distance touring seats; close ratio gearbox; sump shield; fuel tank protective shield; auxiliary touring fuel tank; extra long range fuel tank; alternative axle ratios, 3.9:1, 4.1:1, 4.4:1, 4.7:1; limited slip differential; lightweight differential casing; lightweight clutch housing; lightweight gearbox extensions; high ratio steering box; heavy duty front suspension; adjustable rear shock absorbers; high performance brake pads and linings; oil cooler unit; high performance exhaust system; fuel injection; high performance connecting rods, pistons, camshafts, valves, oil pump; lightweight alloy body panels for doors, bonnet and boot lid.

Taking it easy on the last day, Roger Clark corners gently—for him—in the Cortina Lotus.

Ford foremost

Roger Clark wins Scottish rally

by Hamish Cardno

Pictures by Eric Bryce

IF ever there was a curious motor sporting cocktail it is the Scottish Rally. Last week's event had the mixture as ever—some of the best rallying territory anywhere in Europe, a bevy of top drivers in works cars, and a host of private entries competing in their only international of the year.

But in many ways it was a rally of disappointments, as top drivers dropped out one by one, leaving Roger Clark in one of the new "more" Cortina Lotuses in an almost unassailable position towards the end of the event. He led by a comfortable margin—the third time he has won the Scottish—followed by Lars Ytterbring, the only survivor from the BMC works team, Calle Orrenius in the one remaining works Saab, and Rosemary Smith, waving the Rootes works flag single-handed.

First off the starting ramp opposite the Royal Scottish Automobile Club's headquarters in Blythswood Square, Glasgow, was Tony Fall in the leading works Mini. Fall won the event last year and the prediction merchants were talking of the great battle there was going to be between him and the other works entries—but they received the

first of many disappointments when a valve dropped through a piston in the Mini's engine 10 miles from the start, and the leader of the BMC team was out of the Rally before he had even seen a special stage.

The other Sunday afternoon disappointment was the blank in the line of cars at the start which should have been filled by Bengt Soderstrom with a Cortina Lotus. Ford had discovered after the entry was in that it was impossible to get a car back from the Acropolis in time for it to be prepared.

And so with two of the fastest potential competitors out, 97 cars headed for what was reckoned to be the toughest part of the Rally—800 miles and 35 special stages taking them in a loop round the south of Scotland, and then up to Grantown-on-Spey, which was the headquarters from Monday night on.

Hundreds of spectators had turned out to watch the Rally on the first few stages—Glentress, Cardona, two stages in Ae Forest, and others which have become well known through use in previous Scottish and RAC rallies. The watchers were not to be disappointed. The works cars were all very fast,

142

Clark particularly was very spectacular, and the fastest dozen of the privateers were all worth watching. Behind them came the local heroes, driving as fast as they could bearing in mind that the cars had to take them to work for the rest of the year, and often as spectacular.

Roger Clark, who is probably the only British driver to have mastered completely the Swedish habit of taking a forestry road corner sideways, more sideways and then suddenly forwards, was throwing the Ford about with great enthusiasm, but was being beaten at times by Tom Trana, proving in his first works drive for Saab that speed need not necessarily be spectacular. Ytterbring was the faster of the two works Minis, and Andrew Cowan and Peter Harper, driving identical Imps in completely different styles, were also going very quickly.

BMC's already slightly grim expressions became even grimmer during the night when Larsson's radiator burst, putting him out of the Rally, and then at Bennan, the longest (18 miles) stage Rootes troubles started when Peter Harper's petrol pump disintegrated, petrol splashed on to the exhaust and the Imp went off the road with flames shooting from the rear. Harper and his co-driver David Pollard were unhurt and the fire was quickly put out, but that was the end of the Rally for one Imp.

As a cold grey dawn came up on Monday that old favourite, Rest and Be Thankful was waiting to whet the appetites of the competitors before the breakfast halt at Strechur. The stage is the old road over the Rest, which is used as a hill-climb during the year, with the result that the road surface is breaking up, making the job of maintaining a 50 m.p.h. average speed increasingly difficult. But if the pre-breakfast run was hair-raising, the same stage taken downhill while full of eggs and bacon was worse. After this many competitors felt it a relief to get back to the rough and tumble of forestry roads for the seven stages left before Grantown and a well-earned rest.

After the cars came in, the lists showed Trana fastest, followed by Clark, Ytterbring and Cowan.

Tuesday's run consisted of a loop round the Black Isle, just north of Inverness, and round Loch Ness to Spean Bridge. There were 11 stages to be covered before Spean Bridge, and most of them were run in that special sort of torrential rain which is a West Highland speciality. On the fourth stage Saab hopes faded when a drive shaft on Trana's car broke, he went off the road and a small fire started in the engine compartment. This put Trana out of the Rally, but his car was quickly repaired and in the best Saab traditions he became a service crew—and for the rest of the Rally he must surely have been the fastest service car about.

With a 70-mile run back to the *parc fermé* and 11 stages behind them, most cars had arranged for service points before Grantown, and this was to be the undoing of many.

The RSAC had put in two speed checks on the route from Spean Bridge to Grantown, and very nearly all the competitors were found from this to be exceeding their maxi-

The way the Scandinavians drive cars—Ytterbring kicking up the dust in the works Mini.

Barrie Williams in one of the Imps which won the team award for Team HAS gets a helping hand from spectators after overdoing it somewhat in Clashindarroch.

An unlucky start with the Saab team—Tom Trana pictured just before a drive shaft broke and put him out of the Rally.

Very fast but very smooth, Calle Orrenius hurrying the Saab V4 round an uphill hairpin.

Ford foremost

continued

mum permitted average speed of 40 m.p.h. and were penalised 300 points. While probably a commendable action from the point of view of public safety, this action by the Club did not go down well with the competitors—with 47 stages completed the cars needed service, the Highland roads could not be described as congested, and in any case the north of Scotland police forces (who seem rather less keen on rallying than are the public) had radar speed traps in a very large number of the built-up areas through which the Rally passed.

By Tuesday evening, then, Clark had gone in to the lead, followed by Ytterbring, Cowan, Orrenius, and Roy Fidler in a Triumph 2000 which at times beat even Clark's Cortina for spectacular moves on the stages. In sixth place was Rosemary Smith with her new co-driver Susan Seigle-Morris.

But Rosemary was not to stay sixth for long. Ten stages in the north-east corner of Scotland were scheduled for Wednesday, and significant changes had occurred before five were completed. On Fetteresso Forest, the second longest (15 miles) stage in the Rally, Roy Fidler overdid things, left the road and was stuck in a ditch. Similar excursions had been made by other drivers on other stages when there were spectators to push them out, but Fetteresso was practically deserted, so Fidler was well and truly jammed by the roadside.

One or two people had "moments" on the next stage, Drumtochty 1. The finish of the stage was a long steep hill where the road made a right-angled turn just past the final control. The first few cars found difficulty in

stopping, and then a shower of rain made the surface even more slippery and J. Cotton's Peugeot 404 became the first and most serious casualty, when it came down the hill with all the wheels locked and ran straight into the bank at the side of the road, crumpling the front wing and twisting the suspension. Several others came down in equally dramatic fashion and one or two landed in the rhododendron bushes before the marshals found time to put up "hazard" and "caution" warning notices at the top of the hill.

Andrew Cowan's hopes of repeating his success on home ground (he has won the Rally twice previously) ended on Drumtochty 2, when his engine went sick, and then a con rod came through the side near the final control. He coasted down-hill and across the line to retire—and, like Trana, became the driver of an ultra-rapid service car. There was little excitement after this as by this time most of the privateers were driving to finish, Clark was still in the lead by a fairly comfortable margin, followed Ytterbring and Orrenius, Rosemary Smith, then private entrant Jack Tordoff, in a Ford Cortina GT.

If drivers were easing off on Wednesday, Thursday's sections were even slower. Only Ytterbring and Orrenius were still obviously really trying hard, Clark was still travelling at incredibly high speeds on the straights in the forests—he was timed at 88 m.p.h. on one—but he was taking corners in a much more steady fashion.

And in fact, the final placings were identical to those on Wednesday night. Clark's car arrived at the finish looking in almost showroom condition. It was only on close

inspection that bodywork damage showed where he had "yumped" and landed on the body before the wheels touched the ground, the cars of Ytterbring, Orrenius and Rosemary Smith were also in very good condition (partly because each had had a huge squad of service vehicles to tend them), and then there were privateers Tordoff and J. S. Bate.

Bate's story was an unhappy one: the Morris Cooper S bearing number 25 was the property of Stuart Brown, listed in the entry as co-driver. Brown, a Scot, had entered the car in the name of Bate in order to be seeded nearer the start. In fact, the car was driven throughout all the stages by Brown, who was trying desperately for the prize as highest-placed Scot—which included a free entry in the Scandinavian Rally—but as the entry was in the name of Bate, an Englishman, he missed out. The much-coveted award went instead to Gerry Birrell in a Singer Vogue.

The 1967 Scottish will go down as a tough rally, but one which was thoroughly enjoyed by the competitors—and the mixture seems almost certain to be much the same next year. **M**

Provisional results

1 R. Clark (Ford Cortina Lotus); **2** L. Ytterbring (Mini Cooper S); **3** C. Orrenius (Saab V4); **4** Miss R. Smith (Sunbeam Imp); **5** J. Tordoff (Ford Cortina GT); **6** S. J. Bate (Mini Cooper S).

Class awards. Series production cars up to 1,000 c.c.: L. Cowan (Morris). **Up to 1,300 c.c.:** J. M. Wright (Morris Cooper S). **Up to 1,600 c.c.:** K. W. Edwards (Ford Cortina GT). **Over 1,600 c.c.:** subject of protest.

Touring cars up to 1,300 c.c.: S. J. Bate (Morris Cooper S). **Up to 2,500 c.c.:** G. King (Ford Cortina Lotus). **GT cars:** Miss R. Smith. **GT sports cars:** J. Tordoff.

Best team performance: Team HAS, H. A. Skelton, B. Williams, G. Tripp. **Highest placed private entrant:** J. Tordoff. **Highest placed Scot:** G. Birrell (Singer Vogue).

Ladies' award: Miss R. Smith/Mrs. Seigle-Morris (Hillman Imp).

FORD—
LOTUS-CORTINA

WHEN the Lotus-Cortina (or Ford Cortina-developed-by-Lotus as Ford preferred to call it) was originally introduced in 1963 it offered a pretty exotic specification for a road car. Since then there have been many changes, each one bringing the car back nearer to standard. Strangely enough the more standard the car has become the better it has behaved as a road machine, and the latest version on the Mk. II Cortina chassis is undoubtedly quite the best Lotus-Cortina to be built.

The first Lotus-Cortina had many light alloy body panels, a revised facia, new seats, greatly revised suspension, with trailing arm and coil spring rear end, and, of course, the twin-cam engine with close ratio gearbox. Over the years it lost many of these parts, reverting to the normal steel body panels, leaf spring rear suspension, a less closely ratioed box and so on. Now, the new model is made entirely at Dagenham, and Lotus do not have a hand in building the car, which greatly simplifies production as far as Ford is concerned.

The new Cortina was designed with the Lotus version in mind so that relatively few modifications have been necessary. In fact one could almost say that the Lotus-Cortina is a Cortina GT with a twin-cam engine and not be far off the mark. The interior of the car is exactly the same, with the same facia and the same seats as the GT. Externally the car is also difficult to distinguish from normal GTs, but the black mesh radiator grille of the old Lotus-Cortina is retained and Lotus badges are fitted on the rear of the body sides. Whereas the earlier Lotus could only be obtained in white with a green stripe, the new model is available in any of the Ford colours. Naturally many people will still plump for a white car, and a green stripe is available, but the new body styling does not really lend itself to the stripe, which cannot follow the body contours as on the Mk. 1 Lotus-Cortina. In actual fact Ford have not given any method of designating between the new and old Cortina, so we will call them Mks. I and II. "Sidewinder" stripes with the name "Ford" can also be specified to be fitted along the lower body sill.

ENGINE
The twin-cam engine is supplied in slightly more powerful form than on the Mk. I as the previously optional special equipment engine is now standard equipment. This engine gives 115 b.h.p. (gross), 109 b.h.p. (net) at 6,000 r.p.m. compared with the 105 b.h.p. (net) at 5,500 r.p.m. of the previous engine. Ford have done some development work on the engine in their own engine development department, whereas on the Mk. I the engines were supplied and developed by Lotus. Most of the modifications are aimed at reliability and refinement and especially noise level. The typical Weber carburetter roar has been silenced to a great extent by a new air cleaner, an enormous device which straddles the cam covers and makes plug removal rather difficult. However, the lower noise level will be much appreciated by all but the boy racer element. The engine feels quite smooth and refined and it

starts well, even on cold days, with two or three pumps of the throttle pedal and the choke can be ignored. It warms up quite quickly and idles evenly at about 800 r.p.m., although our test car developed an exhaust leak which made the idling rather rough and also affected performance. We took a set of performance figures with the car in this state but they were rather poor and Ford submitted another car which gave much better results. On the ordinary Cortina GT we achieved a 0-60 m.p.h. time of 14.8sec. and 0-80 in 30.5sec., while on the Lotus-Cortina we reached 60 in 10.8sec. and 80 in 20.1sec., which is, of course, a useful improvement, especially at the higher speeds. However, the cars are not directly comparable because they have different gearbox and final drive ratios and the Lotus version is fitted with a distributor cut-out which shorts the ignition at 6,500 r.p.m., whereas we were revving the pushrod GT engine to 7,000 r.p.m.! The acceleration figures are affected quite noticeably by this cut-out as the engine cuts at 38 m.p.h. in first, 55 in second and 78 in third; if the engine could be revved slightly higher to encompass 40, 60 and 80 in these gears the acceleration figures would be improved somewhat. But as the twin-cam tends to break its crank if revved over 7,000 r.p.m. for long periods in standard form, the cut-out is justified. Strangely enough the performance of the latest Lotus-Cortina is very similar to the early model we tested in January 1964 which gave a 0-60 m.p.h. time of 11.1sec. and a 0-80 of 19.8sec., although the

gear ratios were vastly different. Ford claim a top speed of 108 m.p.h. for the new Lotus-Cortina, but we failed to reach this, putting in a two-way average of 103 m.p.h To achieve 108 m.p.h. the car would have to pull the full 6,500 r.p.m. in top but our rather new test car would not pull much more than 6,000 r.p.m. No doubt when it loosens up the performance will improve. The new engine struck us as feeling slightly more refined than its predecessor, while oil consumption, which can be a problem on the twin-cam, was negligible as the engine only required a quart in over 1,500 miles.

FUEL CONSUMPTION
Despite a lot of hard driving the Lotus-Cortina returned a fuel consumption of 23.4 m.p.g. over a fairly high mileage, although this can be increased to below 20 m.p.g. if continuous high speeds are maintained. The normal 10-gallon fuel tank is retained, which means that the range of the Lotus-Cortina is not much over 200 miles. We feel that this type of car, which is likely to be used for long distance Continental travel, should be able to go at least 300 miles on a full tank of fuel.

TRANSMISSION
In our test of the Cortina GT when it was introduced last October, we criticised the gear ratios, as we felt that second gear was far too low. Early this year Ford introduced a higher second gear for the GT and the Corsair 2000E and this uprated gear is also fitted to the Lotus, although Ford have been strangely reticent about admitting the existence of the up-

THE NEW Lotus-Cortina is available in any Ford colour, but our test car was painted white with the usual green stripe. The stripe does not really lend itself to the new Cortina's body styling. The sidewinder stripe is optional.

rated gear. The early Lotus-Cortina used a modified Elan box with rather high ratios, which were not very suitable for road use, but since 1966 it has used the normal Ford box. The Lotus box is still available for competition use. The box has a very light, but slightly notchy, change which can be whipped from gear to gear very rapidly indeed, although lever travel is fairly long, while the diaphragm clutch is commendably light. There is a slight gear lever "zizz" at certain revs. but nothing to worry about. Using the gears to the full, the Lotus can be made to perform incredibly well, putting up the sort of average speeds which would make Mrs. Castle faint, yet doing so in perfect safety. Acceleration from a standstill is perhaps not exactly vivid, due mainly to the fact that you cannot spin the wheels in the dry, but once motoring in the 60-80 m.p.h. bracket the car really rockets along, while a cruising speed of 100 m.p.h. can be sustained for long periods without signs of stress. Our test car had the standard 3.77:1 axle, but numerous optional ones are available.

HANDLING

We criticised the early Lotus-Cortinas for rather vague, fussy handling on the road, but the new model is a terrific improvement. Our test car was shod with Goodyear G800 radial tyres on the standard 5½in. rims which gave first-class handling in the dry, although a great deal of circumspection was required in the wet as the lightly laden tail would flick out very easily. If you are quick with the opposite lock the situation can be saved but the Lotus-Cortina definitely needs treating with respect in the wet. Experiments with other tyres might well produce better results, but the main problem is the light weight of the car. In the dry when cornering at the limit the car understeers very strongly and the tail needs a great deal of provocation before letting go. Despite our reservations about the wet weather handling we rate the Lotus as an excellent handling car. It feels very safe, is not affected unduly by road surfaces, and tracks very straight at high speed, with little sign of wander except in strong cross-winds.

STEERING

The recirculating ball steering has a higher ratio than on the GT version but is much the same in general feel. There is some sponginess and lack of precision in this type of steering, but it seems less inclined to transmit road shocks than rack and pinion and is generally satisfactory. Some of our staff commented unfavourably on

THE INTERIOR of the Lotus-Cortina is virtually indistinguishable from that of the normal Cortina GT. The only changes are a 140 m.p.h. speedometer and an 8,000 r.p.m. tachometer.

HIDDEN: The cam covers of the Lotus twin-cam engine are now well and truly obscured by the new air cleaner/silencer, which does much to reduce the induction roar of the twin Webers.

the virtual complete lack of self-centring action, which means that the driver has to return the wheel to the straight ahead position after cornering instead of letting it spin through his fingers. The actual wheel, which is the same as that of the GT, will probably be replaced by most people with a less dished wooden type to give more arm room.

RIDE AND COMFORT
The suspension of the Lotus-Cortina is slightly lower and stiffer than that of the GT but the resultant ride is very similar, giving a firm, pitch-free ride on all but the worst surfaces. With four people on board the car feels better than with only one or two, but we feel that few drivers will complain about the riding qualities. Rear seat leg-room is only modest but the front seats are an improvement over those of the earlier Lotus-Cortina, although taller drivers will no doubt prefer more fore and aft adjustment and a reclining backrest.

BRAKES
The brakes are the same as those of the new GT, with 9.6in. discs at the front and 9in. drums at the rear, but the Lotus has a vacuum servo which reduces pedal pressures to a very low level, giving the car very impressive braking from high speeds. The rear brakes can lock up and cause the wheels to judder but slight easing of the pedal pressure stops this quickly. The pedals are well placed for heel and toe changes, but the organ-type throttle pedal of our test car fell off, leaving us only the shaft to depress! The umbrella handbrake is retained in the Lotus-Cortina for some unearthly reason; we would have thought a fly-off central handbrake would be much more appropriate, although the central luggage locker takes that space at present.

INTERIOR
As already mentioned the interior of the Lotus-Cortina is virtually identical to that of the GT, the only real differences being the fitting of a 140 m.p.h. speedometer and an 8,000 r.p.m. tachometer for obvious reasons. The car is well instrumented by any standards and the layout of the minor controls is quite satisfactory.

The latest expression of the Lotus-Cortina theme is probably less exciting to the enthusiast than the original Chapman idea, but as a sensible road car it far outreaches any of its predecessors — we predict a great future for it. **M.L.T.**

FORD LOTUS-CORTINA PERFORMANCE					
Acceleration through gears:					
0-30	...	...	...	...	3.8 sec.
0-40	...	...	...	...	5.8 sec.
0-50	...	...	...	...	7.6 sec.
0-60	...	...	...	...	10.8 sec.
0-70	...	...	...	...	14.6 sec.
0-80	...	...	...	...	20.1 sec.
0-90	...	...	...	...	30.1 sec.
Standing start ¼-mile	...	...	...	17.6 sec.	
Maximum speeds in the gears (6,500 r.p.m.):					
First	...	...	...	...	38 m.p.h.
Second	...	...	...	...	55 m.p.h.
Third	...	...	...	...	78 m.p.h.
Top	...	...	(6,200 r.p.m.)	103 m.p.h.	
Overall fuel consumption:					
Average	...	...	...	...	23.4 m.p.g.
Range	...	...	...	...	20-27 m.p.g.

PRICE: £869 plus Purchase Tax £199 2s. 11d. Total £1,068 2s. 11d.

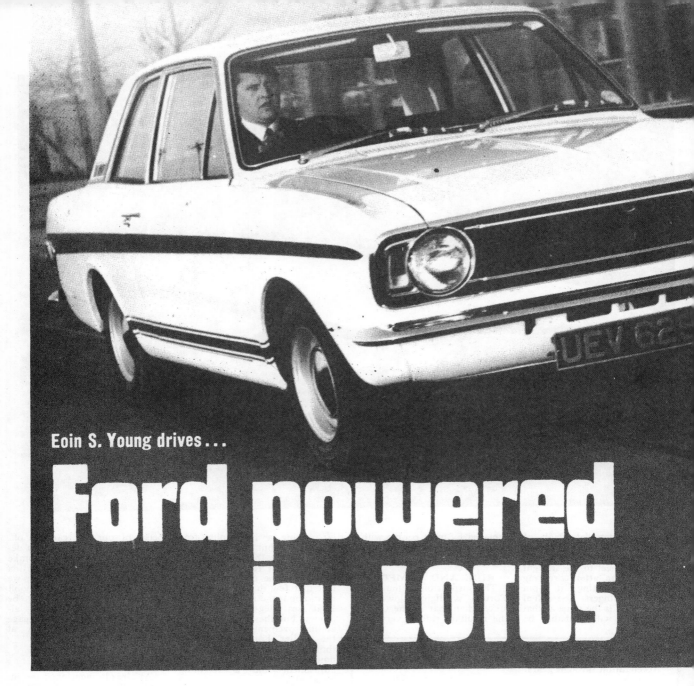

Eoin S. Young drives...

Ford powered by LOTUS

In the darker corners of the Lotus workshops stands a Cortina wearing a Formula Two Cosworth-Ford in its vitals — Webers and all the gear.

A LOTUS-CORTINA was once a fast car if you could keep it out of the repair shop, but now that Ford has stepped in and taken over the complete operation of assembly and sales, the new Cortina-Lotus is one of the fastest, most reasonably priced and reliable cars on the road.

The original Lotus-Cortina (by Lotus) was built up from special bits — the lightweight competition version had aluminium doors, boot lid and bonnet as well as the normal rally-type seats, a

Lotus is already installing the 220 bhp FVA F2 Cosworth-Ford in its works cars. It may become an option. Here Keith Duckworth (left) and Harley Copp, inspect the engine.

Interior is strictly Cortina GT apart from speedometer and tachometer. If you want to fit a wood wheel instead of plastic original, it costs more, but is worth much in status.

Heart of the matter. That tremendous dohc Cosworth-Lotus-Ford 1500, with two twin-choke 40DCOE Webers and genuine polished alloy cam covers. Note power booster at right.

Complete mit hoon stripes on the rocker sills, and blacked-out grille that should chip out well, the 1967 Cortina-Lotus is getting some real drama.

special dash lay-out, a wood-rim wheel, and special suspension — but the new car, based directly on the current new-shape GT Cortina, is a more standard vehicle, making use of existing parts and keeping the price down.

The only departures from GT Cortina trim are the matching tachometer and speedometer, the rev counter red-lined at 6500 (when an ignition cut-out assists your memory and cancels your chances of over-revving the free-spinning engine) and the speedo calibrated to 140 mph. This calibrated top speed isn't all that optimistic in the light of latest Lotus developments fitting the Formula 2 1600 cc FVA Cosworth Ford engine into the racing Cortina-Lotus.

Under the bonnet everything is Lotus, the twin-cam 1500 cc engine hiding under a sprawling air

cleaner that also serves to drown the Weber "suck" from the two twin-choke 40 DCOEs. This big air cleaner also makes it a little difficult to get at the spark plugs. To make room for the larger engine, the battery has been transferred to the boot. The previous optional engine equipment is now standard and power is up from 109 bhp to 115 bhp.

The car will start without the choke if you open the throttle a couple of times. It fires up, spits quietly to itself for a few seconds, and then settles down to a steady idle. The revs race tremendously freely and you immediately appreciate the cut-out at six-five.

The gearbox is the poker-through-butter box that first arrived on the 2000E Corsairs and has since been transferred to the Cortina range. It is delightfully engineered to make gearchanges finger-light, yet also extremely precise and fast. Acceleration in the rather high "low" gear is slightly hesitant, but as soon as it catches it pulls strongly up to the cut-out point which corresponds to 40 mph. Dropping the clutch with a good head of steam usually resulted in a slight bogging-down without wheelspin, then a quick recovery to surge away, but this initial hesitation probably kept acceleration times down a little. Ford says it will do 0-60 in 10 sec but I couldn't better 10.5 sec (the same time as the 2000E Corsair!).

The Lotus comes into its own above 80 mph. Most traffic is easing at this speed, but the Cortina pulled heartily up to around 95. Top speed in second was a handy 60, and third was good for over 80 mph. This third gear slipped in easily on a down-change for a quickish corner if you needed more revs than were left in top. On corners like this the suspension and Pirellis were well able to look after any driver indiscretions. Because we were travelling so much faster than normal, the brakes seemed to be taking longer to do their job, but I'm living proof that we had no moments in 600 of the fastest miles I've ever driven. The suspension is lower and slightly stiffer than the GT Cortina's, but the firmer ride isn't noticeable.

I'm no great fan of the seats in the new Cortina range. They look good, but they flatter to deceive. The 2000E seats have backs adjustable for rake, and the Cortina-Lotus would benefit by a similar arrangement. Back seat passengers have little legroom. You have to part with more pennies if you want a wooden or leather rimmed wheel, otherwise you have to make do with the normal Ford plastic tiller.

The handbrake is the old umbrella-handle under the dash, which seems to annoy the purists because it isn't a fly-off type. As far as I can see the only novelty of a fly-off handbrake is if you're planning on a few Le Mans starts, or wish to flummox the garage mechanic.

At the wheel you realise that the bonnet of the new Cortina looks stubbier than the last, and that the white-on-black rev counter and speedometer are a great improvement on the standard fairground items as fitted to the GT. The tacho was an electric one which tended to be rather hysterical and unreliable after about 25 miles of driving. Like the GT, the gauges for amps, oil pressure, water temperature and fuel live on a little hooded panel above the centre of the main dash. The fuel gauge showed just above three-quarters when it was brimming full, which meant you were never sure how much fuel was left in the 10-gallon tank. Other gripes are that the wipers are only single-speed, a dangerous nuisance on a car that tops the ton, and the light switch is a two-stage toggle unmarked on the dash. A stalk lever pokes out the right-hand side of the steering column to control direction indicators (up and down), flash the headlights (spring-loaded flick upwards) and dipper (balance switch pressed down). Completing the uses of this stalk-of-all-trades, the horn was operated by pushing the end inwards, which wasn't a very satisfactory idea as you could also flick indicators on at the same time. Whatever happened to horn-buttons in the centre of the steering wheel?

Original Ford intentions were to market the Cortina-Lotus with those ghastly black and white side-winder flashes along the base of the doors to aid model identification as Ford was originally frightened that the Lotus version didn't LOOK as though it was worth $500 more than the GT. Fortunately for us all they gave up the idea, although some of the test cars were so adorned. My test car was white with the Lotus green flash down the side, but the chunky shape of the new Cortina doesn't really lend itself to straight flashes like this, and customers will probably prefer to order the color of their choice and leave model identification to the modest Lotus badge on the rear flanks, and the matt-black radiator grille. This grille is painted, and looks as though it will be a failure from the point of view of stone chipping. Ford gives the impression that the Cortina Lotus is only available as a two-door, but sources tell me that four-door versions are available on special order.

I would take a four-door version for several reasons, first being the fact that with the two wide doors extra weight is placed on the locks and these are apt to become faulty. I had to take my test car back for the striker plate to be adjusted, and I understand that this is a fault with the two-door models. Also at speed (which is most of the time in a car like this) there is an annoying draught and wind whistle around the trailing top corners of the doors. This was a bad feature of the previous two-door Cortina. A four-door version wouldn't present such a large slab of fitted metal to the wind. And, of course, four doors are so much more convenient. It's worth the slightly smaller driver's door to avoid having to act the jack-in-the-box act everytime someone wants out of the back seat — invariably in teeming rain.

The engine noise at speed is negligible, although there is a high whining from the twin cams winding up through the gears. Perhaps this was drowned above 80 mph by the wind noise around the square-rigged windscreen. This Cortina-Lotus is the only car I have driven that gives so little impression of speed that passengers sit chatting, unaware that we're motoring through twisty roads at 70 or 80 mph.

The confidence the car instils in the driver is fantastic. You find yourself driving everywhere at least 20 mph faster than normal, just because it feels right, and feels safe. It's also easy to float into a built-up area at what you imagine to be the speed limit, only to glance down and see you're 20 mph over the legal maximum! This happened to me on my way to Silverstone and two radar gendarmes stopped me in a 30 mph zone — fortunately they were more interested in the car than in my offence, and they let me off with a warning.

Top speed is 108 mph says Ford, but I saw an indicated 118, which, allowing for speedometer error, is still a healthy speed. And even when wound out, it wasn't floating or lane-hopping, or doing any of the other alarming features you sometimes associate with cars that suddenly find themselves with more urge than they can handle. This is where Ford's competition program with Lotus, Superspeed and Broadspeed comes into effect, putting track lessons directly into the customer's hands.

The **only** Cortina-Lotuses to be seen of late down under are those of Firth and McKeown — the former having but a short life.

A new Cortina-Lotus will set you back £1068stg in England, but I reckon that on top of a stiff wallop for insurance you'd also have to allow a bit more for speeding fines. It's that sort of car. It runs away with you. And this is one car I'd like to be run away with . . .   #

*"I started to take 60 **thou** off then the milling machine ran amok."*

MOTOR TESTED

Family sports car

*'. . . what it has lost in character
has been made up in other ways
through a massive refining process . . .'*

"**A**NYONE in the market for a £1,000 saloon who doesn't buy a Lotus Cortina must be mad. . . ." While hastily withdrawing the implication that some of our readers are idiots, this forthright view by one of our drivers certainly reflects a feeling among us that the new Ford Cortina Lotus—to use its proper new title—is a very appealing piece of machinery. Of course, not everyone wants a saloon with only two doors that will do 106 m.p.h. and out-sprint a Porsche 912 to 80 m.p.h. Not everyone will be able to afford the high insurance premiums, or be willing to part with their transport every 2,500 miles for servicing (against every 5,000 miles for other Fords).

Unlike the first "Cortina-developed-by-Lotus", which was more or less a Dagenham body shell loaded with Lotus running gear at Cheshunt, the new car is wholly Ford built. What it has lost in character has been made up in other ways through a massive refining process, so successful that it almost justifies the several months spent in exile. It is no longer the raw, uncivilized driving machine it was to begin with; the fragile A-bracket rear suspension, and expensive aluminium body panels are among the things that

went long before the new Cortina body was taken over, of course. But the latest model does not even have a wood-rim steering wheel or the familiar green-flash-on-white paintwork. In fact, the only way you can distinguish it from a GT is by the yellow Lotus badges and the matt black grille. Yet, for all this anonymity, the Cortina Lotus has a number of outstanding qualities that make it a far better all-rounder that it ever was before. Perhaps the most impressive and unexpected of these is its mechanical refinement. The uprated engine, despite its racing pedigree and whirring twin-cam chain drive, is not only very flexible and quiet but also one of the smoothest fours we know; and the ease and precision of the gearchange is superb. Excellent roadholding and handling—different to the previous car's and, on balance, better—have their price in a firm, knobbly ride but this alone caused less discomfort than the disappointing seats and driving position—of which a lot more later.

In its accommodation and trim, the car is similar to other Cortinas—notably the GT—and thus has a cavernous boot, the best ventilation system you can buy without installing air conditioning, and a facia that has more area devoted to instruments and controls than bare panel. If you want, and can afford, further segregation from the lesser Cortina fold, then there is a formidable list of competition extras to choose from, including several alternative axle ratios, close ratio gears, a hotter engine, cast magnesium

Continued on the next page

PRICE: £869 plus £199 2s. 11d. purchase tax equals £1,068 2s. 11d. (this includes delivery charges).

Ford Cortina Lotus
continued

wheels, various lightweight parts and "long distance touring seats" which, we think, ought to be standard equipment. Even if the price *has* gone up a bit, at £1,068 it still undercuts, by a handsome margin, a number of suave and sporting Continental imports chasing much the same sort of market.

Performance and economy

To counter the additional weight and drag of the new body, the gem of an engine has been uprated a little by re-jetting the carburetters and using the old Special Equipment cam as standard. With 109 b.h.p. there is nominally only 4 b.h.p. more than before, but we suspect the real improvement is actually greater than this. Apart from the slightly lower top speed of 105 m.p.h.—3 m.p.h. below Ford's claim—the car is actually even more lively than before. All out through the gears, it will reach 60 m.p.h. in the magic 10 seconds, and 100 m.p.h. in well under a mile from rest. Not that you have to keep the revs soaring to go fast because the car slogs smoothly from 20 to 40 m.p.h. in top in the same time that it needs to rush from 60 to 80 m.p.h. The third and top gear acceleration figures show just how strongly and consistently this engine punches out the power from 1,000 to 6,500 r.p.m. when a centrifugal ignition cut-out prevents even higher speeds. This sensible device certainly does not inhibit fast driving because most drivers, even when pressing on, were content to change at under 6,000 r.p.m., leaving the last bit of thrust for, say, urgent overtaking. Apart from the harsh juddering when accelerating in top from below about

Performance

Performance tests carried out by *Motor's* staff at the Motor Industry Research Association proving ground, Lindley.

Test Data: World copyright reserved; no unauthorized reproduction in whole or in part.

Conditions:

Weather: Good. Warm and dry, 8 m.p.h. wind
Temperature 68°-72°F. Barometer 29.8 in. Hg.
Surface: Dry tarmacadam and concrete.
Fuel: 101 octane (RM). 5 star rating.

Maximum speeds

	m.p.h.
Mean lap banked circuit	105.1
Best one-way ¼-mile	108.4
3rd gear	82.0
2nd gear } at 6,500 r.p.m.	57.0
1st gear	38.0

"Maximile" speed: (Timed quarter mile after 1 mile accelerating from rest)

Mean	104.9
Best	105.9

Acceleration times

m.p.h.	sec.
0-30	3.6
0-40	5.3
0-50	6.9
0-60	9.9
0-70	13.5
0-80	17.7
0-90	25.2
0-100	38.7
Standing quarter mile	17.6

m.p.h.	Top sec.	3rd sec.
20-40	10.1	5.9
30-50	9.2	5.6
40-60	9.4	5.8
50-70	9.7	6.3
60-80	10.3	7.8
70-90	12.9	—

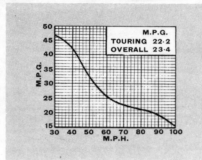

M.P.G.
TOURING 22·2
OVERALL 23·4

Fuel consumption

Touring (consumption midway between 30 m.p.h. and maximum less 5% allowance for acceleration)
 22.2 m.p.g.
Overall 23.4 m.p.g.
 (= 12.1 litres/100 km.)
Total test mileage 1,700 miles
Tank capacity (maker's figure) 10 gal.

Hill climbing

At steady speed
		lb./ton
Top	1 in 8.6	(Tapley 260)
3rd	1 in 5.6	(Tapley 395)
2nd	1 in 3.8	(Tapley 570)

Clutch

Free pedal movement = 1 in.
Additional movement to disengage clutch completely = 4 in.
Maximum pedal load = 20 lb.

Speedometer

Indicated	30	40	50	60	70	80	90	100
True	29½	38	47½	57½	67	76½	86	95½

Distance recorder 3% fast

Brakes

Pedal pressure, deceleration and equivalent stopping distance from 30 m.p.h.

lb.	g	ft.
25	0.33	90
50	0.77	39
75	0.92	32.5
80	0.94	32
Handbrake	0.41	73

Fade test

20 stops at ½g deceleration at 1 min. intervals from a speed midway between 30 m.p.h. and maximum speed (=67.5 m.p.h.)
	lb.
Pedal force at beginning	33
Pedal force at 10th stop	22
Pedal force at 20th stop	22

Steering

Turning circle between kerbs:
	ft.
Left	27.2
Right	28.5

Turns of steering wheel from lock to lock 4.0
Steering wheel deflection for 50 ft. diameter circle 1.0 turn

Weight

Kerb weight (unladen with fuel for approximately 50 miles) 17.8 cwt.
Front/rear distribution 53.5/46.5
Weight laden as tested 21.5 cwt.

Parkability

Gap needed to clear a 6ft. wide obstruction parked in front:

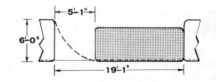

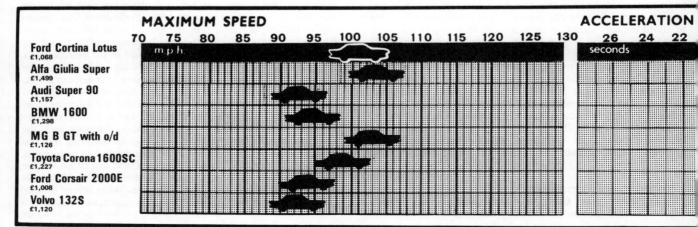

	MAXIMUM SPEED	ACCELERATION
	70 75 80 85 90 95 100 105 110 115 120 125 130	26 24 22
Ford Cortina Lotus £1,068	m.p.h.	seconds
Alfa Giulia Super £1,499		
Audi Super 90 £1,157		
BMW 1600 £1,298		
MG B GT with o/d £1,126		
Toyota Corona 1600SC £1,227		
Ford Corsair 2000E £1,008		
Volvo 132S £1,120		

Above left: The seats themselves are quite comfortable but adjusters made the driving position uncomfortable for some people.

Above: The steeply sloping rear cushion provides good thigh support but there is little lateral location from the squab.

Left: The front seats can be wedged against the front screen pillars to keep them up. The central cubby is a useful oddments box but some drivers found its lid-cum-armrest hindered gearchanging.

Below: The matt black grille and, if you are a keen observer, the lowered suspension distinguish the Lotus from GT models.

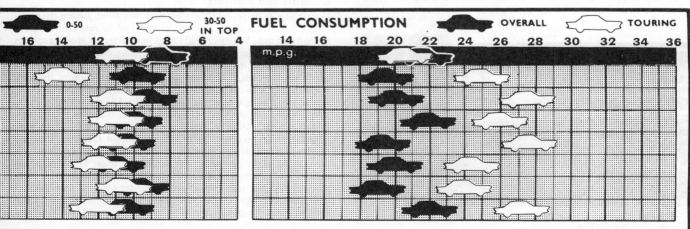

FUEL CONSUMPTION

0-50		30-50 IN TOP				OVERALL		TOURING
16 14 12 10 8 6 4				14 16 18 20 22 24 26 28 30 32 34 36				

m.p.g.

Ford Cortina Lotus
continued

From the back, the yellow and green badges are the only distinguishing marks on the Cortina Lotus. The 5½J spare wheel fractionally reduces the width of the boot but there is still enough room for 10 cu. ft. of our test boxes.

22 m.p.h., the engine is remarkably smooth though it would sometimes hesitate when the throttle was snapped open at low speeds.

Despite changes to the carburation, the engine would still fire from cold without the choke after a couple of dabs on the accelerator, but it sometimes needed a few seconds churning when hot. The even idling speed of about 800 r.p.m. is further evidence of carburetter refining though, as the handbook acknowledges, there is still a metallic clatter from the floppy pistons until the engine has warmed a little—something it takes a long time to do according to the thermometer, even if there is no hesitancy when pulling away after a cold start. Apart from this, there is surprisingly little engine noise, the familiar intake roar having been virtually eliminated by a massive air cleaner that also hides the attractive engine from view.

In top gear, petrol consumption varies from 15.5 m.p.g. at maximum speed to nearly 47 m.p.g. at 30 m.p.h., showing what an enormous influence driving habits can have on economy. On the logical basis that Cortina Lotus owners will not be sluggards, though, overall consumption is almost certain to be in the lower 20s, as our own overall and touring consumptions suggest. This is very similar to that of the lighter but lower geared earlier car. Despite the fairly high 9.5:1 compression ratio, the engine seemed to run happily on our own fleet-car petrol (about 97 octane).

Transmission

We said of the Corsair 2000E that it had one of the world's best gearboxes. This goes for the Cortina Lotus, too. There is no frictional resistance or floppy free play in the stout gearlever and the synchromesh is absolutely fool-proof yet hardly notchy, let alone obstructive. You just go snick, snick with your fingertips and the lever has sliced through the gate. The ratios are good, too, with an untypical (for Ford) high second which can thrust the car up to almost 60 m.p.h. The final drive, higher than before, provides a fairly long-legged ratio in top (17.6 m.p.h. per 1,000 r.p.m.) for motorway cruising yet it does not seem to have made the engine any less flexible at lower speeds.

The clutch is very nearly as light as the gearchange and, despite quite a long travel, works so smoothly and easily that you can drive barefooted without any discomfort: on a hot, muggy day, one driver tried it for 120 non-stop miles and rather enjoyed the novelty.

Handling and brakes

Whether you have Pirelli Cinturato tyres (as on our car) or the alternative Goodyear G800s, the roadholding can hardly fail to be good on covers of such enormous width. It needs a smooth road and one of those nasty corners that tighten up on you to show the car at its best: instead of understeering into the opposite lane or losing stability if you lift off in panic, the car responds magically to more lock, hugging the kerb at g forces that increase to very high values. The firm springs, which make the car about

an inch lower than other Cortinas, prevent the body from rolling much, though the final degree of lurch coincides with, perhaps promotes, the most gentle breakaway of the back wheels. High cornering powers and controllable, progressive oversteer like this are an unusual combination with radial-ply tyres: we enjoyed the previous Lotus Cortina simply because you could chuck it around on opposite lock in complete control, even though its cornering powers on ordinary cross-ply tyres were not all that high. You now get the best of both worlds, plus an important additional bonus in that there is no longer any vicious bump steering. In other words, the car is not deflected by ridges, white lines and manhole covers in the disconcerting way of its ancestors—although it will patter quite violently on a really bumpy road, especially under acceleration.

There was a disappointing frictional stiffness in the steering, which is a pity because it was otherwise quite responsive, reasonably light and sensibly geared. This friction, or whatever it was, damped out the last bit of castor action when the wheels were on a small lock so you had to help the steering to straighten out sometimes. Through an S-bend, going from one lock to the other, some drivers found it hard to judge by feel exactly when the wheels *were* pointing straight ahead, though there was quite a lot of feedback in the steering while actually cornering.

The disc/drum brakes now have a servo which makes them very light to work yet not fierce or over-sensitive to clumsy feet. Our fade test actually turned out to be a revival test: instead of pedal pressures increasing to maintain a ½g stop as the brakes got hotter, they actually diminished by a third, from a modest 33 lb. to begin with to a mere 22 lb. Even a panic stop from 100 m.p.h. calls for only gentle pressure on the pedal. The water splash had scarcely no effect at all and the handbrake not only secured the car very firmly on a 1-in-3 hill but also provided the sort of emergency stop that few rear-engined cars, with lots of weight on the back wheels, can better.

Comfort and controls

If anything is to prevent the Cortina Lotus from joining the ranks of the luxury compacts it is the firmness of its ride and the poor driving position. We can readily forgive the harshness of the springs on account of their benefits to the handling but to endure a bad driving position in what is essentially a discriminating driver's car is another matter. The trouble lies in the location of the seat, in particular with the dreadful notched-arc adjuster that makes the squab more upright (and the cushion flatter) as the seat goes back. The 2000E has been given a decent slide, why not the Cortina Lotus as well? Matters would not be so bad if the squabs were adjustable for rake but, as in other two-door Cortinas, they are fixed—presumably because it is necessary that the seats tilt forward to allow passengers to get in the back. Not that this is much of an excuse because it is quite possible to provide both together. Even a small wood packing under reversed seat brackets confirmed our view that a little penny pinching on the production line has caused a lot of discomfort to tall drivers. As it is, you must

With a small turning circle of 27-28ft., the Cortina Lotus is easy to manoeuvre in a car park.

Engine

Cylinders	4
Bore and stroke	82.57 mm. x 72.82 mm.
Cubic capacity	1,560 c.c.
Valves	twin o.h.c.
Compression ratio	9.5:1
Carburetter(s)	Two Weber 40 DCOE sidedraught
Fuel pump	AC mechanical
Oil filter	Full flow Tecalemit or Fram
Max. power (net)	109.5 b.h.p. at 6,000 r.p.m.
Max. torque (net)	106.5 lb. ft. at 4,500 r.p.m.

Transmission

Clutch	Borg and Beck 8 in. diameter s.d.p.; diaphragm spring
Top gear (s/m)	1:1
3rd gear (s/m)	1.397
2nd gear (s/m)	2.010
1st gear (s/m)	2.972
Reverse	3.324
Final drive	Semi-floating hypoid bevel, 3.777:1

M.p.h. at 1,000 r.p.m. in:—

Top gear	17.6
3rd gear	12.6
2nd gear	8.8
1st gear	5.9

Chassis

Construction	Unitary body/chassis

Brakes

Type	Girling hydraulic
Dimensions	9.62 in. front discs, 9 x 1.75 in. rear drums

Friction areas:

Front	20.64 sq. in. of lining operating on 189.5 sq. in. of disc
Rear	48.0 sq. in. of lining operating on 96.1 sq. in. of drum

Suspension and steering

Front	Independent by MacPherson struts and coil spring damper units; anti-roll bar
Rear	Live rear axle with semi-elliptic leaf springs and two trailing radius arms
Shock absorbers:	
Front and rear	Armstrong telescopic
Steering gear	Burman recirculating ball
Tyres	165 x 13 radial-ply Pirelli Cinturato, or Goodyear G800
Rim size	5½J

Coachwork and equipment

Starting handle	No
Jack	Screw type
Jacking points	Two each side under body sill
Battery	12-volt negative earth, 38 amp. hours capacity
Number of electrical fuses	None
Indicators	Self-cancelling flashers
Screen wipers	Self-parking, single-speed electric
Screen washers	Manual plunger with twin spray
Sun visors	Two
Locks:	
With ignition key	Driver's door and boot
Interior heater	Fresh air type as standard equipment

Extras	Twenty-one high performance racing and rally options—see text
Upholstery	P.v.c.
Floor covering	Carpet
Alternative body styles	None

Maintenance

Sump	7.5 pints SAE 10W/30 or 20W/20
Gearbox	1.75 pints SAE 80
Rear axle	2.0 pints SAE 90 Hypoid
Steering gear	SAE 90 EP
Cooling system	12.5 pints (drain taps 2)
Chassis lubrication	Every 2,500 miles to one point
Minimum service interval	2,500 miles
Ignition timing	12° b.t.d.c.
Contact breaker gap	0.014 to 0.016 in.
Sparking plug gap	0.023 to 0.027 in.
Sparking plug type	Autolite AG22
Tappet clearances (cold)	Inlet 0.005/6 in., Exhaust 0.006/7 in.
Valve timing:	
Inlet opens	26° b.t.d.c.
Inlet closes	66° a.b.d.c.
Exhaust opens	66° b.b.d.c.
Exhaust closes	26° a.t.d.c.
Front wheel toe-in	0.14 to 0.20 in.
Camber angle	0° 15' to 1° 45'
Castor angle	−0° 45' to +0° 45'
King pin inclination	7° 11' to 8° 41'
Tyre pressures:	
Front	24 p.s.i.
Rear	24 p.s.i.

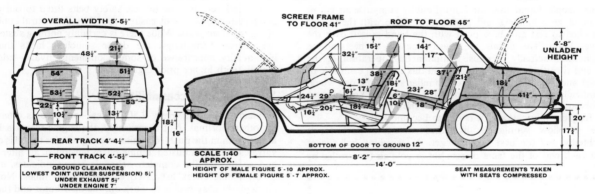

OVERALL WIDTH 5'-5½"
SCREEN FRAME TO FLOOR 41"
ROOF TO FLOOR 45"
4'-8" UNLADEN HEIGHT
REAR TRACK 4'-4½"
FRONT TRACK 4'-5½"
GROUND CLEARANCES
LOWEST POINT (UNDER SUSPENSION) 5½"
UNDER EXHAUST 5½"
UNDER ENGINE 7"
SCALE 1:40 APPROX.
HEIGHT OF MALE FIGURE 5 - 10 APPROX.
HEIGHT OF FEMALE FIGURE 5 - 7 APPROX.
BOTTOM OF DOOR TO GROUND 12"
8'-2"
14'-0"
SEAT MEASUREMENTS TAKEN WITH SEATS COMPRESSED

Safety Check List

Steering Assembly

Steering box position	Good—behind axle line
Steering column collapsible	No
Steering wheel boss padded	No
Steering wheel dished	Yes, a lot

Instrument Panel

Projecting switches	Yes
Sharp cowls	No, but several sharp edges
Padding	Crushable brow over facia

Windscreen and Visibility

Screen type	Zone toughened
Pillars padded	No
Standard driving mirrors	One inside
Interior mirror framed	Yes
Interior mirror collapsible	Probably

Seats and Harness

Attachment to floor	By two clamps over front cross-bar
Do they tip forward	Yes
Head rest attachment points	None
Back of front seats	Hard frame
Safety harness	Yes
Harness anchors at back	Yes

Doors

Projecting handles	Yes, door handles and window winders
Childproof locks	No—but only two doors

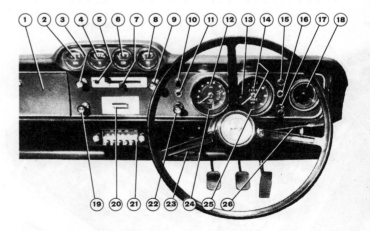

1, cubby. 2, ammeter. 3, Aeroflow control. 4, oil pressure. 5, fan switch. 6, engine temperature. 7, heater. 8, petrol gauge. 9, Aeroflow control. 10, panel lights. 11 and 16, direction indicator tell-tales. 12, rev counter. 13, speedometer. 14, mileage recorders. 15, lights switch. 17, ignition/starter. 18, Aeroflow vent. 19, choke. 20, ash tray. 21, radio (extra). 22, wipers/washer. 23, handbrake. 24, ignition warning light. 25, main beam tell-tale. 26, indicators/horn/dip/flasher.

Ford Cortina Lotus

continued

---

sit fairly close to the wheel and so upright that your body tends to flop forward: some drivers actually preferred to sit knees-up to the wheel so that they could lean back a bit more. Of course, anyone who likes to sit well forward—and we concede that many people do—will probably have no grumbles because the seats themselves, though not so enveloping as we should like, are quite good. They are firmly padded yet fairly resilient and they provide plenty of lumbar support. Raised side pieces on the cushion stop your thighs from sliding about but there is not enough to lean your back or shoulder against when cornering hard. Tilted forward, the squabs conveniently wedge themselves against the screen pillars so it is not necessary to hold the seat up while getting in the back. However, there is no lock to prevent them tipping up in a crash. The back bench seat provides little lateral support but is otherwise quite good and there is enough room to stow longish limbs in tolerable comfort. It is actually the front passenger who has the most comfortable seat because there is plenty of leg room here and the angle of the tilting chair is not so crucial.

Some people found that the central cubby-cum-armrest got in the way of gearchanging and preferred to drive with the lid up: others liked to rest an elbow on it with the hand poised over the gearlever knob. The pedals are ideally located to heel-and-toe (a misnomer, actually, because simultaneous operation of the brake and throttle is most easily done on this car with each side of the sole) and the throttle has Ford's familiar swivelling pad which automatically takes up the best angle for your foot. You have to lean forward for the umbrella handbrake, the sliding rod of which needs frequent lubrication if it is not to become stiff.

The Aeroflow ventilation, like that on other Cortinas, is undoubtedly still the best you can get. A swivelling ball-socket vent at each end of the facia directs hot or cold air (controlled by handy knobs and a two-speed fan by the central heater levers) in almost any direction. The heater, too, is very powerful but a little less versatile than the ventilation system in that it lacks an air volume control. Consequently, you must sometimes endure a stronger blast than is necessary to the footwells. Wind noise is quite modest—though with fixed quarter lights, it might perhaps be even less.

Fittings and furniture

Counting the two air vents, there are nearly 30 items on the facia to look at or to work. The 140 m.p.h. speedometer (with trip and total mileage recorders) and matching 8,000 r.p.m. rev counter are finely calibrated in white-on-black figures—though the rev counter is more of interest than use since the ignition cut-out prevents over-revving. Four other dials (amps, oil, temperature and fuel) are sunk into a raised nacelle above the facia where they are a bit to the left of one's normal sight-line though still on a level with it. Below, the black fabric-covered dashboard bristles with symboled knobs and small flick switches, all of which are just within reach of an outstretched hand, though not even the horn/flasher/dip stalk is within fingertip control when on the pushed-away main beam setting. A shelf under the facia, a cubby in it (not lockable), and the central oddments box provide quite generous shopping carriers, leaving more awkward packages to go under the front seats or on a shelf behind the back ones. Such are the cornering powers of this car, though, that anything left unsecured will rush from side to side on a twisty road.

The jerk-sensitive inertia reel safety belts fitted to our car were comfortable to wear but easily trapped by the central cubby when tilting the front seats. While there is certainly nothing austere about the interior furnishings, the decor somehow lacks that lavish high-quality appearance of some Continental rivals—admittedly, though, with higher price tags.

Servicing and accessibility

Servicing is needed every 2,500 miles—or twice as often as that for other Cortinas. Not surprisingly, the engine wants a lot more attention than the push-rod units: at every service the oil is changed, valve clearances adjusted, timing chain tensioned, air filter cleaned, and so on. As the complete schedule below indicates, it is quite a formidable check list to cover every 2,500 miles. Nor is it a particularly easy engine to work on: the distributor and fuel pump, for instance, are buried underneath the carburetters, and it is not even very easy to poor oil through the filler on the back of one of the cam covers. Oil consumption on our test car, incidentally, was about 500 mile per pint—better than for most previous twin-cam Lotus engines. The pillar screw jack, operated by a ratchet handle that you swing to and fro, is quite easy to work. **M**

Insurance
AOA group rating 6
Lloyd's . . . . On application to underwriters

Maintenance summary

Every 2,500 miles (4,000 km) or three months: Change engine oil; top up steering box, clutch and brake fluid reservoirs, radiator and screen washer bottle; clean sparking plugs, fuel bowl, and air cleaner; adjust and clean distributor and points; lubricate distributor and generator rear bearing, distributor cam; clean crankcase emission flame trap; adjust valve clearances; check timing chain tension; adjust fan belt; check battery; top up gearbox and rear axle; check tyre pressures; check torque of rear spring U bolts; check torque of front suspension cross member bolts; check boot-type gaiters on front suspension and steering joints; check front brake pads for wear; check rear shoes and self-adjusting mechanism and blow clean; lubricate drive shaft sliding joint; inspect all hoses for chafing and leaks; check front wheel bearings; grease handbrake cable at dash grommet; adjust handbrake if necessary; lubricate door locks, hinges, etc.; check lights and controls; adjust carburetter and ignition timing.

Every 15,000 miles (24,000 km) or 18 months: check front wheel toe-in; renew air cleaner; repack and adjust front wheel bearings; check rear spring inserts and replace if necessary.

Every 22,500 miles (36,000 km) or two years: Renew brake fluid and brake servo filter.

Every 45,000 miles (72,000 km) or three years: Check with dealer about changing clutch and brake cylinder seals, brake hoses and clutch fluid.

1, starter solenoid. 2, hydraulic reservoirs. 3, Weber carburetters. 4, cam covers. 5, radiator filler. 6, dip stick. 7, screen washer bottle. 8, brake servo.

MAKE: Ford. MODEL: Cortina Lotus. MAKERS: Ford Motor Co. Ltd., Dagenham, Essex.

LOVE–HATE

WITH A LOTUS-CORTINA

YOU don't live with a Lotus-Cortina, it suffers you to exist with it.

You sit at home cowering at the thought of it lurking just outside the house only waiting for you to dare to start the beast.

Perhaps cower is a strong word but after 18 months of living with one of the projectiles in various states of tune, then the two of you arrive at some sort of compromise—a sort of semi-peaceful co-existance.

The saga of life with NAR363D started in January 1966 when, after coming nowhere in sprints, hill-climbs and autocrosses with a Downton 1100, I finally wrote it off in a fit of rage on a narrow Essex hill one night.

I always tell friends "a tyre burst, you know". They smile knowingly and I suppose we both realise the awful truth but no-one ever gives voice and says "you lost it you bloody fool". I had of course, and rolled twice, finishing the aerobatics sitting surrounded by tinkling glass, securely held by Britax (not Berlei) and wondering how the hell I was going to get home.

After KMT502C had been rebuilt I didn't frankly trust the beast so opted for a change. We took the woodrim and Downton badge off and some old lady bought it I was told. Being told by every dealer in our area that we'd have to wait 16 weeks for a Lotus-Cortina, and brushing off the pleadings of our insurance company who shouted "No" down the telephone, we tracked down one dealer who said he could get one "next week, old boy".

Six weeks later we collected the shining white (then) dream car. Nursing her home for the first time we were impressed with the subtle feeling of power, good handling characteristics and above all the looks we fondly imagined ourselves getting from other motorists.

It wasn't until several days later when we'd read the handbook that we realised the oil pressure was lower than it should have been. About 12½ pounds. The local Ford man protested "Oh, that's OK sir, they're all like that". We discovered later that he'd never seen one before.

Eventually, after much pleading, we persuaded another Ford man to take the pump off and examine it. "We'll have to send it back, sir", he said, whilst I had visions of trekking to Dagenham or the wilds of Cheshunt. "The pump", he added, as I looked my usual shade of blank.

He showed me the erring unit's innermost parts and explained that some congenital lunatic in some factory somewhere had put the wrong vane in or something. It was apparently OK for an Anglia but a twin cam? Anyway, they

fitted a new pump. Our status symbol was fit for combat.

Our grin lasted a week as we continued running the car in. One day, out for a quiet blat round Lancashire (no, Martyn; you don't fall off the edge if you go beyond Potters Bar) we noticed the temperature gauge rapidly going off its head. Stopping and investigating we quickly discovered for the first time just exactly what a core plug is—or was—one had come out.

Two hours later we had another in the block and I had six in my pocket, for by this time I'd realised that maybe this was a "tea-break" car and I'd better hire a trailer to carry all the spares I was obviously going to need.

Driving the beast rapidly became a battle between me and it to see who would win. I was determined to sort out all the bugs even if I bust.

By this time I'd of course made the dealer who supplied the vehicle change the C41's it came on ("they're only good for a steady 80", a voice on the 'phone from Dunlop had said) to Pirelli Cinturatos, which I'd been happy with on the 1100. We managed to neutralise the oversteer by changing tyre pressures to two pounds lower at the front than back, and generally began to settle down to enjoy our Lotus-style motoring.

A circuit sprint at Mallory Park soon altered all that complacency. We were at least 20 seconds slower than anything else in the class and apart from being very frightened by the frequency with which other bods tried to modify the chicane realised that if we were going to do any good with the car we'd have to make it quicker.

So much then for the ads—or was it a feature in somebody's veteran magazine which claimed blandly "the Lotus Cortina is equally at home taking the family for a Sunday spin or on the club circuit at Silverstone". That scribe might have been right if he had a 10-lap start in a seven-lap handicap but I didn't have.

Len Street Engineering in London were now looking after the car after we'd written to Lotus complaining that no Ford dealer we could find knew the first thing about twin-cam engines. Lotus had suggested that as a former Lotus man he might satisfy my rapidly-growing mistrust of the vehicle. Len and his team did, and ironed the problems: Do your dynamo brackets break every other week? Or do the bolts simply unscrew themselves until an autocross scrutineer says " 'ere, what's this?" as he picks the dynamo off the grass underneath where you've parked the monster? Does your heater suddenly decide to deposit the entire contents of your radiator (complete with liberal dosage of Bluecol) at very high temperature all over your feet at a non-BC speed on the M1? Apart from the panic which ensued it ruined a colleague's new suede boots.

Does your cam cover leak so much that your plugs are usually swimming two inches deep in lovely green Duckhams? Mine did until I found that Hermatite on the gasket when refitting seals the whole thing up. At least it did until the whole gooey lot started finding its way up the cam cover retaining bolts; more Hermatite now cures that. Then it found its way through the oil filler cap. We braised on a new fuel filler type with double strength spring and two rubber washers (Len Street thought this up and it works). Now the top was clear of oil but it was gushing out of the breather—scrutineers don't really like that either. Cure?—make sure the rubber junction between the breather tube and the head is not blocked—ours was, and obviously had been since the engine was built.

By now the bolide had a Street Stage One conversion costing about £100. For this they balance the bottom end, take off the distributor cut-out and fit CPL2 cams. I think they'd changed the chokes and jets too.

We were much happier with the performance and began to do better in sprints and hill-climbs, spun for 200 yards going straight in an autocross too! The car still did 25 m.p.g. on a long journey and really accelerated like a scalded cat. We set a new British quarter-mile record using a 4·4 diff, and were happy with the firm ride and fact that she used little oil. Threw it out from every gasket that Ford had thought of and a few others—but didn't burn any! She went well, then and now, on Champions, except that someone has shares in Autolite and changes them over whenever I'm not looking. We'd had other "tea-break" troubles by the way. The water pump bearings decided they'd had enough and we had to arrange for a five-mile tow to Mr. Street's insulting rooms for a cure. A front wheel bearing unscrewed itself or something, and one headlight gave up the ghost. Those few bothers, plus the carb butterfly needles unscrewing themselves once a week, kept us busy.

After a fair season last year we put her away for a quiet winter and didn't think about competing this year until a friend listening to the engine one spring evening said confidingly, "your little end's going, ya know".

We didn't, but hurried off to Uncle Len's to hear the worst. "It's a cam follower", he diagnosed and the head came off to prove him right—as usual.

As putting this spot of bother right meant taking the head off we decided to cut our losses and have Dr. Street and his staff put the motor in stage three trim. This promised "a conservative 140 b.h.p."

The whole operation involved polishing and porting the head, fitting new valves and springs and CPL1 cams, re-profiled to Len's own design. New jets are fitted and Cosworth pistons can be added. The lower end can at the same time be reworked to give better strength and balance.

We settled for the top half work, which set us back around £80. Incidentally, when fitting the stage one conversion we'd had a high pressure oil pump put in too—it helps in competition work we're told.

Incidentally, while doing the work Len found the cam bearings were shot to hell—in about 10,000 miles, I ask you!

Anyway, we took the bolide away and she felt pretty good. Tootled up to see Roy Morris at Morspeed in Birmingham to have a roller brake test and see just how much power we were getting.

Gloom settled undisturbed. We were only getting 75 b.h.p. at the wheels, which means roughly 105 at the flywheel—we felt like driving the bloody thing off Beachy Head or selling it—you know the ads, "immaculate, only 5,000 from new, never raced or rallied". Well, we had only done sprints, drag racing and autocross.

On the brake our projectile declerated from 70 m.p.h. to 30 m.p.h. in seven seconds. A standard Lotus-Cortina took 15 and a Vauxhall 101 Estate 19 seconds.

Verdict—excess drag somewhere between the gearbox and rear end. Back in London we discovered the half-shaft bearings were clapped, the nuts holding the prop shaft to the diff were half off and the prop shaft rubber mountings were soggy.

Apart from the drag business at Morspeed we'd also found the timing was wrong, jets could have been better; Oh, and they prefer Champions too.

This time back at Street's Len offered to drop his own racing engine in for another test at Morspeed, just in case the roller brake gear had been reading incorrectly. He did drop it in and we arrived in Birmingham excited at the prospect of seeing a real engine in our car and performing well.

It did perform, too. After Roy Morris and able electronic gear manager Allan had done their fiddling bits they tweaked it up to 115 b.h.p. at the wheels. Not without four of us sitting in the boot, however, together with a dustbinful of sand, though, for the wild bomb threatened to plunge up and off the rollers with the amount of power it was putting out.

Frankly, I wasn't too happy at the prospect of seeing it shoot off the brake when the large dial reading M.P.H. said something like 130 m.p.h. But all was well and we sorted out power curves giving me the best revs to change at, best distributor settings to gain another 5 b.h.p., best combination of air and petrol jets, best plug gap and so on.

As the car had been well tuned by a respected mechanic before I left London the Morspeed test seemed to prove one point above others. That is that however good a mechanic he is, he must be a genius indeed if he can tune a car as accurately as electronic equipment sympathetically used. The tests Morspeed use, for example, even check on the efficiency of each cylinder and plug, compression, distributor dwell, combustion efficiency, carb efficiency, exhaust gas constitution, etc.

In the end we arrived at peak power in the rev range we wanted—that is always allowing for the variations of the wild cam.

Power came in at about 4,800 and continued upwards to about 6,800. Deceleration on this trip took 14·2 seconds but as we had larger tyres than the standard vehicles tested that probably accounted for the extra second.

All in all we were pretty happy with the car and with Street's superb engine. We had the feeling that now we'd sorted the drag question out our own engine too would have shown up well.

Len's engine we discovered later had been checked on an engine dynomometer at 150 b.h.p., so Morspeed's readings were completely vindicated.

Len's quite fantastic engine takes the car up to 132 m.p.h. very easily although the handling at that speed is very unsteady. After all, the take-off speed of a Tiger Moth is only about 80 m.p.h.

She will do 30 m.p.g. at a steady 4,000 but in town and sprinting this comes down to 15 m.p.g.

Engine vibration and noise at high revs are a bit much but this, we're told, is one of the penalties of high tune. Use of oil is not bad but we're still having breather trouble.

Another breather fitted to the front of the cam cover does the trick. Racing driver Willie Kay has proved this on his very successful Lotus-Cortina.

Our love-hate Lotus relationship continues unabated however. On the way back to civilisation after the second Morspeed test the lower heater hose blew and took the head gasket with it. This was in Tamworth, in the middle of a road works diversion! Those circumstances didn't stop Roy Morris collecting us and rebuilding the engine overnight to race at Santa Pod the next day though. He had to take 10 thou off the head as the excess heat had warped it, so we now have a ratio of about 10·6 to 1. Tribute to the engine and tuning.

We broke our own records for the standing start quarter at Santa Pod and came second in the 'Competition' eliminator —our best performance there yet.

A week later in an Austin Healey Club sprint we didn't win but beat all the other Loti and were only beaten by a 1650 Anglia and Roy Salvadori's ex 3·8. The next week at Kemble aerodrome in Gloucestershire we were in a class of 25 assorted missiles ranging from Brian Cutting's hairy circuit type Anglia to Martin three-valve-head Anglias and full race 1275s. We beat those we expected to beat but were pushed down the list by our own inexperience.

Taking acceleration figures for this feature one week later part of the flywheel decided to part company with its surroundings resulting in £8 10s. worth of expensive noises and a four-mile tow.

The figures we produced are pretty startling for this model but could be improved perhaps by slicker gear changing. We feel that there can be few Lotus-Cortinas about still used on the road and putting up this type of performance. Racing tyres and weight shedding, via fibre boot and bonnet, would probably help improve things as would harder suspension. Hard to believe that we're still running on standard suspension, but true. Rolls like an old mattress at times but the old Kwells help out.

The Cinturatos have now seen us though 15,000 miles of road work, to say nothing of about 30 sprints, hill-climbs, drag races and autocrosses. We've invested in some Dunlop yellow spots for future events and a first try out with them at Lydden Hill really showed us what we've been missing when really trying to push the bolide. We probably can't do much more to the engine, it's a little impossible in traffic now and to go any further would make each traffic light stop a plug cleaning job.

The answer to future development lies, as we've said, in weight shedding and distribution to say nothing of driver experience and nerves.

We'd like to try Mr. Street's great engine (costs about £450 outright—less for exchange) in an Elan, but that's another story, now perhaps if we found another bank manager . . .

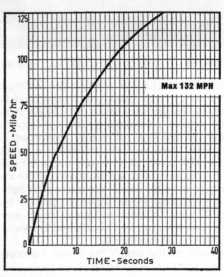

Max 132 MPH

SPEED - Mile/hr

TIME - Seconds

PERFORMANCE

Maximum Speed: 132 m.p.h. approximately.

Acceleration:			
0-30	3·5	0-70	10·3
0-40	5·0	0-80	13·8
0-50	6·7	0-90	15·0
0-60	8·4	0-100	18·0

Standing ¼ mile: 15·89 secs.

Fuel consumption: 18-30 m.p.g. depending on weight of right foot.

The Versatile Projectile

THE Editor of this old established mag has an enormous supply of a quality called "alacrity"; he is wont to display this whenever somebody offers him a particularly quick motor to trundle around the scenery in. The staff also have a smaller quantity of this mysterious ingredient. They displayed oodles of it recently when The Man from Ford Comps Dept offered us a test of the Graham Hill/David Seigle-Morris RAC—prepared Cortina Lotus.

After an emotional scene with Ed, in the course of which one bod hung from the Ed's 3rd floor window whimpering "let ME pick it up, PLEASE", we both went to get the fuel-injected beast—all 137 b.h.p. of it.

When we got to Boreham Airfield, Essex (which is where Ford competitions dept hang out), there was the aforementioned Man, looking suitably impressed by our early arrival.

During the next few days we came to love the beast; it is outstandingly tractable in traffic but has real teeth on the road or rough; for overtaking on a crowded main road it's the cat's whiskers. Once you've got 2,000 r.p.m. on that dial it's off. The great thing about it for road use is that the urge is right where you need it; that's to say from 20 to 100 m.p.h., which comes up bloody fast (too fast for England, of course!). This isn't really a "wot'll-she-do test", because the machine has a low (4·7) axle ratio, Goodyear Ultra Grip "knobbly" tyres (speed limit of about 90/95 m.p.h. sustained) and a rev limit of 7,500, which coincides with about 110 m.p.h. on the speedo. Still, even with all those restrictions it was FUN, FUN, FUN. What with the spot and fog lamps peering out everywhere, Lotus and Tecalemit/Jackson badges strewn round the back end, it was the ultimate boy racer's dream—all this and Graham Hill's name emblazoned on the driver's door! The latter really did provoke the general populace (and the fuzz) into regarding us with totally unjustified suspicion; the fuzz even tried getting us in on a loitering charge during the foggy part of the test period!

It was during this foggy period that we took the car to a friendly farmer's field for a session on the rough stuff, which is what the machine is meant for, is it not? This was even more fun, what with spraying our unfortunate Art Manager—who was taking the pix—with about eight tons of

Gunge-infested—it says Graham Hill on the side but actually it was Walton who did it!

As soon as the mechanics had finished fettling the motor The Man took us for a quick spin round their test circuit (described in the January issue of C&CC). This was an enthralling experience watching just how easy it is to hold a twin-cam Cortina in a 100 m.p.h. controlled slide (yes, fully controlled); even a sudden transition to a damp surface didn't upset the car at all, it merely slid a bit more. While we were on the test track we were shown the car's paces over a section of rough pavé—complete with potholes. Our Man did a few quarter-miles; times varied from the slowest first run of 17 secs, to a final 16·1 secs, which was achieved after many runs when we had not clicked the watch because the posts went past too quickly!

While we were on the circuit there was a prototype of the then secret Escort undergoing reliability trials—it impressed us by its stable cornering and remarkable resemblance to a Viva at the rear, and old model Taunus (Ford's German division) at the front.

Our very first impression of the car was unfortunate—we stalled it twice, once setting off from the main building, much to the amusement of the Comps dept staff; the second time as we trundled down the narrow lane outside. Still, it never happened again.

farmyard slurge and taking on the farmer's turbocharged Dodge truck in a battle of the giants! We also had a frantic session of round the mulberry bush with the poor old A.M., who had scuttled into a patch of nettles (to take all-action shots, he said!) eventually falling over while taking two shots at once as we spun around the nettle clump!

As you would expect, the Twin-Cam is absolutely at home on crud, though even with the Salisbury limited-slip diff. working overtime, traction isn't as good as an autocross Min at low speeds. But when you've got it well and truly screwed on there's little to touch it, being easy to control, once you overcome any Min habits that you may have. We say this because opposite lock plus power seems to see it through most quag-covered bends. Braking on the rough appears to be a waste of time—go sideways, young man!

While the car was with us in our London offices it had to do a considerable amount of traffic work. This is where the versatile bit comes in; you can trickle it through traffic with the clutch out at 1,500 r.p.m. No clutch slipping is required, which is a lot more than you can say for most group 5 cars, be they racers or rally go-wagons.

Which brings up an interesting point; we ran an article on a sprint Lotus-Cortina (November C&CC) which did the

Testing a group 5 Cortina Lotus

Just getta loada them lights. We've seen scooters with more, though.

Comfort in spite of it all—those seats are just the job and the harness helps too!

quarter mile in 15·89 secs and 0-60 in 8·4 secs. This car was a beast in traffic yet the group 5 motor with a 50 m.p.h. first gear managed to just pip it to 60 m.p.h! After this though the group 5's acceleration lags behind it, as it does in fuel consumption, which was 10 m.p.g. in traffic and about 18/20 on a long run. Sprinter's go-juice gobbling rate was 18/30 m.p.g.

There is a secret to the group 5's good traffic manners, as the motor uses the now-standard special equipment cam, so that Graham Hill would have a bit more low-down punch than the other works cars.

Brakes are little altered; drums are still on the rear but are fitted with Ferodo VG95 linings. Up front are the same company's disc pads, graded DS11.

This must be about the most civilised dicer there is, with no Infernal din inside the cockpit and full trim retained. All that disturbs you during your incredible wheel-twirling act is the whine from the fuel injection pumps, which brings up another point; not once did we have any bother in firing it up. On frosty mornings, it always started on the third tweak. Hot starting could be a little dicy if the car was on an uphill gradient. In the end we mastered this; all you do is switch off the fuel pumps.

As we said, the beast is civilised. Inside there is a reclining Microcell seat for the passenger and full safety-harness for both front seat occupants. The passenger has an easy time of it even when flying through the air, as there is a grab handle and footbar for sweaty palms and feet!

In our story on the Ford Competitions department (January

C&CC) we mentioned that the works motors had a new system of four-jet screenwashers from Tudor. These people are to be congratulated, for together with the two-speed wipers they coped with all the quag from that Dodge truck! Lights are operated from within, of course, and they, as you can imagine, are very efficient.

If you think this represents the ultimate in Cortinas, Ford have now added a five-speed box to the list of goodies you can order from the Performance Centre. This features materials by Hewland and assembly by Wooler. Fitted to a full house group 5 rally Cortina this has reduced the standing quarter times down to a remarkable 15 secs, we are told. Cost is around £125.

When we started to take acceleration figures a snag reared its ugly head. A good one, we suppose—the wheels would not spin! This, together with that high first gear, made for a nasty pause as we got off the line. It's those 7J Minilites that do it, you know! (fitted to the aft end only).

You too can build a group 5 Cortina-Lotus. All you have to do is get the Performance Plus booklet from: Ford Performance Centre, Boreham Airfield, Near Chelmsford, Essex. Then find the money, after you've drooled!

As we have said before, the Performance Centre does not fit equipment for ordinary mortals like us, so that you will have to see to it yourself.

There is, incidently, one snag to all this rave review—Mr. Hill's car is valued at at least £3,000. Shame ain't it?

JEREMY WALTON

 Cars on Test

Cortina Lotus Group Five

Engine: four cylinder; 80.98 mm 77.62 mm; 1,599.1 c.c.; twin o.h.c.; compression ratio 11.25 to 1; Tecalemit/Jackson fuel injection; 137 b.h.p. at 7,500 r.p.m.

Transmission: close ratio gear box and 4.7 axle ratio. Salisbury limited slip differential.

Suspension: standard but using heavy duty components throughout. Modified radius arms at the rear.

Brakes: as standard but fitted with DS11 pads at the front and VG95 linings on the rear.

Dimensions: standard except for weight which is 16/18 cwt (standard 21¾ cwt.)

PERFORMANCE

Maximum Speed 110 m.p.h. (see text)

Speeds in gears: First 48
Second 73
Third 90 (estimated)

Acceleration	m.p.h.	Secs.
	0–30	2.0
	0–40	3.5
	0–50	5.8
	0–60	8.2
	0–70	11.8
	0–80	16.9

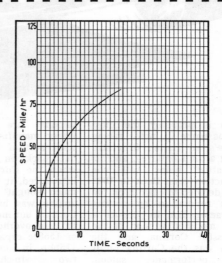

Manufacturers: Ford Motor Co. Ltd., Dagenham, Essex. Car prepared by Ford Competitions dept, Boreham, Essex. Not for sale at present, valued at £3,000.

SECONDHAND SPORTSTERS
LOTUS CORTINA

Lotus is probably the most famous name in motor racing (there's an Italian firm still doing a bit I believe), and its reputation helps sell the production cars. Back in 1962 Ford decided to cash in on the Lotus reputation by getting the racing firm to produce a much modified version of the successful Cortina, and the result was the Cortina Lotus high performance saloon. Some people thought it was a boy racer special, but it was designed for competition, and in that sphere proved very successful.

These days performance saloons are commonplace. Every manufacturer produces some sort of tweaked model, but back in January 1963 when the Cortina Lotus was introduced, it was a rare and much sought after car. The engine was basically a Ford Cortina, but modified by Lotus to twin overhead cam design of 1558cc capacity and giving 115bhp in standard trim on two twin-choke 40DCOE Webers. A competition type clutch was fitted with a specially developed close ratio gearbox (50mph in first!) and this made the car a bit of a beast to drive in traffic.

But the Lotus mods weren't just to make it go. The suspension was modified—the rear drastically with the original leaf springs replaced by coil springs radius rods and an A-bracket mounted to the diff. 5½J wheels and radial ply tyres were standard and the brakes were power assisted with discs on the front. The doors, bonnet and boot lids were made of alloy to save weight and the front end looked different with its quarter bumpers (from a Bedford van actually!) and matt black grille. Inside there were different seats, steering

wheel, dashboard layout and instruments (including a tacho of course) and a Lotus gear lever knob.

In October '64 the Lotus received Aeroflow ventilation as on the ordinary Cortinas, but it wasn't until October '65 that any major changes were made. In the two and half years the car had been on the market Lotus had come across several snags. The major one was that the A-bracket rear suspension didn't do what it was supposed to and in fact did a lot of things it wasn't supposed to—like making the axle bend, which caused oil leaks and toe-in on the rear wheels! Customers complained about the difficulty of driving the car at speeds below 30mph and particularly about starting from rest, and the alloy body panels were easily damaged. From this time then the car lost all these features in favour of the original leaf spring suspension, a standard Corsair GT gearbox and standard steel body panels, and it was also produced on the Ford production line and not at Lotus. Ford also tried to emphasise that it was a Cortina Lotus, but most people had come to know it the other way round and old habits die hard.

In October '66 Ford produced the Mark 2 Cortina with much smoother body shape and so many other mods that it was really a different car. The Lotus carried on being built on the old body shape until March '67 when it became more or less a Mark 2 Cortina GT with the Lotus twin-cam engine, stiffened and lowered suspension and a matt black grille—somewhat different from the original concept, but still a very good car and much more practical.

In September '67 the car received all the safety, ventilation and trim mods as on the standard Cortina and a 'Twincam' motif fitted under the Cortina badge on the boot. The original cars were finished only in white with Lotus green side stripes and rear, but now they were available in any colour.

October '68 saw the last changes made. Useful mods included reclining seats, a better remote control gear linkage, fully fused electrics, floor mounted handbrake and interior bonnet release.

On the road the early cars had excellent performance with a top speed of just over the ton and a 0-60mph time of about 11secs. Steering was

good and roadholding was excellent until things started going wrong with bushes, brackets and axles. The car performed best on Goodyear G800 tyres. Average fuel consumption was 24mpg or so.

The Mark 2 models weren't quite so spritely as they were heavier, but they did have reliable rear suspension and cornering was very good for a saloon car. Average consumption was 22mpg. The most noticeable thing on both models is the strong induction hiss as the twin Webers suck in air. If you're buying the car to race or rally this will hardly be a consideration!

We've already covered the most important points to watch for on a used model. In fact most of the early A-bracket suspension cars have been converted to the later type suspension, so that no major worry should occur. If you're looking at an early model you will soon know it

by the high first gear, in which case you should be sure the box is fairly quiet and working properly as repairs to it are expensive. If it needs a new box a Corsair GT unit can be obtained for under £40. While driving the car watch for wander on the straight which indicates worn steering arm joints.

The Lotus twin-cam engine is generally noisy, but reliable if maintained properly. It should do at least 50,000 miles on the road before rings and bearings are needed. Rings tend to wear early and let oil past and the sump may get pressurised if the breather is blocked. If the sump leaks check this point. Oil pressure should run at 45/50lbs psi when hot (may be only 10lbs idling) and consumption may be under 200 to the pint when the rings are worn. Timing chain and tappets are noisy. The timing chain job isn't very difficult, but redoing the tappets means fiddling with

all those shims after removing the cams—a long job.

If you want more performance from your Lotus Cortina you can take the engine to any number of specialist firms who will tweak it for the road, rallying or racing up to a full-house, fuel injected 190bhp job—but that's likely to cost you £1,000 plus. Top tuners include the mighty Cosworth, Brian Hart, Vegantune, Racing Services, and others. Full car preparation for rallying can be done by Mike Brown Rally Services, Supersport, etc. Race preparation can be done by Jeff Uren (remember the Willment Cortinas?), Broadspeed and others. But for serious competition, remember that the Cortina is now really outclassed by the Escort, although the Cortina is still a good tool for club events.

What do they cost? Well the earliest model (which you don't want really) would cost about £350. The cheapest you could get the late '65 modified suspension model for would be about £475, while an early Mark 2 will be around £700. The later models are better for normal road use, but of course they look externally like any other Cortina—until you get your greasy little customising hands on them!

These days you expect to pay a lot for sports car insurance, but be prepared for a shock with the Lotus Cortina. It used to be classed in insurance group five. Then it became six and now some companies put it in the highest group, seven, along with yer Ferraris and things. This means that your basic premium could easily be over £100 if you live in the country. If you happen to be a 20-year-old musician living in London and have no no-claims bonus, you're going to need all that money you're reputed to earn!   **LAURIE RUSSELL**

Pleasure Machines

Classic combination

When Ford and Lotus got together they produced a sporting saloon of true character

By Graham Robson

MOST CLASSIC car enthusiasts have a very clear idea of what Lotus-Cortina motoring was all about in the 1960s. Memories, and archive pictures, all relate to the same wheel-waving, giant-killing, antics on the race tracks — and, for owners, to the breakdowns and frustration suffered while owning temperamental early examples.

But the Lotus-Cortina had so much character and — when going well — so much performance and spirit, that some of us never lost the urge to own one. John Wood, whose 1966 example is featured here, sums it all up perfectly:

"The Lotus-Cortina was *the* car in the year that I started to learn to drive. I wanted one then, but of course I couldn't afford one. So when at last I had some spare cash — not much! — in 1978, and fancied a restoration project, I advertised for a Lotus-Cortina."

The car he bought was a ruin, a £100 failed-MoT test, trailer job: "But it was original, and it was quite complete. The problem was that when I first looked at it, I turned it down because I couldn't find any alloy panels, and thought it was non-standard. It was days before I discovered that all 1966 models were like that — and that all the special Lotus bits, except the engine and the suspension, had been dropped."

Classic car ownership, however, can become something of a disease, for John not only owns the two cars pictured here, but a third hulk which he hopes to restore one day. The second car, incidentally, surprised and delighted this writer, even though it is by no means as original as it might be. KPU 383C is one of a batch of "works" Lotus-Cortinas built at Boreham in 1965, for use as rally cars, and it was in that very machine that I sat alongside Roger Clark while he used the car to win the Welsh International Rally in December 1965. The win had nothing to do with me, but a lot to do with the car.

Below: John Wood's two Lotus-Cortinas. The one in the foreground is the ex-Roger Clark rally car — and should be painted red. . .

In the beginning the very idea of a Lotus-Cortina was conceived by Walter Hayes of Ford, but I'm also happy to report that *Autocar* was also closely involved. The car itself would not have been possible if the twin-cam Lotus engine had not been developed, and the design of that unit (which was a clever conversion of the Ford "Kent" push-rod design) had been carried out by *Autocar's* technical editor, Harry Mundy, as a freelance project. Mundy, of course, came to us from Coventry-Climax, where he had been chief designer for some years.

Walter Hayes, as Ford's new director of public affairs, was charged with building up a formidable "Total Performance" image, and approached Colin Chapman of Lotus, to help with the development of an "homologation special". His proposal was that Lotus should build at least 1,000 cars based on the new Cortina, that they should engineer all the changes, and that their new twin-cam engine (already slated for use in their Elan sports car) should provide motive power.

History now records the fact that the early cars, complete with Lotus-designed coil spring rear suspension, and A-bracket location of the light-alloy case back axle, were unreliable and frankly uncouth road cars, but that the re-designed cars built from mid-1965, shorn of their light-alloy panels, and reverting to conventional Cortina GT type leaf spring rear suspension, were much more successful.

All the magazine tests made the point that the lowered, and stiffened Lotus-Cortina handled very well indeed, and owner John Wood confirms this: "The roadholding is considerably better than that of the Cortina GT. The overall suspension geometry is different, for the car is lower, the camber of the front wheels is different, the wheels and tyres are much wider, and there is reduced Ackermann effect on the steering."

Colin Chapman's brief, in 1962, allowed him to make all manner of changes to the running gear, but to leave the

styling of the two-door shell strictly alone. The result was that apart from its much lower stance, and its wider wheels and tyres, the Lotus-Cortina of 1963-66 could only be recognised by its badging, and its unique colour scheme. There was, quite literally, no choice. Every production car was white, with that familiar Lotus striping down the side, and across the tail.

[The irony of John Wood's purchase of the wreckage of KPU 383C was that he bought a red car, resprayed it to "standard" Lotus colours during a comprehensive rebuild, then found out that, as a Boreham rally car, it had always been red anyway . . . .]

Even though *Autocar* was closely involved in the birth of this exciting new sports saloon, we were rather cautious about its prospects when describing its engineering. When we tested a car in November 1963, we said that: "it would be a bit like putting a spirited hunter into the shafts of a coal cart to use the car mostly for domestic chores . . ."

We were, no doubt, ready to make allowances for this very brave project, which was intended to put a Ford into the winner's circle in touring car racing, and also to provide a competitive rally car in the fullness of time. Sports Editor Peter Garnier was delighted, no doubt, to be allocated an early Lotus-Cortina (the 20th from the production line at Cheshunt), but he seemed to suffer all the traumas with which most "coil-spring" Lotus-Cortina owners became familiar. In particular, the A-bracket rear suspension strained the axle casing so much, and so often, that no fewer than six replacement final drives were needed in 29,000 miles of exciting motoring.

John Wood has the more reliable and civilised "Mk

Above: The distinctive side striping and subtle Lotus badging

1½" version with leaf spring rear suspension: "At first it didn't seem very quick to me. It was only when I started overtaking people, and noticing how quickly I was leaving them behind, that I realised how deceptive the performance was. Yet it isn't top-endy. It has a remarkably smooth torque curve. There are a few disappointments, of course. The clutch is too sharp, and that wood-rimmed steering wheel, the standard one, is really far too flexible."

The pleasure of owning a car like this Lotus-Cortina (which was built, incidentally, in November 1965, and registered in Edinburgh in April 1966) is not so much in the wolf-in-sheep's-clothing performance, but in the attraction of cheap Ford spares for the non-standard parts. The problem is, as John Wood told me, that very few body panels are still available (none at all, reputedly, in light alloy), and those that can be found tend to be expensive. "The problem with mine, which I only really discovered when I stripped out the shell for restoration, was that it had obviously been involved in a heavy diagonal crash at one time, and there were wrinkles in the floorpan, and the bulkhead."

Rebuilding the Lotus twin-cam engine, on the other hand, was no problem to John, who is a Chartered Engineer. "But when I bought the car in 1978, we couldn't even get the engine to run. *Everything* had been tinkered with — carburettors, distributor cap cracked, plugs fouling, coil shorting out, and timing disturbed. I started again from scratch, and it's as sweet as a nut now."

The delights of a Lotus-Cortina like this, of course, are that it can be an absolute joy to drive around, in all conditions. The Wood Lotus-Cortina works hard for its living. Not only was it entered in the 1982 Lombard-RAC Golden 50 rally with some success (John, co-driven by his wife Ann finished 17th overall, behind a fleet of ex-works cars, mostly Mini-Coopers), but John now uses it for daily transport. In the last year it has covered 10,000 miles, including the commuting trip to a nearby factory in Lancashire. Nor is KPU neglected, for John's wife also uses that one for shopping . . . .: "Yes, we're a two Lotus-Cortina

Cortina GTs, and there is much bare metal in evidence. The steering wheel looks pretty, but wouldn't be considered acceptable today (wood-rimmed wheels went out of fashion when they were seen to be prone to splintering in accidents), but the matching wooden knob for the gear-lever is rather sweet.

The under-bonnet view, of course, is impressive, for the Lotus twin-cam engine looks massive, and powerful. Firing it up, of course, confirms that view, for the grumbling of the big Weber carburettors is matched by the whirr of cam drive chains, and the tappety conversation of bucket tappets themselves.

To follow it down the road is to appreciate Colin Chapman's opinion, that standard Ford wheels were far too narrow, and that the basic car was too high off the ground. The standard body shell creases were ideally placed to accept the Lotus paint scheme — that, at least, being a touch more obvious than the discreet initialled "ACBC" Lotus badges on the rear wings, or on the front grille.

To every true Lotus-lover, by the way, this was the only acceptable type of Lotus-Cortina. The later examples, the Mk 2s with completely restyled bodywork, were assembled by Ford at Dagenham, rather than by Lotus at Cheshunt, and were less specialised than before.

To own a Mk 1 car today, on Britain's increasingly

Left: Ex-Ford "works" rally car — now used for shopping

Above: The black interior complete with wood-rimmed steering wheel and matching gear knob

family, which must make us rather rare, I think."

The miracle of the Lotus-Cortina, of course, was that it was never really intended as a normal road car. Lotus developed it purely as a competition car, and because of the regulations they were obliged to build the 1,000 replicas. It was something of a tribute to their reputation that so many customers queued up at Ford dealer showrooms to buy these machines, knowing that vandals, or just careless accidents, would soon deal grievous blows to the flimsy bonnet, door skin and boot lid panels, and that the ultra-close gearbox ratios, and the relatively highly tuned engine were quite unsuitable for use in heavy traffic. The price asked, of course, was encouraging, for in 1963 one was only asked to pay £1,100 for a Lotus-Cortina, at a time, for instance, when a Jaguar 3.4 Mk II saloon cost £1,463, and an Austin-Healey 3000 sold for £1,064.

To sit in a Lotus-Cortina today is to realise just how much the accepted concept of a sports saloon has changed in so little time. Even this, the "facelift" machine has very basic and gloomy trim and fittings, with black predominant throughout. The seats are the same as those fitted to

Above: The impressive view of the Lotus twin-cam engine

smooth highways, is a delight, and a real journey back into time, even if one has to put up with the baiting of Escort RS owners, pay through the nose for insurance, and worry where the next much-needed spare part is to come from. Good radial ply tyres (strictly non-standard, old boy . . . . but who's complaining?) all help to improve that nervous turn in of the race-intended steering, and the torquey growl of that famous engine makes it all worthwhile.

John Wood, of course, fell for the car many years ago, when it was quite beyond his means, and I believe this sort of impression is essential before one can love a car like the Lotus-Cortina. Only 2,894 Mk 1s were built in about three years, but many of these have already suffered from terminal body rot and been scrapped. Many of the "coil-spring" cars, too, have retrospectively been converted to leaf spring rear suspension. How many now remain I wonder? □

As interest in the original Lotus-Cortinas continues to grow, so does the club set up to help owners of the cars. For more information, and for technical and spares location assistance, you should contact: D. Missions, 47 Leslie Crescent, St. Michaels, Tenterden, Kent.

The new breed

Now regarded as a classic, the Lotus Cortina was a troublesome baby when new, as Peter Garnier, FRSA, remembers. His adventures with car No 20 may have sent him grey but he loved it

NOW that my infamous Lotus-Cortina seems set to become one of the all-time classics, the memory of it has sparked off these thoughts. It was No 20 off the 'production line', and little more than a prototype being developed by its owners. There was absolutely nothing unobtrusive about it, and I would have you proud owners of this newly-arrived classic spare an occasional thought for us unwitting guinea-pigs who helped develop it for you.

It became mine (in a manner of speaking; *Autocar* actually paid for it) in May of 1963 when I was Sports Editor, and I began the task of running-in which, at 10-12mpg, worked out costly (even at 5s 5d a gallon, which was what it cost then). Shortly after taking over, I covered the May Silverstone international, driving proudly into the paddock with what was then a rarity. Friends gathered round to inspect it and, to emphasise a point, one of them clouted the bonnet with the flat of his hand — and it bore the dent until we parted, 29,000 exciting miles later. Subsequent production cars had their light-gauge aluminium bonnets replaced by steel. My arrival in the Silverstone paddock, with some 3000 miles on

the clock, for the British GP in July was also not without interest. I draw up with a shrill and embarrassing shriek from the front brakes — and carried right on to the Ferodo van. With Harold Theyer's help, I removed a front wheel, and found the pads worn through to the backing plates. The original DA4 material was replaced by the harder DS11 against Colin Chapman's advice: "Much too hard," he said, "First time he brakes in the wet he'll be round, facing the way he's coming from". Maybe they did upset the designer's front/rear balance, but the DS11s needed replacement only once during the rest of my time with the car, and any subsequent *têtes-à-queue* could not be blamed on the brakes (or on me, for that matter).

During these early days the managers of the various competition departments grew to know the car pretty well as, in turn, they were summoned to the rescue. Laurie Hands, of Champion, was among them, curing a tendency to oil plugs by fitting N9Ys. But these little problems were as nothing compared with what was to come.

Things started in earnest on the way back from

the German GP at the Nürburgring in August, this particular trick becoming one of the star-turns in its astonishing repertoire.

I had hurtled along the dangerous three-lane road from Liège to Brussels at an indicated 100 mph or so, and as I approached Brussels I lifted-off. The noise from the back axle on the over-run was terrifying. People gazed skywards, under the impression an air-raid was imminent; and an elderly, and otherwise mute, Belgian whose car had broken down and I was lifting to Ostend said, with a blinding glimpse of the obvious, "Le pont arrière", he said, with a blinding glimpse of the obvious, and fell silent again. I dropped him off in Brussels and struggled on to the first garage on the Jabekke road. Anxiously, I clambered underneath as soon as their hoist was high enough. The entire underside at the back was running in oil — from the final drive, which was empty. When it had cooled down enough to touch, we tightened the studs securing the cast aluminium nose to the banjo, replacing those that had disappeared, filled it with oil, and off — very noisily — I went, thinking of the blank pages where the story of the German GP should have appeared.

Like so many of the BBC's programmes, this was to be a 'repeat'. By the time 5000 miles appeared on the speedometer, it had had three replacement crown wheels and pinions.

It was nothing if not versatile, but very fortunately its second escapade was a one-off. In January 1964 I had been covering the northern routes of the Monte Carlo Rally, and had decided to put the story and films on to a plane at

The distinctive Lotus Cortina livery of white with green flash. Despite trials and tribulations, Peter Garnier remembers his 'infamous' car fondly.

The new breed

Brussels before heading south. It was again on the run from Liège to Brussels, but we had decided to give the three-lane main road a miss and take to a minor route to the north. If yours is one of the early cars you will be familiar with the rear axle layout, with coil springs concentric with heavy-duty telescopic dampers, the live axle controlled by radius arms each side, and a wide-based A-bracket in the middle for lateral location; the apex of the A was attached to the final drive casing by a bolt on which it pivoted.

This bolt fell out . . . and the resulting rear wheel steering put us off the road. Had we been on the crowded three-way, doing maybe 90mph or more, the story might have ended abruptly. We summoned help, which was not readily forthcoming as it was a Sunday; it wasn't particularly quick when it did arrive, as the A-bracket was bent, but eventually we were back on the road again and completed the event without further excitement.

It seemed to be allergic to Belgium for the next two excitements happened there. In June 1964 we had been covering the Spa 24 hrs race and were returning, tired and hungry, to the hotel in Spa when we all agreed that the suspension had suddenly lost much of its flexibility. Next day, on the inevitable run to Brussels airport with the copy and films, this view was confirmed — it appeared even to have lost all its movement. We made the airport, put photographer Ron Easton on a plane, and started back for the Nürburgring and the German GP. In the middle of the town the right-side rear corner sat down with a crunch on the pavé, and that was that. We hailed a taxi and asked him to take us to the nearest Ford agent, stupidly omitting to record where the sit-down had occurred. When we eventually reached Mr Ford, and he asked us where the car was, we had sheepishly to confess that we'd no idea

We eventually found it, sitting woebegone where we'd left it, and took it back on a breakdown. This time the attachment of the right rear suspension strut had broken away from the axle casing — the damper having seized. It took two days to repair, and we went on to cover the German GP without further trouble. In May the following year I was bound again for the Nürburgring, at the 1000kms sports car race when, driving through Liège, I had to brake hard on a cobbled left-hand bend as somebody emerged flat-out from the darkness of a tunnel to my right. When I left the cobbles for a smooth surface, there was a continuous squeal from the front tyres — the track rod had bent! We had the bend reduced (to call it straightened would be a gross exaggeration) and the toe-in re-set, and carried on.

In a curious masochistic way I was loving the car as it was such enormous fun to drive. It was like a sort of congenial rogue, possessed of every human failing in the book, but charming with it. By now there were mutterings in the office, each time I returned by the skin of my teeth with the story of an event, that it would have to go — but I fought vehemently on its behalf, explaining that these were but teething troubles and would soon be past. It was given a stay of sentence.

The RAC Rally that year produced a whole clutch of troubles. The bushes fell out of the radius arms, allowing the axle to move backwards and forwards under braking and acceleration — to which was attributed the subsequent complete failure of the clutch. Added to these, the axle lost all its oil again (and why not?), so that our progress amid the whine from the final drive, the clonks from the radius arms, and the graunching from the long-suffering gearbox, became quite a feature of the event. We completed the coverage, and struggled back to London on time with the story — and to have the fourth final drive

fitted. Before the car and I parted, there had been six replacements, and the Voice of Authority was becoming loud and insistent. "This can not continue", it said, to which I replied: "Just one more chance . . . please!. Another stay of sentence was granted. I had to admit, inwardly, that it could scarcely be regarded as having given the high standard of reliability that my job demanded, though somehow it always managed to get the story back on time.

At around this time it trotted out yet another trick when, hurrying back to the office I changed down into third at around 60 mph for a round-about . . . and selected a coupie of gears at once (which couple, I never knew). Luckily, there was a wide grass verge to the left, so that the resulting gyrations, caused by the locked back wheels, caused no damage. I think I did begin to wonder, though, how long I was going to remain unscathed.

Its swansong came during the coverage of the Dutch GP at Zandvoort, when final drive replacement No 5 began its all-too-familiar song — though in fairness to the car, I have to say that it had been fitted without the oil seals. It had to be the end, though, even if we did limp home with the story on time.

Maybe it was because the car contrived to combine the adventures of the very early days of motoring with the performance of a hot saloon of the Sixties; maybe it was because, as is said, you don't get to know and love a car really well until you've been through thick and thin with it; maybe it was simply because it was such enormous fun to drive . . . All I know is that I was sadder to part with that car than any other. And later on, at the wheel of something wholly reliable and unremarkable, I used to see the Mark IIs going by, with their Cortina GT rear axies and suspensions, their steel bonnets and boot lids, and all their other modifications, and say to myself "I wonder whether you'll ever appreciate what adventures we pioneers went through to give you that exciting and reliable motor car." ▲

Below, This particularly nice MkI Lotus Cortina, complete with A-frame rear and a full complement of light-weight panels, was seen for sale in the automart at the recent Beaulieu Autojumble. Below right, the GT Cortinas raced too. Here we see Jack Sears just keeping ahead of John Whitmore's Cooper at Brands '64. The GTs are easily distinguishable from the Lotus versions by the paint scheme.

The Kelly/Lund MkI at the 1964 Spa 24-hours where it finished ninth. Below right, three-wheeling at Brands Hatch and far right below, that same old problem with the rear axle.

'For what is basically a road car — it has even been MOT'd as per the regs — Phil's Lotus Cortina is super fun'

GREEN FLASH

Those distinctive colours of white with a green flash always bring back memories of the Lotus-Cortina's racing heyday. Willie Green tries to emulate Jim Clark in today's top racer

There are certain photographs which seem to capture, in a micro-second, what motor racing at a particular period is all about. Think of the shots of Mercs and Auto Unions yumping at Donington: Fangio in an absolutely classic four wheel drift; and Jim Clark three-wheeling a Lotus Cortina. That last picture (I think it's at Bottom Bend at Brands, but the location and the race are immaterial) has been published thousands of times, but the magic never stops. Jim, a Lotus Cortina, and three wheels are inseparable, and it's quite possible that it did more for Cortina sales than any other factor you care to mention. It all proved that you can turn a sow's ear into a silk purse.

The sow's ear, of course, was one of the most successful cars ever produced in this country in terms of sales — the Ford Consul Cortina, to give it the name with which it was christened. With its dead simple (but light) body, dead simple mechanicals, and dead simple image, you could hardly call it a racer. It was the Ford popular, not Popular, though that might have been a better name than Cortina. It was for dad, mum and three kids, for junior members of staff, for reps and bank clerks. A racer it wasn't.

Ford's first steps

But it appeared in 1963, when Ford had discovered competition on tracks and in rallies. For sure they'd been racing and rallying before, but in 1963 they allocated the vast sum of £43,000 to competitions. Ford were off and running, sometimes with rather unlikely machinery — like the Cortina.

The Lotus Cortina story really started somewhat earlier, with a genius called Colin Chapman. He'd been making the pretty little Climax-powered Elite for some time, but was looking for a replacement engine — the Climax was both small and expensive — for an up-coming new model, the Elan. The little Ford 105E engine had proved highly amenable to tuning from its birth, so Chunky hit on the idea of using the 105E bottom end and topping it with a twin-cam head. He approached Harry Mundy, an engineer who was, at the time, the Technical Editor of *Autocar*. Working in his free time he came up with a classic head, a dream of inspired simplicity, free-breathing yet torquey. It was made of alloy, and held the chain-driven

camshafts which operated the valves, inclined at 54deg, through inverted piston-type tappets.

In the meantime, Chapman was let into a Ford secret — the Cortina 116E engine with its five-bearing bottom end, obviously a much better bet for a high-performance unit. The new head was adapted to this 1498cc block without too much trouble, and the whole engine had a lot of potential. It was given a baptism of fire in May 1962 in a very famous race, the Nürburgring 1000kms. Snuggled into the back of a Lotus 23, it caused a sensation at the end of the first lap when Jim Clark came past the pits with nothing — literally *nothing* — else in sight. The race, and Jim's and the engine's performance in it, are still talked about today with much joy by those who were there,

even if the car didn't survive to reach the finish.

Perhaps as a part of that race, Ford had the inspired idea to approach Chapman and suggest that the engine be fitted into their new car, the Cortina. Chapman, of course, agreed instantly, the idea being for Lotus to produce 1000 off to homologate the car for Group 2. Cosworth took over the development of the engine, which was initially built by the motorbike engine firm JAP, while Lotus would take over the suspension and chassis side of things, and build the car too. One of the first things Cosworth did was to bore out the engine to 1558cc, taking full advantage of the 1600cc class split, in which form the engine gave 105bhp.

Lotus, meanwhile, went to work on the rest of the car. The dead simple back axle, sprung on and located by leaf springs, went. The live axle was retained, but located by links trailing from the original front spring mounting brackets to the axle: sideways location came from an A-bracket, attached to the body at the front, on a bracket welded underneath the same original spring mountings, and on the axle at the centre of the differential underneath via a rubber bushing. The coil springs and dampers picked up on the original damper mountings, these being strengthened by struts from this point back to the original rear spring mounting bracket. At the front the coil springs were shortened and a new forged lower link reduced camber angle.

Distinctive colours

Other mods included a close-ratio gearbox and bigger clutch, assorted castings made from aluminium instead of cast iron, a larger diameter prop shaft, a stiffer anti-roll bar at the front (but none at the back — hence the car's propensity for three-wheeling), higher-geared steering, new instrumentation and seats finished in that most horrid of materials, Vynide. Externally, bonnet, doors and boot were clad in aluminium (no slamming allowed!) and the whole ensemble was finished off in white with a green flash down the side, and discreet 'ACBC' Lotus badges. With its distinctive colour scheme and lower stance, the Lotus Cortina looked ready for the track just standing still.

But it took a long time for it to roll off the lines, and, though the car was announced in January 1963, nothing much happened in that year, so the car really started to come into its own only in 1964. Messrs

One of those classic motor racing memories: Jim Clark three-wheels his Lotus-Cortina at Brands Hatch in 1964

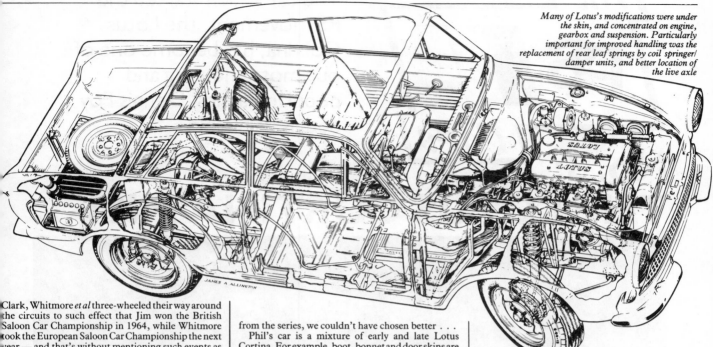

Clark, Whitmore *et al* three-wheeled their way around the circuits to such effect that Jim won the British Saloon Car Championship in 1964, while Whitmore took the European Saloon Car Championship the next year — and that's without mentioning such events as Roger Clark's British Rally Championship in 1965.

Once the 1000 homologation cars had been built, some rationalisation took place, the first step being the gradual deletion of the light but vulnerable aluminium panelling, replaced by steel from June 1964. Some of the alloy castings were supplanted by standard items, while the close-ratio' box was another victim. A split prop-shaft, to remove a vibration period, was introduced.

However, the car had an Achilles heel — the rear end. The strengthening from the coil spring mounting down to the rearmost spring anchorage wasn't strong enough, and any rough stuff could have the tail drooping like that of a frightened dog, accompanied by wrinkled bodywork. More dramatic, though, was the fact that the loads imposed on the axle and casing by the new locating links were excessive — where leaf-spring wind-up used to absorb braking and torque forces, these were now fed into the axle so it warped and soon leaked oil profusely. In addition, the lower A-bracket was vulnerable when rallying — it could be rapidly wiped off by an errant rock.

Thus it was, in July 1965, that a radically altered Lotus Cortina rolled off the lines. This time there were leaf springs at the back, with axle location by a pair of radius arms from under the rear seat pan to the axle. Problems solved . . .

Racer's 140bhp

Back in 1964 a racer straight from the factory was announced at the Racing Car Show, developing some 140bhp, followed in 1965 by the Special Equipment version which gave 'only' 117bhp. The Lotus Cortina was in production at Cheshunt for only three years, 1964, 1965 and 1966, during which time about 2700 were made. In the autumn of 1966 the Mark 1 Cortina was phased out, and when the Mark 2 became available in February 1967, it was a totally Ford project — but that is another story.

Phil Wight could almost be called the archetypal low-key club racer. He's been at it since 1974, mainly in saloons — he's had three seasons of Renault 5 stuff, and won the Classic Saloon Car Championship in 1980 in a very rapid Austin A35. He's had one-and-a-bit seasons in the Pre-65 series, having pulled out last year after a couple of races — "I decided to rescue my business: I was slowly going broke spending all my time and money on *that*!" he said, nodding at the Lotus Cortina. This year he's been the man to beat in the series, invariably the fastest overall, never mind just in his class. Certainly, he is the most consistent of the top runners, and has already won his class in the Championship. If we were going to track test a car

from the series, we couldn't have chosen better . . .

Phil's car is a mixture of early and late Lotus Cortina. For example, boot, bonnet and door skins are alloy, but the rear suspension is by leaf spring. In more detail, the engine is prepared by Oselli to full race specification, including Cosworth rods and pistons, narrow journal steel crank, steel flywheel and so on. It has shown 150bhp at the wheels, which equates to about 180bhp at the flywheel. He had a major blow-up last year when a missed gearchange sent revs soaring, so this year he has fitted a rev limiter — "The best £34 I've ever spent!" Front suspension uses 2½ins springs adjustable for ride height, plus an adjustable anti-roll bar, while at the back, the live axle is located by twin radius rods and a Panhard rod. A limited slip diff with a choice of ratios makes the car easier to set up for different circuits.

Phil bought the car in October 1983 as a fire-damaged write-off, and with the help of Simon Holland, spent the winter rebuilding it from the ground up, only the engine work being farmed out. I'm sure he won't mind me saying that it was all done on a shoestring: he reckons, taking everything into consideration, that it's cost him between £9000 and £10,000 over two years. Considering how much racing he has done, that must make his car more value per £ than any other I can think of!

According to Phil "it chews starters", and in fact it makes some funny noises when you turn the key, but once it catches there's no further problem. Phil and I are about the same height, but he seems to have longer arms and legs than me. The gear lever was a bit of a stretch away (but you get used to this very quickly) and I couldn't heel and toe (Phil: "I don't bother heel and toeing — if I try, my knee hits the steering wheel . . ."). Other than that, there are no cockpit problems with the car.

The engine is superb, even if, as Phil says, it's getting rather tired, having completed a full season, including 32 laps of Oulton in a relay race. It has no

No cockpit problems, but heel and toeing is not possible

vices, pulling cleanly from idle right on up to the red line, though I limited myself to 8000rpm for the purposes of this test. Like all good engines, it's actually unremarkable — it's funny, I suppose, but it's much easier to write about something that's wrong rather than something that's right! Considering that the brakes are standard, too, with DS11 pads at the front and drums at the rear, they work incredibly well, nicely balanced and powerful.

The handling on or near the limit was really a matter of two factors — the fact that the Lotus Cortina is fitted with a live back axle, and the other that Mallory, though one of my all-time favourite circuits, is rather bumpy! Try as I could, I couldn't get it to waggle a front wheel as in days of yore (though the pictures may prove otherwise!) but then, as Phil remarked, they don't build them today as they did in . . . In fact it feels very stiff at the back, even though Phil has softened-up the rear as much as possible and made the front as stiff as possible — when he first took it to the tracks it would, apparently, spin at the slightest provocation!

Plenty of tyre squeal

The problem you have is that, if you hit a mid-corner bump, of which Mallory has its share, the back axle bounces up, loses traction, and you have instant oversteer, which makes it somewhat twitchy, to put it mildly. Thus, if you know Mallory, it is decidedly nervous at the exit to Gerards, but on the fast left hander into the pit straight — which is relatively smooth — it is superb, sliding smoothly and cleanly and very, very quickly. The hairpin is a bit of a hoot — you just throw it into the corner with a foot full of power and come out very, very sideways, accompanied by much tyre squeal from wheelspin. In fact, it's my sort of car — you steer it with the throttle, and only use the sterring wheel if you go too far . . .

For what is basically a road car — it has even been MoT'd as per the regs — Phil's Lotus Cortina is a super fun car, and *extremely* quick. I don't normally quote lap times, since they tend to be a bit meaningless unless you've actually raced something comparable at the same circuit, but I managed to get down to a 60.01sec lap: when Phil went out after me, he recorded a 59.4sec lap, which just goes to show how well the car's sorted. If a complete stranger can get that close then the car can't be at all bad. It's for sale, incidentally, since Phil wants to turn his hand to Renault 5 Turbo racing, for about £7500, so if you want an instant winner on the cheap, now's your chance: contact Phil on 01-204 3936.

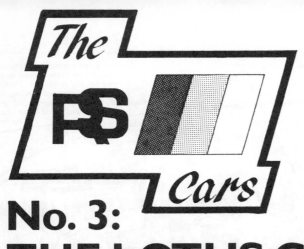

The car which started the RS movement, the Lotus Cortina, has become one of our most enduring and popular classics. Dennis Foy details its history.

No. 3:
THE LOTUS CORTINA MK I

DENNIS FOY

That Ford could ever market a version of their new mid-sized car which features a sophisticated twin-cam engine and a maximum speed comfortably in excess of "the ton" was almost inconceivable back in 1962. Yet a year later they did just that, producing (with more than a little help from sportscar manufacturer Lotus) the all-conquering Cortina Lotus.

Credit for the concept must be lain at the feet of Walter Hayes, presently Vice-Chairman of Ford of Europe, but back in 1962 a newly-arrived member of the Ford Public Affairs Department. Anxious to capitalise on the marketing potential of having Ford cars prominent on Britain's racetracks and rallies, Walter Hayes got in touch with his old friend Colin Chapman, whose Lotus company were already producing their own version of the engine which would power the as-yet-unannounced Cortina range. This engine, which topped the block of the Ford product with a twin-cam cylinder head produced by Lotus to designs by one Harry Mundy, was able to pump out more than 100 b.h.p. — no mean achievement at the time.

Hayes reasoned that combining the two elements — Chapman's engine and Ford's new car — would be a surefire winner in competition, and Colin Chapman was not inclined to disagree. Thus, having agreed terms by the middle of 1962, Lotus were left to it to not only develop the project, but to make deliveries of the first batch by the beginning of 1963.

The car was known within Lotus as the Type 28, and the method of production chosen by Ford was that Lotus would be supplied at their Cheshunt factory with two-door Cortina bodyshells, and a short time later would receive back complete cars, which Ford could market through their dealer network. The first stage of conversion, or more accurately of building up the shells into cars, was to install the 1558cc (125E) engine, which was backed up with the all-synchromesh gearbox of the Lotus Elan, the two components being joined by a specially-cast aluminium clutch housing. These two components fit into the shell without any difficulty, thanks to the generous amounts of space available within the Cortina's engine bay.

Next, Lotus got to work on the rear suspension system of the original Cortina, and developed their own, far more substantial and sporting, axle location system. This involved replacing the original equipment leaf springs of the Ford with a set of coil springs, mounting to the axle via a set of specially-designed brackets. These spring units had internal dampers, and the original damper top-mounts were used to locate the new spring and damper units of the Lotus development. Next, a pair of trailing arms from the original car's leaf spring forward pickup

points to the axle were installed. Finally, an "A" frame was installed, with its apex locating onto the specially-modified differential casing, and its open ends bracketed to the floorpan close to the radius arm pickup points. To ensure that all remained as solid as the designer intended, stiffening tubes were strategically affixed around the rear floorpan of the car.

The front suspension came in for attention also, but not on anything like as grand a scale afforded to the rear. Shorter struts with uprated damping were installed, along with a set of lower, stiffer springs than those found on any other model of Cortina. Forged track control arms were fitted, and a faster (3.0 turns lock-to-lock, as opposed to the usual 4.2) steering box was installed. The braking system was specified at 9.5" front discs

with 9" x 1¾" rear drums, and the car was the only car in the range at the time to have the luxury of servo assistance.

Overall the car sat extremely low — lower, in fact, than any other Cortina ever has, in the showroom. Coupled with the wide steel wheels of 5.5" x 13" with their 6.0" crossplies, the car looked aggressive — an appearance emphasised by the frontal elevation of the Lotus Cortina, which used small quarter bumpers in place of the usual full-width blade affair.

Identifying the car was easy: they came in any colour you like, as long as it was white with a green sidestripe. Discreet Lotus rondels were affixed to each rear wing and to the front grille, but ▷

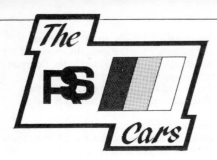

there was no badging whatsoever on the rear of the car. The doorskins, bonnet and bootlid were in light alloy, which kept the weight of those early cars down to about 1700 lbs.

That the original intention of the Hayes/Chapman coalition was to score success on racetracks was immediately apparent upon looking inside the car; it was a bit basic, to say the least. The seats were rudimentary buckets in the front and a bench in the rear, all finished in black vinyl — as were the door liner panels. Ahead of the driver was a binnacle unique to this car which contained four clocks, and there was a wood-rimmed alloy steering wheel. The rest of it was a combination of much painted metal, a bit of padding, and the occasional strip of chromed trim.

But of course these cars were not about luxury — they were built to go, and go they certainly did. The engine was enough to endow the car with a power-to-weight ratio of more than 135 b.h.p./ton, and that is a figure which is creditable today, so

"These cars were not about luxury. They were built to go, and go they certainly did."

back in 1963 it was revolutionary. The top speed of the car was put at about 105-110 m.p.h. depending on the output of that particular engine (they varied quite a bit ...), and acceleration from 0-60 m.p.h. could be as good as ten seconds dead. However, where the car really scored was not in sprinting from traffic lights, but in blasting through curving roads. There, it was almost inassailable with enough power available to push out the tail if too much throttle was applied, even at quite high cornering speeds.

The car could not only go through bends very rapidly and very safely — learn to handle the wayward rear and it was surprisingly

friendly towards the driver — but could also stop quickly and squarely, thanks to those big front discs. Steering weights were always good, and the inter-relationship between controls, both foot and hand, were excellent.

Unfortunately, those early cars also showed a tendency to damaging their own rear axles, and the close-ratio Elan box (a development of the Cortina unit) proved less-than-ideal in a car which weighed some 300 lbs more than the sportscar for which the gear clusters were chosen.

To overcome these problems, one or two revisions were introduced in the early part of 1964. These started with the Elan gearbox being dropped in favour of that of the GT Cortina for production cars — the original close-ratio item was still available for competition use — and this meant a change from cast alloy to cast iron for the casings. To overcome the problem of rear axle vibration, the original one-piece propellor shaft was changed for a two-piece shaft. Production costs too were being looked at more closely by this time, and the result of a cost-cutting exercise was that the light alloy body panels were ditched, and standard Ford steel pressings were employed. It was July 1964 by the time that these changes made their way through to dealership showrooms, and a couple of months later there were more changes to be found, this time inside the cabin of the car.

Ford had by this point developed the Aeroflow "eyeball vent" ventilation system for the entire Cortina range, and the system was introduced to the Lotus Cortina along with a more attractive six-clock dashboard layout.

▲The interior of this early example of the car shows the distinctive fascia arrangement — and the abundance of painted metal.

THE LOTUS CORTINA IN COMPETITION

The list of names who have driven Lotus Cortinas in competition reads almost like a "who's who" of British and Scandinavian motorsport. Jackie Stewart, Jim Clark, Sir John Whitmore, Vic Elford, Roger Clark, Bengt Soderstrom, Graham Hill, Gunnar Palm, are just some of the legends who have successfully piloted the cars to victory in a range of races and rallies.

For Britain the cars were prepared by either Boreham or Lotus Cars at Cheshunt, whilst in Europe they were prepared by Alan Mann Racing.

Examples of the car are still to be found on racetracks, where they compete in Classic Saloons. LCR Secretary David Missions' example, shown here in mid-bend with one front wheel in mid-air, is highly successful, still able to fend off all but the most powerful of V8-engined machines with ease.

▲An original ad from 1963. Notice how the Lotus name only appears later in the ad, the car being pushed as the Consul Cortina ...

Externally another minor change was instigated, with the original car's grille being widened to full-width. Fortunately for fans, those quarter bumpers were retained.

A year later, in the middle of 1965, came the most important change to the specification of the Lotus Cortina. That radical rear suspension system, with its links and coil-over-damper arrangement, was dropped in favour of the conventional "cart spring" system which was to be found under the rear end of the Cortina GT. This too had a pair of forward-reaching radius arms, but true devotees of the marque were still horrified, considering the move to be a penny-pinching exercise on the part of Ford. Be that as it may, the benefits in terms of longevity and reliability outweighed the disadvantages of losing the Lotus-designed rear end.

The last major change to the Lotus Cortina came in the October of that year, when the gearbox was again changed, this time for the Corsair 2000E's set of ratios. Although by the standards of the first examples of the car the 1966 model was the least exciting in terms of equipment and specification, it was undeniably successful in competition, and relatively reliable both on and off the racetracks.

Whilst it could make the heart beat a little faster to even watch an example of this car, let alone actually drive one, they were something less than quick in making an exit from the dealers' showrooms. This was principally because the early cars were dogged with a poor record of reliability – for all of its handsome appearance, excellent power outputs and awesome noises, the

engine could be a real prima donna, slipping out of tune at the slightest excuse. Compound this with the way in which the rear axle could shake loose its bolts and deposit its oil all over the roadside, and the picture begins to come clear ...

By a strange series of twists and turns, it was this car which first gave us the RS dealerships, and subsequently the RS cars. When compared with the simple, quite fundamental, designs of the rest of the car range that Ford were selling at the time, the Lotus Cortina (Ford always sold it as a Cortina Lotus, but out of deference to the amount of work put into the car by Lotus, is is more commonly known as the Lotus Cortina) was so technically advanced and complicated that it scared the pants off a substantial number of dealerships. Consequently, the sales team at Ford came up with the RS concept – Sam Toy was the prime mover, aided and abetted by Walter Hayes and Terence Beckett – whereby a small number of dealers would undertake to train their workshop's leading lights in the care and maintenance of the twin-cammed Cortina. The dealers would also endeavour to offer a competitions unit, which would see a van in the paddock at race meetings in the area, and at local rallies. Even it if meant waiting at the end of a forest stage in the middle of Wales in the middle of a Saturday night, somebody would be there.

BJH 417 B

This particular car, now totally restored by owner Andy Middlehurst, was the actual car which won the British Saloon Car Championship, with the late, great, Jim Clark behind the wheel.

One of the pair of factory cars from 1964, the other bearing the plate BJH 418 B, this particular example is endowed with a slightly milder engine than that which was in place in 1964, but even so it still produces about 140 b.h.p. Ostensibly identical to the other Lotus Cortinas of the day, the car was actually slightly different in the suspension department, the major change being the addition of a rear anti-roll bar by Lotus.

Andy Middlehurst acquired the car almost three years ago, and subjected it to a total rebuild at the family workshops. Refinished in the original colours, the car is as clean underneath as it is from above. It has covered less than 11,000 miles from its date of registration in March 1964, and Andy has the full history of the car from the moment it first turned a wheel at the Lotus factory in Cheshunt.

The main differences between this and a road-going version of the car, besides the anti-roll bar, is the provision of a much larger fuel tank (with filler cap immediately behind the rear windscreen, rather than on the back panel of the car), and the replacement of the original front seats with a pair of vinyl-covered hip-hugging bucket seats. As it is a race machine there are no carpets to be seen throughout the interior, and, naturally, it has no spare tyre. Finally, the bonnet has a quick-release buckle to hold it down, and a matt-black flash across the leading edge.

Interestingly, there is no roll cage fitted to the car – this was the period when drivers wore Aertex short-sleeve sports shirts and, if they felt like, a cork crash helmet. By modern standards the spring rates of the car are very soft, and this led to a good deal of wheel-waving when the car was raced; it was nothing out of the ordinary to see one of these cars cornering on two wheels.

Andy Middlehurst, best-known as driver of a Golf GTi in ProdSaloons, has a fondness for his Lotus Cortinas – he has a second example at present undergoing a total rebuild – which is totally understandable; the car is still extremely rapid even by modern standards, and has that increasingly rare commodity of Character with a capital "C".

Being the way that they are, it took Ford but a little amount of time to instigate the idea and turn it into a reality, and even less time to realise what a potential goldmine they were sitting on. Nowadays, RS dealerships are coveted, but Ford have remained true to their original pledge, and ensure that no new RS dealership sets up in a territory already occupied by an existing dealership. The "network within a network" was an inspired piece of marketing strategy, and continues to provide Ford with a steady band of devoted customers — especially since they formalised everything with the RS 1600 back in the '60s.

"The Lotus Cortina was so advanced and complicated that it scared the pants off a substantial number of dealerships."

But back to the Lotus Cortina. In all, there were less than 2,900 of the machines ever built, and a good number of those have now disappeared from our roads forever — one tailslide too many? Of those, more than half were built with the leafspring rear axle, which means that the chances of picking up a coil-sprung specimen are rare indeed. Having said that, they do come up for sale from time to time, albeit at prices substantially in excess of the £1,100 which would have bought a new model back in 1963. Expect to pay about £9,000 for a pristine example — although less-than-perfect models can be bought for much less. The leaf-sprung (post June 1965) examples come cheaper, but again the differences between a perfect example and one which is in need of restoration can vary tremendously.

Surprisingly, spares are not altogether unobtainable — the owners club is the best source for these. Providing you are prepared to scout around, to pay out substantial sums of money for certain bits and pieces (mainly body panels and trim items), and prepared to take on a lot of work, it can be most worthwhile to buy a tatty example and rebuild it.

What you will get at the end of the day is a car which excites, which stimulates, which needs a lot of attention, which frustrates and delights. All in one — and if not in the same day, then almost certainly in the same week. In standard form the

engine still puts out as much power as a modern XR3i, but with something sorely lacking in the XR3i — that delightful wail as the cams really start to let the gases through, and the power out to the flywheel. And it is still possible to buy a tremendous range of tuning items for the engine, from wild cams to trick pistons, which will see the power approaching nearer to a hundred and fifty brake horsepower without sacrificing driveability. Yes, a well-sorted Lotus Cortina will see even a modern hot hatch, with its sophisticated suspension system and free-revving, economical, ecologically-sound engine, floundering to keep up ...

LOTUS CORTINA REGISTER

The scarcity of the Lotus Cortina has ensured that there is a healthy demand for an owners' club for the car, and this need is fulfilled by the Lotus Cortina Register. Both Mk I and Mk II examples of the car are catered for by the club, which keeps members in contact with each other by a variety of runs and events, as well as a lively and interesting magazine Quarter Bumper, which is produced four times each year.

A major function of the club is to supply information on keeping these cars mobile, not just by the availability of spares but also through the provision of advice and information.

The club can also be found displaying superb examples of the marque at shows up and down the country throughout the summer months.

For more information on the Lotus Cortina Register contact David Missions at Department P.F., Fern Leigh, Hornash Lane, Shadoxhurst, Ashford, Kent TN26 1HT.

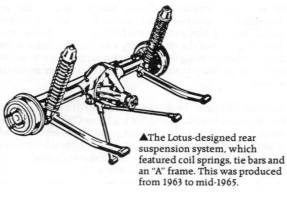

▲The Lotus-designed rear suspension system, which featured coil springs, tie bars and an "A" frame. This was produced from 1963 to mid-1965.

2 of a kind

Chris Graham samples two sporting saloons from the 1960s — the Lotus-Cortina Mk2 and Rapier H120.

Photographs by Chris Graham

The interior of the Lotus-Cortina Mk2 is plain but functional. Visibility from the driving seat is good in all directions and the driving position is comfortable. The steering wheel fitted here is not standard and features an oddly enlarged boss.

The driving compartment in the H120 is rather plushy. The seats are luxurious and the dashboard presents a feast of instrumentation. Rearward vision is, however, somewhat limited.

The 1960s was a decade of change. The last clinging vestiges of the sobering post-war depression finally had been thrown aside and people began to view life through optimistic eyes once again. Development and innovation came to the fore and, what's more, England won the World Cup — could things ever be bettered? The motor industry, not wishing to be left out, responded to this heartening growth with enthusiasm. Flair and style were injected into the latest designs in an attempt to match the mood of the nation. Things they were a boomin'!

One interesting motoring consequence which resulted from this rejuvenated thinking was that the divide between the traditional sports car and the family saloon started to crumble. This, incidentally, is a trend that has continued to the present day; five-seater saloons that boast fiery Ferrari-type performance are now relatively common on our roads. Ford are regarded by many as being the fathers of the sporting saloon and, in 1963, an arrangement with Lotus led to the Lotus-Cortina Mk 1 and the die was cast. This car, which was assembled by Lotus, enjoyed great success in competition and proved popular with the buying public. It set Ford on their way to an illustrious competition career and led quickly to the development of the famous 'RS' cars. At this time Ford's competitors could offer no real opposition and true rivals were few and far between.

In 1966 Ford decided to build on their success with the introduction of the Lotus-Cortina Mk 2. It was based upon the Mk 2 Cortina GT and was assembled at the Dagenham works. By this stage the other major British manufacturers, not wishing to see a repeat of the Mk 1's impressive dominance, were anxiously working on projects of their own and perhaps the most creditable sparring partner to emerge was the Sunbeam Rapier H120.

This car arrived in 1968 and, thanks to the 105bhp developed by its Holbay-tuned 1725cc Rootes engine, it was a snappy performer. It featured Rostyle wheels, go-faster stripes and the distinctive bodyshell of the standard fastback Rapier model. However, beneath the surface the car was based on rather more mundane foundations than its outward appearance might have suggested. The rear lights are a definite recognition point and those in the know should immediately link them with the Hunter. Times were hard within the Rootes empire as the new-generation Rapier took shape and, somewhat inevitably, financial short cuts were taken. The whole vehicle was based on the floorpan and selected internal panels from the Hunter estate. Front suspension also was as per the Hunter, independent with coil springs, MacPherson struts, an anti-roll bar and telescopic dampers. At the rear a live axle was coupled to half-eliptic leaf springs and telescopic dampers. Overdrive transmission was standard (automatic was never an option on the H120) and the car's 5in wheel rims shod with 165 x 13 tyres were controlled by servo-assisted disc brakes at the front and

2 of a kind

drums at the rear.

The Lotus-Cortina offered surprisingly similar specifications with a virtually identical suspension and braking set-up and so, on paper, the two make ideal competitors. Unfortunately, both are in quite short supply today. There were just over 4,000 Mk 2 Lotus-Cortinas made between 1967 and 1970 and some 1,700 of these were sent for export leaving just 2,300 examples for the home market to enjoy. The facts concerning the H120 production figures are a good deal more vague and the Sunbeam Rapier Owners Club can give only an estimated figure at present. Barry Quinnell, the Fastback Registrar, told me that Holbay produced 12,000 modified engines and he considers that about half of these were used for the H120 (the others powered the Hunter GLS). Consequently, it seems that approximately 6,000 H120s were built — but they don't appear to have survived well. Although great hopes were pinned on the 'new' Rapier at its launch it was, nevertheless, rather unsuccessful. Its production period ran from 1967 to 1976, but resulted in the creation of only about 47,000 cars in total, which was disappointly low.

It is arguable that the Mk 2 Lotus-Cortina had an important advantage over the H120 gained from having a rather more established image. It stepped straight into the slot previously occupied by the charismatic Mk 1 and continued, despite being less of a Lotus and more of a Ford, to set a high standard although latterly its popularity suffered at the hands of the RS Escorts. As you would expect from Ford, the Lotus-Cortina was very keenly priced and, at its launch, one could be purchased for just under £1,000.

The fastback Rapier, on the other hand, had a tough job from the start. It was designed on a strict budget and yet was expected to lift Sunbeam's flagging reputation. The Series Rapier had become very dated in all respects and the major facelift that was required was severely hampered by the considerable financial constraints. The H120 was supposed to be the king of the fleet and indeed, to buy one new, cost almost as much as the crown jewels! The asking price was well over £1,500 and it is interesting to note that for just a few hundred pounds more the discerning motorist could choose a Mk 2 Jaguar.

The cars we tested

The H120 Rapier that we chose for this feature belongs to Mrs Muriel Lindo from Romford in Essex. Muriel acquired the car, a 1969 model, from her father a couple of years ago and, since then, has overseen a reasonably comprehensive restoration. The bodywork received the greatest attention but the engine, being in fine condition, was left well alone. The mileometer currently indicates just over 60,000 and this is thought to be a genuine figure. Muriel, despite using the Rapier for everyday transport, has it insured on a limited mileage policy and considers that she covers only 4,000 miles a year.

The taut suspension set-up on the Lotus-Cortina inspires great confidence. The steering is precise but, in this case, was rather on the heavy side due to the wider tyres.

Bob Coombes bought his Lotus-Cortina Mk 2 two years ago and confines its use mainly to the summer months. He does all his own servicing work and gains great pleasure and satisfaction from doing so. The car is basically in original condition although wider tyres and a non-standard steering wheel have been fitted. No restoration work has been necessary so far in his ownership but some small areas of surface rust are starting to appear on the bodywork.

Driving impressions

I drove the H120 first and was immediately struck by its high level of refinement. It was comfortable, relatively quiet and easy to drive. The instrumentation was impressive and the brakes superb. I found the engine

Despite feeling large the H120 is surprisingly manoeuvrable. Saloon car roll is evident but this is very predictable and, consequently, manageable.

The twin-cam Lotus engine (as used in the Elan) produces 105bhp and provides this special Cortina with interesting performance. The battery is housed in the boot.

The H120 Rapier is characterised by its subtle spoiler built into the boot lid and the flashy side striping. The Lotus-Cortina offers only badging at the rear (some owners affix Lotus badges to the front grille as well) to provide a clue as to the contents of its engine compartment. Both cars have black radiator grilles.

responsive but was surprised by how quickly the needle reached the red line; perhaps the rev counter was a little optimistic. It seemed to reach the indicated limit before any real power became evident and this, to my mind, rather tamed the performance. Handling was quite acceptable if somewhat wallowy at times (its Series parents exhibited this tendency too) and the steering was light and manageable. Overall, however, I feel that the H120 is rather too refined for its own good and unfortunately, in my opinion, it lacks the 'killer instinct' to match its sporting reputation.

The Lotus-Cortina was quite different. Despite being considerably more spartan in all respects the car fitted in much more convincingly with my preconception of a true sporting saloon. It was noisy, bumpy and rough but it had guts. The engine provided real urge when pressed and gave enjoyable, if not earth-shatteringly quick, performance. However, on this car the brakes were well

below the standard (servo problems Bob assured me) and the 185 tyres left the steering heavy at low speeds.

Both cars had an excellent gearchange that encouraged rapid and frequent changes. The overdrive fitted on the Rapier afforded it useful top-end flexibility and the clutches in both cases proved comfortable in use. However, for me the Lotus-Cortina came out on top. It couples infectious sporting appeal and saloon car specifications to create an appealing and desirable classic driving machine.

The owners' views

Bob Coombes found the H120 considerably more refined than his car and agreed that the brakes were excellent. One of his immediate criticisms was that he could not see the back of the car through the rear window when reversing. Overall, however, he liked it but did feel that it was smaller inside than the Cortina. He was surprised at how powerful the engine was but added that he did not feel it matched his car despite the manufacturer's claims. We concluded that perhaps the Rapier's extra 275lb might have something to do with this. He liked the instrument layout, appreciated the lighter steering and found it an easy car to drive but felt that it had no real

Specifications

	Lotus-Cortina Mk 2	Rapier H120
No. cyls	4	4
Bore	82.55	81.50
Stroke	72.75	82.55
Capacity	1558cc	1725cc
Comp. ratio	9.5:1	9.6:1
bhp at rpm	109 at 6,000	105 at 5,200
Carburation	2 x Weber	2 x Weber
Length	14ft	14ft 6½in
Width	5ft 5in	5ft 4½in
Weight	2,025 lb	2,300 lb
Front susp.	ifs, coil	ifs, coil
Rear susp.	½-el, live axle	½-el, live axle
Max. mph	104	105
0-60mph	11.0	11.1
Std. ¼-mile	18.2	17.7
Fuel con.	22.2	21.9
Price new (1969)	£1,234	£1,503

Although appearing slightly plain both these cars possess considerable sporting potential and are truly 'wolves in sheeps' clothing'.

Holbay were employed to beef-up the trusty Rootes 1725cc engine for the H120 model and this they did to very good effect. Beware of fakes when buying; the Holbay rocker cover is easily transferable. Surprisingly, the Rapier was rather more expensive than the Lotus Ford.

sporting feel about it.

Muriel Lindo, having returned from her turn in the Lotus-Cortina, commented that it was much bumpier than her car but that it did not roll so much round corners. She admitted that the Lotus engine felt powerful but did not agree it was more so than her Holbay-tuned Rootes unit. Her test run was certainly hampered by the uncertainty of the Cortina's weak brakes but, nevertheless, she enjoyed it and revelled in her ability to see the rear of the car through the back window! Muriel also added that she felt that the Cortina's steering had rather more feel to it than that on the H120 despite being considerably heavier.

Predictably, neither owner would change their allegiance after the test runs but there was evident appreciation from both sides. Despite the similarity of these two cars 'on paper' they are quite different in reality. Potential owners must decide whether it is a fast and refined touring car or a rough and ready sporting machine that they desire — both have their merits. ☐

My thanks go to Bob Coombes, Muriel Lindo, Kent County Council and the staff at The Valance School, Westerham, Kent, for the help given with the preparation of this feature.

LOTUS CORTINA

A Wolf in Sheep's Clothing

Mixed Lotus Cortina track action.

ROBERT DAINES

Cortinas were popular in rallys; this Mark I is a typical example.

In the late 1950's, the parent group of the Ford Motor Company commissioned an inquiry into why their cars were failing to sell in sufficient numbers to the newly affluent youth sector of the market.

The results of the survey suggested that young people viewed the Ford range as 'grocery getters' or a suitable car for the old man to drive. Consequently the Ford company decided to inject some sporting and performance image into their worldwide range of cars. Ford of Great Britain were granted a 12 million pound budget and a brief to produce a car with adequate seating for four and handling and performance to appeal to the young, enthusiastic drivers who were spending large sums of money with Ford's rivals.

In 1962, the Ford Cortina made its debut, to press and public acclaim. The basic Cortina featured a 1200 cc, 55 bhp engine which was a tried and tested Ford unit, noted for its durability. The engine, coupled with superior luggage space and mid-Atlantic styling ensured a favourable reaction from the public and 3000 cars were sold within the first three days, while export orders worth 20 million pounds rapidly filled Ford's books.

Ford intended to produce several variants of the Cortina, to cover every facet of the market, including the high-spending youth sector and soon released the Cortina Super, which was equipped with a 5-main-bearing-crank 1500 cc engine, now putting out 64 bhp. The 1500 engine had already seen extensive use in motorsports with great success, and

Ford capitalised on this proven track record by modifying the carburation, exhaust and cylinder head to produce 80 bhp.

The modified 1500 was augmented by a stiffer suspension set-up, disc brakes, and was released to the public as the Cortina GT. With its race bred engine and suspension, the GT soon proved its mettle on race tracks around the world, competing against cars from 850 cc Minis to the 7-litre Ford Galaxies. At the end of the 1963 season the Cortina 1500 had competed in 18 British races and came first in its class in each. To cap its season's successes, the Cortina GT finished 1st, 2nd and 10th in the 12-hour endurance race held in Marlborough, Maryland.

The serious racing potential of the Ford 1500 cc unit had not gone unnoticed by one Colin Chapman, who had been using Ford engines as far back as 1949 in his special, hand-built racing cars. By the 1960's, Chapman's company,

Lotus Cars, was a force to be reckoned with in both Formula One and Formula Junior racing. Through his continued use of Ford powerplants, Chapman had developed a close relationship with Ford, which gave him free access to the Dagenham engine plant where he encountered the 1500 engine for the first time.

Sensing a potential race winner, Chapman acquired a base 1500 and commissioned his engine designer, Harry Munday, to develop a modified unit to power a Lotus special. The fruit of Munday's labour, the first 1500 Ford Lotus Twin Cam, made its appearance at Nurburgring on May 27th, 1962 powering a Lotus 23 Sports, with Jim Clark behind the wheel. Although the 23 crashed while leading the race, the assembled motoring press had their interest piqued in the new engine and were delighted to learn that it was to be installed in the production model Lotus Elan.

Mark I cornering. Note tiny bumpers of earlier models.

Lotus-Ford Mark I 1500cc Twin Cam.

Mark II Twin Cam. Note huge intake silencer.

Meanwhile, in Dagenham, British Ford executives were flushed with the Cortina GT's success both on the track and in the showroom. Orders came from the U.S. parent company to push on with their performance program. The object was to secure further victories in saloon car racing and rallies and, hopefully, at Indianapolis. To produce the desired wins, Ford of Great Britain turned to the man who had long been making winners from their engines. Colin Chapman eagerly accepted the challenge. Chapman's assignment was to produce a production-trim car, that, in a mild state of tune, would develop more power than the Cortina GT.

Back at the Lotus factory, Chapman wasted little time in slipping his 1500 twin-cam into the company's beat-up Ford Anglia, which he then gave to an unsuspecting Jim Clark to drive to his home in Scotland. Clark was a little upset, as he had just returned from a successful

South African rally and was expecting a Lotus Elite to complete his journey home with. His disappointment did not last long however, as out on the motorway, the humble Anglia moved like it had no right to. Much to his delight, Clark passed a 3.8-litre Jaguar which he estimated was doing about 115 m.p.h. Jim Clark and a rather suprised Jag driver had just learned that the 1500 twin-cam in a small saloon body was a potent combination.

The resulting Consul Cortina Sports Special was announced to the British press in January 1963, and achieved homologation for Group 2 saloon racing with 1,000 units produced on the 9th of May 1963. Although Ford executives and publicity referred to the car as the Cortina, the public called it the Lotus Cortina, a fact that was to cause problems between Ford and Lotus in the future.

Suspension-wise, the Lotus Cortina Mk1, as we shall call it for brevity, was built in the Lotus tradition featuring an

A-frame rear axle design along with uprated brakes. The twin-cam was coupled to a close-ratio gearbox, with a heavy duty diaphragm clutch and a stronger 3-inch diameter propshaft. In order to reduce weight, the bonnet, boot and doors along with the diff case and clutch bell housing were all manufactured in aluminium. Although it was a bona fide production car, the Lotus Cortina had a strong racing influence and that, in practice, was to cause problems on the public road, which would sour the relationship between the two companies.

The 'A' frame rear suspension was a particular cause for concern, as it planted the rear wheels so firmly to the road that excessive shocks were transmitted through to the body shell. Body roll, meanwhile, applied loads which twisted the axle, distorting the aluminium diff carrier, resulting in a loss of oil and premature axle failure. Bodywise, the aluminium doors, bonnet and boot were

No, it's not out of control! Typical Lotus Cortina behavior under hard cornering due to severe roll stiffness. This is a Mark II version.

1967 Cortina Mark II wears Ford badge, but the public still knew it as a Lotus Cortina.

easily pocked and scarred by the minor scrapes that inevitably occur in day-to-day driving. Lotus attempted to correct some of the problems by introducing a two-piece propshaft with a centre bearing and discontinuing the 'A' frame in favour of a heavy-duty leaf spring system which was similiar to the GT Cortina.

Despite criticism over the reliability of some units, the motoring press generally responded favourably to the Lotus Cortina GT's 0-60 time of 10.1 and top speed of 108 mph. *Autosport* dubbed the car, "An ideal carriage for the keen driver who requires four seats."

In addition to the Lotus Cortina, a special was released in 1964, which featured a 145 bhp engine, built by either Cosworth or BRM. The special was nothing less than a showroom racing car, complete with detachable trim and a list of options running from a limited slip differential, to a full-house 165 bhp engine.

The victories were soon mounting for the Lotus Cortina, but all was not well, as Ford felt that the resulting publicity was being directed more to Lotus than Ford. In addition, Ford felt that the Lotus Cortina was growing too far apart from the Cortina GT and that the Lotus Cortina's image of a spartan race car was deterring many potential customers,

who were seeking performance along with some degree of comfort. In fact, the Lotus Cortina was selling slowly despite the racing victories and ensuing publicity.

Ford now bought their considerable influence to bear, insisting that Lotus create a car more geared to regular road use and thus to appeal to a wider band of customers.

The result was the 1964 Cortina, which came with carpets, Cortina GT seats and enough appointments to warrant consideration as top of the Cortina range. Mechanically, the close-ratio box was replaced by a Corsair 2000 unit, while the Lotus high-ratio steering box was ditched for a standard Ford unit.

All of the aluminium parts were replaced with conventional steel. Cosmetically, the 1964 Lotus Cortina gained 'Aeroflow' ventilation and a full length grille. Ford felt they had achieved their object of a sporting car that did not sacrifice driver and passenger comfort. The press agreed and nominated it the '1964 International Car Of The Year.' Ford now began an export drive with the revamped Cortina. The left-hand-drive cars received full width bumpers rather than the sportier quarter items, to comply with safety standards. The bulk of the export models was delivered to

Europe and the United States.

By 1966, Ford decided that the Lotus Cortina had exhausted its potential in drawing sales from the youth market, and the line was discontinued. However, the Lotus/Cortina association was not destined to end in 1966. Ford's competition department began testing a Lotus twin-cam in the new Mark 2 Cortina. With the veteran Jim Clark behind the wheel, the Mark 2 won the 1966 R.A.C. Rally in fine style.

Ford reasoned that, with more control over production and marketing, the Lotus Cortina could still produce some worthwhile publicity, and gave the go-ahead for the Lotus Cortina Mark 2. Assembly took place in Ford's Dagenham plant and the Mark 2 was indeed a car with far better road manners. Gone was the wood-rimmed steering wheel with Lotus badge and even the white with green side flashes - the Lotus racing motif - was shelved.

The twin-cam, however, gained extra power from special equipment cams and bigger valves which netted 108 bhp. To keep things a little more civilized, a huge A.C. Delco air cleaner silenced the twin Webers effectively. While the Mark 2 had more creature comforts, it still performed well in competition and won many rallys. *Autocar*, a British motoring magazine, had this to say of the Mark 2: "The Cortina retains much of its dynamic appeal, yet it is so much more refined that there is scarcely any comparision between them. It is immensely better, and is now a thoroughly satisfying high performance car."

Despite such praise, the Lotus Cortina Mark 2 made only a brief one-season appearance before it was superseded by the Escort twin-cam.

The Lotus Cortina had made an indelible mark on the public. Despite its teething troubles, it was a powerful, fine handling machine, capable of running to the shops as well as blasting around the race track on weekends. For all of its conservative appearance, it's a true example of British muscle; no less than a wolf in sheep's clothing. □

THE LOTUS CORTINA REGISTER

Twenty years on, the Lotus Cortina has an enthusiastic following with members as far afield as Japan and New Zealand. This thriving club supplies a spares location service, parts and spares discounts as well as promoting motorsports events enabling members to see what their Lotus Cortina can do on the track. The register has been serving Lotus Cortina fans and owners since 1979. For further details please contact Jeff Fenton, 10 Manor Farm Drive, Soothill Batley, Yorkshire, England.

North American Lotus Clubs include: Lotus Club West, 1023 22nd St., Santa Monica, CA 90403 (213) 929-1311; Golden Gate Lotus Club, 1393 Gilbert Ave., Fremont, CA 94536, (415) 797-9299; and Club Elite of NA, 23999 Box Canyon Rd., Canoga Pk., CA 91304, (818) 346-5151.